Death on the Hellships

Death on the Hellships

PRISONERS AT SEA
IN THE PACIFIC WAR

Gregory F. Michno

LEO COOPER

First published in Great Britain in 2001 by
LEO COOPER
an imprint of Pen & Sword Books Ltd
47 Church Street, Barnsley, South Yorkshire S70 2AS

©2001 Gregory F. Michno
Annapolis, Maryland, USA

ISBN 0-85052-821-6

A CIP record of this book is available from the British Library

Printed and bound in the USA

CONTENTS

PREFACE

World War II was arguably the single most important event in the lives of millions of men and women who survived its horrors. It has provided the raw material for thousands of books, many of which were based on the written accounts and memoirs of those who experienced the cataclysm firsthand. Soldiers and sailors, from enlisted men to career officers, have given us numerous combat stories, their narratives running the gamut of wartime emotions, from boredom to terror, from camaraderie to glory.

A significant number of survivors, however, have been unwilling or unable to share their experiences. The majority of the returned prisoners-of-war (POWs) have remained silent. With the exception of a number who made their stories public shortly after the war's end, POWs have not readily spoken of their ordeal. The onus of having been captured played a part in their silence, as did the unwillingness to relive a bad experience. In some cases post-traumatic stress disorder, a psychological condition that affected many who experienced the brutalities of war, limited their ability to communicate. Many felt guilty about surviving; others were ashamed of what they had been forced to do in order to survive. They blocked out painful recollections. This "psychic numbing" prevented survivors from talking about their experiences for years after the war (American Psychiatric Association, *Diagnostic and Statistical Manual*, 236–37, 248–50).

It is only within the last few decades that many surviving ex-POWs have finally been able to tell their story. Once the dams broke, a deluge of words poured forth. One ex-prisoner, Robert E. Haney, likened his postwar life to being a tormented, caged dragon. He set up barriers against anything that would remind him of the past. But, he lamented, time did not heal all wounds; it only buried them in very shallow graves (Haney, *Caged Dragons,* 245).

As Haney's book illustrates, prisoners of the Japanese suffered unusual brutality. Though Japan had signed the Hague Convention of 1907, which called for humane treatment of POWs, it refused to ratify the Geneva convention of 1929, and its prisoners suffered the brunt of this decision. Recently published POW accounts, including Manny Lawton's *Some Survived,* Preston John Hubbard's *Apocalypse Undone,* and Van Waterford's *Prisoners of the Japanese* (Jefferson, N.C.: McFarland, 1994), have detailed the ordeals of beatings, disease, and starvation, as well as the prisoners' capture, daily camp life, and eventual rescue. The story of the surrender of Singapore has been told. The fight for Bataan and its attendant Death March has been recounted many times. In contrast, the story of the prisoners who experienced life and death on the Japanese hellships has had less exposure. Some books acknowledge these prisoners, but with no more than a paragraph or, at most, a chapter. (Waterford has a chapter on the hellships, Daws devotes a score of pages to hellships in *Prisoners of the Japanese* [New York: William Morrow, 1994], and Kerr, in *Surrender and Survival,* addresses hellships but concentrates on the American experience in the Philippines.) The hellships have not yet had their own story, an incongruous situation given the great number of prisoners who have claimed that their days on the hellships were the worst of their lives. *Death on the Hellships* is the first book to concentrate on this aspect of the prisoner-of-war experience.

Another comparatively unknown part of the hellship saga is the submarine connection. Thousands of POWs who had survived prison camps on land lost their lives at sea when the Japanese ships they were on were torpedoed by Allied submarines. Chillingly, this "friendly fire" was many times purposely directed by Allied intelligence. Because Japanese codes had been broken, it was possible to know of convoys' cargoes, destinations, and daily positions, facilitating interception. Japanese ships sailed unaware that Allied intelligence knew of their moves and had vectored submarines to attack them. Of the approximately twenty-one thousand prisoner deaths at sea, about nineteen thousand were caused by "friendly fire" from either Allied submarines or planes. Although Allied death rates under the Japanese were much worse than

Allied death rates under the Germans, when one subtracts all of those killed by their own countrymen, the percentages become almost equal.

Can a story of the hellships be written? No, according to Preston Hubbard, former prisoner and retired history professor at Austin Peay State University in Clarksville, Tennessee. Hubbard believes the unrelenting horror of the hellships does not lend itself to a book. Novels or movies need points of contrast, moments of relief, different viewpoints. The hellships, says Hubbard, have no contrasts. Their damned, dark world lies buried beyond the reach of imagination or memory. It was a world unrelieved by humor, light, setting, or routine. Such a story, he claims, would collapse into itself like a black hole, shedding no light and yielding no understanding. Indeed, the hellships may represent a kind of depravity, a supreme form of evil beyond the scope of history (Hubbard, *Apocalypse Undone*, 164). Although Hubbard's observation may be valid when it comes to the creation of a painting, movie, or novel, fortunately (or unfortunately, as the case may be), this is not a novel. Truth does not always follow the dictums of art.

ACKNOWLEDGMENTS

Many people helped me with the preparation of this book. I would like to thank John D. Alden, submariner and author, for his critique of the manuscript and his unselfish sharing of rare English translations of Japanese source material; John Taylor at the National Archives for helping to locate many of the radio intercepts and Ultra information; the late Clay Blair Jr. for permission to use his taped interviews; the folks at the Submarine Force Library in Groton, Connecticut, for locating all the patrol reports; the *Quan,* the magazine of the American Defenders of Bataan and Corregidor, for printing my requests for assistance; the *Polaris,* magazine of the Subvets of WWII, for printing more assistance requests; and the National Maritime Museum in San Francisco for its support of the project.

I consulted many published books and articles; however, this book would not have been complete without the help of so many individuals who saw merit in this undertaking. Those men and women, former prisoners, submariners, and civilians, more than fifty of them, are cited in detail in the bibliography. Their correspondence, interviews, and tapes were of utmost importance in adding a personal touch to these proceedings. Although it was sometimes difficult for them to reveal their thoughts, they assisted me to the best of their ability. I hope this story will illuminate a fraction of what they experienced to a world today in which patriotism and sacrifice are often considered archaic.

Death on the Hellships

1942

RELOCATING THE POWS

In the opening months of the war, the Imperial Japanese Navy and Army stormed through China, Southeast Asia, the Philippines, and the western Pacific. They gobbled up millions of square miles and affected the lives of hundreds of millions of people. Within weeks of Pearl Harbor, the Japanese captured Guam, Wake, and Hong Kong. They landed in the Philippines, Malaya, Borneo, and various islands of the Dutch East Indies. By February 1942, Singapore, Britain's supposedly impregnable bastion, had fallen. Sumatra and Java were attacked. In six months, the Japanese had extended their conquests to Burma, north to the Aleutians, and south to New Guinea and the Solomon Islands, threatening the American lifeline to Australia.

In the course of these conquests, the Japanese killed, wounded, or captured more than 300,000 Allied troops. The most significant surrenders were at Hong Kong, where nearly 14,000 Britons, Canadians, and Indians defended the island; on Java, with 25,000 Dutch and 7,000 British, Australian, and American troops; and in the Philippines, where 75,000 Americans and Filipinos surrendered. The worst single instance was the fall of Singapore, an event Prime Minister Winston Churchill called "the greatest disaster and capitulation in British history." In one swoop, 130,000 British, Australian, and Indian troops surrendered to fewer than that number of Japanese soldiers. It was the greatest land victory in Japan's history.[1]

The Imperial Army was unprepared for this influx of prisoners. What would they do with them? After a time they released the native prisoners—Indonesians who fought with the Dutch and Filipinos who fought with the Americans—and instituted a marginally successful campaign to enlist the Indians against their former British masters. All these actions were logistically sensible and calculated to earn propaganda points for them as racial liberators of Asia. Yet this still left 140,000 or more white prisoners of war.[2]

GUAM

Before the Japanese could make long-term plans for housing POWs, prisoners would have to be moved out of the forward battle zones. The first such move occurred on Guam. On the morning of 10 December 1941, about six thousand men of the Japanese 144th Regiment came ashore, quickly overrunning the island's pitifully small number of American defenders. Cdr. Donald T. Giles, vice governor of Guam and executive officer of its naval station, was bitterly disappointed at what he called a shameful sacrifice by the U.S. government. Facing the Japanese with only a few hundred men armed with pistols and Springfield rifles, the Americans resisted for only twenty minutes. Even so, seventeen men had been killed and thirty-eight wounded before they gave up.

One month later, on 10 January 1942, they received an unusually hearty breakfast of lunch meat, a cold potato, and a sip of coffee. They were told that they would be heading south by ship, so they only needed to take their tropical clothing. From Piti Navy Yard in Apra Harbor they boarded what Giles called a beautiful passenger ship, the *Argentina Maru*. A twenty-knot luxury liner of 12,755 tons, capable of accommodating eight hundred passengers, the ship had traveled the Far East–South America route prior to being recalled for use as a troop transport. There would be no first-class accommodations for the prisoners, however. On deck, the governor of Guam tried to explain to the Japanese commander why they had surrendered. The officer slapped him in the face.

"You and your men are all cowards for surrendering," he snapped, "and we will treat you accordingly. We will give you all the punishment that the human body can withstand!" Thus the Americans quickly learned what the Japanese thought about prisoners. They were sent four decks down and crammed into six-tiered shelves, with eight men lying side by side. There was little space between one's face and the shelf above, and there was no ventilation or sanitation. As luxurious as the ship was, said Giles, she was never intended to carry prisoners: "Except for the lack of chains, we were there as galley slaves."[3]

As the prisoners speculated as to which "tropical" destination they were bound, the Argentina Maru sailed north, unescorted and without zigzagging, causing Giles to worry about submarine attack. The temperature grew colder. The food served was described as "buckets of slop," lowered on lines from the boat deck above. Marine private John B. Garrison complained about being forced to stay right above the engines and only being allowed on deck once a day for exercise. He thought there were about three hundred servicemen and four hundred civilians in the hold, all sleeping on steel shelves, side by side. Garrison weighed 140 pounds when he surrendered, only 110 by the time he got to Japan. Unaccustomed to the meager meals of rice spiced with daikons (pickled white radishes), he found it very hard to eat, even as hungry as he was. No one, said Commander Giles, who was ever a prisoner of the Japanese will ever complain about food again.[4]

On the morning of 15 January, as snow fell, the Argentina Maru sailed into the Inland Sea and anchored off Tadotsu on the island of Shikoku. The prisoners were ill prepared for the frigid cold. Giles remembered 420 of them being taken to Zentsuji Camp, about five miles southeast of Tadotsu. Zentsuji, the first POW camp established in Japan, was administered by reserve personnel, which perhaps worked in the prisoners' favor. The POWs' new home was a shock, yet all things considered, Zentsuji would prove to be one of the "better" Japanese POW camps in the empire.[5]

WAKE

Making a much better fight of it, the defenders of Wake Island actually repulsed the first Japanese invasion attempt on 11 December 1941. The small invasion force under Rear Adm. Kajioka Sadamichi,[6] commanding Destroyer Squadron Six from the light cruiser Yubari, approached too close to the island and was surprised by still-operable shore batteries and planes. Down went the destroyer Hayate, the first Japanese warship to be lost in World War II, and the destroyer Kisaragi. Kajioka retreated. On 23 December he was back with reinforcements, but before surrender, the stubborn defenders inflicted nearly five hundred casualties on the attackers while losing only fourteen Marines and fourteen civilians. The Japanese had been roughly handled, and curses, kicks, and rifle butts emphasized their orders as they rounded up the Americans. Their valuables and clothes were stripped from them, and their hands were wired behind their backs with loops around their necks. "They stripped us down balls and ass naked and hog-tied us," complained one Yank. Then they were lined up and covered by three machine guns. As they waited to be shot, a landing craft rammed onto the beach and out stepped Rear Admiral Kajioka, resplendent in a spotless white uniform. He ordered the machine gunners to remove their ammunition belts, and the prisoners realized they had been saved—for the moment.[7]

Almost sixteen hundred Americans, counting servicemen and civilian employees, were taken to the airfield. Kajioka had won his argument with the commanding Army officer. The interpreter passed along the gist of the exchange: "The emperor has gracefully presented you with your lives." Out of the mass of hog-tied bodies, where civilian construction workers Oklahoma Atkinson and Harry Jeffries surveyed the scene, came the sarcastic response, "Well thank the son of a bitch."

Eventually the prisoners were housed in the contractor's barracks. They stayed until 11 January, when all but 388 of them were ordered down to the beach. Word was that they were going to Japan. Before they were lightered out to the waiting ship, they were sprayed with what Cpl. George W. McDaniel called a "smelly insecticide," and the Japanese guards shook them down one more time. They clawed their way up rope ladders in heavy seas, and once aboard, new guards kicked and cursed them for being devoid of loot. After they were beaten with bamboo clubs while running through a gauntlet, all 1,187 of them were shoved into the forward cargo holds.

The 17,163-ton *Nitta Maru,* built as a luxury liner in 1939, sailed for Yokohama on 12 January 1942. Capable of making twenty-two knots, it was the holder of a transpacific speed record. It could accommodate 278 passengers, but there was no luxury for its current guests. Down in the holds, the POWs were packed in, body upon body, and ordered to sit still. Anyone who moved was beaten. Corporal McDaniel said he wasn't allowed to stand up for fifteen days. Their toilets consisted of five-gallon pails. They were refused water, and some men tried to lick the condensation off the steel bulkheads. They were fed a thin rice gruel, so watery that many men went more than two weeks without a bowel movement. Others were plagued with dysentery. Civilians Jeffries and Atkinson said the gruel sometimes came with a few slivers of smelly pickled radish, other times with rotting fish heads or guts. Men couldn't even make it to the slop buckets to relieve themselves. Not in such dire straits was Capt. Bryghte D. Godbold. He and a small group of men were placed in what appeared to be a mail room. There were even a few bunks for the older officers, while the younger ones slept on deck mats. Godbold ate rice, soup, pickles, and tea a couple of times a day. It was not pleasant, but there was no brutality shown. It was about what you'd expect on a prisoner ship, he said. Not so for the great majority, who would describe their trip on the *Nitta Maru* as the worst time of their captivity.[8]

The *Nitta Maru* was heading north to a freezing Japanese midwinter. The prisoners were issued one thin cotton blanket each, but it was not nearly enough. On 18 January, the engines quit vibrating and *Nitta Maru* docked at Yokohama. To celebrate their homecoming, the guards pulled back the hatches and threw snowballs at the prisoners. The commanders at Wake, Maj. James P. S. Devereaux and Cdr. Winfield S. Cunningham, and a few other officers

Nitta Maru. U.S. Naval Historical Center

were ordered to clean up and report to an upper deck room, where they were photographed, smiling for propaganda purposes, their pictures later appearing in English-language magazines. As compensation for their cooperation, they were allowed to send radiograms to their next of kin. About twenty other men, including Maj. George H. Potter Jr., Maj. Paul A. Putnam, and Cdr. Campbell Keene, all involved in aviation or communications intelligence, were removed from the ship for in-depth interrogation. Later in the month, when the Japanese were finished with them, one dozen were sent to Zentsuji prison camp.[9]

When the voyage resumed on 20 January, the mistreatment turned deadly. A day or two out of Yokohama, five men were brought up from the holds. Seamen Theodore Franklin, John W. Lambert, and Roy J. Gonzales, and Sgts. Earl R. Hannum and Vincent W. Bailey, all with aviation backgrounds, probably thought they were going to be interrogated. Their comrades never saw them again. Blindfolded and bound, they did not know what was happening as they were brought up on deck and surrounded by about 150 guards and crewmen. Lt. Saito Toshio, commander of the guards, stood on a box to read the indictment: "You have killed many Japanese soldiers in battle. For what you have done you are now going to be killed—for revenge. You are here as representatives of your American soldiers and will be killed. You can now pray to be happy in the next world—in heaven." One by one, each man was forced to kneel on the deck while sword-wielding guards stepped up behind them. A Japanese sailor described what happened: "The sword as brought down on the neck of the first victim made a swishing noise as it cut the air. As the blade hit and pierced the flesh it gave a resounding noise like a wet towel being flipped or shaken out. The body of the first victim lay quietly, half across a mat and half onto the wooden deck." Four more times the swords flashed while the Japanese applauded. Afterward, some took turns trying to cut the corpses in two with a single sword stroke, like samurais of old. Then Saito had them propped up against barrels for bayonet practice. Finally the crowd dispersed and the bodies were thrown into the ocean. That evening, Saito invited guests to his cabin to celebrate the occasion.

On 23 January, the *Nitta Maru* made Shanghai, then traveled up the Whangpoo River to Woosung. The prisoners were marched five miles to their new camp—seven unheated, old wooden barracks surrounded by electric fences. Within a week they were joined by captured Marines from Peking and

Tientsin, boosting their numbers to about fourteen hundred. Censored reports filtering back to America did not indicate that much was amiss. The wife of Dan Teeters, superintendent of the civilian construction workers on Wake, had a rosy picture painted for her. "We have no reason to think that the men have not received fairly decent treatment," she told William Bradford Huie, who was writing the story of the construction battalion. Red Cross packages were arriving at the camp, and although there was a lack of warm clothing, she reported, "there have been no atrocities."[10]

SINGAPORE

The capture of Guam and Wake were small operations compared to the invasions in the Philippines, Malaya, and the Dutch East Indies. On the day they bombed Pearl Harbor, actually 8 December 1941 for the entire western Pacific, the Japanese also landed at Kota Bharu, on the east coast of the Malayan Peninsula. Throughout December and January they forced the British and Australian defenders back, as they moved inexorably south toward Singapore. The Japanese appeared unstoppable, and the Singapore area verged on chaos. At the same time that troop convoys were arriving in an attempt to shore up the rapidly deteriorating situation, thousands of people began to flee. Japanese planes and warships had field days. On 5 February 1942, dive bombers sank the arriving 16,909-ton transport *Empress of Asia* carrying units of the 18th Division. Between 13 and 17 February alone, about seventy ships, from small auxiliaries to gunboats, minelayers, and steamers, were lost while fleeing.[11]

One typical escape attempt had a disastrous dénouement. On 12 February, three days before the fall of Singapore, the small steamer *Vyner Brooke* was loaded with more than two hundred elderly men and women, children, and sixty-five Australian Army nursing sisters. Two days later on the north Sumatra coast the ship blundered into an area where a Japanese convoy was unloading under the protection of the carrier *Ryujo*. The *Vyner Brooke* was bombed and sunk. Survivors headed to the nearest land. One group, with twenty-two nurses and a number of wounded men, made it ashore on Bangka Island. They were joined by about twenty-five surviving men from another sunken vessel. All were intercepted by a party of Japanese soldiers, who separated them into two groups. The men were marched out of sight behind a headland. Rifle shots were heard, and shortly thereafter the soldiers returned, cleaning their rifles and bayonets. The twenty-two nurses and one civilian were ordered to walk waist deep into the sea, when the Japanese opened fire on them. Nurse Vivien Bullwinkel took a bullet through her back. She fell and floated with the waves for ten minutes before being washed ashore. The Japanese were gone. Bullwinkel, the only survivor, dragged herself across the beach and into the jungle to hide. Another group of nurses who made it to shore were also captured. Although not executed, eight of them would later die in prison camps. Both the military and civilian population were rapidly discovering what it was like to fall into Japanese hands.[12]

PRISONERS FROM THE JAVA SEA

On 15 February 1942, the same day Singapore surrendered, Japanese forces landed on Sumatra. On the nineteenth they landed on Bali, while Vice Adm. Kondo Nobutake led his carrier armada into the Timor Sea to launch an attack on the harbor of Darwin, Australia, damaging eleven ships and sinking nine, including the U.S. Army transport *Meigs* and destroyer *Peary*. On the twenty-seventh, an invasion force including fifty-six transports approached western Java, and a second force including forty-one transports neared eastern Java. The proximity of all those juicy transports was more than enough to entice the American-British-Dutch-Australian (ABDA) fleet out from Surabaya to do battle. Rear Adm. Karel Doorman, in charge of the combined forces, charged out to fight but succeeded only in destroying his fleet. On 27 February, in the Battle of the Java Sea, he lost the Dutch destroyer *Kortenaer*, the British destroyers *Electra* and *Jupiter*, Dutch light cruisers *Java* and *De Ruyter* (his flagship), and his life. Meanwhile, south of Java, the seaplane tender *Langley* was sunk by aircraft. Damaged ships fled the scene, only to succumb on the bloody first of March. Destroyers *Edsall* and *Pillsbury* were caught south of Christmas Island by Kondo's carrier planes and sunk. The U.S. heavy cruiser *Houston* and Australian light cruiser *Perth* blundered into the western Java invasion force and were sunk in Sunda Strait after a hard fight. Trying to escape the Java Sea, which had become a ship trap, the British heavy cruiser *Exeter*, which had figured in the destruction of the German pocket battleship *Graf Spee*, the British destroyer *Encounter*, and the U.S. destroyer *Pope*, were all sent to the bottom by Japanese planes and surface ships.[13]

These appalling losses resulted in the Japanese reaping more prisoners from the sea. In the Indian Ocean south of Java, the *Edsall*, which had rescued 177 men from the *Langley*, transferred them to the tanker *Pecos*. Returning to Java,

Edsall was sunk by Japanese heavy cruisers *Tone* and *Chikuma*. Only 5 survivors reached land, all of whom later died as POWs. Meanwhile the *Pecos*, fleeing to Fremantle with 670 people on board, was sunk by aircraft from the carrier *Soryu*. This time the destroyer *Whipple* rescued 232 men and finally got them safely to Australia. In the same area on 2 March, the British destroyer *Stronghold* was intercepted by the heavy cruiser *Maya*. The battered DD went down, and 50 survivors were picked up by what appeared to be the Dutch steamer *Duymaer van Twist*. The ship, however, had been captured by the Japanese, and the luckless prisoners were transferred to the *Maya*.

Floating survivors of the Java Sea battle met various fates, depending solely on where they happened to drift, and which, if any, ship's captain happened to discover them. The U.S. submarine S-38, under Lt. Henry G. Munson, was patrolling near Bawean Island, unaware of the great sea battle that was being fought. Late on the twenty-eighth, a call brought Munson to the bridge. The low, dark silhouette on the water could be either wreckage or sampans. Munson wasn't sure, so the gun crew came topside and S-38 sped in for a look. As she neared the object, a voice cried out in the darkness, "My God, they're not finished with us yet!"

Astonished at hearing English, Munson hailed back, "Who are you?"

Several voices called out, "We're men of His Majesty's Ship *Electra!*"

S-38 hove to and began pulling aboard men from life rafts and floating debris. The job was rushed, for dawn was tinting the sky when the last man was picked up. There were fifty-four of them, thirsty, oily, and burned. Seventeen were badly wounded and one was dying, but they were all carried to safety. It was the first of many rescues to be accomplished by submarines. As an encore, S-37, under Lt. James C. Dempsey, rescued two American sailors who had been on the *De Ruyter* and left five days' worth of provisions for a boatload of the Dutch cruiser's survivors.[14]

The Japanese destroyer *Amatsukaze* had been prowling the same area. Cdr. Hara Tameichi's ship had been one of the escorts covering the eastern Java invasion force, when, on 26 February, he spotted a white-painted vessel. Halting it for inspection, he found it was the Dutch ship *Op ten Noort*, built in 1927 as a 6,076-ton passenger ship and recently converted to a hospital ship. Hara hustled the ship over to the care of his supply squadron commander, then sped back in time for the Java Sea fight. After the battle, low on fuel, the *Amatsukaze* was ordered to escort *Op ten Noort* to Borneo. Passing about sixty miles west of Bawean Island, Hara noticed more than a hundred Caucasians floating on wreckage, all with their hands held in the air and crying, "Water! Water!"

"The sight was pitiable," said Hara. "I had no personal hatred for the drowning enemy. But what could I do? My small ship could take only forty or fifty of them, at most. How could I discriminate and pick only half of these survivors?" He radioed his superior about the drifting men. As they steamed close by, one of Hara's lieutenants, who spoke English, called out to them to hang on, for they would soon be rescued. After taking the hospital ship to Bandjarmasin and refueling, the *Amatsukaze* passed the scene once again. The drifting survivors were nowhere to be found.[15]

The *Exeter*, damaged in the Battle of the Java Sea and accompanied by *Encounter* and *Pope*, headed along the Borneo coast in an attempt to reach Ceylon. It was hopeless, for they were caught by the Japanese heavy cruisers *Nachi, Haguro, Ashigara*, and *Myoko*, accompanying destroyers, and aircraft. *Exeter* was the first to be smothered with shells, then *Encounter*.

With the order to abandon the *Exeter*, Lt. R. Geoffrey Blain calmly removed his shoes, placed them at the rail, and stepped into the water. The cruisers moved away and Blain was left floating in his life vest with hundreds of others. That evening he noted how warm the sea was, though any exposed areas above the surface turned very cold. There were no sharks, but several men were bitten by sea snakes. The next morning two Japanese destroyers appeared. Blain later thought how ironic it was that they were so pleased at the time to climb up on a solid deck.

The destroyer *Inazuma*, under Lt. Cdr. Takeuchi Hajime, picked up 376 survivors, while *Yamakaze*, skippered by Lt. Cdr. Hamanaka Shuichi, rescued about 300 British seamen. Said Blain, "The conduct of the Japanese sailors was exemplary, and it was the high point of Japanese behavior during my three and one-half years in captivity." As they headed for Bandjarmasin, they were cared for and given a meal of condensed milk and biscuits. "This standard of treatment," said Blain, "was not to last."[16]

As *Exeter* and *Encounter* succumbed, the old World War I four-stacker *Pope* seemed to have a chance to escape as she beat her way back to the east. But old age, as much as Japanese near-misses, caught up with her. Ammunition was exhausted. The brick walls of the number three boiler had caved in from repeated concussions. One underwater blast gashed the hull. The port propeller shaft went out of line and was shut down. Bomb blasts had opened up seams in the hull and water rapidly filled the compartments. The aft weather deck was awash before Lt. Cdr. Welford C. Blinn gave the order to abandon ship. Demolition charges were set and *Pope* was on her way to the bottom when a last shell hit her upturned bow, applying the coup de grâce.

The cruisers pulled away, leaving 143 men floating on a whaleboat, rafts, and wreckage. Miraculously, only 1 had been killed. Blinn had them all roped together as they rationed their small supply of food and water. Hope was that they would be found by a friendly submarine. That night a red flare was fired, but it accomplished little except to briefly illuminate the lonely sea with an eerie glow. In the gray and drizzling morning they started the whaleboat's engine in the hope that the boat could tow them to Java. Near midnight they spotted four Japanese destroyers, but still hoping to be rescued by friends, they shut down the engine and remained silent. The DDs passed by at one thousand yards but did not spot them. On 3 March, the whaleboat's engine ran out of fuel. A low-flying Japanese seaplane hovered over them for a time, then flew off. Almost out of food and water, many began to think that it might be better to be captured than to die at sea. That night the last of the supplies were consumed and they waited. Bright moonlight rippled the wavelets in silver, and they were settling down for another lonely night when a black shape loomed. A signalman hoisted a waterproof battle lantern. The ship slowed and turned on its recognition lights. It was the *Inazuma* again, back in the area after dropping off *Exeter*'s survivors. A voice called out in Japanese, and Lt. William R. Wilson, fluent in the language, quickly explained their predicament. The DD hove to, turning on her lights and dropping a Jacob's ladder over the side.

Once on deck, Lt. (jg) John J. A. Michel was grabbed by two sailors while a third sprayed him with a carbolic acid mixture and a fourth rifled through his pockets and relieved him of his wallet and a rosary. Michel was taken to the forecastle, where the rest of the officers were assembled. Canvas screens and mats were rigged up, and they were motioned to sit. Michel was happy to comply, especially when given hardtack and a warm, sweet drink with a lemon flavor. They hungrily ate and lay down for a night's sleep.[17]

More prisoners were caught as Allied ships fled Java. The Japanese destroyer *Ikazuchi* spotted an escaping Dutch tanker and tried to capture it, but the crew scuttled the ship. If he could not seize the ship, Lt. Cdr. Kudo Shunsaku would bag the crew. *Ikazuchi* gathered them up and carried them to Bandjarmasin.

Next to run afoul of the victorious Japanese was the U.S. submarine *Perch*. On 25 February off Celebes, Lt. Cdr. David A. Hurt was about to make a night surface attack on a lone merchant ship when its concealed deck gun put a shell through her conning tower fairwater. *Perch* pulled clear. Three nights later she received news of the Java Sea battle and was told to head for the scene. Early in the morning on 2 March, about 20 miles north of Surabaya, *Perch* was on the surface recharging batteries when she was spotted by *Amatsukaze,* once again combing the area. Hara spun his ship around and charged in, letting go several salvos and claiming a direct hit on the conning tower. Following behind, the *Hatsukaze* echoed Hara's moves. But Hurt had already gone to periscope depth and watched the charging destroyers. With a zero angle on the bow, Hurt decided to head for 200 feet. Unfortunately, the sea bottom was at 140. As *Perch* punched into the mud, *Amatsukaze* crossed over with a string of charges, blasting the sub. Hurt cut the motors while *Hatsukaze* dropped her charges, shaking the boat again. The *Perch* was badly damaged: the engine-room gauges were broken or jammed, air banks in the after battery were leaking and the hull had been pushed in, the batteries showed full ground, the hull exhaust duct in the control room was flooded, the conning tower was dented in, the number two periscope was frozen, the crew's toilets were shattered, and several hatches were leaking. The crew waited in silence.

Above, the *Amatsukaze*'s sonar could not pick up a target. The area smelled strongly of oil, and Hara was elated, certain that he had made his first definite kill. The destroyers steamed away. It was lucky for *Perch* that they did, for Hurt, also hearing nothing from above, started his motors and, after struggling for a while, broke free and rose to the surface at about 0300. He had missed the destroyers by minutes.

In the predawn, the crew came topside to assess the damage. The antenna and blinker lights were down and the number one main engine was malfunctioning. Worse, *Perch* had only been up an hour when two more destroyers were seen heading her way, this time the *Ushio* and *Sazanami*. Hurt took her down to rest on the bottom, this time at two hundred feet, but the DDs had seen her and dropped several strings of depth charges. Main ballast tanks one and three ruptured. The engines' circulating water lines leaked. The bow planes were pushed in, and the rigging panel was burned. Torpedoes in number one and two tubes made hot runs. The hull over the officers' staterooms was dished in. The electric and telephone circuits went dead. After these attacks, the Japanese destroyers again steamed away, confident that they had made a kill. This time, however, *Perch* could not free herself from the muddy bottom. Before the crew could go full throttle and blow all remaining ballast in the hope of rising to the surface, they would have to wait until dark.

For thirteen hours the crew suffered in silence, quietly making repairs to ready the boat. About 2000, Hurt gave the command for full power to both shafts. After several tries, full forward and full astern, *Perch* pulled loose. She popped to the surface once more at about 2100 on 2 March. The crew faced a seventeen-hundred-mile trip to Australia, uncertain if they could submerge with any hope of surfacing. The *Perch* crept along, heading east. An hour before sunrise on the third, Hurt decided to make a test dive to assess the boat's condition. It didn't work. They could flood down, but they could not blow out the water fast enough. By blowing all ballast, *Perch* barely clawed her way to the surface, but the water in the engine-room bilges was up to the generators. Only the pumps running at maximum could keep her afloat.

As luck would have it, the breaking dawn also brought back the snooping destroyers, followed by cruisers *Nachi* and *Haguro*. It was over. Hurt ordered *Perch* scuttled and abandoned. Torpedoman Sam Simpson passed through the control room and got the word that they had better hurry because the sub was already sinking. He rushed out the conning tower hatch, then ran aft and sat down and took off his shoes. Classified material was given the deep-six, flood valves were opened, and nine officers and fifty-three men went over the side. Simpson floated in the sea while guns flashed and shells fountained up geysers of water. The *Perch* seemed to slip backward, then her bow rose and she slid below, stern first. Within the hour the *Ushio,* under Cdr. Uesugi Yoshitake, picked up the entire crew and headed toward Borneo.[18]

It was a veritable ABDA sailors' reunion in Bandjarmasin, although under the auspices of the Imperial Navy. Men from *Exeter* and *Encounter* were placed in the bowels of an old tanker, which contained four levels of wooden decks hastily constructed to carry Japanese troops to the beaches. "It was no consolation to us to know that we were being treated no worse than the Japanese soldiers," said Lieutenant Blain. The hatches were open, and Blain complained that the temperature was 90 degrees in the shade. But, he said, "there was no shade, and more important, there was no ventilation in the tanks."

They sat in the sweltering heat for three days. The Japanese had water, but the POWs had no containers to drink from. As men collapsed from heat-stroke, they were brought on deck a few at a time. After another day of heat, thirst, and interrogation, *Op ten Noort* pulled alongside. The Japanese mine-layer (CM) *Tsubame* was in port, and its sailors helped load and guard the more than nine hundred prisoners who transferred to the hospital ship. It was cleaner and cooler than the tanker, said Blain, but the Dutch crew shunned them, refusing even to treat their wounded. "What do you expect?" said one of the doctors. "You are only prisoners of war." The British sailors were fed rice balls supplied by the Japanese, while the Dutch ate their own rations and made no secret of it.

After a few days of chasing Allied submarines across the Java Sea, the *Amatsukaze* also returned to Bandjarmasin for fuel and supplies. Hara, still con-cerned about the drifting sailors he had seen near Bawean Island a week earlier, visited the hospital ship. He was relieved to learn that almost everyone had been picked up and *Op ten Noort* was filled with nearly one thousand prisoners. Seeing the cramped men huddled in narrow spaces reminded Hara of his cadet days. It was distressing, and he made an earnest wish never to be captured. Soon after, *Op ten Noort* weighed anchor for the trip to Makassar, Celebes.

Meanwhile, *Ushio* brought her catch of *Perch* men directly to Makassar, as did *Inazuma* with the *Pope* survivors, reaching port the next day, 5 March. Embarking on a landing barge off *Inazuma*, Lieutenant Michel saw a hospi-tal ship already docked in the harbor. An officer spoke to him. "I am sorry we could not make you more comfortable aboard this ship. When you go ashore you will learn true Japanese hospitality."

Once ashore, however, they were all thrown in a prison. The cells contained a few buckets—some for drinking water, others for toilets. The farther from the ship they got, Michel thought, the worse their situation grew. Soon, *Pope*'s sailors discovered that other cells held men from the *Exeter*. Two weeks later they were all marched to the outskirts of Makassar to a prison camp that held cap-tured Dutch troops. To their surprise, they also saw men from the *Perch*. Michel met a classmate from the Naval Academy, Jake Vandegrift, and his old instruc-tor, Commander Hurt. They were allowed to move in together. It might have been cause for celebration, were it not for the fact that they were all POWs.[19]

After a few weeks of incarceration they received notice that a number of men would be sent to Japan. Thirty-two senior British and American officers were rounded up, including all five from *Perch*, four from *Pope*, and nine from *Exeter*. All the commanding officers went, along with communications and gunnery officers, plus some enlisted radiomen. Apparently the Japanese were selecting those most likely to have knowledge of war plans and codes. *Perch* sailor Sam Simpson recalled that Commander Hurt kindly divided all his remaining money among his crew; each man received sixty cents.

The departing prisoners looked like hobos, bearded and dressed in ill-fitting, cast-off civilian clothing perhaps looted from the Dutch. The *Maru Ichi* (one) left Makassar about 2 April 1942, northbound for Japan.[20] The ship sailed to Yokohama, via Takao, and everyone was taken to Ofuna Camp for interrogation. The *Perch*'s Jake Vandegrift was questioned about his submarine's sonar gear. He pretended not to know what they were talking about. When pressed, he admitted that sonar was used for detection of ships, something they already knew. When asked how it worked, Vandegrift again pleaded ignorance. They asked what he did when it needed repair; he answered that it was sent to the sub tender to be fixed. They asked him why, if he was in charge of this equipment, he didn't he even want to know how it worked. Vandegrift replied that he never liked his job and he was always off relaxing in Manila. At this, the interrogator stood up and shouted, "Get out. You are a disgrace to the American Navy." Blinn's and Hurt's ignorance was not so readily accepted, and they were roughed up. Finally, after the Japanese had extracted all the information they could, the shaken prisoners were sent to their new home in Zentsuji. Nine of *Perch*'s crew would die as POWs.[21]

JAPANESE STRATEGY

The ABDA fleet was unsuccessful in keeping the Japanese off Java. Troops landed on opposite ends of the island and fought their way inland. The *Perth* and *Houston* had gone down in the Battle of Sunda Strait, after making a good fight against numerous destroyers and cruisers of the invasion's covering force. *Perth* lost half her crew, but 320 men finally made it to land. *Houston* sank twenty minutes later. More than 600 went down with her, but 368 of her crew made the Java shore. Many of those who reached land were captured by the Javanese and turned over to the Japanese invaders.

Finding resistance hopeless, the Dutch governor and Gen. Hein ter Poorten surrendered their forces, about 25,000 men, along with a mediocre Indonesian Home Guard force of 40,000, on 8 March. The 7,000 British, Australian, and American troops on Java were forced to follow suit. Commonwealth units included two veteran Australian battalions that had fought in the Middle East and a squadron of British 3d Hussars. Most of the Americans, about 550 of them, belonged to the 2d Battalion, 131st Field Artillery Regiment, 36th Division—the "Lost Battalion."

In Sumatra, escapees from Singapore had been streaming to the north and west coasts in the hope of catching ships to Ceylon. However, about 1,200 British escapees were rounded up in Padang and thrown in a Dutch barracks with men of the 18th Division and even sailors off the sunken *Prince of Wales* and *Repulse*. Swept up on Sumatra were also civilian escapees from Singapore, New Zealanders, and Royal Air Force (RAF) men without their planes. Farther north, some diehard Dutch troops fought on for three weeks after General ter Poorten surrendered his forces on Java, holding out near Kota Cane before giving up. The Japanese were aided by Indonesian rebels who did not want their land "scorched" by the retreating Dutch.[22]

How might this new wealth of prisoners fit in with future Japanese plans? The great majority of Japanese divisions had always been kept in China, where they had waged war for several years. Yet the Chinese would not crack. Supplies helping to sustain them came through the "back door," trucked along the tenuous Burma Road or flown over the "Hump" of the Himalayas in cargo planes. The Japanese could never conquer China while these reinforcement routes were open. Japan took Malaya with relative ease, and her occupation of Thailand was made even easier when the two countries signed a treaty in December 1941, permitting stationing and transit of Japanese troops. Japan was now poised on the Burma border, but crossing over was not easy due to the mountainous spine with four-thousand-foot peaks and steep river chasms separating the countries. Nevertheless, Japanese troops struggled over the mountains, and once in the relatively flat land beyond, hastened their drive across Burma to the Indian border.

Possession of Burma was far from being a panacea; on the contrary, it brought on a host of new problems. At the far end of its empire, Japan was now next door to British and Indian bases and open to counterattack. Poor land connections meant that sea communications were critical. Rangoon, near the mouths of the Irrawaddy and Chindwin Rivers, was the key to land communication in Burma. But to hold Rangoon, one had to control the Andaman Sea and much of the eastern Indian Ocean. It could perhaps be done, but it would take great number of ships and escorts. A round-trip sea journey from Singapore to Rangoon was more than twenty-two hundred miles. Japan started the war with about 6 million tons of shipping. She captured about 800,000 additional tons. Even so, by the end of the initial Burma campaign, in May 1942, Japan had lost about 314,000 tons of shipping. In other words, supplying Burma by sea was potentially a costly endeavor.

The distance from Bangkok to Rangoon by sea is about 2,000 miles; by land it is only 350 miles. Why not connect the two port cities by land? The route would be protected from Allied naval interception, and supplies along it could be moved much more quickly. A good railway already existed between Singapore and Bangkok; in fact, rails stretched west 40 miles from Bangkok to Ban Pong, and from Rangoon east to Moulmein and Thanbuyzayat. The gap between railheads was only about 250 miles. Why not extend the railway over the mountains and connect the railheads? The route had been explored before, by European powers, but the dense, hostile jungle, the engineering problems, and the high costs in dollars and, very likely, in human lives had been more than enough reasons to shelve the idea. Now the war brought a new imperative. There were mountains, jungles, tigers, pythons, kraits, scorpions, monsoons, floods, and diseases to contend with. The human cost, however, would be relatively insignificant: Japan had a great labor pool at its fingertips.[23]

The contemplated Burma-Thailand Railway was not the only project that could employ prisoner labor. With every Japanese soldier needed at the front, prisoners could be used for scores of other tasks: to build and repair roads, load and unload ships, construct and maintain airfields, and toil in the mines and factories of the empire itself. In April 1942, the Japanese began marshaling their prisoners north for the preparations that would culminate in the great railway project. The move would require an increase in rail and sea voyages.

NORTH TO BURMA AND THAILAND

After the fall of Singapore, British and Australian prisoners were moved to various barracks at Changi, on the northeast tip of the island. The Indians were housed separately and were exhorted to break their allegiance to Britain, change sides, and join the pro-Japanese Indian National Army. About 40,000 out of 45,000 switched, becoming guards of their old masters or fighting directly against the British in Burma. On 4 April 1942, 1,125 British prisoners from Changi, under the command of Lieutenant Colonel Hugonin, were sent by rail up the Malay Peninsula to Bangkok and east to Saigon in French Indochina. They worked in the area for a year before half of them were sent back to Thailand to build the railway.

The next party to move north was designated A Force, a group of about 3,000 Australians, mostly from 22 Infantry Brigade, under forty-nine-year-old Brig. Arthur L. Varley. They went down to the wharf on 14 May and began loading. They were divided into three battalions of about 1,000 men each. The first, under Lt. Col. G. E. Ramsay of 2/18 Battalion, boarded *Celebes Maru*. The second, in command of Maj. D. R. Kerr of the 2/10 Field Regiment, and the third, under Maj. Charles B. Green of 2/4 Machine Gun Battalion, boarded the 7,031-ton cargo ship *Toyohashi Maru*.

Ken Williams, a corporal in the 27th Brigade, stood in line. He was already thirty-six years old, had a wife and two children, and probably shouldn't have joined the army. The Depression, though, had hit him hard, especially working as a blacksmith for forty-eight shillings a week. By 1940, with the number of motorized trucks on the increase, Ken had decided that blacksmithing had no future. He joined the Australian Imperial Forces (AIF). And what did they need, but a blacksmith! Talk was that the force moving north was not to be a working party, so there was no need to take medical supplies or equipment. Waiting to board, however, Williams began to have second thoughts as he saw hundreds of picks and shovels being loaded.

"Holy Hell," exploded one soldier who used to work the Fremantle docks and was familiar with *Celebes Maru*. The single-screw freighter of 5,824 tons, built by Kawasaki in 1917, was 385 feet long, with a top speed of thirteen knots and a cargo capacity of about 2,000 tons. The soldier called the maru "old blue-bottle" and complained, "If we are to go aboard that thing we'll be in sheep pens. Pre-war, I helped load thousands onto that old bucket and the poor old sheep had barely enough room to stand."

The "bucket," however, was to be their new home. While waiting for hours to load, a few Aussies managed to purloin some edibles from a nearby godown (warehouse). They were bashed with rifle butts or hung up by their thumbs. The prisoners loaded through the day, slowly crawling up rope ladders, and did not finish until 0100, 15 May. One lad fell from deck level and broke his leg. He was sent back to Changi—one of the lucky ones.

True to the former dockworker's word, *Celebes Maru* contained sheep pens. About 640 men were put in the largest aft hold, and the remaining 360 were put in the forward hold. The air was fetid. When they were fed, the sweat from bodies on the upper levels dripped down into the men's rice below. Those afflicted with dysentery fouled themselves, but not until Lieutenant Colonel Ramsay pleaded for them to be allowed to use the two, three-hole "toilets." Even so, it was not enough; the deck was fouled, and the returning users spread excrement from stem to stern. It was so hot below decks that Ramsay again pleaded to the ship's captain to have a windsock rigged to funnel some air into the holds. They thus made their way to Sumatra.[24]

On 9 May, before A Force was collected, groups of Allied POWs on Sumatra were being gathered on the south coast at Padang. The British Sumatra Battalion, a group of 498 British and 2 Australian officers, all under Maj. Dudley Apthorpe, joined 1,200 Dutch troops and began the journey. They went north by road and rail, through the mountains and past the beautiful Lake Toba district. On the twelfth, trucks carried them to Medan on the north coast, and they were placed in the Uni Kampong Camp, which was then occupied by Dutch civilians. On the fifteenth, they hiked the last miles to the port of Belawan and boarded the ironically named *England Maru*, a 5,038-ton cargo ship built in 1919 and owned by Yamasita Kisen Company. In the holds they packed into a four-foot-high wooden tier that had been built around the hull to accommodate troops. The Dutch climbed on the 5,493-ton *Kyokusei Maru*, a former Canadian ship built in 1920.

After one false start, the ships returned to Belawan to await the arrival of the two ships from Singapore. On the sixteenth, 350 Japanese troops boarded the heavily laden *Celebes Maru*. They were joined by a minesweeper, and the five-ship convoy headed north through the Strait of Malacca. The weather remained hot, and below decks men became seasick, adding to their misery. Constant protests by the officers finally resulted in groups of 50 men being allowed on deck for twenty minutes at a time. The fresh air, plus a brief hose down with salt water, was almost heaven. On *England Maru* the officers were segregated from the men, but Major Apthorpe went down to see them, and on one occasion passed some stolen Japanese cigarettes to a Sergeant Pearce. The next day, Apthorpe was beaten for stealing cigarettes. Pearce sought out the major and said he was sorry for what happened.

"Sergeant," Apthorpe asked, "did you enjoy smoking them?"

"Of course," Pearce replied, though he added that it did not seem worth the beating.

"Then that's all that matters," said Apthorpe. "I enjoyed stealing them, it was just unfortunate that we were caught."

On 20 May, after a voyage described as "appalling," the convoy stopped at Victoria Point, at the southern tip of Burma, where the 1,017 Aussies of Green Force were taken off the *Toyohashi Maru* by barges and the Dutch were unloaded off *Kyokusei Maru*. They were to work either at the Victoria Point wharves or at the nearby airfield. Next stop was Mergui, where on 24 May the *Celebes Maru* disgorged Ramsay Force and *England Maru* deposited the British Sumatra Battalion. They were put to work building an airstrip. *Toyohashi Maru* carried Major Kerr's remaining 983 Australians to Tavoy on 26 May, where they came under command of senior officer Lt. Col. Charles Anderson and were thereafter known as Anderson Force.[25]

The unloaded convoy remained at Tavoy until 1 June, when it sailed back for Singapore without an escort. Patrolling at the north end of Malacca Strait was the British submarine HMS *Trusty* on her third patrol, under Lieutenant Commander Balston. In the predawn darkness of 4 June, he noticed four ships steaming south, about seventy miles southwest of Phucket, Malaya. Picking out the largest target, the *Trusty* fired a salvo of torpedoes at the unsuspecting ships. At 0335, two torpedoes hit *Toyohashi Maru,* striking holds one and seven on the starboard side. Heavy explosions shook her and she flooded quickly. The ship, built by Kawasaki in 1915, owned by the Nippon Yusen Kaisha (NYK) Line, and carrying thirty-five shipping engineers, went down at 0400. Sixteen gunnery force members and one crewmen were killed, while the survivors were picked up by *Kyokusei Maru*. The remaining three ships quickly headed for Penang, Malaya. The *Toyohashi Maru* was the first of the hellships to be sunk. Had *Trusty* found the convoy on its outward voyage, there might have been a disaster for the Allies.[26]

TO AND FROM SINGAPORE

On the same day *Toyohashi Maru* was torpedoed another ship was bringing more prisoners to Singapore, among them Frans J. N. Ponder of the Royal Netherlands–Indies Army (KNIL). Ponder, who had been ashamed when General ter Poorten surrendered almost without a shot, had been shifted to a number of camps in Java before ending up in Batavia. On 4 June, he and about five hundred Dutch prisoners boarded *Maru Ni* (two), an old freighter of about three thousand tons. Most of them were packed into the hold by the liberal use of rifle butts, but Ponder was lucky enough to be given a spot topside.

The maru steamed laboriously out of the harbor, only to be buffeted with strong winds and rough water. Since the toilets were located on deck, those below who became seasick could not climb up in time; many vomited on the ladders or on deck. Said Ponder, "In no time there was an unbelievably smelly mess." In addition to seasickness, many had diarrhea. Japanese guards were posted to control toilet usage, but it was a losing battle. During the five-day journey to Singapore, a number of POWs died and were buried at sea. When they disembarked on 9 June, the filthy men were lined up on deck and washed down with hoses. The Dutchmen were marched to Changi.[27]

Not all the parties passing through Singapore went by sea. A group of six hundred prisoners left Changi on 18 June for the Singapore rail depot, where they were packed in boxcars and sent north. They were followed by four more six-hundred-man trainloads at two-day intervals. This was a mixed group of incomplete units, consisting of III Indian Corps, the British 18th Division, Singapore garrison troops, and the Federated Malay States Volunteer Force, a unit consisting of local Europeans. The tired, underfed, dispirited work force of three thousand detrained at Ban Pong, the junction where the rails went either east to Bangkok or west, up the new railway to Burma. Over the next two years, Ban Pong would be the transit camp where thousands of workers would assemble.

Not all the prisoners leaving Singapore were destined for the Burma Railway project. In early July, Yamada Masaharu, a staff officer at Kuching Headquarters in Borneo, visited Changi looking for laborers. He selected about 1,500 Australians, including 145 officers, to sail to another one of those mythical new camps where work would be light and food plentiful. B Force, under Lt. Col. A. W. Walsh of 2/10 Battalion, boarded *Ume Maru*, a 5,859-ton cargo ship built by Kawasaki in 1919. The prisoners filed into three holds—340 in the forward, 760 in the center, and 400 aft—and sailed on 7 July. Pvt. Tom Burns, 2/20 Battalion, wrote in his diary that there were only two water tanks, about two square meters each, at the bow and stern. In three days they were empty, and the men had to scrounge water from the winches or Japanese supplies—both prohibited. The ship had recently carried coal, and between decks everything was covered with fine black dust that seeped into every pore of the body.

"It reminds me of those pictures of the slave ship days," Burns wrote. "Well I say that nothing can compare with this dreadful boat." Noticing that they had no escort, and seeing very few sailors or guards, the prisoners discussed the possibility of taking over the ship, but the senior officers decided to wait for a better opportunity.

William Young, a sixteen-year-old private in 2/29 Battalion, AIF, had a presentiment. He couldn't help but feel that *Ume Maru* was a ghost ship and the passengers only spirits embarking on their final journey. He knew it would be a one-way trip. They were crammed together like sardines in the holds, the men trying desperately to breathe in the humid steam. Finally, the Japanese rigged a canvas sail that scooped air into the holds. "Not wanting to spoil their record against humanity," Young sarcastically commented, "they proceeded to feed us rice, green with lime and smelling of sulphur—making a most appropriate gruel for a hell ship." Many came down with dysentery—the "squitters," as Young called it. He said he finally came to know what was meant by the phrase "To shit through the eye of a needle." The *benjos* (latrines), built over the sides of the ship, were too few and too far away. Many could not wait in line long enough, before the "bomb bays" opened prematurely. There was one consolation, however: they believed that the bad smell kept the guards away.

"My God, this is dreadful," Tom Burns wrote a few days after sailing. "I am sure there will be a lot who won't survive the trip, as most are very sick men just out of hospital."

With a cruising speed of only nine knots, *Ume Maru* crept eastward along the equator. "Talk about the Slow Boat to China," complained Young, "this thing we were on went backwards more often than forwards." And it was hot. "If we had the eggs we could have fried them on the deck," he said, adding, "Umm, if only we had the eggs, and some salt—perhaps some tomatoes and bacon?" Someone speculated that they were going to Japan, another said Sandakan.

"Where the hell is Sandakan?" one man asked.

"In Bloody Borneo!" came the reply.

"Borneo! Where's Borneo?" said another.

No one knew for sure. Their first stop was at Miri, an oil town two-thirds of the way up the west coast. That night, Bill Young and Joey Crome stood at the rail in a niche between the *benjos* and a storage box. They saw the lights of Miri twinkling across the surface of a black, calm sea, and they talked about trying to swim to shore.

"Whaddya think? Just a bit of a paddle," said one.

"Yea, piece of cake," came the reply.

"You go first."

"Naw, you go first."

Just then the galley door opened and out came a Japanese cook with a bucket of swill that he cast overboard. The garbage no sooner hit the water than the sea boiled up with a hundred fish, streaking fluorescent trails, fighting over the meal. Then up from the depths came a great shark, scattering the small fry and making off with the prize. The two soldiers stood silent for a moment. The ghostly lights of Miri looked a little colder, and the ship's hold took on a cozier glow. They went below.

The *Ume Maru* reached Sandakan on 17 July. The capital of North Borneo, Sandakan was home to only seventy Europeans, who were not incarcerated until May 1942, four months after the Japanese landed. They were then rounded up and sent to Berhala, a small island off the coast containing a leper colony. B Force unloaded. Tom Burns, black with coal, haggard, and unshaven, was glad to get out and stretch his limbs. He thought Sandakan was picturesque, framed by cliffs and interspersed with many single-story, red-roofed buildings. Native huts were built on pilings at the waterfront, while beautiful homes dotted the surrounding hills. They marched, singing "Waltzing Matilda," about eight miles inland from the port, to an internment camp on what had been a British experimental farm. The site was first meant to hold two hundred Japanese residents of Borneo. With the tables turned, however, fifteen hundred Australians now occupied the camp. The prisoners were to build an airfield and a road to connect it to the port at Sandakan.[28]

The Japanese could find many uses for their prisoners, not all of them requiring muscle power. On 4 March 1942, a telegram was received by the Japanese War Ministry, sent by Gen. Itagaki Seishiro of the Chosen Army in Korea: "As it would be very effective in stamping out the respect and admiration of the Korean people for Britain and America, and also in establishing in them a strong faith in [our] victory, and as the Governor General [Taisho Minami] and the Army are both strongly desirous of it, we wish you would intern 1,000 British and 1,000 American prisoners of war in Korea. Kindly give this matter special consideration." A reply was sent the next day that a thousand "white prisoners of war" would be sent to Korea. The appearance of British and American POWs in chains was deemed to be of great psychological value in winning the hearts and minds of the Koreans. Consequently, in May, Lt. Gen. Kusaba Tatsumi of the 25th Army in Malaya was ordered to hand over white POWs to the Korean Army.

On 12 August, fifteen hundred prisoners were marched to the Singapore docks. Lt. Tom Henling Wade of the East Surrey Regiment stood in line with the rest. His unit was one of many that had voted for the trip to Japan. The rationale: a temperate and healthier climate. Wade wasn't convinced. He abstained from voting but decided to go along to keep the unit together. On the waterfront they were confronted by a rusty old freighter so low in the water that only the bridge and funnel were visible above the pier. They were supposed to fit themselves in among the loads of bauxite. Groans were heard. "You could sink that ship with a .303 bullet," said one man.

Standing in line with the rest was Lt. Gen. Arthur E. Percival, the man who carried the stigma of having surrendered Singapore. About four hundred of the fifteen hundred men were high-ranking technicians, engineers, and officers. For three hours the generals vehemently protested that there was no way sixteen hundred men could be crammed into that ship. Surprisingly, they won their argument. The four hundred were put into the hold of the larger *England Maru*. As on most voyages of this type, there was a complete lack of privacy for basic latrine functions. Percival's aide said he "felt terribly sorry for the General," adding that he was also "bloody sorry for myself."

Wade, with the eleven hundred remaining POWs, were put aboard the 3,829-ton cargo ship *Fukkai Maru*. It was ancient and rusty, built in England in 1898 with an extra-tall, old-fashioned funnel. Wade called it a "fumigation ship." The men undressed, were disinfected and powdered for lice, then redressed and embarked. They were divided between the forward and aft holds. The upper part of each had been divided by a shelf, leaving about three feet of space above and below the tiers. No one could stand or kneel; they had to lie, sit, or crawl. It was four days before they got underway, and the men stripped down to their shorts and sat motionless on the straw matting. There was not much more room on deck, as it was crowded with winches, vats, rafts, crates, a cookhouse, an icebox, and a water tank. They were fed rice twice a day, with a thin soup made of flour and water. The big treat came when eighteen tins of Irish stew was divided among them. The contingent was all British except for about one hundred Australians. Wade was pleased to have the Australians aboard, for he loved to hear them sing "Waltzing Matilda" late at night. As the Southern Cross slowly dipped below the horizon, Wade dreamed of freedom and wondered if he had made the right choice.

The convoy made a brief stop at Saigon, then on to Formosa, arriving at Takao on 29 August. According to H. M. "Dutchy" Holland of 2/4 Battalion, "The trip was pretty rough, we ran into three typhoons in the China Sea. Food was fair, we were in the 'dog houses' in the hold; double tiered bunks with about three feet of head room and limited space to lie down." At Takao, *England Maru* disgorged its party of officers, which moved on to Heito. Percival noted the camp had "no redeeming feature." They were paraded in front of the silent Formosans and forced to sign a "no escape" paper. Some stayed at Heito; others were sent to the east coast at Karenko, where they would meet other high-ranking American officers from the Philippines.

Those on *Fukkai Maru* were forced to work as stevedores, unloading bauxite, coal, and rice for a fortnight before continuing the voyage. Twenty-four seriously ill dysentery patients were left at Takao. The weather turned chilly and stormy. The food ran low, and the "icebox" was opened to expose its contents of rotten pork, bright with emerald patches. The cooks sliced off the worst parts and the rest went into the prisoners' soup. Said Lieutenant Wade, "All eleven hundred of us developed diarrhea." The lines to the six wooden latrines grew longer.

Finally, on 22 September, forty-one days after boarding in Singapore, they docked in Pusan, Korea. One ritual shared by almost all POWs landing in the empire was to drop his trousers and bend over, while Japanese doctors inserted glass rods up their rectums. No one was quite sure what was done with these "specimens," but the procedure certainly resulted in no special medical care. Within two weeks, ten men died of dysentery.

After the prisoners pulled up their pants, they were photographed and given another going over by the Kempeitai, Japan's secret police, an organization similar to Germany's Gestapo. A whole company of them in their red pigskin boots, with *ken hei* (thought soldier) on their brassards, inspected the sorry prisoners, stealing their last few rings, watches, and personal items.

The Koreans of Pusan had been marshaled along the streets, and the POWs were lined up in columns of fours and marched up and down the main thoroughfares. Mounted Japanese officers rode at the head while guards walked alongside. They marched under the hot sun all day, only twice allowed to rest, both times near the playgrounds of schools, where children were allowed to spit on them.

The ordeal completed, they were taken to the train station and shipped to Seoul, where they once again performed the parade of jeers. Finally, they reached the camp that was to be their home for the next two years. Several of them died within the next few days. The Kempeitai was pleased with the public propaganda spectacle. Official humiliation of the enemy, which would become common practice in Japanese-occupied areas, went well.[29]

PRISONERS FROM THE BISMARCKS

Lying between the tail of the New Guinea "bird" and the equator, the Bismarck Archipelago was the scene of some of the toughest fighting in the Pacific in 1942–43. Simpson Harbor and Rabaul, on the east end of New Britain, was the major Japanese base in the area for two years. The initial landing came on 22 January 1942, with an amphibious assault under the Japanese Fourth Fleet, which had much the same composition as the one that attacked Wake. This time it was supported by Admiral Nagumo's carrier force, and no Allied ships opposed it.

For years the only "defenders" of New Guinea, the Bismarck Archipelago, and the Solomon Islands were the Australian coastwatchers, a network of local volunteers under the auspices of the Royal Australian Navy who kept an eye on the vast unguarded coast. By 1941, there were more than seven hundred coastwatchers on the rolls, placed at one hundred coast watching stations along a twenty-five-hundred-mile crescent of islands. The station at Rabaul coordinated operations in that sector. These men were watchers only; any serious defense would need armed troops. With that in mind, 23 Brigade of the 8th Division was sent as a nucleus of forces to be placed at various islands north of Australia. The 2/40 Battalion, or "Sparrow Force," went to Timor, 2/21 Battalion, or "Gull Force," went to Ambon, and 2/22 Battalion, "Lark Force," went to Rabaul.

Australia had neither the naval nor air power to support these forces in the event of a major Japanese thrust. There seems to have been no contingency plans to assist the battalions after being placed in such exposed positions. In fact, it was thought that their only function was to "put up a jolly good show."

Montevideo Maru. U.S. Naval Historical Center

When the Japanese landed, they quickly punched a hole in the coastwatch-ers' fence. The volunteers and about four hundred men of Lark Force either fell back into the jungle or retreated along the coasts back to New Guinea. The remaining eleven hundred men put up a brief fight, but the next day they sur-rendered the city and airfield. Thereafter they languished as prisoners at the Malaguna Road Camp until 22 June 1942, when they were separated into *kumis* of fifty men each, then bundled off to Simpson Harbor. Perhaps fearing an uprising, the officers were left behind, awaiting another ship.

About 1,050 men, mostly of 2/22 Battalion, together with 200 civilians, many of them Australian administrative personnel, were loaded on the *Montevideo Maru.* She was a passenger-cargo ship of 7,266 tons built by Mit-subishi in 1926 and was capable of eighteen knots, which was probably enough to outrun all but the latest fleet submarines in a surface chase. Subsequently, she was not escorted. *Montevideo Maru* cut through the dangerous "Red Channel" west of New Ireland, then northwest through the Philippine Sea, heading for Samah on the island of Hainan. Conditions were crowded, with little food, water, or amenities, much as on other hellships. However, no Australian soldier or civilian left a record of the voyage, for *Montevideo Maru* was fated to cross paths with the USS *Sturgeon.*

Late on 30 June, Lt. Cdr. William L. "Bull" Wright conned his submarine about sixty miles northwest of Cape Bojeador, Luzon. At 2216, lookouts sighted a darkened ship to the south. After a few minutes of tracking, it was decided that the ship was on a westerly course, running at high speed. Wright guessed the ship had gone through Babuyan Channel and was headed for Hainan. *Sturgeon* worked up to full power and headed west in an attempt to get ahead. However, logged Wright, "for an hour and a half we couldn't make a nickel. This fellow was really going, making at least seventeen knots, and probably a bit more, as he appeared to be zig-zagging."

It looked hopeless, but Wright hung on, hoping the ship would slow or change course. The range stayed about eighteen thousand yards, but sure enough, about midnight, the ship slowed to twelve knots. Said Wright, "After that it was easy."

Sturgeon altered course to get ahead in good firing position, dove, and waited. At five thousand yards, Wright discovered the maru's course was a little south of west, so *Sturgeon* altered her own course to compensate. With only three torpedoes left in the forward tubes, Wright maneuvered to expose the stern tubes. Even so, it was nearly four thousand yards to the target—a very long shot.

At 0225 on 1 July, the four stern fish were racing toward the darkened, unsuspecting ship. Perhaps all of the prisoners were sleeping in the holds; perhaps there were a few on deck who witnessed the approaching torpedo wakes. At 0229, Wright heard and observed an explosion less than one hundred feet abaft the stack. Finally, lights came on, but they soon flickered out as the ship lost power. In six minutes the bow was high in the air, and in eleven minutes the ship was completely gone. "He was a big one," Wright noted in the log. *Sturgeon* surfaced at 0250, completed her battery charge, and proceeded unconcernedly out of the area, unaware of the human toll she had exacted.

On board *Montevideo Maru,* Japanese survivors indicated that two torpedoes struck in the number four and five holds and in the number five oil tank. Oil gushed into the engine room. Pumps were started but were unable to quell the rapid flooding. Holds filled, and the ship listed to starboard and down by the stern. Within minutes the captain ordered abandon ship. No one bothered about the prisoners deep in the holds. Three lifeboats were lowered, but all capsized, one severely damaged. After being righted, the two remaining boats searched the area until midmorning, then headed for the coast of Luzon, reaching there the evening of the following day. They set out on a trek to find

Sturgeon (SS 187). U.S. Naval Institute

the nearest Japanese base but were harassed and attacked by the natives. Not until 25 July did eighteen wretched survivors reach an Army outpost.

No Australians survived. Either they all went down with the explosion and crush of water or those who escaped were abandoned by the Japanese in their lifeboats. The relatives of the men of Lark Force perhaps endured more anguish than any, having to wait almost four years before being informed by the Japanese what had happened to the men taken prisoner in Rabaul. *Montevideo Maru* was the first hellship loaded with POWs to be sunk by a U.S. submarine. It would not be the last.[30]

Lark Force soldiers had been separated from their officers in Rabaul. Whether this was because the Japanese feared a mutiny is unknown. In any event, on 6 July, six days after their men were already dead, sixty officers under Colonel Scanlan, six Australian military nurses, and thirteen female Australian civilians were taken to Simpson Harbor. They boarded the *Naruto Maru*, a 7,148-ton passenger ship built in 1934, now serving as an ammunition supply ship. The only concession to privacy was a rope across one hold, separating male from female quarters. One nurse called it "a dirty old freighter" and said, "We were all mixed together and spent nine days sweating and starving before we reached Japan." The convoy reached Yokohama on 15 July. The Aussie officers ended up at Zentsuji Camp, the women at Totsuka. They all survived the war. The Japanese destroyer *Akikaze* was a convoy escort as far as Saipan, where she was detached and returned to Rabaul via Truk. *Akikaze* would herself be involved in an incident resulting in a prisoner massacre the following year.[31]

CAPTURE OF THE PHILIPPINES

In December 1941, the Japanese landed on Luzon, the main northern island of the Philippines. Unlike Japan's other conquests in Southeast Asia and the East Indies, the Philippines proved a tougher nut to crack. Several landings were made between the tenth and twenty-fourth of the month, at Aparri, Vigan, Legaspi, and Lamon Bay, but the main force boiled ashore in Lingayen Gulf. The Japanese 16th and 48th Divisions and supporting elements pushed rapidly inland, racing south down the central valley for Manila. Gen. Douglas MacArthur's troops fought holding actions while other elements, including soldiers, sailors, civilians, and Filipinos, fell back to defend the Bataan Peninsula. As in the Malayan campaign, the Allied force was pushed back by a Japanese force inferior in numbers. The Japanese were doing so well that, against the protests of Gen. Homma Masaharu, the 48th Division was recalled to prepare for the East Indies operation. Once the U.S.-Filipino army caught its breath and consolidated, however, the Japanese were stymied. They battered themselves against a series of defensive lines stretched across the Bataan Peninsula. By mid-February, battle casualties, disease, and short supplies forced a temporary end to offensive operations. Both sides waited.

By early March, elements of the Japanese 4th and 21st Divisions had arrived to renew the battle. Ordered by President Franklin Roosevelt to vacate the Philippines, MacArthur left by PT boat on 11 March, leaving newly promoted Lt. Gen. Jonathan Wainwright in charge. To many of those left behind, "Dugout Doug" MacArthur had fled, leaving them holding the bag. The remnants of the U.S. 11th, 21st, 31st, 41st, 51st, 71st, and 91st Divisions would fight on, without additional supplies or reinforcements.

The end on Bataan came on 9 April, more the result of a lack of food, medicine, and supplies than Japanese assaults. Unable to continue the struggle, Gen. Edward P. King Jr. called it off. Some men were struck by the date; the last time a U.S. army had surrendered was also on 9 April, when Robert E. Lee did so at Appomattox in 1865.

Still holding out on the island of Corregidor were Wainwright's eleven thousand men of the 31st Division, 4th Marine Regiment, and soldiers of various units that had managed to get ashore from Bataan. They fought for twenty-seven more days, until the Japanese landed on the island and Wainwright, facing the annihilation of his entire command, went to see General Homma.[32]

Those who surrendered on Bataan suffered through the hell of the Death March. The Japanese had plans for taking prisoners, but they were based on faulty assumptions. First, they assumed that the prisoners would be in good physical condition, which they were not. There was no plan for caring for sick, hungry, and wounded men. Second was the assumption that their own food supplies and logistical planning would be up to the task, which it was not. Third, the Japanese assumed they might have to transfer twenty-five thousand captives to POW camps. Their estimate was far from accurate.

About ten thousand Americans and sixty-two thousand Filipinos were forced to walk sixty miles up the Bataan Peninsula and east to the railhead at San Fernando. They then rode in boxcars for twenty miles, finally marching an additional ten miles to Camp O'Donnell. Along the way they were subjected to countless robberies, brutalities, and killings. Many Filipinos were able to escape from the columns, darting into the jungles and villages, relatively safe among their own people. Even so, perhaps five thousand Filipinos and seven hundred Americans died before reaching the camp. But O'Donnell was no haven, for even more were to die there in the upcoming months from disease, starvation, and beatings.

The soldiers and marines who surrendered on Corregidor did not suffer the same death march, and their casualties were less horrific. There were other prison camps on Luzon, among them Cabanatuan, Tarlac, Las Pinas, Nichols Field, Pasay, Fort McKinley, and Bilibid Prison. Civilian internment centers were opened at Santo Tomas, Camp John Hay, and Los Banos, among other sites, containing about seventy-eight hundred men, women, and children.[33]

PRISONER MOVES FROM THE PHILIPPINES

Other than on Luzon, the main strength of the U.S.-Filipino force was on Mindanao. Brig. Gen. William F. Sharp commanded the 61st, 81st, and 101st Divisions, composed almost entirely of Filipino troops. Their surrender came on 8 May, two days after Wainwright's. Many of the Filipinos were able to melt back into the countryside, whereas the Americans were imprisoned at Del Monte, on the north coast, or at Malabalay, in Mindanao's central valley.[34]

Almost immediately the Japanese began moving prisoners among the islands. At Camp O'Donnell in July, groups of volunteers were asked to move

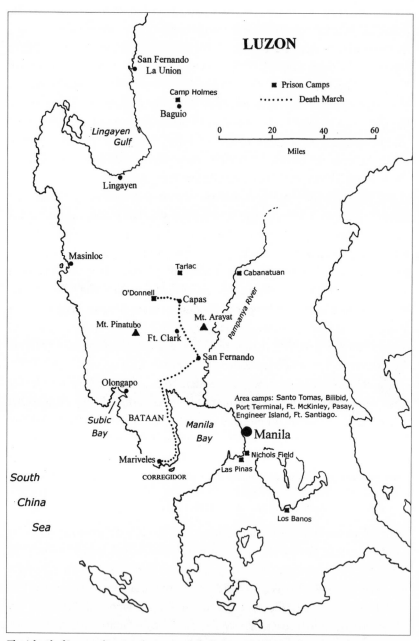

The island of Luzon, showing the route of the Bataan Death March and prison and internment centers, 1942–45.

to several Philippine islands. Many grasped the chance, willing to try anything to get out of the O'Donnell hellhole. One group included Sidney Stewart, a peculiar sort of soldier who became ill every time he saw blood or saw someone get hurt. Stewart found himself on a small interisland steamer with a few hundred others, traveling from Manila to Cebu City, to Zamboanga on Mindanao's southwest peninsula, then to Davao. Conditions on the steamer were much better than in the camp. There was sufficient food, and the guards even joked and laughed. In the ports, they allowed Filipinos to throw fruit to them. They disembarked at Davao and were trucked north to the former Davao Penal Colony, whose criminal occupants had been sent to the leper colony on the island of Palawan. During the following weeks, Army Air Corps arrivals from Del Monte swelled the prison camp's numbers.

In July, Camp O'Donnell was closed down and most of the prisoners were removed to one of the Cabanatuan camps. On 24 July, another call for men was made, and 346 prisoners from Cabanatuan were selected. They traveled, a hundred men to a rail car, to Bilibid Prison, and from there to the famous million-dollar Pier Seven on the Manila waterfront. On the twenty-ninth, they boarded the *Sanko Maru,* a 5,461-ton turbine steamer built in 1939. The entire party was quartered in one hold, where the interpreter told them they were going on a "three-month detail," they would be fed "American food," and things "would be very enjoyable."

Among them was 4th Marine Sgt. Donald H. Thomas, who was captured at Corregidor and had spent the previous few months in Bilibid Prison. Thomas called the steamer a "middle-sized freighter, hauling supplies and Jap soldiers." Generally a man did not take many trips on a prison ship, but Thomas called it "one of the best prison ships I was on." The voyage was uneventful, and the prisoners even had the freedom to roam the vessel. The steamer made the 350-mile trip to Palawan, stopped at a leper colony, and docked at Puerto Princesa on 1 August.

Making the journey was PO Henry Clay Henderson, who had been aboard the sub tender *Canopus* and was left to fight on Corregidor after the tender had been bombed and scuttled. Henderson said they were all in a weakened condition after months of immobility at Cabanatuan. He thought it would be impossible to work, until they were "immediately introduced to the 'vitamin stick,'" which was "adequate incentive to work." They cut down mahogany and coconut trees, and in no time their hands were bloody pulps from using the *juji* (pick ax) and *impi* (shovel). "We worked almost naked in this boiling hot sun for the next twenty-seven months," Henderson said.

They lived at Camp 10-A in unused, dilapidated constabulary buildings. Fourth Marine corporal George Burlage actually thought the site was pretty. It was built in a hollow square, each building had a veranda, and the central plaza was filled with coconut trees. Their building was on a slope, with a first floor galley and storeroom. More than three hundred men were expected to live in the barracks. "We were allotted a space of about six feet long, three feet wide," said Burlage, "a burial plot!"

For two years they built an airfield. Clearing the jungle, crushing coral with hammers, and mixing and pouring acres of concrete, they constructed a strip more than fifteen hundred yards long and seventy-five yards wide. During the ordeal, about fifty prisoners died from overwork, starvation, and lack of medical care. Back in Manila, prisoners who worked on the docks, among them J. D. Merritt, hauled supplies for those on Palawan whose "lot was much harder than ours." Merritt worked the old-fashioned hand winches that loaded the small interisland steamers, the *Naga* and *Isla Princesa,* which occasionally ferried supplies to Palawan. Merritt had "some real donnybrooks" with several of the "miscreants" among them who tried to steal precious Red Cross parcels meant for "our little brothers" in Palawan.[35]

On 15 August at Camp Casising, near Malabalay, Mindanao, all the generals, colonels, and their orderlies, about one hundred men in all, were gathered for shipment north on a small freighter, the *Maru San* (three). Among them were Brig. Gens. William Sharp, Guy O. Fort, Joseph P. Vachon, and Manuel A. Roxas. The latter would become the first president of the Philippines after the war. They were sent to various camps in Formosa and Korea.

At the same time, a larger party was being assembled on Luzon. General Wainwright, who had been in Manila since the surrender, was taken to Tarlac Camp on 9 June, along with other senior officers from O'Donnell and Bilibid. On 11 August, they were fed an early breakfast and shuffled along the road to the train station. Fifteen generals, 106 colonels, and a number of orderlies rode the rails south. They were then trucked back to the Manila docks, where they found a "good-sized" ship that they called the "Stinko Maru."

The *Nagara Maru* was a 7,149-ton passenger-cargo ship built in 1934 by Yokohama Dock Company and owned by the NYK Line. After standing on the pier for more than an hour watching the ship being loaded, the prisoners were

Nagara Maru. U.S. Naval Historical Center

abruptly ordered to about-face. Wainwright peered over his shoulder to see why. A long line of Japanese soldiers, like men in an old fire-bucket brigade, stood on the pier. For the next two hours they passed hundreds of small, labeled cardboard boxes onto the ship. Each box contained the ashes of a Japanese soldier being sent to the home shrines, and they did not want the POWs to know about their casualties.

While waiting, Wainwright was engaged by an English-speaking Japanese officer. They were being sent to Karenko, Formosa, he said, not to Japan. Wainwright would love Karenko, said the officer; there was plenty of fish, fruit, meat, and sugar, and even a fine bathing beach. Wainwright wanly smiled, having heard similar promises before.

There were only about 180 prisoners making the two-day voyage. Even so, all but Wainwright and General King were stuffed in a hold like cattle. They made their beds on two long, wooden shelves that extended six feet out from the bulkheads. Each man had about two and a half feet of space. Wainwright and King shared a cabin on the boat deck. They were ordered not to leave the room. Even so, it was perhaps the most comfortable accommodations any POWs ever had.

On 14 August, *Nagara Maru* pulled in to the nearly landlocked harbor of Takao, on Formosa's southwest coast. She anchored astern of a large liner. They recognized her as the SS *President Harrison,* which had been captured early in the war and renamed the *Kakko Maru,* and was later to be named the *Kachidoki Maru.* She too would become a hellship.

The POWs were lined up on deck and subjected to another distressing physical exam, which, Wainwright explained, "centered around the rectum." This time all of them were sent back into the hold, which was alive with millions of bedbugs, and battened down in temperatures exceeding 100 degrees. The next morning they were released. Wainwright, the big prize, was forced to pose for photographers and a Japanese artist. His group then boarded an "evil little steamer" for the trip up the east coast to Karenko.

They were the first to reach their new home. Arriving in the next few weeks were contingents from Southeast Asia, the East Indies, and Philippines, including Sir Arthur Percival and British generals Ian McRae, L. M. Heath, and Merton Beckwith-Smith, along with General Sharp and the rest of the Mindanao contingent. Karenko was loaded with 405 of the top officers and administrators from the southwestern Pacific theater.[36]

The first group of prisoners from the Philippines to reach Japan assembled in Manila in early September. As usual, the rumor mill was pumping. Talk was that the Red Cross had negotiated a prisoner exchange. One of five hundred men selected from the Cabanatuan camp, Lester I. Tenney of Company B, 192d Tank Battalion, was trucked to Manila in an exultant mood. He was going to board a ship to freedom.

In Manila Bay, Tenney's hopes were dashed. Their destination was Japan, and they were traveling there on a small, dilapidated freighter that appeared to be at least thirty years old. Said Tenney, "It needed a paint job just to keep the steel from rusting out." Tenney walked up the gangplank to the *Toko Maru,* watching as a contingent of American prisoners working on the docks flashed them the "V" sign. The boat did not look seaworthy, even to a landlubber like Tenney.[37]

Although he knew nothing about the job, Tenney volunteered to be a cook so he would have more hours on deck. The *Toko Maru* sailed on 5 September, but it did not take long for Tenney to realize he had chosen the wrong job; a seasick cook was not needed. An old salt soon realized why Lester was spending so much time hanging over the railing. He baited him, telling him how a real sailor could swallow a piece of salt pork tied to a string, then slowly pull it back out without vomiting. That was all Lester needed; he was quickly back at the rail, heaving his guts out. A Japanese officer saw him, and that was the end of his days as a cook. Back he went into the hold with 496 other men.

Without fresh air and a horizon to look at, Tenney only got sicker, and the trip north was pure hell. The box was fifty by fifty feet; about five square feet per man. It was twenty feet to the top, where the only light and air came from the occasionally open hatch. A single ladder led to the deck. They disposed of their waste matter by carrying pails up the ladder and heaving the contents overboard. Wooden planks covered the lower metal deck, for on a previous trip, the ship transported horses. They slept on the wooden planks, which had soaked up all the horse urine. Their clothes and bodies were permeated with the smell of horses. Tenney would have given anything for a hot bath and to be rid of the horrible stench.

Japanese officers suggested that they exercise in the hold to keep fit, which was laughable for men starving on a daily ration of a couple of rice balls and a cup of watery soup. They were all between 30 and 40 percent underweight. Every night someone would have a malaria attack, crying for blankets because he was freezing or screaming that his body was burning up. Tenney hated the noises in the darkness. Every minute was everlasting. The sounds of men breathing could tear through him like fingernails scratching on a blackboard. Men broke down and cried because they could not take it any more.

To keep sane, Tenney managed to join up with a corporal from New Mexico, Jesus Silva of the 200th Coast Artillery. Silva had a pair of dice, and after negotiating a deal, they began to run a craps game. Over the days they won a good sum of money, before another soldier with a hot hand eventually broke them. At any rate, it distracted them from their worries for a time.

Badly in need of repair, *Toko Maru* took fourteen days to reach Takao. While being fixed, the POWs were put to work picking bananas and hauling them aboard for shipment to the empire. They were warned not to eat any. After six days, *Toko Maru* was seaworthy enough to resume her voyage. Before sailing on the twenty-fifth, the prisoners were given a written set of instructions: they should eliminate bowels and bladder before boarding; they would only get one portion of rice, twice a day; they should not complain about the food; when toilet buckets were full, they should notify a guard and haul up the bucket to throw its contents overboard; no one was to climb the ladder without orders; no one was to touch anything on the ship; no one was to disobey an order; no one was to talk loudly; and no one was to move anywhere except within the hold.

The Japanese meant business. One night, a prisoner suffering from malaria and dysentery screamed that he had to be let topside for some air. They could not stop his yelling, or his rush for the ladder. A guard opened the hatch and motioned him up. As the sick man stuck his head up to deck level, the guard shoved a bayonet into his neck. He toppled and fell. It was an hour before the medics could stop the bleeding and sew him up. Because one man had disobeyed the rules, the rest would only get one ration of rice that day—Japanese justice.

Tenney hoped with all his might that he could end this horrible journey, and almost in answer to his pleas, he heard the ship's horn. It was 7 October and they had reached Moji, Japan. In a dockside godown they stripped and were sprayed with delousing chemicals. They were given split-toed sandals and Japanese-style clothing, all too small. Tenney and his group of five hundred were sent to Fukuoka 17 Camp to work in the coal mines.[38]

A smaller contingent left Cabanatuan on 17 September. About three hundred men marched south to Manila, where they waited for three days in Bilibid Prison before boarding the 6,989-ton *Lima Maru*. The twin-screwed vessel, owned by the NYK Line, was built in 1920, was 445 feet long, and had a cruising speed of twelve knots. Otis H. King, Fourth Marines, called it "an old rusty freighter." He heard that thirteen POW colonels and three generals were in the group, some of them with their orderlies still carrying their golf clubs. He doubted that the Japanese would allow the officers any golf time.

The three hundred were placed into a small forward hold, where the air immediately became stale as they packed in shoulder to shoulder. The hatch was covered, and only two forty-watt bulbs swinging overhead provided illumination. There were also two thousand Japanese soldiers in the other holds. "I was reminded of pictures I had seen of crowded slave ships of old," King said. He was lucky to be against a bulkhead on which to rest, but those in the middle had to lay on top of each other to sleep. There were no toilet facilities. One prisoner guessed they were headed to Japan; another disagreed, believing Japan was too overpopulated to accommodate them. Not yet having lost his sense of humor, another man suggested that they had already killed enough Japanese in the Philippines to make room for them, and, he said, "maybe their women need our services."

The *Lima Maru* sailed on 21 September. After four days the men were let out on deck to use the outboard latrines and wash in salt water, letting the

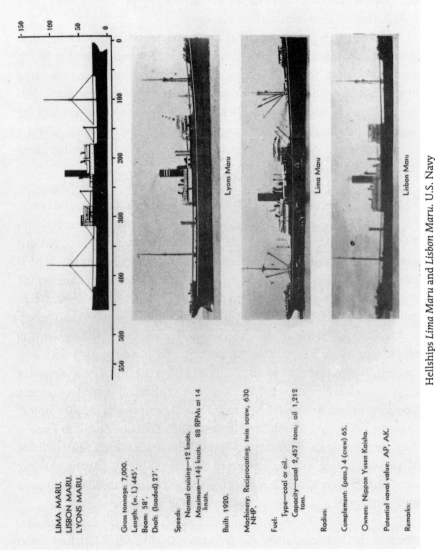

LIMA MARU.
LISBON MARU.
LYONS MARU.

Gross tonnage: 7,000.
Length: (w. l.) 445'.
Beam: 58'.
Draft: (loaded) 27'.

Speeds:
　Normal cruising—12 knots.
　Maximum—14½ knots.　88 RPMs at 14 knots.

Built: 1920.

Machinery: Reciprocating, twin screw, 630 NHP.

Fuel:
　Type—coal or oil.
　Capacity—coal 2,457 tons; oil 1,212 tons.

Radius:

Complement: (pass.) 4 (crew) 65.

Owners: Nippon Yusen Kaisha.

Potential naval value: AP, AK.

Remarks:

Lyons Maru

Lima Maru

Lisbon Maru

Hellships *Lima Maru* and *Lisbon Maru*. U.S. Navy

waste water run down the decks and over the side. Daily meals came in individual boxes consisting of two rice balls and a watery soup. No one was pleased with the accommodations, but, King admitted, "it was like a tourist trip on an ocean cruise liner compared to the 'Hell Ships' that followed in our wake." Even so, eight men died on the voyage.

It took thirteen days to reach Takao. The next morning, 5 October, they debarked and took a train north, to a town that King remembered as Tychu. Their trip to Japan would be delayed, as they spent the next month working in a rock quarry. Before sailing, the prisoners were required to indicate their professions, and King and a buddy said "telephone line repairmen" in the hope that they would be given outdoor work and, consequently, a better chance to escape. When they eventually reached Japan, they would end up in an electric shop in Yokohama.[39]

By September, more prisoners were being shifted to Changi, Singapore, which was a collection point for distribution to Burma, Borneo, and Japan. More than one thousand Australians of Sparrow Force had been captured on Timor and were put in Usapa Besar Camp for six months, where conditions were fair and treatment reasonable. The prisoners could sit among the coconut trees near the beach and wistfully wonder when the Australian forces would rescue them; after all, they were only four hundred miles from Darwin. There would be no rescue. Instead, on 26 July, the 1,871-ton *Samurusan Maru*, an ex-Dutch ship, carried a number of them from Kupang, Timor, to Java, arriving on 5 August. In early September, *Nishi Maru*, called "a dirty, rusty old tramp steamer," sailed from Timor, to Java. It had been the British ship *Kalgan*, a 2,655-ton passenger-cargo vessel built by Scott's Shipbuilding and Engineering Company in 1921 and seized in Bangkok in December 1941. After a stop at Surabaya, *Nishi Maru* took fifteen hundred Dutch KNIL and Aussies to Tanjong Priok, arriving on 12 September. Following behind was the 5,813-ton *Dainichi Maru*, built in 1922 and now owned by the Itaya Shosen Company. Hauling more Dutch POWs and the remainder of Sparrow Force, it sailed from Kupang on 23 September and arrived in Surabaya on the twenty-ninth.

The men from *Nishi Maru* found themselves in Bicycle Camp, Batavia, which at this time contained about 500 British, 500 American, and 2,000 Australian prisoners under Brig. A. S. Blackburn. Notice was given to the British to start packing. After midnight on 14 September, they were rousted out of bed to begin the march to the harbor. There were 473 British POWs, mostly of the RAF, and 1 Australian. Flt. Lt. Charles Johnstone was born near Melbourne but joined the RAF in 1940 when it was recruiting Australian pilots. Now he trudged along with his unit, exhausted upon reaching the docks in the late afternoon. Waiting for them was ship "No. 2106." They were lined up, counted, and their kits were sprayed with a disinfectant. Once aboard they were given a towel ten inches by twenty-seven inches. With a piece of string to secure it, it would become a loincloth—standard clothing. The guards ordered them not to mix with the other prisoners, but they could not tell RAF from AIF, and the men mingled freely. Johnstone was glad to see the last of Batavia. "We thought we had been given a bad time and things could not be worse," he said. "What little we knew of the future."

The RAF contingent was placed in one small hold, where tiers of bed spaces had been built up along the sides. They couldn't fit. The other POWs who had been aboard since Timor, told them it was best to have some men sleep at night, and some during the day. Only half of them were allowed on deck at any one time, so a roster system was instituted to assure every man had a turn. Six small "cabinets" were built over the side, but with dysentery rampant, they were crowded twenty-four hours a day. But, said Johnstone, "we were allowed to urinate over the stern."

They ate rice and fish-head soup, served twice a day in buckets carried down to the holds. One storage room was packed with fish. The cooks cut off the heads and tails and boiled them up with some stale Soya sauce. The heads floated on top. "With all these eyes looking up at you and the stuff smelling, looking, and tasting like vomit," said Johnstone, "there were always plenty of leftovers." The guards ate clean slabs of dried fish, laughing at the POWs' discomfort. Charlie sarcastically concluded, "This soup was a masterpiece. Not only did the Japanese get square with the white races, they got rid of their offal, and at no cost."

It took four days for *Nishi Maru* to reach Singapore. Three men died and were buried at sea. No cause of death was given, but dysentery was the likely agent. Many men were afflicted and unable to reach the latrines. The stench and the rolling of the ship caused an overpowering seasickness that could not be overcome. Johnstone recalled one man who climbed up the ladder, was unable to control an abdominal cramp, and defecated in the face of the man below him.

They nearly cheered when the freighter dropped anchor. Such a dirty, smelly lot created amusement for those watching along the waterfront. With their heads recently shorn of all hair in Batavia, they looked more like pigs just released from a sty. As they marched the ten miles to Changi, one more man collapsed and died. It was midnight when they reached an old, empty Indian barracks, found bags spread on the floor, and flopped down to a fitful sleep. In three weeks they would continue their journey.[40]

THE OCTOBER VOYAGES

By the fall of 1942, Japanese prisoner distribution had formed a pattern. First, the large manpower pool still in Java and Singapore would be tapped for the Burma Railway project, resulting in a flow of men from the outer islands to the Asian mainland. Second, the successful experiment to bring white POWs north for the edification of the Koreans would be continued. Realizing, however, that the POWs could be used for more than propaganda purposes, they were shipped in droves to the empire as slave laborers. Prisoners could work at scores of jobs, in dockyards, factories, cottage industries, shipyards, coal and copper mines, and on construction gangs. Third, on a smaller scale, and almost as a cross-current to the first two trends, ad hoc prisoner groups continued to be shipped among the conquered islands for a number of reasons. At least eighteen POW shipments during October was the highest number for any month of the war.

In Hong Kong, few prisoners had been moved prior to October. The British colony had already suffered its own miniature "Rape of Nanking" when, on Christmas Day, 1941, Japanese troops had entered St. Stephen's College and the temporary Jockey Club hospital in Stanley, systematically bayoneting, raping, and killing about 160 prisoners, wounded men, and nurses. Those who managed to surrender and live were segregated by nationality. The Americans and other European nationals were kept at an internment camp on the island at Stanley. About five thousand British were imprisoned on the mainland at Shamshuipo Camp, on the waterfront in Kowloon. The Canadians went to North Point on the island, and the Indians went to Mautauchung. As in Singapore, the Indians were pressured to join the Indian National Army, and about two hundred of fifteen hundred complied.[41]

In September, the Canadians at North Point were moved across the harbor to Shamshuipo. With their arrival, a draft of 616 British POWs departed from Hong Kong for Japan on the *Maru Shi* (four) on 3 September. Later that month, it was decided to move a larger contingent of British soldiers to Japan. About

1,816 men were assembled on the parade ground of Shamshuipo Camp and were addressed by Lt. Wada Hideo, assisted by interpreter Niimori Genichiro. "You are going to be taken to a beautiful country," Niimori translated, "away from Hong Kong, where you will be well looked after and well treated. I will be in charge of you. So remember my face."

Wada may have been in charge, but Niimori, the chief interpreter in the Hong Kong area, wielded more power than his appointment would indicate. He was a small man with pointed ears and usually wore military field boots and a khaki cloak, although he held no Army commission. Nicknamed "Panama Pete" by the prisoners, he had been educated and lived for a time in the United States, where he worked at rodeos and amusement parks and picked up many colloquialisms. He could sound like a American gangster, with his oft-repeated use of "Youse guys." Other times his mispronunciations or misunderstandings could be comical. He, and Col. Tokunaga Isao, commandant of the Stanley camp, liked to play bridge. Often, unwilling Europeans would be asked to join them. During one evening game, Niimori suddenly asked an internee, "Do you know anything about fucking?"

"Yes, a bit," replied the puzzled man.

"I used to own one," Niimori said proudly.

"Is that so?" said the prisoner, unsure of just what Niimori was talking about and trying to maintain his composure.

One learned not to laugh in Niimori's face. He would blow hot or cold, becoming a kind friend or a sadistic brute, on a whim. When some Canadians were recaptured after an escape attempt, Niimori and a lieutenant spent an hour bashing them with baseball bats.

Niimori Genichiro would be responsible for the POWs on their journey. The men were divided into *kumis* of 50, given the usual medical inspection, and loaded on the 7,053-ton passenger-cargo ship *Lisbon Maru*. The twin-screwed vessel, built in 1920, was 445 feet long, with a beam of 58 feet, a loaded draught of 27 feet, and a cruising speed of twelve knots. It was owned by the NYK Line and had a crew of 65. The number one hold took contingents of the Royal Navy and the 1st and 2d Battalion Royal Scots. Number two hold took the Middlesex Regiment, and number three held Royal Artillery men. Lastly came 778 Japanese troops returning home, plus 25 guards.

Men had to take turns lying down, shoulder to shoulder on roughly constructed platforms. Surprisingly, the food was decent by POW standards: rice and tea in the morning, and rice, tea, vegetables, and a bit of bully beef in the evening. There was an adequate supply of drinking water, but none for washing. The prisoners were allowed on deck to queue up for the wooden latrines hanging over the side. Half of them were given kapok life belts.

Lisbon Maru steamed off on 27 September. Four days of uneventful sailing passed until early in the morning of 1 October. Patrolling the East China Sea south of Shanghai was the *Grouper,* on her second patrol and skippered by Lt. Cdr. Rob Roy McGregor. On the surface in the darkness, lookouts had spotted nothing but sampans until, at 0400, a freighter appeared on the southern horizon. McGregor approached for a closer look but figured a night surface attack in the bright moonlight was too risky. *Grouper* ran parallel to the target to determine her course and speed, hoping to get in position ahead for an underwater daylight attack. The freighter appeared to be heavily laden, moving at a speed of eight knots.

At daylight *Lisbon Maru* changed course 50 degrees, leaving *Grouper* in a poor attack position. McGregor dove, and at 0704 fired three torpedoes from thirty-two hundred yards. All either missed or failed to explode. The *Lisbon Maru* continued on unaware, and McGregor fired a fourth fish. Two minutes and ten seconds later a loud explosion was heard. McGregor peered through the scope. He could see no sign of damage, but the ship changed course another 50 degrees to starboard and slowly came to a stop. She hoisted a flag that resembled "Baker" and began firing a small-caliber gun in the direction of the periscope.

On board *Lisbon Maru,* first warning that they were being stalked by a submarine came when *Grouper*'s torpedo slammed into the starboard coal bunker. The engines stopped and the lights went out. No POWs were injured by the explosion, so they could only guess what had happened. The few of them topside were immediately sent below, while extra sentries were placed at the hatches to make sure they stayed there. Niimori ordered tarpaulins stretched across the hatches and fastened with ropes.

Meanwhile, McGregor closed to one thousand yards and at 0845 fired again. Another miss. McGregor was furious. He was sure his calculations had been accurate and the poor results were due to malfunctioning torpedoes. He conned *Grouper* to a new position about one thousand yards off the port bow and, at 0938, fired a sixth fish from a stern tube, set to run at zero feet. Upon firing, McGregor spotted a plane and dove to one hundred feet. About forty

Grouper (SS 214). U.S. Naval Institute

seconds into the dive, he heard another explosion. Two minutes later the plane dropped three depth bombs in the submarine's vicinity but caused no damage. The torpedo might have been a premature, for no one aboard the *Lisbon Maru* felt additional hits.

Grouper popped back up to periscope depth at 1000. The plane was still there, but McGregor could see no target. Since it hadn't moved for two and a half hours, McGregor logged, "Assume she sunk." They went back down and stayed in the vicinity throughout the day, hearing occasional explosions of distant depth charges. At 1905, under an overcast sky, *Grouper* surfaced and hauled clear.[42]

After the initial shock of the torpedo hit, the Japanese calmed down, but they became very uncooperative. During a long, uncomfortable day, it was apparent to the POWs below that the ship was listing to starboard, but they were given no information. The water supply had run out, there was no food, and the battened hatches left the air supply foul. British officers appealed to Niimori to be allowed on deck for air and to use the latrines, but to no avail. "You have nothing to worry about," Niimori said, "you are bred like rats, and so you can stay like rats."

Later in the day, the old *Momi*-class destroyer *Kuri* and freighter *Toyokuni Maru* came to help. Since they were unable to restart the engines, it was decided to transfer the 778 Japanese soldiers to *Toyokuni Maru* and tow *Lisbon Maru* to shallow water. After removing the troops, Lieutenant Wada, Niimori, and *Lisbon*'s captain, Kyode Shigeru, discussed what to do with the POWs. Wada said it would be impossible for his small guard force to supervise the transfer of so many men. His solution was to leave the hatches closed and tow them to shore. The captain protested, saying that the ventilation was very bad and in case of another attack the ship would sink with needless loss of life. Not until 2100 did Wada make up his mind; the POWs would remain under closed hatches. They were his responsibility and the captain should not interfere.

Conditions worsened through the night. Hold three was slowly taking on water, and the prisoners had to man the pumps for their lives, although lack of food, water, and air meant a man could only manage about six strokes at the pump before fainting. By 0400 on 2 October, they could pump no more. The many men with dysentery and diarrhea had already fouled the entire area. Niimori, with a sick sense of humor, temporarily opened one tarp and let down a bucket of liquid. The men thirstily grabbed for it but quickly found it was filled with urine.

At dawn, about twenty-four hours after being torpedoed, *Lisbon Maru* gave a lurch. It was apparent she was in imminent danger of sinking. The captain requested permission for everyone to be allowed to abandon ship. He was refused. In the holds the prisoners felt the ship stop, probably when the tow lines were cut. It was time to take matters in their own hands. One of the soldiers somehow produced a long butcher knife, climbed the ladder, and sliced through the tarp. Lieutenant Colonel Stewart organized a small party to try to break out. Still hoping not to antagonize the Japanese, Lieutenants Howell and Potter, with a few other prisoners, calmly climbed through the opening and walked toward the bridge to negotiate their release from the holds. Seeing the ship nearly abandoned, they realized at last what a predicament they were in. Instead of talking, however, the Japanese guards began to shoot. Lieutenant Howell took a mortal wound. The men ran back to the hold.

Had the ship gone down then, almost everyone would have drowned, but the shallow water gave them a few more minutes. *Lisbon Maru*'s stern sank, but hit bottom on a sand bar. Panic set in. There was no more holding the prisoners below decks. They came tearing through the tarps, swarming on deck, and diving overboard while the Japanese fired on them from above. The men aft were in the most danger, since the water was about to pour into the number three hold. Lt. G. C. Hamilton of the Royal Scots led men in cutting the tarp and removing the timbers. They formed lines and climbed out in as perfect order as possible. It was not fast enough. The sea reached the now-open hole on the deck and rushed in. Many drowned. Lieutenant Hamilton heard gunfire. He saw some small islands about three miles away, dove in, and began swimming.

Four small Japanese boats were nearby, rope ladders dangling from their sides, but they were only picking up their countrymen. Prisoners were kicked off as they tried to climb up. All of the survivors would probably have drowned had it not been for a number of Chinese junks and sampans that came to the scene. Seeing some prisoners swimming to the nearby islands and realizing that there might be escapees to tell the story, the Japanese had a change of heart and began picking up survivors. After swimming for half an hour, Lieutenant Hamilton noticed a Japanese craft rescuing British soldiers and he swam over. Someone threw him a rope. He spent the next three days on the patrol vessel with a number of other prisoners, sheltered by a tarp on deck, until taken to Shanghai.

About two hundred British prisoners managed to escape the Japanese net and reach the nearby islands. They were fed and cared for by the Chinese until Japanese destroyers came during the next few days to collect them all. Even so, three were hidden by a villager who arranged their escape to Chungking.

By 5 October, the survivors were collected on a Shanghai quay to resume the journey. Of the original 1,816 POWs, 842 had drowned or been killed. They were brought in piecemeal, destitute, nearly naked; some had waited on the pier for three days. Except for what some of them had been given by the Chinese, they had not been fed until the morning of the fifth. Niimori was there to further harass them, telling the guards to beat those who could no longer stand at attention.

Thirty-five seriously ill or wounded men were left in Shanghai, and 3 were still in hiding. The remaining 936 were loaded aboard the *Shinsei Maru,* a 4,476-ton supply ship. Before they embarked, Niimori ordered them to hand over all that was left of their clothing. One sergeant refused and Niimori viciously kicked him in the testicles. Once at sea, Niimori spoke to his charges, leaving them in no doubt that their survival was a great disappointment to him. "You should have gone with the others," he said. Five more POWs died during the trip to Moji. Of those left behind in Shanghai, or distributed among the POW camps in Japan, about 244 more would die. Thus, only about 40 percent of those who embarked on *Lisbon Maru* and *Shinsei Maru* would live to see freedom in 1945.[43]

In early October, 5th Air Base personnel and 268 "specialists" from the 14th, 28th, and 30th Bomb Squadrons left Camp Casising, Mindanao, for a march north to the harbor at Bugo. The Japanese had called for a group of men with a variety of technical skills for "special" projects in Japan, a promise the men had heard before.

Capt. Alfred B. Dreher was commander of the 440th Ordnance Company. His unit had spent much of its time at Del Monte Plantation and had been forced to surrender after the fall of Corregidor. As "specialists," they were rounded up and loaded on the *Tamahoko Maru*, a 6,780-ton passenger-cargo ship built in 1919, originally named *Yone Maru*, and now owned by the Kaiyo Kisen Company. It was 425 feet in length with a 53-foot beam, and driven by a single propeller capable of a maximum speed of twelve knots. *Tamahoko Maru* left on 3 October for a three-day trip to Manila. It was not crowded and was not nearly as bad as subsequent hellships. The prisoners were quickly unloaded, marched to Bilibid Prison for one night, then hurried back to the docks the next morning. There, Dreher found more than one thousand additional prisoners gathering to board another ship.[44]

The chief of staff of the Kwantung Army (Manchuria) had made a plea for fifteen hundred prisoners with technical expertise to help run the Manchurian Machine Tool Company, a plant involved in aircraft production. A new POW camp would be opened nearby to house the workers. They hoped to have the operation up and running before winter and wished to expedite the transfer.

At the Cabanatuan camps, rumors abounded. Most men thought they would be going to Japan and that anything had to be better than the treatment they were receiving in the Philippines. Those with no experience at all instantly became mining engineers or airplane mechanics. Assembling on 6 October at Pier Seven in Manila were about 31 officers and 1,930 enlisted men. They boarded the 5,973-ton *Tottori Maru*, built in 1913 by Russell and Company in Glasgow, now owned by the NYK Line and operating out of Dairen. It was 423 feet long with a 56-foot beam, and its coal-burning power plant and single screw could generate a cruising speed of eleven knots.

Most of the prisoners were funneled into two large holds, which were soon filled to capacity. The remainder of the Americans had to stay on deck, actually not a bad deal given the conditions below. Army Air Force private Sigmund Schreiner, who kept a secret diary, said it was so crowded that "you couldn't put a piece of paper between the bodies." The holds were divided by horizontal wooden sleeping racks with very little headroom. Wooden latrines were constructed and draped over the sides off the top deck.

TOTTORI MARU.

Gross tonnage: 5,973.
Length: (w. l.) 423'.
Beam: 56'.
Draft: (loaded) 25' (light) 8'.

Speeds:
  Normal cruising—10 knots.
  Maximum—12½ knots.

Built: 1913.

Machinery: Reciprocating, single screw,
  556 NHP.

Fuel:
  Type—coal.
  Capacity—1,650 tons.

Radius:

Complement:

Owners: Nippon Yusen Kaisha.

Potential naval value: AP, AK.

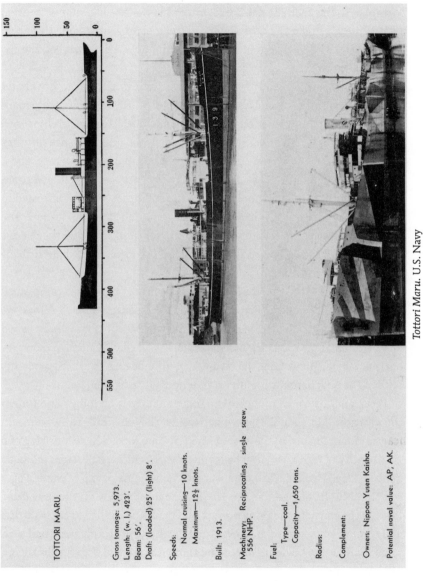

Tottori Maru. U.S. Navy

They waited all day in the harbor. The ship's steel sides grew hot, and the air in the far corners was almost unbreathable. Once in, few could get out in time to use the latrines. The stench became so bad that Joseph A. Petak, a photographer in the 228th Signal Corps, forced his way to the center, prime real estate, directly under the open hatch. In the morning, about one thousand Japanese troops were placed in an upper central hold. On 8 October, the engines finally started and they got underway.

Captain Dreher's men from Bilibid were some of the last to board and spent the next thirty-three days on the open deck. They were given cardboard boxes, each containing three buns, but the buns tasted like soap. Dreher timed the lines: one hour and twenty minutes to get food and forty-five minutes for water. Below, the men were unable to get out to use the latrines, and a relief pattern developed. They urinated in the corners because no one could breath in the unventilated nooks nearest the bulkheads. Others defecated in the central space under the hatch when they couldn't climb out in time. The men moved into zones, avoiding the central morass of feces and the regions next to the hulls, which were awash with pools of urine. Petak had to abandon his central real estate.

The odor was so bad that the Japanese troops in the central hold complained about the smell. Petak wondered at the way the Japanese planned things. He thought they had screwed up handling the men on Bataan. It was almost as bad on Corregidor. The O'Donnell fiasco was worse, and the Cabanatuan move was horrible. It was no wonder the Japanese could not take the Philippines any faster. "The poor bastards couldn't plan properly," Petak thought.

Petak and his cousin, Johnny Urban, could take it no longer and fought their way topside, shouldering a place against the outer rail. The air and sun revived them. At sunset, they got in line for some food, which consisted of a small cloth bag with a few sugar balls and hardtack crackers, the latter promptly dubbed "dog biscuits." Each man was given one canteen cup of water. Petak was thankful he had gotten out. He slept uncomfortably on the steel deck, hearing the constant moaning from the hold. One man tried to cut his wrists and commit suicide but was stopped and patched up. Already there had been more than twenty bodies removed and thrown overboard. Fighting broke out after midnight, and the Japanese guards threatened to shoot into the hold. A cool wind with rain developed during the night, and finally the majority drifted off into a fitful sleep.

Petak awoke with the sunrise. He and Johnny exchanged places with two other men to give them a place at the rail. They pretended to cook breakfast, flipping pancakes, pouring syrup, and savoring every bite. Those around them figured they were crazy and gave them wide berth.

After "breakfast," Petak was trying to relax when he heard the shout, "Torpedoes!" He did not know which direction they were coming from. He looked around the deck wildly. There were no life jackets.

Perched high on a winch and wearing nothing but a G-string, Sgt. Angelo H. Sakelares of the 200th Coast Artillery stoically sat and watched the torpedo approach. Cpl. Cone J. Munsey of the 200th had a similar reaction: "I felt if this was the way it was to end, I would welcome it."

Pvt. Wallace R. Phillips, also in the same unit, didn't know which way to run. "Then I decided it wouldn't matter," he said, "so I went to watch them coming. They were shallow, and as they'd cross a trough, they'd make spray. Three were coming at us, and another far off."

Joe Petak climbed on the hatch cover, looking east. He could see two frothy trails approaching. Finally, men on the starboard side began to scramble to port. A bell clanged and the ship's whistle shrieked. Japanese troops emerged. Many of the men in the holds heard the commotion and began clawing their way topside. Some remained. Sgt. Russell A. Grokett and a buddy sat in their wooden berth and watched prisoners run by in panic. They decided to open and eat a can of food they had been saving. If they had to go into the water, they might as well have a little strength. As they ate, someone shouted, "The ship's going to be blown up. Why are you just sitting there?"

Grokett replied, "Tell me which end will be hit by the torpedo and I'll be on the other."

On deck, Phillips could see the captain on the bridge. "He was a little fellow in a navy-blue suit and white whiskers. He waited until he saw the divergence of the torpedoes, then turned and backed into the widest space, so they went on either side."

The ship heeled hard to port and the deck tilted. To Petak, it seemed that everything was moving in slow motion—the torpedoes, the turn, the men running as if slogging through molasses. He saw the wakes pass by on the port side and disappear.

"One didn't miss us more than eight feet," said Phillips. "That maneuver saved our bacon."

Prisoners and Japanese whooped and hollered, applauding the captain. From the bridge, the whiskered little man turned and bowed. Petak was astounded. "Believe in Fate if you wish," he said, "but somebody up there sure had something to do with it." He recorded the time as 0815 to 0830, 9 October, and said, "If I find any guy that was on that sub I'll buy him a drink." There would come a time on later hellships when men wished the torpedoes would hit.[45]

When the excitement died down, the Japanese responded by shoving all the men off the decks and into the holds. The situation became even more intolerable, but there were no more submarine attacks. Joe Petak managed to get into the central hold, where the Japanese troops were berthed. He had been studying Japanese and wanted to practice what he had learned. He didn't know how his intrusion would be received, but he managed to strike up a tentative conversation. It turned out that the soldiers he met weren't bad fellows. They appeared to get a kick out of teaching an American their language. Once, while talking and bumming cigarettes, a shot rang out, echoing in the steel hull. When the commotion subsided, Petak asked what had happened.

"It is in the prisoner section," a soldier answered.

"What prisoner section?" Petak asked.

"We have prisoners," the soldier explained. Joe learned that the troops were also guarding a number of their own men who were being returned to Japan for various offenses. One had wrested a gun from a guard, and to prevent the disgrace of going to prison, he had shot himself. It was an honorable way out. There were no condolences. Everyone returned to his own business.

The eleventh of October was a rough day. The weather was making up, the seas heavy, and many were seasick. On deck, Captain Dreher held on as giant waves broke over the bow and spray cascaded over them. They seemed to have lost the other ships in the convoy; word had it that the ship had a bent prop and could only make five knots. One Japanese guard forced Dreher to trade his wristwatch for a boiled duck egg. The threat of a bayonet sealed the deal.

On 12 October, to everyone's relief, *Tottori Maru* pulled into Takao. They remained in the harbor four days, and most of the Japanese troops disembarked. The men began fighting over rations, for they received only one eight-ounce can of milk for forty-five men and a pail of rice and seaweed for every thirty men. Johnny Urban was sick with malaria and dysentery and was getting worse. Once again, Petak used his Japanese on an officer to plead for help.

He couldn't believe his luck, for the next day, hospital orderlies came to take Urban and three other very ill men ashore, and Joe got to accompany them to the hospital.

The *Tottori Maru* took on coal and water and headed north once more. Half way up the Formosa coast, she turned around and headed back to Takao, docking again late on the sixteenth. No one knew what the problem was— engine trouble, waiting for another convoy to form up, avoiding U.S. submarines, or just typically poor Japanese planning. Dreher saw *Tamahoko Maru* and the hospital ship, *Manila Maru,* in the harbor.

They sailed again on the eighteenth, but only as far as Bako in the Pescadore Islands. There, storms and rough seas kept them at anchor for eight days. Dreher was in misery; cold, wet, hungry, sick—and to top it off, a filling fell out of one of his molars. He saw at least three men die topside, and one Japanese noncom committed suicide. On 27 October, they finally sailed, but back to Takao once again.

This time all the POWs were offloaded while a crew of Korean laborers boarded to scrub and fumigate. They commented about the ship being one giant *benjo* and wondered how men could be kept in such unsanitary conditions. The prisoners were given soap and water and allowed to scrub down. Everyone had body lice, and most of them shaved their heads. They tried to clean the bugs out of their clothes and blankets, and although they were unsuccessful, they felt better. Sadly, however, Petak learned that his cousin had died in the hospital.

When they pulled out on 30 October, the latest word was that they were going to a very cold country to work in a factory. All correctly assumed it was to be Manchuria. In no time, the holds became almost as bad as before. The only saving grace was that they were now in a temperate climate and the heat was not so overwhelming. "Sig" Schreiner noticed an increase in diarrhea and intestinal problems. The reason for it, he said, "was discovered when someone happened to glance into the water tank and saw a pair of dirty shorts floating around." The tank was cleaned, but they had no medicine to help those who had become ill. "A few men died," Schreiner said, "and were thrown over the side with a piece of scrap iron tied to their feet."

Captain Dreher felt better because they were now getting two meals a day of rice and fish soup. Unfortunately, there were worms in the soup. Petak, assigned to a chow detail, had managed to steal some onions, which were bought, sold, and traded like gold. Japanese noncom Suzuki Yukinoro, from whom Petak had been learning the language, suspected Petak had been stealing but refrained from turning him in. He was thinking about the future. One night while talking, Suzuki suggested that their families visit after the war was over.

"Japan will win," he said. "We must win. We are small and China is full. No place to go. Korea . . . cold. Only place to go is United States. . . . Japan is very old. More than three thousand years. We know what to do to survive. United States young. Not very smart. We will make a colony there. We have plans for the next hundred years. We will go there."

On 9 November, *Tottori Maru* finally docked at Pusan. A large group, about 14 officers and 1,288 men, received winter clothes and were sent by train north to Mukden, Manchuria. About 580 Americans, including Dreher's men, were placed back aboard, and, after a stop at Moji, *Tottori Maru* reached Osaka, Japan, on 11 November. They were sent to Kawasaki and Omori to work in chemical plants and steelworks. More than 50 men had been left in the hospitals of Takao and Pusan, and about 30 had died on board. Many more would not survive the subzero winter of Mukden.[46]

Other ships carried prisoners to Japan from various islands. The 16,975-ton liner *Tatsuta Maru* brought two hundred laborers to Wake Island on 12 March 1942. The 9,816-ton *Heiyo Maru* took off two hundred civilian contractors from Wake in July, and the 1,772-ton *Tachibana Maru,* built in 1935 and requisitioned as a hospital ship, steamed to Wake in September. She was there to pick up two hundred more civilian contractors. They sailed off on 20 September without incident, arriving in Japan about 1 October.

Japan reached as far south as the Celebes to bring men with technical expertise to the empire. Many officers had been sent in April, but now the Japanese demanded information on everyone in the Makassar camp. About 1,000 men—25 American, 225 British, and 750 Dutch—were selected because they supposedly had special skills. In answer to complaints that the men had no warm clothing for a northern climate, the Japanese sent a party through all the Dutch homes in the area to clear out the closets. The prisoners donned trousers, pajamas, tropical suits, lightweight shirts, and even sarongs, looking like "as fine a group of scarecrows as one could wish for." It did not matter to the American and British POWs that they were leaving, but Makassar was home to many of the Dutch, and the sounds of weeping women tore at their hearts.

The *Op ten Noort* was still anchored in the harbor, along with several other ships, the largest being the transport *Asama Maru:* 16,975 tons, 583 feet long, with a cruising speed of seventeen knots. It had been a luxury liner before the war, with berths for 680 passengers, and it still made a favorable impression. The British and Americans were slated to have third-class accommodations, but the Dutch got to the Japanese and persuaded them that it would be better to put the British and Americans in the hold because there were fewer of them and they would have more room. The Dutch plan did not last. Finding the holds "hotter than hell," the British enlisted men forced their way into the Dutch area. If they couldn't have rooms, they would bed down in the passageways. The Dutch protested to the British officers, but were told that if they didn't like it, they would have to throw them back into the hold by force. Both sides backed off in an uneasy truce.

Officers of all nationalities were given "state rooms." As the only American officer, Lt. John Michel roomed with the British, where eleven of them shared six bunks and a transom—not a bad deal, all things considered. Michel saw to it that the twenty-four American enlisted men under him stayed out of the hold and had them camp on the companionway near a ladder leading topside. Before they left, Michel instructed them to always remain together. He had a bad feeling that they might be torpedoed and saw to it that they got life jackets. He hoped that if the worst happened, they would all be plucked from the sea once again.

They sailed before sunset on 10 October, following a small steam frigate. The next morning they were fed rice and stew, a rather tasty fare. At times they even received fresh scallions and considered it quite a luxury. When the weather got rough, the British and American sailors collected food from seasick Dutch soldiers. They had never eaten as well during the past half year at Makassar.

It still remained hot below decks, and the men were given permission to go to the forecastle for fresh air, and there was plenty of water for drinking and washing. Lieutenant Michel and British lieutenant Geoffrey Blain did have one complaint: they had to share their washroom with a crated Komodo dragon on its way to the Tokyo Zoo. The huge lizard, which was fed live chickens by one of its handlers, ate better than the men. Said Michel, "The stench was overwhelming, and we prayed regularly that the awful thing would die and be tossed overboard." But the reptile remained healthy the entire trip, smelling worse every day.

Some believed they would make a stop in the Philippines, but they sailed on, making a steady fifteen knots with few course changes. The temperature became cooler, and they began to don and layer the assortment of clothing given them at departure. The last day before arrival, cold winds buffeted the ship and the men shivered too much to fall asleep. Peering out of the portholes they could see uninviting islands shrouded by cold mists. On 23 October, *Asama Maru* dropped anchor outside of Nagasaki, and the next day ferry boats came alongside to take them to shore. Most of them were destined for Camp Fukuoka No. 2 and the Zosen shipyard. They were exhausted and demoralized, and, said Blain, "that caused us to lose more people that first winter, mostly from pneumonia, than we did during the rest of our time in Nagasaki."[47]

After depositing her human cargo, *Asama Maru* promptly took on supplies, sailed to Yokosuka, then headed for Wake Island. Reaching there about the last day of October, she picked up the last twenty servicemen who had been wounded or too sick to make the trip on the previous ships. They were served sugar and rice, all they could eat, and actually got to use the ship's swimming pool. They sailed to Yokohama, then went to Ofuna Camp, and, after one month of questioning, ended up at Zentsuji. This left about 168 civilian contractors who remained behind to strengthen Wake's defenses. They were worked so unremittingly, with a lack of nourishment and medical care, that about 45 of them died by December. The Japanese had another surprise planned for the survivors.[48]

The prisoners from the *Nishi Maru* deposited in Singapore on 18 September were moved in to a vacated barracks that once housed Indian troops. Changi at this time housed the remnants of six divisions, including the British 11th and 18th. Since many thousands had already been shipped north to Burma and Thailand, conditions were not crowded, and Changi appeared to many as a haven. Lieutenant Johnstone hardly saw a Japanese guard. "What a restful, peaceful camp it was," he said. The worst problem was in walking between divisions, when one had to be escorted by the sometimes brutal Indian Sikhs. The idyll came to an end in three weeks when they were told to be ready to move to a new overseas destination.

The initial RAF party was joined by some British soldiers, increasing their number to about 810. Flt. Lt. Peter E. Lee thanked their 18th Division hosts, especially for sharing some of the recently received Red Cross packages, and they smartly hiked to the wharves. Through the afternoon of 9 October, they sat on the dock in the hot sun and watched a large passenger liner, painted white with a large red cross on the side, sail through the harbor. The guards said it was loaded with diplomats and internees returning to Japan after an exchange for British and American civilians. The ship was likely the *Teia Maru* on a return voyage from India.

Late in the afternoon they boarded "a big, dirty, rusty cargo ship," an old ex-British freighter of about six thousand tons. Japanese medical orderlies had the newcomers drop their pants and bend over. Those not quick enough were cracked in the head with batons. The glass-rod-in-the-anus routine was greeted by ribald laughter and cheering from the twelve hundred POWs already aboard the ship. They sailed to Singapore Roads and anchored for the night, sailing on the morning of 10 October. At sea, the Japanese told them that their destination was Borneo.

Lieutenant Lee thought that conditions were better than on the *Nishi Maru;* it was less crowded, but the facilities were fewer. There was little drinking water and none for bathing. The 810 RAF and infantry, called "Java One Party," were placed in the forward holds and on deck. Those topside watched the miles of endless sea sweep by. At nightfall the ship began to zigzag. The food was better, without the fish heads of the previous voyage and with an occasional piece of meat. On 13 October, they reached Kuching, Borneo, and a thousand prisoners were offloaded by diesel-engined lighters. The food became so poor that they had to dip into their precious Red Cross packages to supplement it.

Loading of supplies continued the next day, the men hungrily watching the passing of hundreds of bags of sugar and tapioca, depressed by the backdrop of "the steamy swamps of Kuching." The picture brightened for a few, however, when some of the bags dropped and burst. Airmen and soldiers scrambled for the spilled treasure. Major Suga, commandant of all the prisoners in Borneo, came aboard to give them a speech on how they were to conduct themselves in his domain. The POWs were not impressed.

The next day the ship continued up the coast. The water shortage became so serious that men's tongues were badly swollen. Some crept up to the steam winches and opened the taps to release a few drops of water. A few careless ones were caught and bashed for their efforts. The ship stayed in sight of the coast, reaching Miri on the sixteenth, what Lee called "the last place God made." They unloaded crates, batteries, paints, engineering equipment, and about five hundred tires. Sailing north the next day under a gray sky with alternating drizzles and downpours, the men were forced to spend much of the time in the holds. Those who braved the elements were caught in the gusty wind and rain and coated with black soot from the smoke stack. Dysentery was rife again, and the stench of vomit and excrement was shocking. Nine men died. One fellow who had spent much time hanging on the rail and staring out to sea, could take no more of the strain and terror and jumped overboard. The officers told others he had fallen. Said Johnstone, "We did not want our men to learn of this suicide as it would have further depressed them."

Deep in the holds, some men pried up a plank on the floor and got into a room of bagged sugar, tinned fish, and meat. Much of it was quickly consumed, and the rest went into kit bags and pockets. They put the room back in order and no one was any the wiser. On 19 October, they anchored at Jesselton, lying on the coast with the forested 13,455-foot Mount Kinabalu looming on the horizon. The eight hundred British POWs were taken to a camp and lodged in atap huts; the officers were put in a native jail, two to each six-by-eight cell. They would remain in Jesselton for six months.[49]

The October transports also moved men from Java to Burma. Construction of the main line of the Burma Railway was about to begin, and manpower levels were upped accordingly. A Force had been preparing the ground along the Burma coast for the past several months. Ken Williams worked at the Mergui docks, unloading petrol drums. He felt humiliated. A few months ago, he and his mates had tossed pennies to the natives, and now "the natives were tossing us cigars." They received many "bashings," from both the Japanese and the natives. Beriberi struck. Wooden coffins were supplied by the Burmese. Solemn rites were read, "Last Post" was played, and at least, said Williams, the dead "would know no more barbarous treatment from the Japanese." There was no escape. Three Australians tried, but they were caught by the Burmese and returned, then tied to trees and shot. The Burmese were paid two hundred rupees a head.

In August, some of Green Force was trucked from Victoria Point north to Ye, then marched to Thanbuzayat; others were taken to Tavoy on a 200-ton coaster. Ramsay Force also suffered another sea journey on 16 August when shipped from Mergui to Tavoy. The men thought the voyage was worse than on *Celebes Maru*. They were forced into the holds of several small ferries, the largest being the 501-ton *Tatu Maru*. They sat with knees to chin, unable to move, and had to eliminate bodily wastes where they sat. It was a two-day trip to move 150 miles, and only near the end of the voyage did the Japanese rig up a *benjo* (which hung dangerously over the side of the hull). The only food for the entire trip were five-ounce loaves of bread covered with blue mold, but, said Williams, "it filled the empty spaces." They pulled in to Tavoy on 18 August, where they met up with Anderson Force. At Tavoy they worked on either an "aerodrome" or road construction. There, said Williams, the Japanese man in charge "was nothing else but a lunatic. Bashings were plentiful and severe. A favorite place for the Japs to kick the men was in the crotch, which resulted in excruciating pain." Two men who had stolen a few bits of soap were nearly beaten to death.

The unpredictability of the Japanese character was clearly demonstrated on the first Tuesday in November. Knowing the Australian enthusiasm for horse racing, the Japanese suggested that they hold their own "Melbourne Cup," even providing the trophy: a polished coconut shell with two brass handles. A sham race was held, with big, strong men as the "horses" and small men as the jockeys. Bets were placed, and thirty-four "horses" and riders lined up for the big race. There was a collision at the first bend, with many going down. After much pulling, shoving, kicking, and cursing, "Walla Walla," at one-hundred-to-one odds, won by "a toe." Bets were paid out in cigars. Said Williams, "We wander back to our beds on the cement and wooden floors, and so ends one of the brighter POW days."

With the preliminaries complete, they were ready to lay the first rails in October. A Force had been concentrated at Thanbuzayat, Burma, under Brig. Arthur L. Varley. Still the assembled numbers were not enough. The enormity of the project meant that thousands more would have to be collected. In October and November, trainloads of POWs moved almost daily from Singapore on the twisting journey to Ban Pong. Drawn from River Valley Road Camp, Sime Road, Adam Park, and Changi, this almost exclusively British labor force worked at the Thailand end of the road, heading west. The Burma side, however, also needed more bodies.[50]

This time the additional men would come from Java. After the surrender, prisoners had been shifted from camp to camp, many eventually ending up in Bicycle Camp in Batavia. Once a Dutch compound, Bicycle Camp would later be thought of as quite a haven, much as Changi and Zentsuji would prove to be. Survivors from the *Houston* were kept there, where they later cheerfully greeted the men of the 131st Artillery because they were fellow Americans, and because they had extra clothes to share. In early October, the Japanese said they wanted men, but it was the Allied officers who took the rosters and made the selections.

Two contingents were assembled. The first, about 1,500 men under Australian Lt. Col. J. M. Williams and Lt. Col. C. M. Black, consisted of elements of 2/2 Pioneer Battalion, 2/3 Reserve Motor Transport Unit, 2/6 Field Company Engineers, RAAF personnel, some men of the 2d Battalion, 131st Field Artillery, some Dutch troops, and survivors from the cruisers *Perth* and *Houston*. The American group, 191 men, were under Capt. Arch L. Fitzsimmons.

Houston sailor Donald C. Brain was pleased when he heard they were going to Singapore. He had shipped there several times and thought it was a beautiful place. However, on 7 October, when they marched from Batavia to its port of Tanjong Priok and saw the ship that awaited them, they had misgivings. The transport, Brain said, "was just unbelievable." One of the first aboard, he got stuck in the bottom. "There were sacks of grain and stuff down there," he said, "and it had gotten damp and started to rot. It was hot down there, damp, and stinking."

Aussie Tom Fagan was also worried. From dockside, he thought it would be utterly impossible to squeeze everyone aboard, especially on top of all the cargo being loaded. However, the excited guards pushed and prodded them up the gangplanks, "yelling and screaming as if all the demons in hell were scrambling up the side of the rust bucket." In no time they were shoved down almost vertical ladders "into the very bowels of the rodent-infested hulk."

The ship was the 4,574-ton transport *Kenkon Maru*, owned by the Ken Steamship Company. The fifteen hundred men were divided into two holds, each of which went down three deck levels. Between each level wooden platforms were built, with crawling room height, giving each man a space of about two by five feet. Brain was in the narrowest bottom level where the bulkheads angled in toward the keel. Water sloshed in the bilges. He found himself a rotting sack of grain for a bed. As usual, there were no toilet facilities below, and the area soon became intolerable. Said Tom Fagan, "The stench from sweating bodies, urine, and those suffering from dysentery, was indescribable."

They languished dockside for thirty-six hours. Finally the Japanese fed them a half pint of tea, a ball of rice and some soya soup. At first, some men disdained the food and ate the tins of beef that they had secreted aboard. It was not enough in either case. Water was needed, but not one drop was available. Fagan asserted, "Men dreamed of luscious, gushing, clear mountain springs. Visions of waterfalls were with them every moment." The Japanese guards tormented them by playing around with the hoses, spraying and wasting water.

Marine corporal H. Robert Charles managed to come aboard with his buddies, James W. Gee and James McCone, all survivors of the *Houston*. McCone, called "Packrat," lived up to his name by hauling aboard a water-filled five-gallon tank. It saved the lives of several men. The three of them managed to get topside for some fresh air. Deep below, Don Brain sat on his grain sack and listened for the rats he couldn't see. There was only one light bulb dangling from a cord, swaying with the motion of the ship. In the far corners it was still pitch black. One fellow said the odors from the rotting grain and rice would produce methane gas.

Charles, Gee, and McCone spent a night near the ladders, as close as they could get in case they had to rush on deck. They talked, dozed, and listened to the pounding of the giant propellers churning the sea, and the sounds of a creaking, ancient freighter moving in the night. What bothered Charles most was that the ship sailed alone, flying the Japanese flag, with no watertight compartments, no life jackets, and no chance at all if attacked.

It took three days for *Kenkon Maru* to reach Singapore, docking on 11 October. Despite the hardships of the voyage, only one Australian had died. They unloaded and were marched to Changi, but those who believed they were to have a nice rest in Singapore were sadly mistaken.[51]

The second contingent of POWs left Java four days later. It consisted of about 200 Dutch troops, 385 Australians under Maj. L. J. Robertson of the 2/6 Field Company Engineers, and 450 Americans under Lt. Col. Blucher S. Tharp of the 2d Battalion, 131st Field Artillery. Included in the groups were more *Perth* and *Houston* survivors. The core of this group was later known as Branch Party Five.

A radio operator in the 131st Regimental Headquarters Battery, Kyle Thompson learned of the preparations to move when the Japanese uncharacteristically gave them international post cards to send to their families. They consisted of short, preprinted lines for the sender to check, including "I (am) (am not) well," "I (am) (am not) working," and "I am with a friend," and so on. Thompson was pleased that his family would finally know that he was all right. The Japanese were not quick to dispatch the cards, however; his parents received one on Christmas Day 1943.

Sgt. Frank Fujita of the 131st was a special case. He was Japanese American, and only one of two such people captured by the Japanese during the war. He was also in the "lost" Battery E of the "lost" 2d Battalion. While the majority of the unit was captured and kept in Batavia, Battery E had been separated, captured, and held in Surabaya. They were sent by train to Batavia, where they briefly united with those who had not sailed on *Kenkon Maru*. Guards split the group in half and distributed red ribbons to one group. Fujita tied a ribbon to his arm as instructed. His party would go to Japan, the other would go to Burma.

Early on 11 October, they were taken on barges out to the 5,813-ton *Dainichi Maru,* which had recently carried prisoners from Timor to Java. Fujita called it a rusty cargo ship that "looked as if it would sink at any moment." Lt. Julius B. Heinen of the 131st explained that the Japanese had an easy way to fill a hold: they just pushed men in. When it looked completely full, they simply jabbed rifle butts and bayonets at the closest men, who reacted by pushing their way back against the crowd. Now more could fit in—and the process was repeated. Artilleryman Roy M. Offerle said, "Sardines had more room in a can than what we had in that ship."

Houston sailor Seldon D. Reese described the hold. About three feet from the bottom a wooden shelf had been built, and three feet above that, another shelf. They wormed their way into the nooks and laid down, for it was impossible to sit up straight. The only time they were allowed out was when they had to use the *benjo.* "It was hotter than holy hell," said Reese, "and it stunk. God, that place stunk!"

Another *Houston* seaman, William Weissinger Jr., noted the maru was outfitted to accommodate the smaller stature Japanese. He remembered the platforms being stacked four high, with only two feet between layers. Weissinger said he was lucky. Boarding with the last men, he found himself in the center of the hold, about six feet from the ladder. There was constant traffic, but, he said, "this space had one advantage. If and when any air—

fresh or otherwise—got down that far, I got some of it. We were four decks below main deck."

There were two holds, forward and aft, each about sixty feet square and each, Fujita thought, carrying about five hundred men. In his section the men had to sit between each other's legs. The ship was a coal-burner, and the heat from the engine room was felt right through the bulkhead. Combined with the tropical heat associated with an equator crossing, the men guessed that the temperature was about 120 degrees. The floor was alive with vermin. A Japanese cavalry unit complete with horses took up lodging right over the prisoners. The openings to the lower holds were boarded over with heavy planks with one- to two-inch gaps between them, and when the horses relieved themselves, the waste dripped down on the POWs below. Fujita, sick with dysentery, could not climb outside fast enough and soiled his clothes. The Japanese did not want sick men contaminating their horses, so Fujita and other sick men were booted out of the holds. Fujita was forced to remove his pants and throw them overboard, but he didn't mind. He thought that being allowed to stay topside was the only thing that saved his life.

Kyle Thompson was positive that had they not been in fairly good health, many of them would have died before reaching Singapore. They were only allowed out of the holds twice a day for the usual cup of rice. Someone, however, broke into a closed storeroom and stole a large quantity of dried potatoes. Thompson called it a "God-sent treasure."

The trip to Singapore only took three days, but the agony was prolonged when *Dainichi Maru* languished in the harbor for two additional days before disgorging its passengers. They were trucked through town to the barracks at Changi, which were similar to those at Bicycle Camp: concrete floors, poorly plastered walls, open doorways, and no windows. Those not slated for Japan would make this their home for a time. They quickly learned that they did not care for the British in charge, who walked about with swagger sticks and mannerisms the Americans found pushy. They also learned that two days before their arrival, the men of Williams Force had already departed for Burma.[52]

Those who had disembarked from *Kenkon Maru* a few days earlier lined up on the dock in time to watch another ship, *Maru Go* (five), unload about one thousand Indonesians, black from head to foot with coal dust. The groups intermingled. *Houston*'s Bob Charles noticed that the Indonesians had soot in their eyes, ears, and nostrils, even ground into the pores of their skin. They had come from Timor and were soon herded into waiting trucks. Among them was the Dutch doctor Henri Hekking, who was removed and placed with the Americans under Captain Fitzsimmons. Hekking was a medical officer for the KNIL when the Japanese invaded Timor. He escaped being shot by caring for a Kempeitai officer. Still, he was forced to leave his wife and children behind and accompany the native work party to Singapore. The Indonesians were a gentle people, Hekking said, exposed for the first time to man's inhumanity. When they were invited aboard the ship, they thought they were going to work for the "Greater East Asia Co-Prosperity Sphere" and would be treated with dignity. Instead they were thrown into a bilge of coal dust, kicked, and starved. Hekking was sad to see them trucked away; he thought a way of life was evaporating before his eyes. The Americans grew to like Hekking, and he would save many of their lives on the railway.

The mixed contingents were taken to Changi, but their respite lasted only two days. They were back on the docks on 14 October to load on yet another vessel, this time the 7,005-ton *Maebashi Maru*. Built in 1921, it was owned by the Nanyo Marine Transportation Company but was currently operating under control of the Imperial Army. *Houston* POW Don Brain thought it was a "good-sized Jap freighter," one of half a dozen being loaded that morning in busy Keppel Harbor. Brain ended up in the bottom again, just as on *Kenkon Maru,* and he was not happy about it. Bob Charles and Hekking were there also, in a bilge covered with straw and fresh cattle manure. Rumors spread concerning their destination.

This group of perhaps eighteen hundred men—Williams's Australians, Fitzsimmons's Americans, Dutch prisoners, and some Japanese troops—was packed like nothing they had seen before. They sweltered aboard ship for fifty-six hours, all sweat seeming to boil off their bodies. Houston T. "Slug" Wright of the 131st Artillery was completely dried out. As the ship moved up the west coast of Malaya, his tongue was huge in his mouth. He had only a small canteen. He went topside, found hot water dripping from a leaking joint in a steam pipe, and tried to fill his container. A guard saw him and knocked him on his back. He had been beaten enough times to know how to protect his glasses from being knocked off and stomped on. The guard left, Wright adjusted his glasses, and he continued to fill the canteen. A second guard saw him and knocked him down again. He tried a third time and was beaten once more. Slug Wright decided he would wait until dark before trying again. His attempt to get water had cost him a broken nose and some smashed ribs. In terrible pain, he forced his nose back into shape with his fingers. His glasses no longer fit right and he could hardly breathe. He passed out, having crazy dreams of meadows and cool spring water. He believed he had visited the twilight world between life and death; he wished he could pass away and be in heaven.

The accommodations aboard were much the same as on the trip from Java to Singapore, but the food seemed to be scheduled and rationed better. It was still basically rice, a watery stew, and a spoonful of sugar water at night. Cooking vats were assembled on deck, and there were many sacks of grain and rice, which became home to thousands of weevils and hundreds of rats. Roy Cornford, a private in 2/19 Battalion, AIF, did not accompany A Force in May but rejoined his unit after a trip on the *Maebashi Maru*. He had managed to secure a place on deck for part of the voyage. Cornford watched the Aussies play with a pet monkey that they somehow brought aboard. The monkey caroused on deck, eventually hopping on one of the hot, dripping steam pipes that Wright had tried to tap. The monkey landed on the hot pipe, screamed, and jumped off. Unfortunately, the panicked leap carried it over the railing, and Cornford and others watched the monkey sail out of sight into the sea. The owner was saddened—as were a few others who viewed it as a loss of a future meal.

Quickly learning that either Japanese promises or logistics were not always up to par, some men came better prepared on this trip. Arthur Bancroft, called "Blood" for his flaming red hair, was a sailor off the *Perth*. In Singapore, he managed to secure a Red Cross parcel, the only one he would get during his entire captivity. His share was a tin of condensed milk, which he swapped with a Dutch prisoner for a full water bottle. The bottle was invaluable on what he called a "rust bucket Jap transport" ride to Burma, and it was his most precious possession during the next year and a half.

Maebashi Maru sailed up the estuary to Rangoon on 22 October. Soldiers and sailors finally got topside, looked over the railings, and speculated as to where they were. Wright dragged himself on deck. Don Brain said, "Hell, I know where we are now."

A few soldiers just called him a smart-ass sailor, but Wright wanted to know.

"Where are we?" he asked.

"Rangoon, Burma," Brain answered. "I used to live here. My dad was an oilman, so when I was a boy, I was right here in Rangoon."

The *Maebashi Maru* anchored, and the prisoners were hustled off the ship, but they were not to see the sights of Rangoon. Their voyage was not over.[53]

Almost immediately the prisoners were moved along the pier and up the gangways to a smaller vessel, the 3,807-ton *Yamagata Maru,* a cargo ship built in 1916 and owned by the NYK Line. About 150 Australians were removed because of sickness or to remain as a harbor work party. The remainder again filed into the holds, or spread out on deck because the ship's innards were not large enough to hold them all. Even so, there were too many prisoners, and the overflow had to load on a few small coastal craft for the next part of the trip.

Yamagata Maru left the next day for the short trip across the Gulf of Martaban. Roy Cornford was able to talk to an English-speaking crew member and learned that the crew and ship had been to Sydney before the war and had received Australian hospitality. As a result, the crew was kind to them, feeding them better food and even sharing their own biscuits.

It was only a one-day trip, but it was late evening on 24 October when the ship lowered its gangplank and the prisoners debarked. Once again they wondered where they were. They marched down a dark street to a wrought-iron gate. Guards waved their lanterns and motioned to them to go inside and lie down. They found a well, and a stone dropped into it proved there was water. Someone loaned Slug Wright a peach can with a wire handle. Another man produced a long string, and Slug lowered the can into the well. They retrieved several cans of water, boiling them to make sure they would be safe to drink. Slug could not wait, and he drank his share while it was still hot. His swollen tongue immediately started back down to normal size. Someone else gave him some concentrated soup stock. It was delicious, and Slug could feel his strength returning.

At night they could hear wind chimes tinkling in the distance, and across the fence they could see the outline of a huge pagoda. With dawn just lighting up the eastern sky, dogs began howling and the men stirred. The pagoda stood in stark outline on the horizon.

"Welcome to Moulmein, Burma, folks," said James Gee of the *Houston.*

They asked him how he knew.

"Ever hear of Rudyard Kipling?" he asked. "He wrote a poem called 'Road to Mandalay.'"

With that, Pvt. Fred Quick Jr., who had a fantastic baritone voice, began to sing, "By the old Moulmein Pagoda, lookin' lazy to the sea, there's a Burma girl a waitin', and she's waitin' there for me."

They sat and listened to the song. In a short time it was too light to sleep, and the stiff, tired men got up to search their surroundings. Bob Charles, Wright, and the others noticed the jail's other occupants. Some shrank back into their blankets, while others slept uncovered. The POWs looked and saw disfigured faces, missing legs, arms, and hands: they had been placed in the prison's leper section. Not inclined to spend any more time there, they needed no additional prodding to move along to the train station. Burmese women cried for them as they trudged past, occasionally slipping them food. They were loaded on flatcars and rode to the village of Thanbuzayat.

While *Yamagata Maru* was crossing over to Moulmein on 23 October, another ship was loading in Singapore. A mixed group of Australian and Dutch POWs and thousands of railroad cross beams went aboard the 4,621-ton cargo ship *Shinyu Maru*. Early the next morning they left Keppel Harbor, but within twenty-four hours their convoy was spotted off Penang by the Dutch submarine O-23 on its third patrol. Commander Valkenberg maneuvered his boat into position and fired a spread of torpedoes at what appeared to be the largest ship.

One torpedo connected. Valkenberg claimed a sinking and sailed away. Although damaged and abandoned for a time, *Shinyu Maru* did not sink. Lifeboats were launched, and much flotsam went over the side, including many of the wooden beams. Frans Ponder, along with an Aussie and two more KNIL soldiers, clung to a floating beam for hours before being picked up by a tugboat and returned to Singapore. They were placed in the Harbor Jail and celebrated both Christmas and New Year's Day there. In January 1943 they were reunited with their countrymen in time for a train ride to Ban Pong. The other POWs from *Shinyu Maru* were picked up and transported to Rangoon and, eventually, Thanbuzayat.

Thousands of other Allied prisoners—among them Ramsay Force, Green Force, and Anderson Force—were at Thanbuzayat, where the coastal rail line's spur headed southeast. Williams Force arrived and was split into two groups, Williams Force and Black Force. Apthorpe's British Sumatra Battalion was there, as well as Dutch and American POWs and native laborers. There were a total of approximately forty-five hundred Australian, forty-six hundred

Dutch, five hundred British, and two hundred American prisoners. It was only then, according to *Perth* sailor "Blood" Bancroft, that they finally learned they were going to build a railway. They would work west to east, hopefully meeting with the twenty-thousand British working toward them from Ban Pong on the Thailand side. The great Burma Railway project was about to go into high gear.[54]

More prisoners left Java on the October transports. Lt. John Fletcher-Cooke wondered how he had gotten into this predicament. He had been posted to Malaya in the Colonial Administrative Service and had only joined the RAF on 7 February, during the chaotic days prior to Singapore's surrender. He had been one of the last to escape, only to be captured on Java. He had been imprisoned at Boei Gloduk, Batavia, since April. On 21 October, Fletcher-Cooke's group of 120 RAF and 380 British Army POWs left the prison and rode a train to the harbor at Tanjong Priok. Awaiting them was the 5,425-ton, *No.* 1 *Yoshida Maru,* a cargo ship owned by the Yamashita Kisen Company. The 500 British POWs were crammed into one small forward hold. Amazingly, the Japanese forced about 2,200 more men, Dutch soldiers and Javanese laborers, into the remaining three holds.

"The conditions were indescribable," said Fletcher-Cooke. The sides were fitted with rows of rough shelves with about two feet of headroom. Many had to sit on the wet deck, and no one could stretch out to full length. Two steep wooden ladders led up to the deck, where armed Japanese guards peered down at them. They spent the first night anchored, and the heat was unbearable. Finally, a sack of bread was tossed down to them. As "men fought like animals for the loaves," Fletcher-Cooke said, both bread and men "were trodden underfoot."

They had been buoyed up by the thought that the Allies would soon retake Java; now they were moving from the perimeter deeper into the heart of the empire and realized it might be years before they were rescued. They looked for positives; perhaps there would be medicines where they were going, perhaps fewer tropical diseases, or perhaps no Korean guards that enjoyed bashing the prisoners.

Fletcher-Cooke heard Japanese shouting orders from above. He knew they had never ratified the Geneva Convention regarding treatment of prisoners of war, and their contempt for its tenets was shown as they transported troops and war material in the same ship as POWs.

The ship got under way on the morning of 22 October. The movement channeled some air into the forward hold, but those aft, blocked by the bridge structure, got no relief. Many suffocated. Finally, they were allowed on deck, ten at a time, to use the two wooden *benjos* built over the side of the ship. Since many of them were suffering from a variety of intestinal ailments, they became unspeakably filthy before the first day was over. There was a water spigot, but men had to be fast; all too often impatient guards would laughingly knock the canteens from their hands. Below, men clustered at the ladders cried out in agony. Their fear was that the Japanese would halt the operation before they had their turn. The fear was justified.

The officers organized a food distribution system, which made the next bread drop go more smoothly, and everyone got at least one mouthful. Fletcher-Cooke theorized that a starving man can always be induced to wait a little longer, as long as he knows that some food is coming. Dysentery sufferers could not wait; neither could men dying of thirst. They were only given three cups of water a day. In the unrelenting heat, officers begged the Japanese to remove the tarpaulins from over the hatches—then it rained and soaked them to the skin.

They arrived off Singapore after three days at sea, and the next morning, 26 October, they tied up in Keppel Harbor. Still they were kept aboard one more hot night before being allowed to disembark. Two incidents marked their first day waiting on the waterfront. The first was a pleasurable shower under a hose on the quay. The second was very unpleasant. They lined up on the dock in groups of fifty, dropped their trousers and bent over. The inevitable glass rod was inserted into each man's anus, revolved, removed, and placed in an inscribed cardboard box, much to the amusement of hundreds of coolies witnessing the spectacle. Meanwhile, the cargo from *No. 1 Yoshida Maru* was being unloaded, including a number of British Bren-gun carriers. Then, to the POWs' horror, they were marched aboard once more to spend a last sweltering, oppressive night.[55]

The following day the POWs and laborers left the ship. The prisoners were taken to a disinfection center where they were given baths. Their kits were fumigated—and pilfered. That evening, to their consternation, they were marched back to the pier. This time they were to board two ships. About twelve hundred went on the *Dainichi Maru*, which had been waiting in the harbor since 16 October after disembarking POWs, including Lieutenant Colonel

Tharp's Branch Party Five. Eleven hundred boarded the *Singapore Maru*, a 5,859-ton cargo ship built in 1919 that had just made an eight-day trip up from Batavia with almost three thousand prisoners, mostly Dutch. *Dainichi Maru*'s cargo bay was still ripe with the waste from a unit of cavalry horses.

They sailed on 30 October, but it was not the same group that had come over on *No. 1 Yoshida Maru*. Most of the British Boei Gloduk Party remained, but they lost some native laborers while picking up other prisoners. As they sailed north, battened down in the stifling holds, they realized they were not going to the rumored railway project in Burma. They were in the South China Sea, and from contacts on the Singapore docks they learned that Allied submarines were sinking Japanese merchant ships all over the Pacific.

Their first port of call was at Cape St. Jacques, outside Saigon, where they arrived on 3 November. However, something went awry, for they never dropped anchor. On *Singapore Maru*, Lt. Col. E. R. Scott asked that all sick prisoners be removed, but his request was refused. The *Dainichi Maru* turned around in a great hurry and sailed away. POWs on deck were forced into the holds, which were battened down for a full twenty-four hours. Said Fletcher-Cooke, "Our hold became the cess-pit it was to remain for the rest of our voyage."

On Armistice Day, 11 November, the first POW died aboard *Dainichi Maru*, an RAF man named Glenister. A request was made for a funeral, and to everyone's surprise, the Japanese complied. In fact, they staged a very impressive ceremony. A Union Jack was produced to cover the body, which was tightly bound in a shroud. While the prisoners stood at attention on deck, a solemn procession of senior Japanese officers emerged from amidships, wearing medals, white gloves, and samurai swords. Buglers followed, along with four soldiers bearing trays containing milk, fish, sweets, and other Japanese dainties. An officer read the burial service, the bugles sounded, and the corpse was slipped into the ocean. Each officer in turn took a food item and threw it overboard in the wake of the body. The ceremony was complete.

Although the POWs were impressed with the ritual, many noted that if Glenister had been given some of that food while he was still alive, there might have been no need for it. Fletcher-Cooke, who believed he knew something about the Japanese character, explained to other prisoners that the Japanese had a great respect for the dead, especially for those who died in the service of their country. Unfortunately, he added, "they have no respect for POWs who, in their view, do not exist as human beings. To reestablish himself in their eyes it is necessary for a POW to die."

The scene would be repeated. The next few deaths got the same VIP treatment. But soon, with additional deaths, the senior officers failed to show up. Then the buglers. After that, the Japanese ceased contributing food for the departing spirit. Finally, the only Japanese representative was a slovenly guard who was rather irritated by the entire affair. Eighty men were consigned to the deep.

In the holds, Fletcher-Cooke could do nothing for the dying men other than talk to them and offer them comfort in their last moments. He was deeply moved. Some men gave up on living; others clung to the spark of life as long as they could. They all turned into nameless, shroud-covered corpses dropped into the sea.

For a few days in the South China Sea the weather was glorious, and the ambulatory were allowed on deck. The dying, too weak to drag themselves up the ladders, lay in their own filth. It was so dark that many of the dead remained wrapped in their blankets, undiscovered for days.

In mid-November the ships reached Takao, Formosa. Again Lieutenant Colonel Scott asked that 100 sick men be removed, and for once the Japanese agreed, perhaps fearful that the ship would arrive in Japan with nothing but corpses. The other prisoners were also offloaded and remained ashore for three days, while more bodies were removed for cremation. On the second day, a few hundred prisoners from *Dainichi Maru* formed a work party that would remain on Formosa. They were replaced by 286 Americans who had come over from Manila the previous month on *Lima Maru,* plus a mixed group of 200 from Singapore. In addition, 600 more Japanese troops were packed aboard *Singapore Maru.*

On 14 November, they headed for the Pescadores, what Fletcher-Cooke called "a group of very bleak islands to the west of Formosa." They remained at anchor for three more days, waiting out a storm. All lights were extinguished, but it made little difference to those in the Stygian darkness of the holds. The burials at sea commenced once more. On the fourth day, they joined in a convoy with five other ships and a destroyer escort. They remained blacked out. A Malay-speaking Japanese sentry told Fletcher-Cooke that they were passing through an area where many ships had been sunk by American submarines. "Roosebelto no goodo," the guard added for good measure.

The food had never been adequate. Now, the portions were even smaller and poorer. Otis King could have cried when he saw the ship's cooks toss overboard big chunks of pork fat. No amount of pleading could get them to add the fat to their thin soup. What was worse, the water supply was cut, and for the fever-racked men, that was unendurable. Fletcher-Cooke believed the conditions were much worse than on the trip from Java to Singapore. He also believed that nature had a way of blotting out some of a man's worst experiences however, because the next days evolved into a blur of horrible dreams. Men were forced, Fletcher-Cooke asserted, "into depravities of which I, for one, did not realize the human race was capable." Some men knelt above other men's faces so that the dying could drink their urine. Others cut open veins with razor blades or metal scraps so they could suck each other's blood. Most died for their attempts. Others gave up and willed themselves to die, believing they would never see the light of day again.

On 25 November, the ships steamed up to the wharf in Moji. Now it was bitterly cold, and the POWs wrapped themselves tightly in any scraps of clothing they could find. The inevitable anal probe followed, but Fletcher-Cooke didn't mind. At least, he thought, he would die on dry land. He affirmed that the voyage was undoubtedly the "grimmest part" of his captivity. His group was separated from the rest, embarking on a ferry across the Straits of Shimonoseki. Not everyone could make the march, and whispers passed through the files that those who couldn't were bayoneted where they lay. The British were taken to the Habu camp on the island of Innoshima, in the Inland Sea. The sole purpose of all their sufferings, Fletcher-Cooke thought, was simply to boost the morale of the civilian Japanese dock workers.[56]

The deplorable conditions brought comment from the War Ministry. About 140 men had died aboard the two ships, and 280 more were too weak to walk away. They were taken ashore, but within six weeks, 127 had died of malnutrition and various diseases. This was a waste of manpower. An order dated 10 December stated, "Army Asia Secret Order No. 1504. Recently, during the transportation of prisoners of war to Japan, many of them have been taken ill or have died, and quite a few of them have been incapacitated from further work due to their treatment on the journey, which at times was inadequate." Instructions followed stating that those responsible for the prisoners should ensure that they reached their destination in a condition that would allow them to be constructively put to work. Dead or seriously ill POWs would be of no benefit to the Japanese. The order was rarely followed.[57]

Besides the generally northern movement of prisoners to Singapore, Burma, and Japan, there were cross currents of interisland traffic among the October transports. Officers and specialists had departed Camp Casising, Mindanao, in previous shipments. On 18 October, all remaining American prisoners left the camp. They rode north to Bugo on open flatbed trucks. Carl Nordin, a private in the 2d Quartermaster Supply unit, used to drive the road in peacetime. He noticed Filipino families that he had known watching silently from the roadside. Now he was a prisoner in his own truck.

About one thousand men were loaded aboard *Maru 760* at Bugo. The freighter took them through Surigao Strait and down along Mindanao's east coast. They were unescorted, and the prisoners were allowed on deck for much of the time. Said Nordin, "The weather was warm and sunny, and with the gentle South Sea breezes blowing, we were really quite comfortable." They were fed rice twice a day and slept on the relatively clean steel deck. Nordin had read that east of Mindanao were some of the deepest waters in the world, almost seven miles down. He hoped that no U.S. submarines would attack them.

On 23 October they disembarked from *Maru 760* at Lasang, north of Davao. Carrying packs under the hot sun, they were forced to walk about sixteen miles to the Davao Penal Colony. Many fainted along the road. They were allowed one stop to fill their canteens from a slow-running water spigot. There was not enough time. Nordin was about fifteen men from the spigot when they were forced back into line to continue the march. They reached the Penal Colony under a bright moonlit night, and the men ran to the water spigot to quench their terrible thirsts. Davao Penal Colony was built to be self-sustaining. They would have to grow their own food.[58]

Also headed for Mindanao was another group collected from Luzon. Those who missed the trips to Japan on the *Toko Maru* or *Tottori Maru* had another chance to leave Cabanatuan. The story was that they would be going to a plantationlike camp where they would be taught farming and other trades. There was a sawmill, a rice mill, farm equipment, and groves of coconuts, avocados, and bananas. The idea of moving south sounded good to Lt. Donald H. Wills, a regimental transportation officer in the 26th Cavalry Scouts: it was seven hundred miles closer to the Allied forces. Capt. Manny Lawton, of the 1st Battalion, 31st Infantry, also thought it was a good idea. Working on a large farm would give him the opportunity to get fresh fruits and vegetables. On 26 October, they took a train to Manila, stayed in Bilibid Prison one night, and, the next morning, hiked to the docks.

Waiting for them was the 5,493-ton *Erie Maru*, built in 1920 by Asano Company and operated by Nanyo Kaiun. Wills noticed a plate on the super-structure labeled "Erie" and believed it was the ship's place of origin. He and one thousand others were moved aboard. Filipinos were being placed in the forward welldeck, while most of the POWs went aft. They sailed on 28 October. Unlike many other transports, said Lawton, they had ample room to stretch out. It was hot, but the hatches were left open and the air was fresh. The most pleasant surprise was the food. Helpings were generous: rice, fish, an occasional piece of corned beef, and cups of cabbage soup with slivers of pork. Capt. Bert Schwarz of the 27th Bomb Group said the food was the best he had while a prisoner, remembering the salted cherries on rice as particu-larly good. When Cdr. Alan McCracken became ill, the ship's doctor got him a can of pineapple juice and some vitamins. Probably the most unusual gift was a small vase of flowers presented to him by a shy Japanese sailor. There was, thought the POWs, just no way to judge the Japanese character.

Though better than most prison transports, there were still discomforts. Captain Lawton noted that toilet facilities consisted of several open-top, five-gallon cans placed on the deck. Seeing that they were filled, Lawton decided he would dump one over the side. He placed it on the rail and slowly tilted it. All was going well until he felt his legs getting wet and warm. Looking over, Lawton saw that he had been pouring the contents into a scooplike projec-tion in the hull, which funneled it back through a scupper, soaking him from the knees down. He dropped the "honey-bucket" and figured it would be the last time he would try to tidy up his area.

Lieutenant Wills slept on the open deck, where it was cooler, except one night when it rained and he went below. The only place he could find to sleep was in a coal bunker. While sleeping he was attacked by giant, two-inch long, flying cockroaches. He learned to sleep with a cloth over his face, but he could still feel them crawling all over him. Wills noted that after a few days of a bet-ter diet, fewer men suffered from diarrhea. It was a ten-day trip, however, and eventually the food supply dwindled. They broke open an iceless ice locker and found fish and carabao meat turning green. Nevertheless, most of it was consumed, beginning the diarrhea cycle all over again. Lieutenant Wills and Capt. Cecil LeBrun were on food detail, washing rice. Japanese rules said that the officers must be fed first, which brought the usual complaints from the enlisted men.

The *Erie Maru* stopped at Iloilo, Panay, where some Filipinos disembarked, then on to Cebu City, Cebu, where the remainder went ashore. They followed the east coast of Mindanao, rounded Cape San Augustin, and docked at Lasang on 7 November. They reached Davao Penal Colony about two weeks after the arrival of those from Malaybalay. There were now about twenty-one hundred prisoners in the camp. But, hoped Lieutenant Wills, anything had to be an improvement over Cabanatuan.

Although the prisoners thought they had experienced a relatively easy trip, two men had died. Although they got to rest and eat better for ten days, the Japanese commandant of the penal colony was not happy with the men he received. Maj. Maeda Kazuo, portly and balding, lectured the new arrivals: "POWs are here to work, not to sit around idle and eating. They must forget lazy American ways and learn Japanese industry and frugality." Disappointed, he concluded by saying, "I asked for laborers, not walking corpses."[59]

On Ambon, the survivors of Gull Force were being split up. Originally, 1,131 men of 2/21 Battalion and perhaps 1,000 Dutch troops defended the island. When the Japanese landed on the last day of January, the Dutch did not put up a stout fight, and the Japanese captured key positions without much trouble. The Australians who defended the airfield at Laha fought with more determination, causing many casualties among the 1st Kure Special Landing Force. The Japanese, incensed over the death of their commander, Yoyoshihara, executed a number of surrendered Australians in February. All told, about 229 men were killed, mostly from Companies B and C. The 789 remaining Australians who were captured on Laitimor Peninsula, across the bay from Laha, never knew what happened to their comrades until after the war was over.

Australian and Dutch survivors were imprisoned in the camp at Tan Toey, where harsh treatment, poor food, and disease cut rapidly into their numbers. In October, it was decided that the sickest would be removed, with the promise of being sent to a "convalescent camp." On the twenty-fifth, 263 Australians and 267 Dutch were loaded on the 2,984-ton *Taiko Maru*. It had been built in 1937 as a steamer, then requisitioned and converted to a gunboat and minesweeper. The holds were covered with thick planks and tarpaulins, leaving a space of only one square yard through which to enter. Stretcher cases went into the number one hold and the rest of the POWs into the other two holds. When a portly Dutch naval officer protested to the captain of *Taiko Maru* that there were no lifeboats aboard, the officer replied that "should they be torpedoed, he would float on account of his bulk."

The first six days of the voyage were uneventful, and the food—rice, sweet potatoes, bully beef, and canned fruit—was surprisingly good. But the tropical heat made the holds unbearable, especially in number one, where the dysentery cases lay. The food supply rapidly ran out, and once into the South China Sea, they caught the tail end of a typhoon. On 4 November, the ship's captain called for the Australian and Dutch officers and pointed to the land on the horizon. "There is the island of Hainan," he said, "where there is much hard work for you all."

On the fifth, they docked in Bakli Bay, near Yulin, on Hainan's southwest coast. They would be kept at Hashio Camp and used to work the copper and iron deposits nearby. Three months earlier the Australians of Lark Force had been sent from Rabaul to Hainan to work when their ship, the *Montevideo Maru,* was torpedoed. At last the Japanese had their work force. Unlike the tropical island camps where most POWs were kept, this part of Hainan was desertlike, clumps of prickly pear dominating the terrain. Escape would be doubly hazardous, for Chinese bandits lurked nearby, killing Westerners as readily as they killed the Japanese. About eighty-five prisoners would die in camp or be killed by the Chinese on Hainan.[60]

FINAL MOVES OF 1942

One particularly obscure voyage with disastrous results did not become fully known to the Allies until after the war. Sometime between late September and mid-October, a convoy left Singapore with the eventual destination of Rabaul. Six hundred British soldiers, the "Gunners 600," embarked, possibly on the *Nagara Maru,* the same ship that had carried General Wainwright's group from the Philippines. The convoy, also consisting of the *Noto Maru, Sagami Maru, Kinugawa Maru,* destroyer *Matsukaze,* and two other escorts, left Singapore on 29 September. They cruised to Belawan, on the northeast coast of Sumatra, on 4 October, where they loaded an Army unit and horses. On the sixth they headed east, calling at Surabaya, Java, and finally continuing to Rabaul, which they reached on 19 October.

Another report said the Gunners 600, mostly of the Royal Artillery, did not leave Singapore until 18 October, reaching Rabaul on 6 November. They were slated to build an airfield on the island of Ballale in the Shortlands, south of Bougainville. One man died on the voyage. The *Nagara Maru*, which had been at Rabaul since 19 October, formed up in another convoy, this time with the *Arizona Maru, Toyo Maru, Yamazuki Maru, Teiyo Maru, Yuri Maru, Toyokuni Maru, Oigawa Maru,* and *Shinanogawa Maru*. The men of Gunners 600 remained at Kapoko, New Britain, for a time, then reembarked, leaving behind eighty-two men who were too sick to continue the voyage. The convoy, escorted by the minelayer *Shirataka,* torpedo-boat *Hiyodori,* subchaser (SC) 16, and minesweeper (AM) 15, sailed for the Shortlands on 6 November. Heavy squalls were encountered, but the convoy made a consistent nine knots down the north side of Bougainville. The next day, a U.S. submarine was contacted, but the escorts dropped depth charges, preventing an attack. Bad weather temporarily prevented the convoy from entering the harbor, but on 8 November, it arrived safely in the Shortlands.

The Gunners 600 party, now reduced to 517, was taken to Ballale, which contained a Chinese compound whose occupants had already started airfield construction. Upon first setting foot on Ballale, one white prisoner apparently disobeyed an order. He was beheaded on the spot by Lt. Cdr. Ozaki Noriko. Conditions would deteriorate from then on. The only witnesses to upcoming events were Korean guards, Chinese laborers, and a few captured Japanese. There were no British survivors.[61]

Another group of prisoners from the Royal Artillery had better luck than the Gunners 600. About a thousand British POWs, most of them members of the 155th Field Regiment, were chosen to go to Formosa. In late October, they left Birdwood Camp near Changi and marched to the quay, where they were to board the much-traveled *England Maru*. Gunner John McEwan, who had been on a work detail dockside, had recently unloaded cattle from the ship. He was shocked. He thought the ship was a "battered old rust bucket" with faded, peeling paint—a "stinking, rat-infested, disreputable hulk."

"It seemed that this potential mass coffin was to be our mode of travel," said McEwan. They were bullied down, 250 men into each of four holds, gingerly stepping over the piles of cattle excrement that still fouled the decks.

Each hold was lit by one small electric bulb in an overhead socket. McEwan and his mates, John Kane and "Taffy" Morgan, fought with rats that scuttled across their bodies during the night and battled two-inch cockroaches and voracious bluebottle flies. The voyage lasted more than two weeks, and three men died. Their bodies were unceremoniously tossed overboard, accompanied by the constant "Speedo! Speedo!" calls from the guards.

The ever-present latrine hanging over the side of the ship was called "the Stage" by the POWs, because of the endless laughter it produced in the Japanese guards, who came by to enjoy the discomfiture of the prisoners as they did their business while hanging on for dear life. The only benefit of the contraption came when the pounding waves lifted cold seawater spray to cleanse the men's exposed bottoms.

The *England Maru* pulled in to Keelung in early November. Perhaps because many of the men were Scottish, Welsh, and Irish with mining backgrounds, the Japanese sent McEwan's group of five hundred to work in the copper mines at Kinkaseki. They were stranded on Formosa for the entire war.[62]

Other hellships traveled to Japan. On 1 November, names were drawn up from the prisoners at Cabanatuan for another special detail. There were the usual takers and decliners, depending on how one saw his chances. For Pvt. Robert Davis of Battery D, 515th Coast Artillery, there was no doubt. "I was about to crack up and go over the wall," he said. "A man could get killed for that. When the Japanese asked for volunteers to work, I jumped."

Those selected were allowed to take the few belongings they still owned, plus they were each given a large breakfast and a piece of meat two inches in diameter and a quarter of an inch thick. However paltry, this was the most meat they had seen since being captured, and they relished it. They were trucked to the train station, then loaded in boxcars, packed in as they had been on the way up to O'Donnell during the Death March. Lt. Col. Ernest B. Miller of the 194th Tank Battalion slowly chewed the tough piece of meat, making it last almost to the depot. An old Japanese officer, shedding crocodile tears, told them how sorry he was to see them go; they must guard their health, for they were being taken to Japan, where they would receive better treatment and lots of food. Miller was sick of this "drivel" he had heard so often.

While fifteen hundred men assembled at Pier Seven, some managed to sneak away to inspect the cargo in the godowns and on the docks. Twenty-year-old 4th Marine corporal Robert E. Haney found bales of compressed,

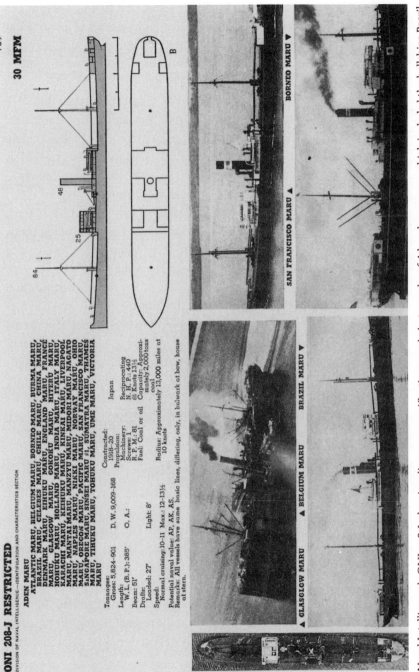

Naval Intelligence's ONI 208-J, showing diagrams, specifications, and photographs of *Aden*-class marus, which included the hellships *Brazil Maru*, *Celebes Maru*, *England Maru*, *France Maru*, *Nagato Maru*, *Singapore Maru*, *Thames Maru*, and *Ume Maru*. U.S. Navy

dried fish. He and his buddies stole and ate some, later finding out it was to be used as fertilizer. Lieutenant Colonel Miller found a stock of uncured leaf tobacco. He and several others grabbed a considerable amount, securing bunches of the leaves to the insides of their trouser legs. It was, said Miller, "the most terrible stuff I have ever smoked."

When all were assembled, they trailed out on the pier to see their ship. "My new hell was the *Nagato Maru*," said Bob Davis. "An old freighter—dark, drab, and bulky—marring the sparkling blue waters of Manila Bay." He walked up the gangplank, then, he recalled, "the Japs crammed us in. They stacked us like animals, 550 men to a hold, so crowded we touched. As temperatures in the holds rose, tempers did likewise. This was a Hell Ship."

The *Nagato Maru* was a passenger-cargo ship of fifty-nine hundred tons, 385 feet long, with a single propeller and a normal cruising speed of ten knots. It was owned by the NYK Line. Davis heard that *Nagato* meant "everlasting gate." Was this to be a cruise to eternity's gate, he wondered?

It was late evening when they loaded. One of the first aboard was Bob Haney, and he headed to the forward hold, thinking the air flow would be better there. However, being first meant that he went to the farthest bottom corner, while the men pushed in behind him. A steep, open ladder led down against the aft bulkhead. At the bottom were triple tiers of shelves. In the middle of the hold was a large slop bucket that smelled of pickled daikons. Another barrel contained water, which was used up in minutes. Lights high up in the rigging didn't illuminate the bottom, and a single light bulb hanging in the hold didn't help much.

There were more than five hundred men in each of three holds. Davis was first reminded of a dungeon. Then the riblike timbers lining the sides of the hold made it appear that he had been swallowed by a huge whale. Miller thought of an old movie he had seen, depicting Spanish galley slaves. When it seemed like no more men could be forced into the holds, almost fifteen hundred Japanese troops filed in to the decks above. Miller calculated that ten men were allotted a space of only about five by six feet. They cried out for water and air. Guards appeared at the rim of the hatch, threatening to open fire if they did not quiet down. Some prisoners panicked and vomited on their neighbors. When it seemed that they were on the verge of rioting, the Japanese sent water buckets down on ropes, but only enough water for about one teaspoon per man.

Nagato Maru moved out into Manila Bay on 7 November, in a convoy of three ships. Getting under way was somewhat of a tension release; suddenly the lines to the latrines grew longer, but there were only two *benjos* hanging outboard from the top deck. The slop bucket in Haney's section was soon occupied by three men at a time, with lines of men standing impatiently by. Some couldn't wait, and soon the rims, base, and deck around the barrel were a mess. It got on shoes and trousers, and before long the entire deck and even the ladders were coated. Prisoners had to grasp the ladder rungs then use the drinking water to wash their hands. Said Haney, "The slop bucket was soon filled. But diarrhea and dysentery wait for no man." The hold became a cesspool. Haney thought that Dante's *Inferno* might have been aboard *Nagato Maru* in 1942. "For much of the rest of my life," he stated, "this nightmare Pacific passage would color my impression of the Japanese."

Late in the afternoon, a soldier appeared at the top of the ladder with buckets, indicating that they were to begin emptying the barrel. As the prisoners dipped the buckets and carried them up the ladders, much of the contents splashed out. After emptying the barrels, ten men were called to carry rice and water down the same ladders. Feces and rice! Haney could not consciously remember eating for the entire seventeen-day trip. He surely must have, but the revulsion of the experience no doubt blocked it from his memory.

After a few days of sailing, Davis could think of nothing but food. He became detached and apathetic, but visions of food consumed him. The men talked of food and only got hungrier. Davis and his friends Reardon and Potter talked about opening a restaurant after the war.

"We'd serve my best dish," Davis said. "Mexican enchiladas smothered in cheese and hot sauce."

"Steak dinners," Reardon said. "We'd have those too. Steak, potatoes, salad, vegetables, milk, and coffee, all for forty-five cents."

"Candy bars," said Potter. "Mounds, Baby Ruth, Hershey's."

"Shut up you guys!" someone would yell. Then silence for a while.

"Pizza!"

"Beer!"

And on it would go until a fight started or they quit from exhaustion.

Two days later the hatches were suddenly closed. Prisoners returning rice buckets to the galley were brutally forced back down, one man losing teeth in the process. The hatch was closed for four hours. It was a submarine attack.

They could feel and hear the concussions of the explosions right through the hull. Depth charges were dropped and the ship's deck gun barked. Below, no one knew what was happening, only that they were trapped with no way to escape. A few men died for lack of oxygen. Haney fainted and awoke when a fellow prisoner fanned him back to life, telling him about how good it would be to drink down a cold draft beer. By the time they reached Takao, on 11 November, about seventeen men were dead.

The *Nagato Maru* docked in Formosa for three days then sailed to the Pescadores, where a storm held them up for several more days. They pulled out on 18 November. Next was a two-day stop in Taipei, on Formosa's north coast, and then the final leg of the journey. A canvas scoop rigged up over the open forward hatch funneled some air into the holds. That, and cooler temperatures, helped keep the death rates down during the run across the East China Sea. By this time the prisoners had become infested with lice, and they spent the last days scratching in misery.

North of Shanghai, the hull became cold to the touch. Skirting the Yellow Sea, a Siberian air flow dominated the weather, and spaces fore and aft farthest from the boilers became intolerably cold. Whereas prisoners once pressed their bodies against the metal sides for coolness, they now avoided contact. Whereas they once shunned resting against warm bodies, they now curled up together for warmth. Haney no longer had trouble breathing; it was now a matter of maintaining heat in a body that had no fat reserves. Bob Davis thought in biblical terms. "Men shivered in their thin rags," he said, "seventeen hundred Jonahs in the dark, damp belly of hell."

Nagato Maru finally pulled in to Moji on 24 November. Davis couldn't remember the last time he saw the sun. "I remember our first time up," he said. "We hit the decks squinting like moles." Men hobbled down the gangways, almost unable to walk, using some muscles for the first time in weeks. On the wharf they were stripped, hosed down, disinfected, and inoculated. They got showers and received sets of what seemed to be Philippine Army denims. It was almost like heaven.

Lieutenant Colonel Miller looked back on the trip, wondering how something so horrible could have occurred. Faces looked strange. It seemed that they had all grown years older in only a few short weeks. Before they entrained for Osaka, Davis turned around for a last look at *Nagato Maru*, and shivered. He yearned to watch her roll over, moan, sink, and disappear from the surface of the water. It all seemed like a nightmare that should never have happened.[63]

The last ship to Japan in 1942 left from Singapore on 28 November. Frank Fujita of the 131st Artillery was moving again. He was one of Colonel Tharp's men wearing the red ribbons when they had come from Java on *Kenkon Maru* in October. After missing out on previous transports, they were finally going to finish the journey. Fujita thought that the same group was being shipped, but many of Tharp's Branch Party Five remained in Changi.

The day before sailing, the Americans were issued British wool uniforms and hobnailed boots that an officer had managed to purchase with some of Battery E's payroll. The well-dressed men were loaded onto trucks and taken to the harbor, where 2,213 POWs, designated C Force, were gathered: 500 Americans, 563 Australians, 200 British airmen, and 950 Dutch. The Australians, under Lt. Col. A. E. Robertson, had come from the Adam Park camp, where they had been working on a memorial to the Japanese dead at Bukit Timah. Their work at this camp probably saved some of their lives later. Said Aussie Mervyn Gronow, "That's where I picked up my health. The work was bugger all . . . and you could get something to eat. We got a South African Red Cross parcel."

It was a large group, but the ship they boarded was large. It was built by the Yokohama Dock Company in 1930 as the *Chichibu Maru,* a 17,256-ton, twenty-one-knot passenger liner. In 1939 it was owned by the NYK Line and renamed the *Kamakura Maru,* and in 1941 it was requisitioned as a transport and hospital ship. The Japanese were converting several of their large liners to escort carriers, and *Kamakura Maru* was slated for conversion in 1943.

Pvt. William A. Visage, also in Battery E, said the ship was loaded with contraband goods that the Japanese were removing from the East Indies. There was so much cargo aboard that most of the POWs had to stay on deck; not a bad experience, at least while still in the tropics. Fujita noticed that one Japanese sergeant they called "the Bull," who had accompanied them on the trip from Java, was still with them. He was amazed at how much authority the man had, being in charge of a thousand prisoners. The Bull was a short, massively built man who hulked around like a gorilla. If a POW stepped out of line, he would be beaten unmercifully, but he would do the same with the guards under him. Fujita watched several times as the Bull beat his own men in plain sight of the prisoners.

The trip through the South China Sea was pleasant, the food was adequate, and the weather fine. The only hardship, said Fujita, was that there was plenty of water aboard, but they were only issued one canteen of tea per man and told that it would have to last for the seven-day trip to Formosa. They reached Taipei, about 5 November, but stayed there less than half a day. After leaving, they were given all the tea they wanted. Fujita said, "We were never able to fathom Japanese reasoning."

Heading northeast across the East China Sea, the weather turned much colder. They donned all the woolen clothing they had, but it was not enough to counteract the ice and sleet storms. Huge waves splashed over the sides of the ship and soaked them, making them wish they could go into the holds for shelter. They had few blankets. Food was cut to three scoops of rice once a day. Bill Visage said that after their clothing was soaked, they stripped off everything down to their shorts and packed close together for warmth. No Americans were lost, but a few Dutch POWs contracted pneumonia and died.

On 7 December, the anniversary of the Pearl Harbor attack, *Kamakura Maru* docked in the harbor of a large city. Fujita had a strange feeling of déjà vu when he was told that the city was Nagasaki; it was the very city his father had emigrated from when he went to the United States in 1914. He wondered if any of his distant relatives might be watching them from shore.[64]

One last hellship would yet leave port in 1942. On 21 December, an eleven-ship convoy of three sections, under the name No. 6-GO Transportation Operation, left Shanghai for points south. B section, consisting of the *Oigawa Maru, Kenkon Maru, Kyokusei Maru,* and *Panama Maru,* and escorted by the destroyer *Shiratsuyu,* was destined for Truk and Rabaul. The 5,289-ton *Panama Maru* carried 130 Chinese prisoners. It went to Formosa, Palau, and Truk, where, on 19 January 1943, it disembarked the Chinese, who would be used as slaves to build up Truk's defenses.[65]

1942 CURRENTS

The first full year of the Pacific war ended with some notes of optimism for the Allies. There had been no sweeping territorial gains, but the Japanese Army and Navy had been halted. The Australians had stopped them in Papua, New Guinea, on the Kakoda Trail, and at Milne Bay. The Americans had checked them at Guadalcanal. Few miles had been gained on the long road to Japan, but the most important results were psychological. The Japanese could be beaten.

The Japanese came to believe that the turning point in the war was the six-month-long Solomons campaign. It was then that their logistics system began to deteriorate. The Solomons fight was a war of transportation, and one of the prime causes of defeat was Japan's inability to supply its island garrisons. There simply was not enough infrastructure to carry on a successful war. The Imperial Navy was top-heavy: numerous warships but not enough of a merchant marine to adequately supply its troops.[66]

The insufficiency of the merchant fleet was not immediately apparent in 1942. It was estimated that Japan needed about 6 million tons of shipping to sustain its war effort and meet civilian needs. She began the war with about 6,376,000 tons, with the Army controlling 2,150,000 tons, the Navy controlling 1,560,000, and civilians owning 2,666,000 tons. The division did not expedite matters, as the various authorities often worked at cross-purposes. During the first several months of the war, Japan captured many Allied and neutral ships, adding more than 345,000 tons to her fleet. During 1942, her shipyards built 361,000 tons. Losses in 1942 amounted to 978,000 tons, leaving 5,942,000 tons still afloat at the end of the year. In fact, as late as October 1942, Japan had slightly more tons afloat than she had at the war's start. Increased submarine and aircraft attacks in October and November accounted for the net loss by the year's end. Still, it was not much to be concerned about.[67]

The sustainable merchant ship losses and relatively poor showing by the Allies gave Japanese war planners a false sense of security. A cavalier attitude often sent Japanese merchant ships sailing alone, or in small convoys without escorts, or on nonzigzag courses across thousands of miles of ocean. Although the voyages were intolerable for thousands of prisoners, other thousands found the experience satisfactory or, sometimes, even pleasant. The Japanese were not yet feeling the pinch of food, fuel, and shipping shortages. They were not yet being pursued every mile by U.S. planes and submarines.

Even so, there was no great economy of planning and movement. Army, Navy, or civilian-controlled shipping often would not cooperate. Ships might sail to one destination, unload, and return sailing in ballast. Williams Force sailed to Singapore on the *Kenkon Maru,* got off, then loaded for Burma on the *Maebashi Maru.* The *Dainichi Maru* took Tharp's Party to Singapore, where they disembarked. There *No.* 1 *Yoshida Maru* from Java unloaded its POWs, which then climbed aboard *Dainichi Maru* and *Singapore Maru.* Battery E men of Tharp's Party went on neither, waiting instead to board the *Kamakura Maru*. An attempt was made to ship POWs from Rabaul to Hainan, and POWs were successfully sent there from Ambon, although a shift of POWs from the Philippines would have been much more efficient. Australians were taken out of Rabaul, then British prisoners were brought there from Singapore. Moving prisoners out of the Moluccas necessitated bringing more in from Java. Prisoners were moved north from Makassar to Japan, while some in the northern Philippines were moved south to Mindanao. Some Chinese prisoners were even taken to Truk. In spite of the apparent haphazardness, the main axis of prisoner movement was south to north, with about twenty ships destined for Japan or Korea and a dozen going to Singapore or Burma. Prisoners were put to work as laborers in factories, mills, farms, shipyards, and mines and were used to construct roads, railways, and airfields. They were also used for propaganda purposes. The Japanese were winning, and it did not appear likely that they would ever be held accountable for their actions. Thus far their losses were acceptable. Only two hellships had been torpedoed while carrying prisoners: *Montevideo Maru* and *Lisbon Maru*. All told, fifty-four ships carried 49,459 prisoners. The average time of each voyage was about ten days. There had been to date about 2,240 deaths—a 4.5 percent loss rate. It would get worse.

1943

AN UNEASY STASIS

Many prisoners of war survived beatings, starvation, and disease on land only to die at sea, through either the inhuman treatment of their enemies or the torpedoes and bombs of their friends. Prisoners also died at sea in the European theater. In July 1940, the *Arandora Star*, transporting 1,190 Italian and German prisoners from Britain to Canada, was sunk by the German U-47, killing about 800. In August 1942, the Italian ship *Nino Bixio*, sailing from Africa to Italy, was torpedoed with the loss of 37 of the 201 Australian prisoners on board. The next month the British passenger ship *Laconia*, carrying 800 Italian POWs, was torpedoed by U-156 off the west coast of Africa.

RED CROSS PROPOSALS

Such incidents may have been avoided had the belligerents listened to the pleas of the International Red Cross. It had struggled to get governments on both sides to agree on a method that would ensure the safety of prisoners transported by sea. Both Axis and Allied powers, however, were reluctant to make a reasonable accommodation. In 1940, the Red Cross suggested that countries refrain from attacking prisoner ships, or at least notify the other side when and where the ships would sail. Initially, the British felt little legal or moral obligation to respond to the Red Cross appeal. They blamed Germany for beginning unrestricted submarine warfare, they did not want to reveal the routes of their convoys, and they did not want to compromise passenger traffic with the United States, which was not yet officially at war.

By 1942, the situation had changed, with thousands of Allies becoming Axis prisoners in the Mediterranean theater and in the Far East. Concerned with potential disaster in both hemispheres, the Red Cross renewed its appeals. It asked that both sides assure that ships had sufficient life jackets and lifeboats, that all ships carrying POWs fly recognition markers and refrain from carrying troops or war materials. Again, Britain rejected the proposals, believing that if such vessels were clearly marked and announced, it would only make them easier prey. They would surely be sunk, for it "would probably be considered by the enemy to be of greater value than the saving of the lives of their own or allied nationals'."

Axis and Allied powers had the same cynical suspicions of each other. Distrust and the fear of losing some sort of strategic advantage combined to leave the Red Cross suggestions in limbo. The Germans made a counterproposal that prisoners and internees simply be transported on hospital ships, which were already immune from attack according to international law. The Allies rejected the suggestion, unwilling to believe that the Axis would not use hospital ships as a cover to transport war material and troops. Both Italy and Japan, having the same concerns, objected to any significant increase in the number of Allied hospital ships. It appeared that any concessions would not come from humanitarian reasons but only coincidentally, if the concessions also conformed to strategic interests. In November 1942, the Allied Joint Chiefs of Staff concluded that, "in view of the extreme importance of attacking enemy shipping and of the relatively small number of casualties to prisoners of war so caused, no prohibition should be placed at present" on the attack of enemy ships. The directive was specifically focused on Mediterranean operations. Apparently the Joint Chiefs did not think through the implications of their decision for the POWs in the Far East.

In the Pacific, the United States had little interest in the Red Cross plans. It had been practicing unrestricted submarine warfare against Japanese shipping since the opening gun. The strategic edge lost in granting concessions would outweigh the potential benefits gained in saving the lives of Allied POWs. Japan never even responded to the Red Cross proposals. Prisoners of war on both sides would just have to take their chances once at sea.[1]

RELIEF AND REPATRIATION

If the Red Cross could not negotiate an agreement on prisoner sea transportation, perhaps it could facilitate relief efforts for them. In January 1942,

U.S. and Canadian Red Cross societies met to make arrangements to send food packages to the Far East. In May, the American Red Cross and U.S. government worked through the International Red Cross and Sweden to negotiate with Japan for the exchange of diplomatic personnel and civilians. Not until June were the Americans able to charter the Swedish ship *Kanangoora* and load it with a million dollars' worth of supplies for the prisoners in the Far East. By August, the Japanese still would not grant a safe-conduct pass for the ship, and the charter was canceled. The British, in the meantime, tried to use the Vatican as an intermediary to arrange supply shipments on a reciprocal basis. The attempt met with no more success than the U.S.-Canadian plan.

Japan was receptive, however, to a diplomatic exchange. The first voyages went smoothly. In June 1942, the *Asama Maru* loaded U.S. diplomatic personnel and civilians at Yokohama, then traveled to Hong Kong, where it anchored in Lamma Channel. About 390 American civilians left the Stanley camp and were ferried to the ship. It sailed on 30 June for Saigon and Singapore. The *Asama Maru* was joined by the Italian liner *Conte Verde*, which was bringing 636 Americans, Canadians, and South Americans from Shanghai, and both ships sailed across the Indian Ocean to Lourenco Marques in Mozambique.

Meeting them there on 23 July was the U.S.-chartered Swedish liner *Gripsholm*, which left New York carrying Japanese diplomats. The Americans and Canadians saw this as a way to get food supplies to the Far East and loaded the *Gripsholm* with three hundred tons of food, clothing, tobacco, and medicine. This achievement drew criticism from Britain, because it believed this was preferential treatment for U.S. and Canadian prisoners. They protested to Canada, but Canada would not reconsider.

It took four days to transfer the cargo, but thirteen hundred Americans happily boarded the *Gripsholm,* and the *Asama Maru* and *Conte Verde* now brimmed with Japanese citizens and tons of supplies, increased more so by a contribution of bulk foodstuffs from South Africa. The transfer made, the *Gripsholm* headed for New York while the *Asama Maru* and *Conte Verde* went east to Singapore and Yokohama.

While those ships were sailing, the Japanese also decided to evacuate the British embassy staff from Tokyo, Yokohama, and Kobe. Harassed all the way by the Kempeitai, the British were loaded aboard the *Tatsuta Maru* on 30 July. Treated at times like POWs, they were locked below decks in the searing heat of Yokohama Harbor. Additional British civilians were placed aboard the

Kamakura Maru. The voyages, via Singapore to Lourenco Marques, took ten weeks. This time transfer was made to *El Nil* and *Narkunda,* which traded Japanese diplomats and tons of supplies from England, Australia, and India. The *City of Canterbury* was also there. It had left Melbourne with 871 Japanese civilians and the ashes of Japanese submariners who had died in Sydney harbor. All it received in return was 30 Australians, 71 British, and 9 Dutch. The Australians felt cheated. They released the most, gained the least in return, and still had no word about the people that had disappeared in New Britain. The *Kamakura Maru* and *Tatsuta Maru* took the relief supplies to Yokohama and Shanghai, while the *El Nil* and *Narkunda* carried the repatriates to Liverpool.[2]

Further relief efforts were hindered by British and American bickering over details such as which countries would supply European POWs versus Far East POWs, which ships should be used, who should provide what supplies, and whether money should be sent. Canada most often acted as an intermediary, caring not which plan was used as long as it provided relief to Canadian POWs. In 1943, a plan to send supplies through the Soviet Union was agreed upon; however, the United States wanted occasional large shipments, whereas Britain wanted small loads sent at regular intervals. Canada suggested a compromise, but the United States was unenthusiastic. Then the State Department figured there was no point in arguing, as Japan had not agreed to a plan anyway. Lack of cooperation among the Allies was the prime reason for the poor relief results.

When Japan agreed to let the Soviet Union collect supplies at Vladivostok for distribution, Britain and the United States fell into bickering again. Britain felt that the parcels should consist only of food and medicine and be unloaded at all points for the use of all POWs. The United States wanted parcels to also include clothes, cigarettes, and books, and wanted them sent only to camps with American prisoners. Australia joined in and sought her own deal with the Soviet Union to get relief supplies to her prisoners. Finally, they compromised: food was the priority, but Americans would get American parcels and Commonwealth prisoners would get Canadian parcels whenever possible.

The arrangements to stockpile Red Cross parcels in Vladivostok were moving at a snail's pace—a possible reason being the Allies' delay in releasing information about Japanese atrocities. Stories brought back by repatriates and a few escaped POWs exposed Japanese barbarism. Three Americans who escaped from the Philippines brought first word of the Bataan Death March in the summer of 1943, but their story was kept under wraps for fear of reprisals against the POWs and in hopes that the Japanese would not obstruct delivery of supplies then being carried by *Gripsholm*. That ship had set sail in September 1943, carrying Japanese nationals and 140,000 food packages. Because of the escapees' information, last-minute changes were made to the parcels, adding butter, meat, clothing, and drugs aimed at combating vitamin deficiencies, malaria, and dysentery.

The *Gripsholm* met the *Teia Maru* at the port of Mormugao, India, in mid-October. Cargoes were exchanged, and *Teia Maru* headed home to deliver the parcels in Manila, Shanghai, and Yokohama. In Manila, POWs from Bilibid prison helped unload the ship. As thousands of boxes piled up on the pier, the Japanese were awed by the amount of goods earmarked for the prisoners. Not surprisingly, not all of the packages were received by those for whom they were intended. The *Gripsholm* made another trip all the way to the Far East, but this time supplies only reached Shanghai and Manila, for the Japanese refused to allow the ship to enter Hong Kong or Singapore. In Manila, a number of American repatriates were allowed to board. At the civilian internee center at Santo Tomas, Robert H. Wygle was skeptical of the selection process. It seemed to him that those on the selection committee chose for repatriation themselves or their friends. The sick and aged were supposed to go, but the young, healthy, and wealthy were the ones embarking. Wygle, who along with his family was left behind, also thought that many of those leaving were willing propagandists who would spread the word of Japanese magnanimity. "Politics and payoffs were the items that largely filled the boat," he concluded.

The Red Cross packages were unevenly distributed. Some prisoners got one or two a year for three and a half years of captivity, some got one per year, some got one parcel, period. Generally, prisoners in the north received more, while many in the Indies, at the tail end of the distribution system, never saw a package. In Changi, after *Gripsholm* departed, American Bill Weissinger found out what it meant to apportion parcels according to nationality. With the British in charge of the distribution, the Yanks lined up for their portions but came away from the depot with considerably less than their British counterparts. When they complained, they were shown the boxes, which were clearly stamped "For British and Dominion Prisoners Only." A British officer told them they were lucky to have received anything at all. Weissinger couldn't argue with that. The Americans left, disgusted with the "short-minded" folks who had thought up such a system. In contrast, Americans in German prison camps received one Red Cross food package per week and mail fairly regularly. Prisoners of the Japanese only got what was left after their captors had finished looting. Said one former captive, "Boy, we could have owned Japan with a full box once a week!"[3]

FIRST TRANSPORTS OF 1943

In the summer of 1942, Brig. A. S. Blackburn, the senior Australian officer captured on Java, had refused when the Japanese insisted that all prisoners sign a "no escape" oath. Despite cutting rations and issuing threats, Blackburn held fast until the morning of 4 July, when machine guns were set up around the perimeter of Bicycle Camp. Blackburn and Colonel Searle, an American, were arrested. With the prisoners' lives in jeopardy, the two finally gave in and allowed the men to sign the oath, knowing full well that, taken under duress, it was not binding. Still, the Americans were not happy having to sign the humiliating paper on their Fourth of July. Some months later, the Japanese removed all high-ranking officers, assuming that leaderless men would cause less trouble.

On 28 December 1942, seventy-four military men and civilian authorities were taken to Tanjong Priok. The former governor general of the Dutch East Indies, Tjarda van Stachouwer, and a few generals were placed in automobiles. Other civilians and officers followed in three trucks. They were allowed to take their bedding and luggage. In the harbor, they boarded the *Maru Roku* (six), "an old, rusty steamer" of about four thousand tons. Before embarking, they were met by Maj. Gen. Saito Yaheita, commander of the 25th Army. He had presents for Stachouwer: mosquito coils, eau de cologne, and twenty-five cigars. Saito conversed with them, talking about their families. "War is not pleasant," he said.

On board they descended past the first level, which contained two platforms thick with Japanese soldiers. On the second level they found similar accommodations. It was too low to stand up straight and too cramped to sleep comfortably. However, one officer noted in his diary, "Japanese soldiers were in the same situation. No angry mood. Food the same for everybody: rice, three times a day." The latrines were "wooden huts." The diary continued:

"Urinating done in public view—difficult for some. Stinking mess. We wash ourselves in our own sweat."

After more than three hundred years of Dutch rule, long after the "golden age" of Holland, the governor general and important Dutch officials were herded together in a tramp steamer and whisked away, never to see the Indies again. The ship pulled away from Java on 30 December and headed for Singapore.

A three-day trip brought them to Keppel Harbor, where they unloaded to wait for their next ship. In the meantime, another force was readying to move. Lt. Col. Edward E. "Weary" Dunlop, a doctor in the Royal Australian Medical Corps, debarked from the *Orcades* in Java in February 1942 with elements of the 2/3 Machine Gun Battalion, 2/2 Pioneers, and 2/6 Field Company Engineers. After surrender, they had spent nearly a year moving from camp to camp in Java. November found them in Batavia, and late in December it was announced that they would be going to Japan. Believing the known to be safer than the unknown, Dunlop wished to stay in Java, but it was not to be. On 4 January, Dunlop's force of 878 Australians were given four eggs and two buns each and marched to the pier. There they were joined by another group of 1,000 officerless Aussies, most of them of the 2/40 Battalion from Timor, and 100 Dutch troops.

In the dim early morning light, they boarded the six-thousand-ton *Usu Maru*. Dunlop's men went last and split evenly into two holds, which Dunlop likened to "the black hole of Calcutta." He described his hold as a "rusty old tramp," square cargo openings covered by heavy planks, with cobwebs, rats, and cockroaches. Every inch of space was crammed with men, and baggage was hopelessly piled in the center. It was a one-funnel coal-burner that was very lightly loaded, for the Plimsoll line was nearly as high as the quay. After some hours of immobility, Dunlop requested that men be allowed topside for exercise. Permission was refused because, he was told, they would only be at sea for two days until Singapore was reached.

The *Usu Maru* docked on 7 January, and the men were trucked to Changi. That evening, Dunlop visited with the officers who had debarked a few days earlier, including Brigadier Blackburn and Air Vice Marshal Maltby. They learned that Dunlop's force would not go to Japan but would head north to work the railroads. On 10 January the officers and some high-ranking officials would continue their trip to Formosa. The 11,409-ton *Aki Maru*, ex-*Mishima Maru,* was a fast liner, built in 1942 and converted to a troop transport. Former governor Stachouwer climbed aboard, as did Sir Shenton Thomas, the former governor of Malaya, Sir Mark Young, former governor of Hong Kong, A. I. Spits, former governor of Sumatra, Dutch general Hein ter Poorten, Major General Sitwell, A. V. M. Maltby, and Brigadier Blackburn. Despite *Aki Maru's* speed, interminable delays prevented her reaching Formosa until 30 January. The officers and officials made their dreary way to Karenko, to join Percival, Wainwright, and other high-ranking prisoners in their captivity.[4]

There was a never-ending need for men to work on the Burma Railway. Branch Party Five, which had come from Java in October 1942, was on the move again. About 450 Americans and 385 Australians, all under Lieutenant Colonel Tharp, were trucked to the Singapore railroad depot on 9 January. *Houston* sailor Seldon Reese was looking forward to leaving Changi because he figured he would be fed more if he worked. He didn't know how good he had it. About thirty-five men were mercilessly jammed into each metal boxcar, measuring only eight by twenty feet. "The tropical sun transformed the cars into ovens," said Kyle Thompson of the 131st Artillery. "This was no scenic tour we were about to undertake."

Bill Weissinger from the *Houston* said the men had one canteen of water each, and that was soon exhausted. They managed to jimmy the door open to let in some fresh air. After sundown, the metal cars finally cooled. It was past midnight when they pulled in to Kuala Lumpur and were taken off for a quick rice-and-stew meal. The train took on water and was off again. Next stop was at Ipoh, where Malayans furtively flashed them the "V" for victory sign when they were allowed off the cars to fill their canteens.

The two-day trip brought them to Penang, on Malaya's west coast. They got out of the boxcars and breathed the fresh air, then groaned when they saw they were heading down to the docks.

"Oh, no! Not another ship trip," Thompson heard someone complain. "This is too much."

"Speedo! Speedo!" the Japanese guards yelled as they were forced onto several small boats that took them to a tramp steamer anchored in the bay, the three-thousand-ton *Moji Maru.* It was not as crowded as was *Dainichi Maru;* they were allowed on deck, and it was cleaner, with new bamboo mats to sleep on. The Americans went into the forward hold and the Aussies into the aft. The *Houston*'s petty officer, George E. Detre, met the ship's captain, who once lived in Missouri and spoke English. He and Seldon Reese talked to him. He was very friendly and spoke candidly of their chances: if they got to Moulmein it would be a miracle. Even if they did, the captain doubted that he could get out again. Allied submarines and planes were making the trip around Malaya very dangerous, emphasizing the need to complete the railway. The captain allowed the Americans full run of the ship back as far as the bridge, plus they had all the water they could drink and were even allowed salt-water baths.

Also docked in the harbor was the 4,693-ton *Nichimei Maru,* owned by the Nissan Kisen Company. It had been in Singapore when Tharp's Party was boarding the train. It took on 965 Dutch prisoners, plus 1,562 Japanese soldiers and their baggage, then sailed up the coast to Penang. On the eleventh, the small convoy, designated S28 and consisting of the *Moji Maru, Nichimei Maru,* auxiliary netlayer *Choko Maru,* and SC 8, sailed for Moulmein. Kyle Thompson called the naval escort "a tiny corvette that appeared to be an old pleasure yacht armed with a three-inch gun mounted astern." It was typical, he believed, of the lack of value the Japanese placed on their human cargo.

The trip north was quiet at first. Weissinger thought the food was adequate: two meals a day consisting of rice and barley and a watery stew with some sort of green leafy vegetables, plus hot tea. He was bored. "There was nothing to see topside but the murky brown sea, so the trip was very monotonous for the first two days." The coverings were removed from the holds and the men were free to roam. Said Thompson, "Most of the time was spent lounging in the holds, reading, or playing cards." It was, he said, "a state approaching POW elegance."

The idyll was violently interrupted in the afternoon of 15 January, when they were in the Gulf of Martaban, about fifty miles from Moulmein. Thompson was engrossed in a game of bridge when he heard a sudden scurrying of feet on the deck above. He dropped his cards and went topside in time to see a flight of B-24 Liberators. The low rumble of their engines grew louder and cold chills went up Thompson's spine. He was about to be bombed by his own countrymen. One deck down, Weissinger remained where he thought he would be safer. He heard the *Moji Maru*'s whistle shriek and felt the ship speed up. Topside, the gun crews manned the forward and aft 5-inchers and began to track the incoming flight. A few shots barked out, but the flight zoomed past, heading for the larger *Nichimei Maru.*

High-level bombing of ships at sea produced few sinkings early in the war. Not until the low-level tactic of skip bombing was introduced did Japanese ships lose their immunity to land-based aircraft. These Liberators, however, were either good or lucky. On their first pass, three near-misses straddled the *Nichimei Maru,* cutting the radio antenna and communications systems. On the next pass one bomb hit midway between the number two hold and the engine room, while a second bomb struck the rear of the bridge. The planes dropped additional bombs, all near-misses, then returned to strafe, leaving the ship peppered with holes. The *Nichimei Maru* came to a halt and quickly took a 15-degree list.

As the bombers worked over the *Nichimei Maru,* Reese said that he and other Americans were screaming as if they were at a football game: "Hit the son-of-a-bitch! Sink the bastard!" The bombers then turned their attention to the smaller *Moji Maru.* The guards hurriedly forced all the prisoners below decks. Only a few managed to peek through the hatches to give a running commentary on what was happening.

"They're making a turn and coming back," Weissinger listened as one watcher reported. "I think this is going to be a firing run. Yeah, I see them falling." To Weissinger, the falling bombs sounded like sand sliding down a tin roof. He felt like a sitting duck. Thompson commented, "Being bombed at sea is one of the most helpless experiences imaginable. The target is precisely and indisputably the very ship which is your temporary shelter." He closed his eyes and wrapped up in a fetal position. "Never had I known such fear," he said. Weissinger thought the sound of falling sand was going to come right into the hold, when suddenly the deck flew up and dust and rust cascaded through the air. He lost his breath. Trying to grip the steel deck he succeeded only in grabbing a fist full of air, because he was suddenly several inches above the deck. A second later he was slammed back down.

The bombs were near-misses amidships, but they cascaded water over the decks and blew shrapnel holes in the sides. Aft, there were some Australians who did not get into the hold. Capt. Harry Bishop of the 2/2 Pioneers saw the bombers coming in close formation at ten thousand feet. He found a spot on the poop deck and lay down. The inexperienced forward gun crew spun their weapon around, managing only to shoot the stays away on the main mast and clip the corner of the bridge, killing some of their own men. The rear gun crew had worse luck. On their third or fourth shot the breech exploded and the blast killed most of the crew, in addition to several Aussies who had sought shelter nearby. Bombs from the second run hit about the same time, exploding near the fantail. Nearby, Captain Bishop was hit in the head by flying iron and a Japanese sailor was thrown dead at his feet. The ship vibrated, he said, "like a dog coming out of the water." About one dozen Australians were killed, including two sailors off the *Perth*. George Detre said the blasts tore the lifeboats from the side of the ship, set the ammunition off on the aft gun platform, and blew one Japanese officer overboard.

Seldon Reese praised the ship's captain. He had a crewman lay on the deck and report when the bombs began to drop, then zigzagged *Moji Maru* left and right, avoiding any direct hits. He ordered everyone to the starboard side of the ship, which caused a list, then gave it hard right rudder. The tight circle, low to starboard, must have looked like the ship was sinking. Reese thought the trick saved them. More likely, the Liberators were out of bombs, and they headed back to base, their motors fading in the distance.

The *Nichimei Maru* sank at 1550, only half an hour after the initial attack. The Americans thought that about five hundred Japanese soldiers died, but the Japanese themselves reported only ninety-seven killed, plus five gunners and crewmen. Also lost were a load of rails, hundreds of picks and shovels, and a locomotive to be used on the railway. About forty Dutch soldiers died. *Moji Maru* circled the area for three hours, picking up all the survivors it could. Thompson saw a Dutch survivor crawl up a rope ladder and collapse on the deck. He was covered with blood and died with his hands gripping the entrails that oozed out of his stomach. Another Dutchman who climbed up the ropes was not so grim. In fact, he had a small orange and white cat sitting on top of his head. Right then the cat was named Shipwreck, and it stayed with them until one night at 100 Kilo Camp on the railroad, when it ran into a bigger cat in the jungle. Rescue completed and heading to Moulmein, a Japanese guard suddenly turned on Thompson and clubbed him with his rifle, smashing him in the head and stomach. He thought the guard would kill him when a Japanese sergeant intervened. Thompson could figure no reason for the attack, other than that he was an American.

The bombing shook up George Detre. He was as frightened as he had ever been, he said, and it wasn't just a temporary thing. "I was scared for about three days." After the rescue, Detre and a friend managed to talk to the ship's captain again. The captain was fed up with the war. He thought the prisoners should take over the ship. "It's not far to India, you know," he said. Detre and others passed along the word to the Army officers and a serious discussion was made. They outnumbered the Japanese soldiers aboard, and those that were plucked out of the ocean had lost their weapons. "We had enough people to man five ships," Detre said. Yet there was still an escort nearby that would fire on them and alert other warships should they take action. They would probably be sunk before they reached India. To Detre's disgust, the idea was rejected. If they had known what they were getting into, they would have taken the ship, he said. "Somebody missed out on being a big hero. We had to stay prisoners."

On the morning of 16 January, *Moji Maru* entered the muddy Salween estuary and made its way to Moulmein. On the way in there was another airplane scare. A Japanese bomber flew low overhead and two prisoners panicked and jumped overboard. They were fired at before they turned around and swam back to the ship. Like other prisoners who had entered Burma through Moulmein, many were familiar with the works of Rudyard Kipling. Reese claimed to know "On the Road to Mandalay" by heart. The prisoners' situation, however, was far from romantic. After several days in the city prison, they were marched down to Thanbuzayat, reaching there on 26 January. Next stop was 18 Kilo Camp, and a bit of railroad construction.[5]

Three months after the *Lisbon Maru*'s fatal voyage, the Japanese shipped more POWs out of Hong Kong. This time, 663 Canadians boarded the nineteen-knot *Tatsuta Maru,* which had previously been involved in repatriation and hauling relief supplies. Of the 1,972 Canadians from the Royal Rifles and Winnipeg Grenadiers captured defending the British enclave, 1,184 men would sail in to Japan in 1943. About 290 Canadians died while battling for Hong Kong; about 264 more would die as prisoners of war. It was just as lethal to be a captive of the Japanese as to fight them. The fast transport sailed on 19 January and was in Nagasaki three days later.[6]

There were numerous short voyages made among the islands of the Southwest Pacific, although to the prisoners and internees being uprooted, the voyages were anything but minor. When the Japanese landed on Borneo on 19 January 1942, there were forty-five European men, twenty-four wives, and eleven children in Sandakan, a town of fifteen thousand. The men were soon imprisoned, and in May the women and children were forced aboard a small launch that took them on a twenty-minute ride to the island of Berhala, where they were moved into an abandoned settlement about one mile from a leper colony. They had no experience in community living, and the isolation and close quarters quickly wore them down. "How we women hated each other there on Berhala!" said Agnes Newton Keith, an American married to a British civil servant in Sandakan. "We horrified ourselves with the strength of our antipathies."

Six months later they had grudgingly learned to work together, but on 12 January 1943, their lives were disrupted again. Colonel Suga, newly promoted and in charge of the POWs on Borneo, ordered that they be moved to Kuching. The internees, their numbers now increased to forty-seven women and fifteen children, boarded a small steamer for the 350-mile trip. They were frightened, not knowing what to expect. Some thought they were going to a new, clean camp; some thought they would be repatriated; others figured a brothel would be their new home. The steamer had only one cabin, which was occupied by Japanese soldiers and three Japanese women, who had, according to Keith, "the ugliest legs that I have ever seen detached from pianos."

The Japanese officers leered at them. One, Capt. Takakuwa Takuo, who had been commandant of all Sandakan's civilian internees, Keith described as a greasy-looking, disease-ridden "rump rubber." But the women became so unattractive after several days of sweat, seasickness, and vomit, said Keith, that even he left them alone. They burned on the open deck in the sun and shivered in the cold night. There was only one latrine, which soon overflowed, running under the door and along the deck. The children vomited constantly, then complained of being hungry. They were given limed rice and tinned fish balls. They ate it and were sick again. "The journey was hell," Keith said.

The steamer stopped at several small ports, including the larger one at Jesselton. Native peddlers came alongside and tried to sell them food, but the officers would not allow it. One evening a young Japanese soldier with a thin face and large glasses approached Agnes Keith and spoke to her in hesitant English. He told her he had read the Japanese translation of Land Below the Wind, which Keith had written before the war, how much he had liked it, and how sorry he was to see her there. She asked him if he could persuade the officers to let them have some extra fruit or eggs. That night he returned, apologizing that he could not get approval. Then he put his finger to his lips and whispered, "Do not tell." He handed her an envelope with ten dollars and a note in it. The money was his entire monthly pay. He regretted he had no more because, the note read, "I am only soldier. Please don't fear. Take this money. I don't need money because I may die in battle and have no wife, no child, no father, only mother."

The gift made Keith's journey bearable, if for nothing else than the warmth it brought to her heart. It took nine days to reach Kuching. The steamer pulled up the Sarawak River between nipa palms and mud banks. Keith thought of the Englishman James Brooke, the first "White Rajah" who had built his empire here. Certainly he did not arrive as Keith did—wet, nauseated, with diarrhea, a cold, and fever, off the deck of a prison ship. The Kuching area held eight POW and civilian camps, with about three thousand people. Keith's group went to a woman's camp at Batu Lintang, which held about two hundred women and children internees from all across Borneo.[7]

Other voyages took place in the Dutch East Indies. On 9 February, the 3,328-ton *Roko Maru* took a British contingent from Batavia to Singapore. The usual complaints were lodged about overcrowding, unsanitary conditions, and beatings. On 26 February the *Kamakura Maru* was back in action. The liner left Makassar, carrying 709 tons of maize, 194 tons of sesame seeds, and 730 tons of copra. It sailed to Singapore, arriving on 1 March, where it refueled and continued to Japan. Among the items to be ferried to the homeland were 686 passengers and their luggage, 10 Dutch prisoners, "and 55 coffins with the remains of departed heroes."

Additional freighters plied China's rivers, in a never-ending distribution of captives among the conquered territories. On 20 February the *Dainichi Maru* carried 86 "enemy citizens"—41 American, 13 English, 18 Belgian, 10 Canadian, and 4 Dutch—from Hankow and up the Yangtze River to Nanking. In late February, another group of 235 "enemy aliens" was to leave Shanghai on the 6,680-ton *Koryu Maru*, bound for Nanking. Interminable delays held up the voyage until 11 March, however, when 107 men, 115 women, and 13 children finally sailed. The shipment was followed by four similar voyages in March, one more on the *Koryu Maru*, and one each on the *Raihei Maru*, *Nitikoku Maru*, and *Kaiun Maru*. More and more Europeans were being transferred from the once cosmopolitan Shanghai to more secure areas inland, perhaps to the dubious protection of the International Safety Zone, which had been created in Nanking during the infamous "rape" of the city in 1937. In May, in conjunction with a plan to operate a camp for enemy nationals in South China, a shipment of internees was sent from Shanghai to Canton on the 2,600-ton *Seikyo Maru*. The transfer was completed, and on 25 May, *Seikyo Maru* was tied up at Amoy and fumigated due to the suspicion that its latest passengers had been carriers of cholera.[8]

MASSACRE AT SEA

The Japanese destroyer *Akikaze* had been operating in and around New Britain and New Ireland as part of Destroyer Division 34 since the summer of 1942. It had escorted the *Naruto Maru,* carrying Australian soldiers and nurses out of Rabaul in July, and it had towed the torpedo-damaged *Noto Maru* into Rabaul in November. The ship would be repaired to carry its own human cargo in 1944. The *Akikaze* was an old *Minekaze*-class destroyer, built by Mitsubishi in 1920. Still, at 1,552 tons, powered by double-shaft, Parsons-geared turbines, it could reach a speed of thirty-six knots. Its main armament was four 4.7-inch guns and six 21-inch torpedo tubes.

In March 1943, *Akikaze*'s captain, Lt. Cdr. Sabe Tsurukichi, was ordered to sail to Wewak, New Guinea, to deliver food and medicine to the garrison. This part of New Guinea, and the coastal island of Kairiru, had been a German colony until 1918, when Australia took over. There were still many Germans living in the area, however, and although allied with the Japanese, German civilians were suspected of harboring American pilots who had been shot down in the vicinity. The Japanese had never secured wholehearted German cooperation, and they feared the Germans might even be collaborating with the local people, who were rabidly anti-Japanese. In addition, the Allies seemed to know every move of the Japanese fleet. A convoy had recently been destroyed in the Battle of the Bismarck Sea. Unwilling to believe that their codes had been compromised, the Japanese believed that local civilians must have been using radio equipment to report ship movements to the Allies.

Sabe was ordered to remove the suspects, and after leaving Wewak on 17 March, *Akikaze* arrived at Kairiru. About forty civilians were brought on board, almost all of them German clergymen, along with a few nuns carrying infants and a couple of Chinese servants. The *Akikaze* next sailed to Manus Island, where it picked up twenty more neutrals, mostly Germans, and one Hungarian missionary and a few Chinese prisoners, including six women. The two groups were placed in two crew cabins, both of which became hot and crowded, while crew members were forced to sleep on the deck. The ship docked at Kavieng, New Ireland, but no one was allowed off. A courier brought the captain a message. Shortly after noon on 18 March, *Akikaze* sailed for Rabaul.

Lieutenant Commander Sabe assembled his officers and told them he had received a message from 8th Fleet Headquarters to dispose of all the neutrals on board. Preparations were made for the executions. A plank was set on the aft deck and a wooden scaffold was erected where each victim would hang by the wrists from a rope and pulley. They would be shot by four riflemen while the ship was traveling at high speed, and the wind and bullets would propel the bodies overboard, minimizing blood stains on the deck. A white sheet was hung across the breadth of the ship to shield the executions from the other civilians. The victims were led from the cabins one by one, taken to the bridge for some questioning, then blindfolded and taken aft. Speed was increased to twenty-four knots. The engine noise, wind, and waves made it impossible for the civilians forward to hear the rifle shots on the stern.

The men were killed first, then the women. Two children were taken from the arms of the nuns and thrown overboard. It took three hours to execute them all and clean the blood from the deck. Afterward, the officers conducted a funeral ceremony for the deceased. Sabe instructed everyone that they must not mention the executions to anybody. *Akikaze* reached Rabaul at about 2200, 18 March.

As long as it seemed that Japan would win the war, there was no urgency to cover up the deed. One year later, however, the war's outcome was seriously in doubt. By February 1944, Allied naval and air forces had virtually isolated Rabaul and Kavieng had suffered heavy bombings and naval bombardment. At this time there were still twenty-three Australian plantation owners and nine German clergymen imprisoned in Kavieng. To prevent the internees from being recaptured in the invasion the Japanese assumed was imminent, they were trucked to the wharves on 17 March. One by one they were taken off the trucks, blindfolded, and made to sit on the edge of the dock. Two nooses were slipped over their heads, while two men pulled violently from each side. When the victim had been strangled, he was kicked into a barge floating below the dock and his body was tied to a concrete block with wire and cable. Two barges hauled the bodies out to the west side of Nago Island, where the water was the deepest. It took about three hours for thirty-two executions.

Thinking that Allied troops would be landing soon, the Japanese concocted a story to explain what had happened to the internees, both those killed in Kavieng on 17 March and those shot on the *Akizaze* one year earlier. The fact that convoys were no longer able to travel safely in and out of the Bismarcks would assist them in the fabrication. The last convoy to leave Rabaul—consisting of the *Kowa Maru, Kokai Maru,* fleet tug *Nagaura,* and subchasers 37 and 38—departed on 20 February 1944. The convoy hoped to reach Palau, but on the twenty-first, just north of New Hanover, it was attacked by B-25 bombers. Both marus were sunk, and the *Nagaura* was sunk the next day by Allied destroyers. The ships carried four hundred Japanese soldiers and civilian workers. Only fifty of them survived from the two freighters. Cdr. Yoshino Shozo and Capt. Sanagi Tsuyoshi said that all the internees in question had been kept in Kavieng until loaded on *Kowa Maru* on 17 February. They had been placed safely aboard, they said, and were on their way out of the danger zone in Convoy O-003 when it was attacked by Allied bombers and all the internees were killed.

It was not until 1947, when the Australian War Crimes Section interrogated many former members of the Japanese naval garrison that the story began to unravel. First one, then two, then three men broke under questioning and admitted what had happened. Although a number of those involved received prison sentences of from four to twenty years, only one, Tamura Ryukichi, commander of the 14th Naval Base Force, was sentenced to death by hanging.[9]

POWS TO BORNEO

The movement of B Force to Sandakan and Java One Party (RAF and British troops) to Kuching and Jesselton in 1942 were not the last of the prisoner shipments to Borneo. On 28 March 1943, E Force, consisting of five hundred Australian and five hundred British troops, all under Lieutenant Colonel Whimster, left Changi for Kuching. They sailed on the one-thousand-ton *DeKlerk,* a captured Dutch freighter. The Australians, under Major Fairley, had the choice of staying in the aft hold with a leaking cargo of petrol, two small, very hot holds adjoining the engine room, or a double-tiered section of cattle stalls. They wanted none of the choices until Japanese bayonets forced them in. Conditions were "appalling," but some of the POWs managed to alleviate the situation by breaking into the storage areas and consuming a large quantity of beans, sugar, and cigarettes. All were offloaded in Kuching on 1 April and put to work on the wharves. They managed to sabotage some of the cargo by "accidentally" dropping goods into the water or allowing cargo nets to smash into the wharf.

In the women's camp, Agnes Keith heard the shouting and commotion when the newly arrived prisoners marched by. The Japanese warned them to stay away from the main gate—no communication was allowed. E Force was temporarily housed in shelters about a quarter mile away, and in no time the women applied the last bits of makeup they had been saving. Before it was dark one Australian, Private Picken of 2/18 Battalion, the poor rations apparently not affecting his sex drive, tried to make a rendezvous but succeeded only in stumbling over a charged fence and electrocuting himself. Undaunted, other Australians paid nightly visits, crossing the women's camp fence and chirping through the barracks' open windows.

"We ain't seen a lady for a long time," they said. "Look, we've got lipstick and cigarettes that we brought from Singapore for you."

"Sssh!" the women whispered back. "We've got our children here with us, and whenever the Nips get angry with us they cut the food ration. Now go away before you get caught."

Nevertheless, some gifts were left in the grass and some trysts were made. In only a few days, however, the soft whistling of "Waltzing Matilda" in the woods was not heard again. The Australians were again packed up, this time to go to Sandakan.

While E Force worked on the wharves, about 600 British men from Java One Party who had been dropped off in Kuching the previous October boarded DeKlerk and sailed to Jesselton. About 200 British from Jesselton were about to board when the ship's diesels broke down and they were sent back to camp. With repairs completed, they sailed on 6 April. Lieutenant Johnstone thought that he and Lt. Vernon Smith were the only two Australians in the group that he said numbered 760 men.

The weather was good, and although few men suffered from seasickness, those with dysentery had another intolerable journey. Rounding the northern tip of Borneo, DeKlerk experienced more engine trouble, and they pulled into the bay at Kudat for more repairs. Finally, on 8 April, they arrived at Sandakan, where they offloaded and, as it grew dark, marched one mile to an Anglican Church camp for the night. The next day they hiked the remaining eight miles to the aerodrome. They were housed in Camp Two. No contact was allowed with the Aussies of B Force.

While this occurred, the Australians of E Force, who had been pried away from the women in Kuching, were loaded on the five-hundred-ton *Taka Maru* on 9 April. The British who had sailed with them from Singapore were left behind. The Japanese decided that no officer above the rank of captain would accompany any more parties to Sandakan, and the remaining five hundred Aussies, now under Capt. R. J. Richardson of 2/20 Battalion, continued the journey. *Taka Maru* had just unloaded a consignment of cement, and the prisoners had to contend with cement dust for the rest of the journey. The ship slowly made its way up the coast. Several officers, including Captain Steele and Lieutenants Blow, Gillon, and Wagner, discussed escape plans. They approached Captain Richardson.

"Let's take the ship over!" said Steele. "There are only 20 guards—we can handle them and we'll head for the Celebes!"

Richardson refused to agree. "It's my job to get these men home," he said.

The *Taka Maru* stopped at Labuan for coal and reached Sandakan on 15 April. Since a third camp was not yet ready, they unloaded on Berhala, two miles off the mainland.

Japanese lieutenant Hoshijima Susumu had his guards perform an immediate search. He climbed on a makeshift platform and gave the prisoners a speech. He knew all about Australians, he said. They were thieves, sons of convicts, and tricksters. Hoshijima was not far off the mark, but luckily for the Aussies, his soldiers did not discover the contraband they managed to smuggle into camp, including Rolls Royce headlights, a power transformer, a wireless set, and a .38-caliber pistol. As Hoshijima continued his oration, warning them that any escape attempt would result in the death penalty, Lt. Rex Blow turned to his mate, Lt. Miles Gillon, and said, "We won't be staying around with this bastard for too long!"

They began to make plans for their escape. Meanwhile the Sandakan area now contained about 1,500 Aussies in Camp One, 750 Brits in Camp Two, and 500 Aussies on Berhala.[10]

POWS TO THE MOLUCCAS

The Moluccas, a scattered group of hundreds of islands, rest between Celebes and the western end of New Guinea. The southern cluster consists of the larger islands of Buru and Ceram, which appear to hover over the two smaller islands of Ambon and Haruku. The cluster lies in an east-west line, dividing the Ceram Sea to the north from the Banda Sea to the south. When the Australians of Gull Force and the Dutch KNIL were captured on Ambon in February 1942, the Japanese had in them a ready supply of laborers. Some Aussies were shipped to Hainan. Some Dutch POWs went to Java, while others took the short trip to Ceram to work on an airfield. When the Japanese realized they needed more airfields on the perimeter of their conquered islands, they did not have enough laborers. The prisoner pool on Java would be the ticket.

Two POW camps in Surabaya, Darmo and Jaarmarkt, contained the largest number of prisoners in eastern Java, at times housing more than four thousand men. Most of the prisoners were Dutch, but a good number were British, mainly RAF men, with a sprinkling of survivors from the destroyer *Jupiter*. In mid-April 1943, the prisoners of Jaarmarkt were given a "treat": they were shown a movie, a propaganda film with actual footage of Japanese triumphs at Pearl Harbor, Malaya, and Ceylon. Donald Peacock, an RAF motor mechanic, was rather dumbfounded, for it seemed that the Japanese were pleading their case that they were fighting for a good cause and winning. "And who cared a rap what the POWs thought anyway?" he asked. Apparently the Japanese figured it would be good for recruiting, for a few days later they asked for two thousand men to go to a new camp. They were paraded and inspected and given a speech by a wizened little officer they named "Nitty Whiskers."

"Look at my face," he spoke in reasonably good English. "Remember me. . . . Do not fear for your lives . . . you are going to a holiday camp where the food will be very good and the work not too strenuous." Those words made the more savvy of the POWs rush to "borrow" stool samples from POWs with dysentery to prove they were too sick to make the trip. A work party to the boondocks did not sound like a holiday. Peacock, who was judged unfit for Jaarmarkt's normal work parties, was nevertheless selected for this one. The only item issued for the trip was "one pair of tree-climbing, separate-toe, rubber boots per man," said Peacock, "the only clothing I received from the Nips in three and a half years." Arthur Strock, also in the RAF, remembered getting boots, a shirt, shorts, a G-string, and an inoculation. Before departure they met the soldier who was to be a terror to them during the upcoming months: Gunso (Sergeant) Mori Masao, who swaggered about with his bamboo club and beat several men senseless, seemingly for the fun of it. His nickname became "Blood," and he was usually followed by the small, squat interpreter Kasiyama Yoshikichi, known as "Slime."

At dawn on 18 April, 3,071 men marched to the harbor. The smallest vessel there was the 3,165-ton cargo ship *Amagi Maru*, owned by the NYK Line but now under Army control. Anthony Cowling of the RAF called it "a prison ship with a vengeance." The men were split in two groups and sprayed with what Cowling thought was a disinfectant. "The thought that we were in such diseased condition that we might infect this scruffy, nondescript freighter was almost laughable," he said. On deck they had to slosh through a large trough as if they were cattle being dipped. Cowling went down a vertical ladder into the aft hold and was pushed onto a shelf with about three feet between layers. Little did he realize that he would remain in a horizontal position for the next two weeks.

About 1,071 men boarded *Amagi Maru*. Another 1,000 climbed on the *Cho Saki Maru*, what Don Peacock called "a forbidding-looking ship" of perhaps eight thousand tons. The ship's holds also had been fitted out with layers of shelves, but Peacock's group of 410 went into a hold with not enough "bunk" space. He thought they might have to stand for the entire trip until they found an area where they could squat down. Stamped on a girder above him were the words "Made in Skinningrove, England." The old scrap bucket had been built only thirty miles from Cowling's birthplace. A third cargo ship, the 3,127-ton *Kunitama Maru*, took on board 1,000 Dutch prisoners.

It was hot, even by Javanese standards, but the ships sat in the harbor for four days. The smell below was overpowering; thankfully the Japanese let them on deck to use the *benjos*, but with only two contraptions hung over the side of each ship, the lines grew very long. Night brought cooler temperatures, but also tropical rainstorms. On *Cho Saki Maru* the hatches were covered, said Peacock, "to stop us drowning." On *Amagi Maru*, men parked themselves under the open hatches and opened their mouths to catch the cool rainwater.

The next day, while the POWs waited in misery, the harbor was rocked by a tremendous explosion. At first the men thought they were being bombed, but there was only a single blast, louder than anything they had heard before. Eventually they learned from an interpreter that another ship in the harbor, being loaded with bombs, ammunition, and aviation fuel, had blown up. As both ships the POWs were on carried similar cargoes, this caused a bit of consternation. After another day of receiving only a small cup of steamed rice to eat, however, the POWs decided that they would probably starve before they were blown to pieces.

On 22 April, the ships finally got underway, escorted by a small launch and two destroyerlike vessels. Off Bali the next day, Peacock fantasized about topless dancing girls and reflected on the glorious flaming sunset and the majestic volcanoes of Lombok—all from the majesty of his perch on the *benjo.* Yet, he thought, he "would have preferred to see a plate of fish and chips."

On Easter Sunday they were allowed to wash down under a seawater hose. Two ships left the convoy in a southerly direction, perhaps heading for Timor, while *Amagi, Cho Saki,* and *Kunitama* followed the chain of islands for a time before turning north. A few days later, on 28 April, they reached Ambon, where the prisoners were ordered to help unload cargo. Opening a hatch on *Amagi Maru,* they found that several nets of oranges had split, sending mountains of oranges between the bombs. The heat had cooked them into a slimy mess that sported a hairy growth of fungus. Cowling was one of those selected to unload the hold. He noted wryly that "trying to pick up a 50 or 100 pound bomb that has been lubricated with rotten oranges requires a skill that we did not have time to develop." Some of the cargo being unloaded left Cowling incredulous. "Carrying bamboo to Ambon was like giving refrigerators to the Eskimos," he said. Being expected to work for brutal captors with little food, in the rain, and hauling slippery bombs was a shock to many men. They realized they had no control whatsoever over their destiny. "This was probably the first time," said Cowling, "that most of us became really fatalistic."

They shoved off on 30 April and the next day were in the bay at Amahai, on Ceram's south shore. Unloading commenced again. The scheme was to ferry the bombs in small lighters and to lower the fuel barrels into the water and have the prisoners dog-paddle them ashore. One man was so exhausted he could do nothing but float while the barrel was carried out to sea. Cowling said, "When we finally came out of the water we were like prunes, dehydrated and literally dying of thirst." They were fed wet rice. Peacock was stuck man-handling bombs up the beach and to the inland dumps. The barrels could roll, he said, "but moving the bombs was purgatory." After the munitions, the rest was easy. *Cho Saki Maru* disgorged crates and cartons of edible roots, beans, wheat, rice, picks and shovels, and even a steamroller—all surrounded by thousands of loose oranges. *Kunitama Maru* dropped off her cargo of Dutch prisoners, who would construct an airfield on Ceram.

It took three days to unload. Only half a day's sail on 4 May brought them to the small island of Haruku, south of Ceram and east of Ambon. They arrived at midnight in the rain and were ferried ashore by native canoes. Guided by candles, they stumbled ashore, around coconut palms and through dripping undergrowth, tripping over roots and slipping in the mud. Finally they found their bamboo-and-atap barracks. Their main job would be to construct an airfield by leveling two camel-humped coral hills with chisels and hoes and filling in the valley between. By December, five hundred men were dead. About 70 percent of the prisoners would die.[11]

LEAVING SINGAPORE

Once containing 130,000 prisoners after the surrender, Singapore had been rapidly denuded of its manpower. After each outbound shipment, those left in Changi and the work camps on the island had more and more room to stretch out and make better use of their limited provisions and resources. Moving by sea, A Force had gone to Burma, B Force to Borneo, and C Force to Japan. In January 1943, Dunlop Force took trains north to Thailand, and in March, D Force, consisting of 2,780 British and 2,220 Australian men, mainly of artillery units of the 8th Division, headed north. They rode in steel boxcars on a five-day journey to Ban Pong, then were transferred to open flatcars and traveled up the newly built line to the ancient walled city of Kanchanaburi, which at the time marked the end of the rails.

In April, five more trainloads with 600 men per train, carried 3,000 men up the same line. They were all Dutch except for about 150 Aussies and a few Americans. In Thailand they were joined by 700 prisoners who had previously been working in Saigon.

E Force had sailed to Borneo in April. That same month, the 7,000-man F Force moved north. It consisted of 3,334 British POWs, many from the 18th Division under Lieutenant Colonel Harris, and 3,666 Australians, mainly from 27th Brigade under Lieutenant Colonel Kappe. The first of them left Singapore on 18 April in the familiar boxcars, 600 men per train. The first six trains carried Aussies, the next seven carried British POWs and Japanese troops. Tamil coolies were squeezed aboard at Ipoh. This time when the trains unloaded at Ban Pong there were no flatcars waiting to move them beyond Kanchanaburi, and F Force had to hike another 180 miles.

While F Force was rolling up the Malayan Peninsula, G Force, under Maj. R. V. Glasgow, was readying for shipment to Japan. One thousand Dutch, three hundred British, and two hundred Australian men boarded the Army-controlled, 6,783-ton cargo ship *Kyokko Maru,* which sailed on 26 April. Ventilation forward came through the open hatch, but in the aft holds, a wind-sock had to be rigged to circulate the air. Each man had about two by five feet of deck space. No medical officers were allowed on this voyage, but several orderlies were unofficially slipped in, and they were quickly overworked by the number of dysentery cases that broke out. The voyage was long but compara-tively uneventful, and they successfully landed in Moji on 21 May. Two Dutch prisoners died that same day. Most of the POWs crossed Shimonoseki Straits and traveled by train to various camps on Honshu. The Australians went to Taisho Camp, where they worked at the Osaka Iron Works.[12]

In mid-May, J Force—six hundred Brits, three hundred Aussies, and fifty Americans under Lieutenant Colonel Byrne—was sent to Japan. As all the "healthy" men had already gone, this was a very sickly lot. Pvt. R. Keith Mitchell, a Royal Signal Corps operator who had been placed with III Indian Corps, was slated to go, along with his mates Stan Faunch and Bill Titcombe. They had just missed the last upcountry draft and figured they might as well stick together and travel to "a better land" where "all men get health quickly."

J Force stumbled out of Changi on 15 May. Each man was given a cup of peanuts, half a loaf of rice bread, and a bottle of cold tea. As night fell, they stepped down into the dark holds of a cargo ship. Mitchell was sandwiched between two men whom he could not even see, although their faces were only inches apart. They managed to interlock legs and arms so that they could lay down. In the morning they counted between three and four hundred British prisoners in the hold. Along the hull were double tiers of wooden sleeping shelves that could accommodate about half their number. A wooden com-panionway went up the after bulkhead to the deck. The hatch was open to admit the morning light.

At 1000 on 16 May they weighed anchor. Someone chirped in with a trav-elogue spiel—"And so we say farewell to Singapore the romantic gateway to the East!"—and was shouted down with numerous vulgarities. The light allowed them to see a number of life belts labeled *Wales Maru.* The vessel was an Army-controlled cargo ship of 6,586 tons owned by the Kawasaki Kisen Company. As they made their way across the South China Sea, no food was forthcoming, so the men who had not done so already finished off their peanuts. Mitchell, who thought he would never take a bite of the blackened rice bread, now succumbed. "I found that it needed a lot of chewing and improved in flavour when one got used to it." Actually, one could get over the hunger. Once the stomach was completely empty, the pangs would go away and there was no great longing for food. But thirst, said Mitchell, was "another matter entirely."

Eventually, they were served a welcome meal of rice and bean-shoot soup. As usual on these voyages, dysentery was a problem and the number of *benjos* was inadequate. Mitchell observed that the entire China Sea became "our latrine, borehole, cesspit or sewer." The hull beneath the *benjos* was liberally splattered with excrement. They nicknamed the ship "Mucky-maru."

Flies seemed to gather in great clouds. One officer who had a stock of cigarettes began a clean-up contest, passing out one cigarette for every ten dead flies. Mitchell thought the idea was wonderful, for it gave the men an objective during the long voyage. The only danger, he observed, was that there were now hordes of crazy prisoners chasing around the decks in pursuit of luckless flies. Whether or not the fly catching had an impact, dysentery was not a killer on this trip like it was on many others.

Four days into the voyage they stopped for a short time at Cape St. Jacques, thirty miles from Saigon. Only four hundred yards from shore, some talked about jumping overboard and escaping—until they saw a shark fin glide by. On 23 May, *Wales Maru* pulled out, now in a twelve-ship convoy escorted by only one patrol boat. Not only were the ships slow, but they did not zigzag; the Allied submarine threat was still not being taken seriously. The men were given access to the main deck for two twenty-minute periods a day and were allowed to draw up buckets of seawater over the side for bathing. Below, they were still packed in tightly. Mitchell could see his friends, Faunch and Titcombe, in an upper sleeping rack only twenty feet away, yet he could not get over to them for several days. When he did, he found Bill with both of his forearms covered with suppurating ulcers. The only treatment was the universal seawater bath. Whenever it rained the hatches were closed and the air quickly became foul. After three hours or more, the men were gasping for breath. When the covers were thrown open, the hot, fetid air escaped with a great uprush and left the prisoners shivering and gasping with relief.

On 29 May, the convoy pulled in to Takao, and the Japanese forced all men below, presumably so no one would see how the harbor defenses were laid out. When allowed topside, they began their seawater bucket baths again, only to find that they were dumping polluted sewer water on their heads. Mitchell found it interesting that the Japanese allowed them to purchase bananas from a large consignment that was hauled aboard. Perhaps they were finally concerned about the health of the prisoners who were about to be delivered to the homeland.

The convoy, designated No. 268, sailed on 2 June. It still consisted of twelve ships covered only by coast defense vessel (CDV) 36. On the last leg of the voyage they found that the ocean had turned decidedly cold—too cold for bathing. On the morning of the fifth, lookouts began to yell, signals were given, and the guards forced all the prisoners in the holds.

Submarine! Guns began to blaze in the convoy, and *Wales Maru* opened fire to port. One Aussie who managed to hide topside saw two torpedo tracks—one missing the stern by only twenty yards. They were fired by Cdr. Roy L. Daspit in *Tinosa*, making an underwater periscope attack. That salvo missed, but another caught *Tsushima Maru*. Fortunately for the Japanese ship, the torpedoes were duds. The Americans were still experiencing the frustrating torpedo problems that would plague them for nearly two years. CDV 36 counterattacked with depth charges, but *Tinosa* made her escape. *Wales Maru* zigzagged violently and the convoy scattered. The prisoners below prayed, fearfully looking upward. For some reason they all felt it was an air attack.

The hatches were battened for two hours. When the men were allowed on deck again, the rest of the convoy was gone and *Wales Maru* seemed to have damaged her engines during the high-speed maneuvering. She slowly chugged northward alone. Aussie Vic Mirkin thought the inside of the ship was held together with two girders welded across from side to side. The ship's exertions had split some of the seams. "We sprung a big hole in the ship, in the side," he said, "and we all had a bath and then we told them the ship was sinking with a hole. Oh, it was a great joke." It wasn't funny the next day, however, when panic erupted again and the guns blazed. The POWs thought that surely a sub wouldn't miss them this time. Suddenly, the shooting and shouting stopped. The Japanese, said Mitchell, "somewhat shame-faced, returned to normal, grinning broadly. So far as we were able to make out, they had mistaken the branch of a water-logged tree for a periscope."

That was the last of the excitement, for early the next day, 7 June, the "Mucky-maru" pulled in to a nearly deserted wharf in Moji. However, the public glass-rod treatment soon brought out the amused locals to watch another group of humiliated, woebegone scarecrows welcomed to the empire. Five hundred Brits were sent north to Hokkaido, and 250 Aussies headed for Kobe. The sickest remaining 150 men were to be sent to a "convalescent camp," which turned out to be the Hakensho mine in southern Kyushu. No one was too ill to work for the emperor.[13]

Another ship out of Singapore in May was the 5,871-ton *Thames Maru*, owned by the Kawasaki Kisen Company but taken over by the Army. Unlike most of the documented hellships, *Thames Maru* carried Indian and Indonesian prisoners and laborers. The majority of POW shipments prior to this time had involved the removal of white Europeans from the outer perimeter to the inner sanctum, where it would be harder for them to escape. A countermovement replaced those Europeans with Indians and *romusha*, native laborers, whose possible recapture the Japanese were not as concerned about. About 522 Indian POWs who had not joined the Indian National Army were put aboard the *Thames Maru*, along with about 1,500 Malay, Chinese, and Indonesian laborers. The Indians had been given a rough time—worked, starved, beaten, and even beheaded because of their obstinacy. Finally they were told that they had forfeited their status as prisoners and would be regarded as *heiho*, voluntary collaborators, and subject to Japanese military law.

The Indians were from all ranks of the 2/12 Frontier Force Regiment and the 1st Battalion of the Hyderabad Regiment. They pulled out of Singapore on 5 May 1943. After stops in Batavia and Surabaya, they reached the Palau Islands in the Philippine Sea on 30 May. Conditions were harsher than usual, for about 200 died during the month-long voyage, some, no doubt, because of the brutal treatment of Captain Gozawa of the 7th Special Service Company of the Japanese Army. They reached Babelthuap Island on 8 June, where they broke coral and cleared land for an airfield, dug trenches, and loaded ships. In 1945, the Indians were told that they were no longer prisoners—they had officially been taken into the ranks of the Japanese Army—an honor they did not want. By the time the island was liberated in August 1945, 117 more Indians had died.[14]

WORKING ON THE RAILROAD

By the spring of 1943, the major prisoner shipments had been completed. Work forces were parceled out to where they needed to be, and a tentative stasis was reached. In Burma, railroad construction was proceeding at a moderate pace. Ken Williams of A Force had reached 26 Kilo Camp in December, the start of what he called sixteen months of "one of the grimmest tragedies man could witness." Each man was given a daily quota of earth he must move; at the start it was 1.2 cubic meters, then, when the Japanese realized the prisoners could complete the task, the quota was increased to 1.4 meters, then 1.6 meters. If a man met his quota, his quota was increased; if he did not meet it, he was beaten. It was a no-win situation.

Harold D. "Curly" Martin, a private in 2/10 Ordnance Unit, thought he was lucky to go straight to Burma without a chance to "get soft" in Changi. The hardest part for him at first was breaking up stones for ballast. Pieces would fly off the hammers, causing cuts and bruises that later developed into tropical ulcers. When the earth quota went up to three cubic meters, the prisoners tried to fool the Japanese. Someone would distract the guards and others would move the measuring pegs a few feet. Usually one man dug while two carried the full dirt basket on a pole between their shoulders to the top of the embankment. If the guards weren't paying attention, the men might walk back downhill with the dirt, pretend to fill the basket again, then carry the same dirt back up. They figured they could all do their little part to sabotage the Japanese war effort.[15]

Hardly had the work begun in earnest when, in January 1943, Japanese planners decided that the project must be completed by May. Even the men of the Japanese railway regiments were shocked. The deadline was impossible. Commander of the Railway Construction Unit, Major General Shimoda, flew off for an aerial inspection of the trace, but the plane crashed into a teak-forested mountainside. The completion deadline was moved to August. On the Thailand end, the "speedo" period would necessitate rounding up more workers. F Force had been deposited at Ban Pong. Behind them came H Force: two thousand British, seven hundred Australian, six hundred Dutch, and twenty-six American POWs under Lieutenant Colonel Humphries rolling in by train between 5 May and 17 May.

With 60,000 POWs and *romusha* assembled all along the line, it was just possible that the Japanese would get their railroad done by August. In May, however, the monsoon season began with a vengeance. There were few shelters, communications slowed, rivers rose, embankments washed away, supplies diminished, the amount of food was cut, men grew weaker, and less work was accomplished. The monsoon "speedo" was perhaps the sorest trial of all. With pressure at its height, and men's resistance weakest, cholera struck the camps. Hitting first and hardest among F Force, the disease spread up and down the line, doing most of its damage on the Thailand side. F Force lost 637 men, while in H Force 217 died. The *romusha* were hit even harder. At one camp near Nikhe, 1,750 perished, many of them Tamils (Indians who had been living in Malaya). The situation was so bad that the Japanese relented and tried to rush in medical personnel and supplies from Singapore. K Force, 30 medical officers and 200 orderlies, was entrained from Changi on 25 June. In August, L Force, another 15 medical officers and 100 orderlies, was sent north. However, at the end of June, only 700 out of the 7,000 men of F Force were fit to work. The August construction deadline passed.[16]

The Japanese were frantic to complete the job. Hundreds of thousands of tons of earth had been moved, carried a basket at a time, to build railroad embankments over the swamps. Thousands of logs were felled, hewn, and measured to build innumerable bridges over chasms and rivers. In the estimation of Hiroshi Abe, a lieutenant in the Fifth Rail Regiment in charge of Songkrai Camp near the Burma-Thailand border, it was the Burmese and Japanese soldiers who did most of the work. Abe's unit built the bridges and only borrowed laborers from the prison camps, having to ask for the use of POWs on a daily basis. The prisoners, Abe said, only turned over small rocks or dug up soil. They weren't given any important tasks and they never worked very hard. In fact, Abe's men were actually humane. They might beat up the Burmese, he said, but they "never took it out on the elephants."

Although Abe's recollections of prisoner treatment were less ghastly than the POWs' remembrances, the bottom line was the same. The captives had little to eat, and they caught malaria and cholera by the thousands. Each morning they would collect perhaps thirty new corpses from the huts and could do nothing but cremate them. They cut firewood and tried to ignite it,

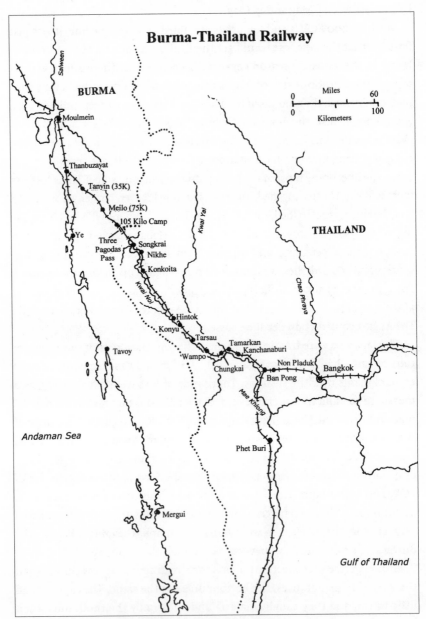

The Burma-Thailand Railway as completed in late 1943.

but the constant rain made the bodies difficult to burn. "Here and there," Abe said, "bodies just piled up like cordwood. Sometimes the wind from those burning bodies blew toward me." But, he concluded, "I really didn't do anything wrong."[17]

On 17 October 1943, the two stretches of railway joined at Konkoita, Thailand, about twenty-five miles south of the Burma border. In November the "Railway of Death" finally opened for full traffic. More than 150 million cubic feet of earth had been moved and nine miles of bridges built. The most famous span, immortalized in a book by Pierre Boulle and in a movie called *The Bridge on the River Kwai,* was actually built across the River Kwai Yai (Big Kwai), near the POW camp at Tamarkan. In reality, it was a minor operation that took about two months to finish in the spring of 1943. Soon after the line was open, Allied bombers struck. By April 1945, the bridge had been blown to pieces. After the war, the British sold the railroad to the Thais for $6 million. Most of the track in the border area was torn up, the sleepers (ties) used for firewood or housing. Today, the line runs about sixty miles into the jungle and stops; the apotheosis of "utter futility," according to one surviving POW.

About 12,000 Allied prisoners, and perhaps 90,000 Burmese, Thais, Malayans, Chinese, Tamils, and Javanese died building the railway. At the start of construction Colonel Fukuda preached to the prisoners, "The Japanese are prepared to work—you must work. The Japanese are prepared to eat less—you must eat less. The Japanese are prepared to die—you must be prepared to die." His words were prescient. About 412 men died for each of the 250 miles of track: one man dead for every three yards of rails.[18] Yet even with track connecting Burma with Singapore and Bangkok, Japan struggled to keep its troops supplied. Its ships were sunk in the Malacca Straits and the Andaman Sea, but its railroad was also bombed. The Allies were too strong. The 1,650-mile shortcut was a delusion, a will-o'-the-wisp. In the end, the railroad and the suffering were all pointless. Yet all of the Allied fatalities on the Railway of Death would not equal the number that were to die on the hellships.

STATUS QUO

There was less hellship movement in the last half of 1943 because most prisoners were already engaged in numerous projects. The Japanese were on the defensive. The Allies advanced inexorably up the Solomons and along the New Guinea coast toward New Britain, yet inside the vast Japanese perimeter few inroads had been made, except for the increasingly troublesome attacks by Allied submarines.

There was some POW movement from the Philippines. On 23 July, 490 enlisted men and 10 officers boarded the 5,498-ton *Clyde Maru* in Manila Bay. Conditions at Cabanatuan had been horrible in 1942, but by 1943, the number of monthly deaths had slackened as men became acclimated to the situation. Daily routines had become bearable, and the Philippines always were thought to be, in the minds of many POWs, first in line for inevitable liberation by a returning Douglas MacArthur. The call for 500 men to go to Japan was not enthusiastically filled. The voyage of this group, known as A Detail, was typically uncomfortable, but it was not molested by submarines and there were no deaths en route. The ship pulled in to Moji on 9 August. Most of the men stayed at Omuta, Kyushu, at Fukuoka 17 Camp, and worked for the Mitsui Coal Mining Company in coal mines and zinc smelters. Fearful that POWs in the mines would mean job losses for themselves, stone-throwing villagers pelted the prisoners as they marched through the camp gates.[19]

The next month 800 more Americans took a train from Cabanatuan to Manila. S.Sgt. Thomas E. Gage Jr., in the Army Air Corps 34th Pursuit Squadron, had fought as an infantryman on Bataan and participated in the Death March. On 19 September he joined the latest draft "and sailed to Japan aboard the small steamer, the *Taga Maru*," a 2,868-ton Army-controlled cargo ship owned by the Hinode Kisen Company. At least fifteen New Mexicans from the 200th Coast Artillery were aboard. The ship stopped briefly at Takao, Formosa. A "press" conference was held in the captain's cabin with Japanese reporters from Takao. A lieutenant colonel represented the officers, a private represented the privates, and Smith L. Green, a technical sergeant in the 31st Infantry, represented the noncoms. Smith recalled being fed tea, sweets, and cigarettes while being asked various questions regarding their war experience. When the POWs volunteered information that there was no way the Japanese could win the war, the conference was abruptly terminated.

They continued to Moji, arriving on 5 October. The fifteen-day trip on the small, heavily laden cargo ship, with inadequate food and medical attention, took a heavy toll on the already weakened men. "The water was the worst part of it," said Pvt. Henry Stanley of the 27th Bomb Group. "For a few days we could make it without too much food, but you cannot live without water." The only air came from one open hatch, and many in the far corners suffocated. "A lot of the guys drank their own urine," Stanley said. "They died like flies!"

All told, seventy died. Gage ended up west of Osaka, at Hirohata Camp 12-B. About four hundred men were placed in the area, working for the Seitetsu Steel Company or Osaka Ironworks. The rest took the long train ride north to Niigata on Honshu's west coast, to work at Niigata Ironworks or Rinko Coal Company. It would be a cold winter.[20]

Although escapes from Borneo had been attempted since the first Aussies had landed, the situation became increasingly tense after the three camps were established at Sandakan. On 31 July 1942, eleven men made a break into the jungle. Within a month, six had been recaptured, and they, along with two officers who supposedly had encouraged them to flee, were removed from Sandakan on 30 August on the small coastal vessel *Burong.* At Labuan Island they shifted to another small ship, the *Margaret,* and reached Kuching on 6 September. Lieutenant Hoshijima wanted no troublemakers at his camp. In September 1942, the prisoners were forced to sign a no-escape document. This time, Lieutenant Colonel Walsh and seven other "troublemaker" officers were removed from Sandakan to Kuching, sailing on another small coastal craft on 27 October, subsisting on raw cucumbers during their seven-day trip.

On 20 February 1943, Pvts. Bill Young and Miles P. Brown decided to break out. They were on the sick list and made their run one day after the rest of the prisoners had been assembled on the airfield. Only a few miles away they were jumped by a few Japanese soldiers and natives eager to collect the twenty-five dollar reward for anyone returning an escaped prisoner. They received the usual beatings, tortures, and interrogation. Young was confused by questions such as "What have you done with the guns?" and "How did you contact the submarine?" The Japanese apparently were on to something big, but Young knew nothing about it.

Young and Brown suffered through a month of questioning and confinement. On 20 March, they were taken out of their "little boxes, handcuffed together, bundled into a truck, and taken down to the dock." Joined by Jimmy Darlington, an Australian Aborigine who had had the gall to strike back at a Japanese guard, they were put aboard the *Treasure,* the former private yacht of the "White Rajah" of Sarawak. Just before sailing, a handcuffed group of five more Aussies were brought aboard, all of them from Young's battalion, the 2/29th. Alan Minty, Bruce McWilliams, Bill Fairy, Normie Morris, and Fred New were the last of the group that had escaped the previous July. They had wandered in the jungle before being taken in by friendly Chinese. They obtained a junk and tried to sail to Australia, but grounded on a mud bank in the Celebes. A Japanese patrol boat came by and returned them to Sandakan.

As the boat chugged along the coast they were unchained and allowed to sit at the stern, being warned that any "funny business" would get them thrown overboard. In Jesselton they slept overnight in what Young called "the smallest jail cell this side of Lilliput," eaten by "the thirstiest blood-sucking mosquitoes in all Borneo." A few days later they were in Kuching, awaiting trial.[21]

Less than two weeks after the arrival of E Force on Berhala, an escape was made from Camp One on the mainland. On 24 April 1943, three Aussies ducked out into the jungle and hid for two weeks. Two of them were recaptured in a native hut about twenty-four miles away. After a quick trial, both were shot on 12 May. The camp was put on half rations because of the escape. The man still at large, WO Walter Wallace of the 2/15 Field Regiment, could not get out of the area. He had been housed by some natives, but they were getting nervous and wanted him out. Wallace sounded out Capt. Lionel C. Matthews to see if he could sneak back into camp. Matthews and the other officers would not allow it. The escape had made it tougher on those remaining, and Wallace would have to go it alone. With more native help, Wallace was taken to Berhala, where another escape was being planned.

Lt. Rex Blow, who had commented on arrival that he wouldn't stay around very long, was making good on his word. On 4 June, Pvt. Jock McLaren, Driver Rex Butler, and Sapper James Kennedy took a native canoe and paddled for ten days to the island of Tawi Tawi. Following behind them in a Filipino kompit, a twenty-four-foot craft with a square sail, came Lieutenant Blow, Lt. Miles Gillon, Lt. Charles Wagner, Capt. Ray Steele, and Walter Wallace. In August, Butler was killed by pro-Japanese Moros on Tawi Tawi. The group went to Mindanao, where they joined the American-Filipino guerrillas, and Wagner was killed by a Japanese sniper. In an ironic turnabout, they captured some shipwrecked Japanese seamen and, unable to keep or feed them, took them out to sea and killed them with parangs (native swords).

In the meantime, the Japanese figured there would be less chance of revolt if the officers and men were separated. Lieutenant Hoshijima ordered that twenty-two more men be sent to Kuching, including Pvt. Eric "Mo" Davis of the 2/20 Battalion and Bill Young's mate, Joey Crome. They boarded the *Treasure* and sailed from Sandakan on 8 June.[22]

Bill Young and his seven Aussie mates had been awaiting trial for three months. Finally in court on 26 June, they convinced the judges that they were not involved in any other illegal activities but had simply escaped from prison. Five local Chinese had been thrown together with them and each was convicted of espionage, taken outside, and beheaded. The Aussies remained to hear their sentences. The tension among the eight chained men was unbearable. Miles Brown was first in line, and Young, next to him, could feel a tremor in the handcuffs as the sentence was read in simple, public school English.

"Miles Pierce Brown, you have been found guilty of escaping from a Japanese prison camp. Your sentence is to serve eight years hard labor in Outram Road Jail, Singapore." The chained men instantly relaxed with sighs of relief. "William Young, because of your youth, the Court in its mercy, has decided to reduce your sentence to four years hard labor in Outram Road Jail, Singapore."

"Oh, what a nice man!" Young thought. He breathed again, and even the air suddenly smelled sweeter. Similar sentences, ranging from six months to five years, were given to Fairy, New, McWilliams, Minty, Morris, and Darlington. Young believed they were the last people to escape from a Japanese prison camp and not be executed. He also learned a great lesson, eloquent in its simplicity: "When death is the alternative, all other choices grow more desirable, by the second."

Outram Road Jail was to be no picnic. With the trial over, the men were hurried to the harbor and nailed shut in a crate carpeted with straw and horse manure. The box was hauled below, and they huddled there in the dark, finding it nearly impossible to breathe. Young, who had still managed to keep his sense of humor, said they were so cramped that "claustrophobia never had a chance even, to fit into the box." The smell, he added, "was guaranteed to send any French perfumer into a frenzy."

After being spun around on the boom and dropped into the hold, they lost all sense of time and direction. They had been loaded on the old Dutch ship *Sibijac*. Working on the dock at that moment were Mo Davis and other Aussies who had recently arrived from Sandakan. They were ordered to avert their eyes from a large crate that was being swung onto a ship. They had no idea the crate was filled with their mates. The trip to Singapore took six or seven days. Sometime in midvoyage, when all were ready to cash in their chips, the top of the box was pried open. As they crawled out their eyes opened wide, for they found themselves packed in among hundreds of Japanese troops, who lined the bulkheads in tiers from wall to wall; they did not appear friendly and the Aussies stayed near their box. They felt lucky when several Japanese soldiers gave them the leftovers from their own rice dinners. Upon reaching Singapore, they were nailed back in the box and swung out to the wharf. The march to Outram Road Jail was the last time they would see the sun in many months, and once through those great green-painted timber doors, they entered a new kind of hell. But at least they still had their lives.[23]

The escapes led the Japanese to believe that civilians must have been providing assistance, and they began to watch their activities more closely. Australian doctor James Taylor had been left in charge of the hospital in Sandakan, where, indeed, he had been sending medical supplies to the camps and acting as liaison between the natives and the POWs. Captain Matthews had a radio, and plans were being made to smuggle in arms from the guerrillas in Tawi Tawi for an uprising. Unfortunately, a native courier was arrested, and under torture by the Kempeitai, he divulged the names of others in the plot. A search was made, and a diary and other incriminating evidence of espionage was found. Matthews was implicated; he was seen coming back from the latrine one night with a shovel. He was arrested on 22 July. Still unable to find the radio, the Japanese confronted Lt. Rod Wells with a list of wireless parts obtained from others who had confessed. On 24 July, Wells, hoping the Japanese would not know the difference, sacrificed the transmitter in order to save the receiver. In all, about seventy-two POWs and civilians were rounded up.[24]

On 16 August, thirty of the forty British officers were placed aboard what Lieutenant Lee called "a small steamer of about four hundred tons, formerly belonging to the Sandakan S.S." Company. It was 125 feet long, driven by diesel engines, and crewed by about twenty Malays. The officers were berthed on the open deck at the stern of the ship. A tarpaulin shielded them, but spray and rain still cascaded in. The Japanese set up a machine gun on the central deck above them.

They stopped at Jesselton, where they were able to buy some fruit from native peddlers in canoes when the Japanese weren't watching. Next it was

Labuan for coal, then to Miri, where they unloaded forty-four-gallon drums. Past Miri they caught the tail of a hurricane, and had to sail further out into the South China Sea to prevent being driven ashore. The ship rocked terrifically, and many of the Japanese guards were hugging the railings in seasickness. Lieutenant Johnstone and others stole some rope to secure themselves to the deck to prevent being washed overboard. No one could cook because the hot coals were either tipped out of the ovens or drenched with rain. The day after the storm ended, on 26 August, they sailed up the Sarawak River to Kuching.

On 10 October, an abortive uprising by Chinese and natives occurred in the Jesselton area of northwest Borneo. In response, the Japanese moved about 104 Aussie officers out of the Sandakan camps, leaving 8 behind. They were given no time for farewells to their men, but were hustled aboard the coastal steamer *Tiensen*. The ship left on 16 October for Kuching, arriving on 3 November. The next day Colonel Suga assembled all the prisoners from the Kuching camps, announcing that the day was special, for it was the anniversary of the death of the Emperor Meiji, the founder of modern Japan. As Suga spoke, Lieutenant Lee and others got their first good look at the internees from the women's camp. Lee was impressed, noting that "most of them looked very attractive this morning, some even having obviously some make-up left."

Back in Sandakan, all those who had been arrested during the summer crackdown were collected: Captain Matthews and about twenty officers, five European civilians (including Taylor), and forty-seven natives. On 25 October, they were placed aboard the small steamer SS *Subuk* for the trip to Kuching. They would spend months awaiting their trial for possessing a radio, contacting the local guerrilla forces, and planning a revolt.[25]

As always, the Dutch East Indies was the scene of more prisoner reallocations. On 26 September, the 4,026-ton *Makassar Maru*, owned by the Nanyo Kaiun Company, left Batavia, packed with thirty-five hundred British and Dutch POWs. Conditions were deplorable, according to RAF men C. L. Cobb, J. B. Mackie, and R. J. Baldwin. The ship was terribly overcrowded, medical supplies and treatment were nonexistent, and the ordeal was made worse by frequent beatings by Japanese and Korean guards. The ship reached Singapore, took on more cargo, made some prisoner transfers, and continued on to Japan.

Leaving Makassar on 2 October, the 9,627-ton *Rio de Janeiro Maru* ferried two hundred POWs across the Java Sea. A passenger liner built in 1930 by Mitsubishi for the Osaka Shosen Company, it was requisitioned ten years later as a submarine depot ship. It served with the Imperial Navy in that capacity until September 1943, when it was again employed as a transport. In May 1943, it had carried two hundred British prisoners from Java to Ambon; the POWs noted that although the ship had red crosses painted on it, it carried ammunition. In October, the prisoners taking the three-day trip to Java had plenty of room and the food was adequate. Perhaps the most shocking thing they saw was at Tanjong Priok. It was by no means a bustling port serving scores of ships. "The harbor was empty, completely devoid of shipping," said one of the POWs, "except for our own transport and a salvaged wreck rotting with rust. They've lost the war," he concluded. "The end is only a matter of time." The end, however, would take nearly another two years.

On 5 November, a shipment of Dutch and British prisoners left Tanjong Priok on the 5,828-ton *France Maru*, owned by the Tochigi Kisen Company. According to Lieutenant Marinus of the RNAF and British flight lieutenant J. S. Owen, the conditions were very overcrowded and unsanitary. The prisoners were routinely beaten by guards under Japanese sergeant Hoshino. The ship carried its human cargo to Palembang, Sumatra, for plans were brewing for the construction of another railroad.

Frans Ponder, who had been shipwrecked when *Shinyu Maru* was torpedoed, had gone from Singapore to Thailand with nine thousand Dutch POWs in January and February of 1943. He worked for much of the year out of the camps at Tarsau and Krian Krai, then near the Burma border, then back near Tamarkan. With the railway complete, Ponder took the train back to Singapore, where he was billeted in a camp near the harbor. About 5 November, he boarded the *Maru Shichi* (seven) for Japan. In comparison with the other ships he had been on, Ponder thought they had much more room. "The food too was somewhat improved," he said. "At least we could taste the bouillon in the soup." It was a long journey, but they were allowed to swim in the cold ocean during a stop in Formosa. They reached Moji about 4 December, and Ponder went to a camp near the navy base at Tanagawa.

Unlike the great majority of POWs, Ponder was not to stay in the empire once shipped there. He went to the coal mines at Kamo for two months, then, with a work detail of mostly British and Australian prisoners, he was assigned to a ship to work as a stevedore at various ports of call. His ship, carrying munitions, went back south to Haiphong, where beans were loaded, and to Saigon, where rice was loaded. From there the ship went to Bangkok, where the munitions and POWs were unloaded. Once more, Ponder found himself working on the railroad out of Kanchanaburi, this time on a repair crew to fix Allied bomb damage. He had come full circle.[26]

Convoy O-305, leaving Rabaul on 13 November 1943, carried nine Allied POWs, some of whom had been aided by the German missionaries who were subsequently massacred on *Akikaze*. Lt. Robert R. Martindale's B-24 was shot down near Wewak in January 1943. The surviving crew members made it to Wokeo Island, off the New Guinea coast, where they were helped by the natives. After recuperating, they made an excursion to Kairiru for more assistance. Word of such clandestine exchanges eventually reached the Japanese, resulting in the evacuation and eventual murder of many of the missionaries. The downed pilots figured they had better move farther from the Japanese and sailed down the Schouten Islands to the New Guinea coast, where they hoped to trek safely to Allied lines. Instead, they were captured their first night ashore and taken to Wewak and Kairiru. In May, they were taken by subchaser to Rabaul, where they were imprisoned and interrogated.

In November, eight American airmen and one Australian engineer were selected to go to Japan for interrogation. The convoy consisted of the *Hokkai Maru, Taisho Maru, No. 7 Hoshi Maru, Makassar Maru,* and *Lyons Maru,* and the escorts SCs 24 and 39. Martindale did not know what ship they were on, only that it was a hulk of a freighter about forty years old. After a few days at sea the POWs were allowed on deck, and they thankfully breathed in the fresh air. They were allowed topside twice a day to "relieve ourselves over the scaffolding on the side of the ship." In the aft hold was a contingent of Indians, Gurkha prisoners who had not joined the Indian National Army and were being used on the islands as laborers. Martindale admired them, as "they seemed as proud and defiant in captivity as Rudyard Kipling depicted them in his novels."

The convoy headed to Palau, where they sweated in the stifling forward hold with many Japanese soldiers until allowed out during a rainstorm. Martindale used a small piece of soap given to him by a Gurkha, reveling in his good fortune by washing himself in the fresh rain on the open deck.

In Palau on 20 November, the convoy stopped while the Gurkhas were offloaded. The nine POWs continued on their journey, what Martindale described as "more endless and uncomfortable days," made somewhat tenable only because they broke into a cask and ate handfuls of pickled onions. They made Moji and boarded a train for Omori Camp, on an island in Tokyo Bay, reaching there on 7 December. At the end of 1943 there were about 566 POWs in Omori: 399 American, 112 British, 28 Dutch, 9 Norwegian, 7 Italian, 5 Australian, and 6 of other nationalities. There were American civilians from Wake, China Marines, merchant mariners, men of the 131st Artillery, men from the *Houston,* and other survivors from battles in the Java Sea. Martindale was to meet many U.S. submariners at Omori, including men from the *Perch,* who had been there for a year and a half, and men from the *Grenadier,* who were comparative newcomers.[27]

ORDEAL OF THE GRENADIER

In April 1943, the USS *Grenadier,* under Lt. Cdr. John A. Fitzgerald, was patrolling in Malacca Strait, where no U.S. submarine had operated before. The area was usually the domain of British and Dutch submarines, but the British had requested that U.S. fleet boats be sent there to help interdict the supply line between Singapore and Rangoon—the sea route the Burma Railway would hopefully make unnecessary. Fitzgerald spent 21 April lurking off Penang, hoping a fat Japanese transport might come along. On the surface only a few miles from shore, Fitzgerald spotted two ships heading his way. While maneuvering for a shot, a lookout shouted, "Aircraft on the port quarter!"

Fitzgerald gave the order to dive. When passing 130 feet, the executive officer, George H. Whiting, said, "We ought to be safe enough now." Within seconds his words were punctuated with a violent explosion, and *Grenadier* was driven down into the mud at 270 feet. A bomb had exploded between the maneuvering room and after torpedo room. The explosion caused the stern to twist out of shape and the hatches and valves to warp, resulting in innumerable leaks. Numerous small fires burned away insulation cork and rent cables, causing short-circuits in most systems. It took half an hour for the damage control party, wearing respirators, to extinguish the fires. Next they tried to stop the leaks and formed a bucket brigade to move some of the water away from the main motors and into the forward torpedo room. Working to near exhaustion throughout the day, the crew made the boat ready for a nighttime surface attempt.

At 2130, they managed to blow ballast and bring *Grenadier* to the surface. The smoke and foul air were cleared out, but Fitzgerald realized how badly his boat had been damaged. The hull of the after torpedo room was dished in about four inches. The tubes had been bent to port, as had the propeller shafts. The hatch between the after torpedo room and maneuvering was sprung and would not close. All hydraulic lines to the after torpedo tubes were broken, as were the gauges. The conning tower radio transmitter was also out of commission.

The engineering officer, Lt. Alfred J. Toulon, tried to straighten the shafts and get some unobstructed revolutions out of them. One shaft managed to turn over, but in doing so it pulled almost 3,000 amps instead of the normal 450. It was a no go. Upon discovering that the deck gun was useless, Fitzgerald realized that *Grenadier* could neither fight, run away, nor submerge—and dawn was breaking. As a last desperate measure, the men tried to rig up a sail so they could get closer to shore, abandon the boat, and scuttle it. While lookouts kept a close watch for planes, the boat's radio, radar, torpedo data computer (TDC), decoding machine, and code books were destroyed.

Suddenly a plane appeared and made a beeline for the stricken sub. Fitzgerald held fire until the plane was almost on them, then opened up with his remaining 20-mm and .30-caliber machine guns. The plane was hit, veered away, and came in from another angle. Again the gunners blasted away, causing the plane to drop its bomb two hundred yards short. The wounded pilot managed to guide his plane back to shore where he crash-landed and died later that night.

The action brought a Japanese merchant ship and escort in to investigate. While the ships circled, taking pictures, Fitzgerald had his men assemble on deck with life jackets and calmly step off into the water as the scuttled ship began to sink. After an hour in the water, the entire crew of seventy-six was recovered by the merchant ship and taken to Penang.

They were taken to an old schoolhouse, not fed for five days, and frequently interrogated, with especially harsh treatment for the officers. Fitzgerald was tied to a bench with his head hanging over the edge and his feet elevated. His captors forced water through his nose until he nearly drowned, then with his stomach bloated, pummeled his abdomen. In spite of this, he maintained his sanity and composure, leaving encouraging messages on the walls of the latrine for the men to read: "Don't tell them anything. . . . Keep your chins up."

After a week, Fitzgerald and three other officers were sent to Japan and the radar operator was sent to Java for further questioning. Lieutenant Toulon was the senior officer remaining. On 6 August 1943, the remaining submariners were removed from Penang to Singapore, where they were put to work building roads.

When their work was done in Singapore, orders were received to send the men to Japan. On 21 September, they sailed on the *Asama Maru,* reaching Moji on 9 October. Fifty-two submariners went to Fukuoka POW camps; twenty-nine, including Lieutenant Toulon, went to the Ofuna Naval Interrogation Center, then to Omori Camp. Four men died as captives, the causes of death listed as pneumonia and beriberi. Toulon thought the likely agents were malnutrition and beatings.[28]

ATROCITIES

Not all atrocities were committed at sea. Ruthless acts occurred across the length and breadth of the Pacific. As we have seen, 229 Australians were killed after surrendering at Laha, Ambon, in February 1942. About 110 Australians and 50 Indians were killed after surrendering at Parit Sulong during the Malayan campaign in January 1942, many gunned down or bayoneted while lying wounded in trucks. The survivors were kept at the Pudu jail in Kuala Lumpur. Other killings of surrendered men took place at Tol Plantation on New Britain. In August 1942, 220 Marines of the 2d Raider Battalion under Col. Evans Carlson assaulted Makin Island. They had been dropped off by the submarines *Narwhal* and *Argonaut* and wiped out the small Japanese force of 83 men. Heavy surf and Japanese planes hindered the evacuation, and in the confusion, 9 Marines were left behind, only to be captured when Japanese reinforcements landed. The raid temporarily succeeded in diverting Japanese attention from the Guadalcanal operation, but it also resulted in the Japanese reinforcing the Gilbert Islands, much to the chagrin of the 2d Marine Division, which would assault Tarawa the next year. Washington called the raid "a piece of folly" and canceled further operations. The captured Marines were treated well at first. They were sent to Kwajalein, awaiting what they thought would be transportation to Japan. Adm. Abe Koso did not know what to do with them, until he received word that the prisoners did not need to be sent to Japan and he could dispose of them as he saw fit. Abe ordered them all beheaded by the sword.[29]

None of the Gunners 600 party on Ballale survived the war. They built an airfield with Chinese, Koreans, and natives from the nearby island of Choiseul. Two Korean witnesses saw them working for some months, but they knew little about them except that they wore khaki clothing, they were British, and they had been captured in Singapore. They were kept in separate compounds. Some prisoners died of diseases and were dumped in the ocean. Those who couldn't work were beaten with bamboo poles. When the Allies began to bomb Ballale's airfield in 1943, the Japanese took cover in trenches but forced the prisoners to remain in their huts. After several bombings, only about one hundred prisoners remained. The airfield was never finished. On 30 June 1943, Ballale was shelled from the sea. Said one of the Korean guards, Kateshiro Fukukan, "The Japanese were afraid of a landing and killed all the PWs next day by bayonets or swords."

Chinese laborers also witnessed the events. One remembered forty bodies being put in rice sacks and taken out to sea to be thrown overboard. Three Chinese recalled that in May, a white man dressed in the overalls of a pilot was tied up on the ground. A drum of boiling water was placed next to him while a number of Japanese soldiers filed by, each one pouring a cupful of scalding water over him. While the prisoner screamed in pain, the soldiers either beat him or clapped their hands and laughed. By July, there were no prisoners left alive. In November 1945, the War Graves Unit exhumed 438 European bodies on Ballale. As in the *Kowa Maru* incident, a story was fabricated that the men were all killed on a Japanese ship that had been bombed by U.S. aircraft on its voyage from Singapore to the Solomons. This is still the story given at the war graves registry at Bomana Cemetery, near Port Moresby, where the bodies were eventually reinterred. The eighty-two men of the Gunners 600 party who were too ill to make the trip from Rabaul to Ballale would face diseases, medical experiments, and executions. They asked themselves, "Who will bury the last man?" Only eighteen survived to be liberated in September 1945.[30]

On Wake Island, more than a year had elapsed since the *Tachibana Maru* and *Asama Maru* had removed prisoners and civilian contractors. Deaths among the 168 remaining civilians were heavy; by October 1943, only 98 were left alive. Raids on the island grew more frequent, and the civilians huddled in their poor shelters now dodged U.S. bombs and shells. A doctor, Lawton Shank, treated the wounded as best he could with the few medical supplies allowed him.

After one attack, the Japanese became convinced that the civilians had a radio and were in contact with the U.S. forces. They also worried that if they were recaptured they would reveal just how weak the Japanese defenses were. On the night of 7 October, Adm. Sakaibara Shigematsu ordered them to be rounded up, hands tied behind their backs and blindfolded, and led down to the beach. They were placed in a long line and all ninety-eight of them were machine-gunned. In September 1945, the U.S. Navy returned to Wake. The inspection found much of what had been expected—and something quite unexpected. Along the island's north shore was a long trench marked with freshly painted white posts, the bushes surrounding it neatly trimmed. Using thought processes alien to the Americans, the Japanese had tidied up the scene of the massacre for the occupying forces.[31]

HAGUE, GENEVA, AND BUSHIDO

Why did the Japanese disregard the conventions of so-called civilized warfare? In the first thirty years of the twentieth century they had shown their wartime enemies exceptionally humane treatment. In 1900, during the Boxer Rebellion, a xenophobic Chinese secret society attacked Christians and Westerners and besieged them in Peking. An international military force, which included Japanese troops, eventually rescued them, and the Japanese conduct was exemplary. When the siege was lifted, some Western troops, particularly the Germans and Russians, went on a rampage, looting, raping, and killing, whereas the Japanese were models of chivalry and restraint. Although witnesses agreed the Japanese were not only the bravest but also the most humane, they were still called "laughable yellow monkeys" by some Westerners. When they fought Russia in 1904–5, the Japanese felt they must demonstrate that they were not an inferior people. Even though they had been given much cause to hate the Russians, they proved chivalrous in warfare, rescuing the crews of Russian cruisers who had just sunk unarmed Japanese merchant ships or, as at the Battle of the Yalu River, capturing and treating humanely many Russians who had mutilated Japanese war dead. When Port Arthur was taken there was fear of an impending massacre, but the Japanese restored order and went out of their way to comfort the Russian prisoners. Likewise, after the sea battle of Tsushima, the rescued Russians were treated well, fed, clothed, and cared for. Japan's hard fighting and good conduct notwithstanding, the 1905 Treaty of Portsmouth, which ended the war, left the Army disgusted. The Japanese were forced to withdraw from almost all the territory won at such a dreadful cost. They had won the war but lost the peace.[32]

In 1907 Japan participated in the Fourth Hague Convention, a preliminary accord dealing with warfare and treatment of belligerents and prisoners. The agreement stated that treatment should not be left up to the arbitrary judgment of military commanders. Prisoners were to remain under the protection of the principles of law as practiced in civilized nations, under "the laws of humanity, and the dictate of the public conscience."

When the Japanese entered World War I, they abided by the convention, treating German prisoners they captured in the Pacific as men, not animals. After the war, as the Western powers attempted to put down the Bolshevik rebellion, the Japanese went with them to Siberia. Red Cross observers gave top marks to two nations for scrupulous treatment of prisoners: the United States and Japan.

At the Paris peace conference of 1919, Japan was there as a member of the "Big Five." The Japanese did not believe that the fledgling League of Nations would be effective unless they all agreed to ban racial discrimination. When the Western powers either opposed the suggestion or refused to vote on it, Japan felt rejected. This time the insult would have far-reaching consequences. The Japanese began to declare themselves a morally superior people, an idea that already had deep roots in their culture. The concept of *kokutai*—the existence of unique, spiritual Japanese values and virtues—took on widespread emphasis. Increasingly the Japanese saw themselves as morally superior, as a people whose divine destiny was to spread their culture to the rest of the world. (Much the same as when Americans invoked Manifest Destiny in the nineteenth century.) Japan was angered at the Washington Conference in 1922, which saw the nation relegated to a second-class naval power, forced to retain capital ships at a ratio of no more than 60 percent of the U.S. and British ships in service. When the United States passed a law to close off Japanese immigration in 1924, the reaction was violent, and thousands of demonstrators marched in Tokyo with calls for war.[33]

In 1929, ideas about the humane treatment of prisoners of war were advanced by the Red Cross at Geneva, Switzerland. Japan, along with forty other nations, signed the accords, but its home government never ratified the convention's position on POWs. Japan believed the agreement would entitle prisoners to a softer time than its own soldiers would have while fighting for the emperor, which to them appeared absurd. Japan did not plan on any of its own men being taken prisoner. They would die before surrendering. So why bother with the Geneva Convention? There was nothing in it for them. Fighting in China in the 1930s, Japan was well out of compliance with the accords, resorting to barbarities that it never would have engaged in just a few years earlier.

In early 1942, Foreign Minister Togo Shigenori gave formal assurance that, although Japan was not bound by the Geneva Convention, it would apply it, mutatis mutandis, to all the Westerners it captured. In other words, Japan would give consideration to national and racial customs about food, clothing, treatment, and so on—at least where practical—but not if doing so would conflict with existing Japanese policies. In effect, this meant Japan would do just about anything it wanted with prisoners of war. In keeping with this expedient approach, general and prime minister Tojo Hideki made prisoners work in war industries and on related projects, issued the dictum "No work, no food," and sent strict orders to the heads of the prison camps: they must not succumb to mistaken ideas of humanitarianism. Treatment of captives was up to the discretion of the local Army commanders—in direct contradiction of the Hague Convention.[34]

In the twentieth century Japan tried to emulate the Western world's self-proclaimed code of civilized warfare, but it saw little of chivalry while observing the Westerners fight. Its own code of Bushido, the "way of the warrior," had been a facet of its culture for a thousand years. After the Meiji Restoration in 1868, Bushido stressed compassion, kindness, and consideration for one's enemies. The imperial precepts issued to soldiers and sailors in 1882 exhorted them to be valorous, loyal, righteous, respectful of superiors, and considerate to inferiors. The experiences Japan had with the Western way of war and diplomacy, however, had shattered its expectations. Disparagement and racism led not to emulation, but to rejection of the West. In addition, the growing military presence in Japanese politics and education led the nation along a new path. Politicians not in line with the military's way of thinking were assassinated. Military reforms brought about brutal discipline in the armed forces, and propaganda engendered a hatred of the enemy. Bushido was a casualty of the new frame of mind. Loyalty now belonged only to the emperor. Surrender was no longer an option, and an enemy who surrendered was beneath contempt. Compassion for the defeated was forbidden. Death in warfare was seen to be lighter than a feather, likened to the fall of cherry blossoms. Victory would be sought by any means necessary, honorable or not.

The result of all this was bad news for captives of the Japanese. Even so, although they were in the minority, there were some conscientious commandants of Japanese prison camps and ship transports. Most, however, ranged from average to horrible; some couldn't care less, others were drunks, some were sadists, and a few were homicidal.[35] Compassion or brutality depended on the individual, not on the race, and often a prisoner's fate was decided with no more rhyme or reason than in the proverbial luck of the draw.

THE SUEZ MARU INCIDENT

The prisoners who had been captured on Ambon, or sent to Ambon and Haruku in April 1943, had experienced some of the worst conditions of any camps. In the southern territories, the camps were administered by the Navy and Army. The Army controlled north and west Borneo, Java, Sumatra, Malaya, Burma, and Thailand. The Navy was in charge of south and east Borneo, Celebes, the Moluccas, Timor, most of New Guinea, the Bismarcks, Guam, and Wake. Some of the highest death rates of all were in the Navy-controlled Moluccas, particularly on Ambon and Haruku.

Hard work, starvation, disease, and the beatings of Gunso Mori, nick-named "Blood," took their toll. On Haruku, Tony Cowling caustically commented that in November 1943, the Japanese suddenly became concerned with the POWs' welfare. Almost 400 of them had died since their arrival six months earlier, and the hospital had 700 patients. The men weighed an average of seventy-five pounds each, and the Japanese decided they would send the sickest back to Java. On the twenty-third, 650 men gathered on Ambon. Two of Cowling's good friends were in the draft. "They were human skeletons just capable of sustaining souls," he said. "How could they survive the hazards of prison ship transportation?" Then again, Cowling thought, anything had to be better than remaining on Haruku.

He was wrong.

In Ambon's fine natural harbor was the *Suez Maru*, a 4,645-ton passenger-cargo ship built in 1919 and owned by the Kuribayashi Syosen Company. The ship was 360 feet long, and its coal-burning engine and single screw could generate a maximum speed of only twelve knots. The unit commander,

Lieutenant Colonel Anami, in charge of loading the POWs, saw to it that the first two holds were occupied with sick Japanese patients. The two after hatches were filled with 546 sick prisoners, most of them British. About 20 of them were stretcher cases.

The last aboard was Lt. Iketani Masaji, who would be in charge during the voyage. Knowing the seas were becoming increasingly dangerous, he turned to Anami and asked, "If this ship is attacked by torpedoes from enemy submarines and sinks, what measures shall be taken? And what should be done if the escort ship is a small minesweeper which hasn't the capacity to accommodate everybody?"

"You may shoot them," Anami responded. "Shoot them!"

On 25 November, the *Suez Maru, Nichinan Maru,* and minesweeper 12 pulled out from Ambon. The next few days were uneventful, but on the night of the twenty-eighth, the minesweeper disappeared. Iketani was concerned. He learned the escort had spotted a submarine and had gone off on a chase. Then *Nichinan Maru* left for its own destination. He increased the number of guards at the number three and number four holds, then looked at the lifeboats and life jackets. He thought that, "generally speaking," they would be sufficient.

In the morning, Iketani was relieved to see the minesweeper far to the rear and steaming forward at full speed. They settled down to breakfast, and by the time they were finished, the escort had pulled ahead and was leisurely sailing at the same speed as *Suez Maru,* emitting clouds of thick black smoke.

It had been raining steadily throughout the night, and the poor visibility made *Bonefish*'s lookouts weary. The submarine, flagship of Adm. Ralph Christie's Task Force 71, had pulled out of Fremantle on 20 November, for her third patrol. She had coursed through the dangerous Lombok Strait on 28 November, and made a beeline to the middle of the Java Sea about seventy miles northeast of Kangean Island. At 0525, the rising Monday morning sun brought with it an end to the rain. The curtain was raised, visibility was unlimited, and entering the stage were two ships making heavy black smoke.

The ships were at twenty-five thousand yards, but closing. Cdr. Tom Hogan calculated that they were on course 267, apparently headed west, either to Surabaya or Batavia. He maneuvered his boat into position and watched them come to him. At 0817 the maru and its escort were at twenty-six hundred yards, speed eight knots, apparently unaware they were being stalked.

EHIME MARU.
MORIOKA MARU.
SUEZ MARU.

Gross tonnage: 4,469–4,654.

Length: (w. l.) 360'.

Beam: 51'.

Draft: (loaded) 23' (light) 8'.

Speeds:
    Normal cruising—10 knots.
    Maximum—12 knots.

Built: 1919–20.

Machinery: Reciprocating, single screw.

Fuel:
    Type—coal.
    Capacity—about 1,700 tons.

Radius: 15,000 miles at 10 knots.

Complement: (pass.) 6.

Owners:
    See Remarks.*

Potential naval value: AP, AK.

Remarks:
    *Ehime—Yamashita K. K. K.
    Morioka—Nippon Yusen Kaisha.
    Suez—Kuribayasi Syosen K. K.

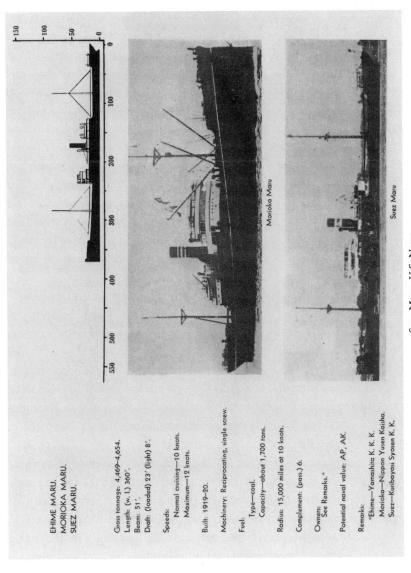

Morioka Maru

Suez Maru

Suez Maru. U.S. Navy

Hogan steadied the *Bonefish* on course 030, speed three knots. He had taken the boat down and limited periscope exposures because the sea was glassy calm. With a last look, Hogan noticed an airplane stowed on *Suez Maru*'s forward well deck. At twenty-two hundred yards, four Mark 14 torpedoes were fired. It was a long run, but the setup looked good, the target speed slow and running on a straight course.

"Torpedo!" Lieutenant Iketani heard the shout. He looked to the stern and saw two white traces approaching. *Suez Maru* picked up speed and tried to turn away. Said Iketani, "For that moment, we prayed to God." The ship was not agile enough, however, and two blasts rocked the stern. Iketani sent men to assess the damage; two of them were blown into the open holds. Prisoners were climbing out of the number three hold, but in number four, which had taken a direct hit, there was much destruction and no one was emerging. The propeller shaft was broken and the engine rooms were flooding fast. It was impossible to keep up steam. Iketani ordered the Korean guards to free the rafts and pass the word for the prisoners to abandon ship. Many of them had already done so. When the ship's list became steeper, Iketani and the last of the crew jumped off.

On *Bonefish*, Hogan watched the first two of his torpedoes hit, one amidships and one under the main aft mast. Immediately the target began to settle by the stern. The escort finally began heading his way, and he took the sub deep. Minesweeper 12 dropped one depth charge from afar, then two more near the spot where *Bonefish* had submerged. Hogan found a temperature gradient at 250 feet but took the boat down to 350 just to be safe. Five more depth charges were dropped, including two very close ones. Then silence. The entire time, the sound gear picked up faint noises of a ship breaking up. By 0917 there was no noise but the pinging of echo-ranging.

While minesweeper 12 chased *Bonefish*, Iketani was desperately swimming to get away from the suction of the sinking *Suez Maru*. Less than twenty minutes had elapsed from the torpedoing to the sinking. The sea was littered with debris, and hundreds of men bobbed about, trying to find and cling to bits of flotsam. The minesweeper returned and began the slow process of picking up survivors, taking the Japanese and leaving the British behind. At 1004, *Bonefish* rose to periscope depth and surveyed the scene. The minesweeper was about four thousand yards away, apparently rescuing survivors. Hogan decided to leave it alone; he crept away, submerged.

Bonefish (SS 223). U.S. Naval Institute

Iketani was in the water for hours and was one of the last picked up. The minesweeper was jammed with exhausted, wet, and wounded Japanese. Its captain, Kawano Osumu, was against picking up any prisoners because his boat was already full, and he believed more men would cause it to capsize. Iketani nodded his head in agreement. Kawano continued, saying that they should not leave the prisoners adrift, because they might be rescued. "Have you received any orders from higher authorities?" he asked.

"We have orders instructing us to shoot them if the ship were sunk," Iketani answered. "I request that proper disposal be made by the escort ship."

"Is that so?" said Kawano. "Then we shall shoot them."

Iketani made a weak protest. "I think it would be all right to leave them alone since the boats are afloat."

"It is the express wish of the Army," Kawano insisted. "Also the enemy submarine is bound to emerge after we leave and rescue the survivors. Then information about Japanese forces will come known to the enemy and affect operations adversely. . . . If we cannot accommodate all of them, death is the only answer."

Iketani stared down from the bridge. He guessed there were still 250 men floating in the sea. He demurred, but Kawano snapped an order to his executive officer. The ship's whistle blew, and men went running. Kawano ordered Iketani to assist his crew in killing the prisoners. "He ordered me to shoot them," he said. "I thought it was futile murder, but that was the situation, furthermore, we were facing the enemy submarine."

There were only twelve rifles on the ship. Iketani armed and positioned twelve of his men on each side of the foredeck. He told a warrant officer in the rifle unit to be careful of its targets, because about twenty Japanese were still missing. The 750-ton minesweeper 12 was armed with two 4.7-inch guns and nine 25-mm machine guns. It was about 1600 when the machine guns and rifles began barking out. Iketani tried to avert his eyes from the killing but remained on the bridge with Kawano to help supervise. The minesweeper slowed to a crawl, circling within fifty yards of the prisoners. At first the survivors were lying prone, floating, unaware of what was about to happen. When the bullets started ripping into them, they tried to hide behind any bits of wreckage they could find. There was no real shelter.

Petty Officer Yoshino was on the bridge with binoculars, scanning the sea, directing fire to groups right and left. Iketani saw a man, completely naked, with close-cropped black hair, lying on a board. He was a *Suez Maru* crew member and they slowed to pick him up. The flesh was torn off his back, and he was barely alive. A crew member of minesweeper 12, Fujimoto Takeshi, was standing topside and saw a prisoner in a life preserver floating near the hull. He wondered if they were going to rescue him, when suddenly he was shot, blood spurting from the back of his head. Fujimoto went down to his cabin. He was shocked. "I had never before seen a man killed," he said. A little later, he went topside again. There he heard one of the rescued Japanese calling out, "Shoot every POW in sight!" Fujimoto tried to count all the dead bodies bobbing in the sea; he thought there were about two hundred.

The minesweeper made several slow circles of the area. "The water in the vicinity was colored by the blood," Iketani said, "and the scene was so distressing it made one cover one's eyes." The last few POWs, knowing they were going to die, stood up bravely on their little rafts and stuck out their chests, inviting the bullets. Their defiant gesture was answered.

"What an inhuman thing to do—to kill unresisting men," Iketani said to Lieutenant Tanaka, standing beside him. "Even if it is war, it is a distasteful thing, isn't it?"

"It is pitiful, isn't it?" said Tanaka in a low voice. "However, if this was one of the means of winning the war, it had to be carried through at any cost."

Soon it was dark. The ship picked up speed and cut through the few lifeboats that remained afloat, then sped off to the west, heading for Batavia. Iketani was overcome with gloom. He dejectedly nibbled at his meager supper, crouched alone in a corner of the officers' cabin. They had rescued 93 Japanese soldiers and crewmen and 205 Japanese patients. Sixty-nine had died. Minesweeper 12 radioed word of the attack to Batavia, concluding with the statement that the prisoners had attempted to escape (*ryuushutsu*) and were disposed of (*shobun*). Back to the east of them in the Java Sea, there was nothing left but scattered debris and an oil slick. Not one of the 546 captives survived.[36]

ULTRA ENTERS THE PICTURE

As 1943 drew to a close, Japan was plagued by ever-growing shipping losses. Her yards delivered slightly over 1 million tons of new shipping in 1943, but her losses were more than 2 million tons. The 5,942,000 tons afloat at the end of 1942 was reduced to 4,944,000 tons at the end of 1943. Submarines accounted for 1.3 million tons. Several factors brought about the increase in submarine successes: more submarines were prowling the sea lanes, tactics had improved, and the serious torpedo problems were being remedied. Another important element was that, unknown to the Japanese, their codes had been compromised. Prior to the Pearl Harbor attack, intelligence units had broken several of the Japanese codes. Two years later, the majority of Japanese communications sent over the airwaves were being intercepted and decoded.[37]

Radio intelligence involved interception of radio messages, traffic analysis, direction finding, translating intercepted signals, collating, and evaluating the material. In September of 1943, the Joint Intelligence Center Pacific Ocean Area (JICPOA) was established to collect worldwide intelligence source materials. The product was known simply as Ultra or Magic, from the British calling it "ultrasecret" or the Americans referring to the code breakers as "magicians." By whatever name, radio intelligence was a boon to the Allied war effort; Gen. Douglas MacArthur believed it saved thousands of lives and shortened the war by two years.

The twelve months fighting on the defensive after Pearl Harbor allowed the radio intelligence units to hone their skills and forge them into a powerful weapon. The Japanese never remedied fundamental flaws in their communications security, perhaps under the impression that their codes were too complex and numerous to admit any sustained eavesdropping. They used up to twenty-four codes at one time, including three strategic, eight tactical, nine attaché, and four extranaval—and these were just the naval codes. The Japanese Army used another thirty or more codes.[38]

Very important to the U.S. submarine effort was the breaking of the Japanese Water Transport Code and JN 40, the merchant shipping code of four-syllable kana groups. The former, broken in the spring of 1943, gave detailed information about shipping that the Army had allocated for its exclusive use. The latter, also called the "Maru code," was the prime source of information on the Japanese merchant marine convoys.

Breaking JN 40 was an Allied effort, although cooperation was not always smooth among the Allies or between American commands. The Army and Navy competed against each other, and both tried to cut out the British. Nevertheless, all the intelligence sections eventually broke the codes. Understanding the maru code allowed the Allies to plot Japanese convoy routes from their positions, which the merchant skippers would obligingly transmit at 0800 and 2000 every day. The ability to know exactly where the convoys were heading was vital. Before that time, the broken naval code, JN 25, allowed the occasional routing of submarines against major warships, but with unsatisfactory results. With the cracking of JN 40, submarines could be vectored at slower, poorly escorted convoys, effectively cutting supply lines. Breaking this code sent the sinking rates skyrocketing in 1944. It was impossible for the Japanese shipbuilding industry to overcome this attrition rate.[39]

SINKING OF CHUYO

By the end of 1943, Vice Adm. Charles A. Lockwood, commander of submarines in the Pacific (ComSubPac), was still uncertain whether to concentrate his boats against large Imperial Japanese Navy warships, in the hope of getting one or two big scores, or scatter them along the major convoy paths to maintain a war of attrition against the Japanese merchant fleet. Ganging up a large number of submarines against Ultra-located capital ships might look rather suspicious if the trick was pulled too often. Yet in December 1943, the opportunity was too good to pass up.

This remarkable story had its beginnings in 1939, when the submarine *Squalus* sank off the New England coast. The sub's main induction, which supplied fresh air to run the diesels, failed to close during a dive, the sub settled on the bottom in 240 feet of water, and twenty-six men drowned. By the use of an experimental diving bell, thirty-three men who had managed to seal themselves off in the forward compartments were rescued. Her sister sub, *Sculpin,* was instrumental in locating the sunken *Squalus* and assisting in the rescue. *Squalus* was eventually salvaged, repaired, and renamed *Sailfish.* In the fall of 1943, *Sailfish* and *Sculpin* were fighting the Japanese in the central Pacific. On *Sailfish* were some crewmen who had been aboard her when she went down as the *Squalus.*

During Operation Galvanic, the invasion of the Gilbert Islands, *Sculpin* was one of a number of submarines placed in the Caroline Islands to attack any Japanese ships that sortied to oppose the invasion. She was under Lt. Cdr. Fred Connaway, but also aboard was Capt. John P. Cromwell, who was to direct a wolfpack of submarines, to include *Searaven* and *Apogon,* that would form up near Truk. Cromwell was privy to the plans of Operation Galvanic, plus much top-secret Ultra information. The pack was to deploy north of Truk to intercept a group of cruisers and carriers that radio messages indicated were traveling from Japan.

Late on 18 November, *Sculpin* tracked a large convoy, and at dawn the next day she submerged to make a periscope attack on what appeared to be one freighter, five destroyers, and a cruiser. Before she could shoot, the convoy zigged toward them and Connaway took the boat down for another approach. At 0730, both Connaway and Cromwell decided that the convoy must be very important; they decided to surface. Charging in from behind, however, was the destroyer *Yamagumo,* left trailing as a "sleeper." *Sculpin* barely got under before a string of depth charges blasted her. Over the next two hours, she was attacked repeatedly. An exhaust valve in the after engine room ruptured, sea valves were jarred loose, and the depth gauges filled with water. As the sub became heavy, speed and up-angle were increased to keep her from sinking. The crew pumped the bilges to regain trim, but neither the drain nor the trim pump would take suction. The men formed a bucket brigade to try to transfer the water from the engine room when, suddenly, *Sculpin* broached. The broken depth gauges still read 170 feet.

Yamagumo saw the wounded submarine and charged. Damaged by more depth charges, *Sculpin* dropped to 500 feet before regaining control. Both torpedo rooms had developed cracks around the tubes, and they were shipping more water. The batteries were nearly exhausted. Cromwell insisted they remain submerged, but it was Connaway's boat. He saw no alternative but to fight it out on the surface. At least the men could abandon ship and hope to live. At 1330, *Sculpin* surfaced once more. Her crew manned the deck gun and actually got off the first few shots before being answered by a salvo from *Yamagumo*'s 5-inchers, which straddled the boat. The second salvo pierced the conning tower, killing Connaway and three others.

Lt. George E. Brown passed the word over the intercom: "Abandon ship, and God have mercy on your souls." Brown, with motor machinist's mate Philip J. Gabrunas, remained behind to open the vents and scuttle the ship. While ensuring that all men had heard the order, Brown had a hurried conversation with Captain Cromwell. He urged Cromwell to evacuate, but Cromwell told Brown to leave. "He told me to go ahead, that it was the right thing to do," said Brown. Cromwell said he knew too much, and he was afraid the information he possessed would be injurious to his shipmates if he were captured and revealed it under torture. Cromwell sat down on an empty ammunition box, gazing at a photograph of his wife, oblivious to the chaos around him.

Lieutenant Brown tried to get everyone else off, but Gabrunas was killed by a shell burst upon exiting the conning tower. Other men refused to go, including Eugenio Apostol, Cromwell's steward, and Ens. William M. Fiedler, who felt responsible for broaching the boat. About twelve men rode the boat down.[40]

More than fifty men made it into the water. Seaman Edwin Keller, who had been blown out of his clothes, bobbed in the water thinking how peaceful everything had become. Then he noticed the destroyer, moving in fast and blasting the water with its machine guns. *Yamagumo* sliced past him. Radioman Julius Peterson called out, and they swam toward yeoman Delbert Schroeder, who had on a life jacket. When they reached him, they found Schroeder had been shot, with at least two bullet holes in his chest. It was 1500 when the gunfire stopped, and this time the destroyer passed by and threw lines over the side. Almost everyone had a chance to grab one, but only one chance. If one missed, it was too bad. Others chose not to accept the lines and swam away. Once on deck, the prisoners were herded to the bow. The seriously wounded quartermaster striker, Claiborne Weade, was ordered left behind. He was rolled into the sea by the Japanese. There were three officers and thirty-eight enlisted men left.

They were given a large tarpaulin for shelter and left on deck while *Yamagumo* headed for Truk, about two hundred miles to the west. The survivors were incredibly thirsty, but only a few tins were passed around, with barely enough water to wet their lips. Interrogations began, and torpedoman Herbert Thomas was beaten until he "confessed" to fabricated Navy secrets. That night a storm arose, and the men, most of whom were wounded, were left on deck exposed to the elements. The next day they pulled into Truk's lagoon and docked at Dublon Island.

At Pearl Harbor, JICPOA was aware of what had happened. On 19 November, the code breakers had intercepted *Yamagumo*'s signal to Truk. The destroyer had radioed: "At 1304, sank enemy submarine with gunfire. Have 41 prisoners. Will send action summary later." The next day, another message was intercepted, this one indicating that the prisoners would be turned over to Base Force Commander at Truk and *Yamagumo* would commence refueling.

The prisoners were placed in three small cells for the next ten days. Whenever anyone cried out for water, a guard with a club would enter and beat the culprit. They got one rice ball and a few ounces of water per day. Wounds were left untreated, and all of the men were interrogated. The three surviving officers had it worst. Lieutenant Brown, Ens. J. W. Gamel, and Ens. C. G. Smith Jr. were pummeled with fists and bats but could reveal nothing of substance to the Japanese. Edwin Keller, who was clubbed in the groin, said, "I still believe that on Truk, they had no intentions for us to survive." However, on the fifth day, a group of well-dressed officers visited them. "They could smell the gangrene," Keller believed, and ordered that their wounds be treated. One man lost an arm to amputation and another lost a hand. They were given more food and the interrogations ceased.

In the meantime the 13,950-ton light carrier *Zuiho* and two 17,830-ton escort carriers, the *Unyo* and *Chuyo,* had arrived. Prisoners from Wake Island rode the latter ship in January 1942, when she was still the transport *Nitta Maru.* However, Japan's carrier losses had caused them to convert several large transports into carriers. *Nitta Maru* was taken to Kure Naval Dockyard in July 1942 and commissioned as *Chuyo* in November. The three ships had brought planes to Truk, but not nearly enough to turn the tide of battle. When the carriers returned to Japan, it was decided to send the captured submariners along with them.[41]

On 30 November, the prisoners were blindfolded and taken aboard. Ensigns Gamel and Smith, and those with the most severe injuries, twenty-one total, boarded *Chuyo*. Lieutenant Brown and nineteen enlisted men boarded *Unyo*. They sailed the same day, accompanied by the heavy cruiser *Maya* and the destroyers *Akebono, Urakaze, Sazanami,* and *Ushio,* the latter two of which had contributed to *Perch's* destruction.

Code breakers were aware of the ships' movement and sent out Ultras to submarines along the intended path. It was *Chuyo's* thirteenth voyage along that route since the previous December. In the previous two months, the *Unyo, Chuyo, Zuiho,* and escort carrier *Taiyo* had made several trips between Truk and Yokosuka, but no submarines had been able to claim a sinking. In September, *Cabrilla* hit *Taiyo* in the Bonin Islands and damaged its propeller and rudder. *Jack* attempted to pick off the cripple, but with malfunctioning engines and an aggressive escort, she could not make an approach. *Chuyo* towed *Taiyo* to Yokosuka. In October, *Chuyo* was twice attacked, by *Mingo* and *Flying Fish,* but no torpedoes connected. *Tarpon, Gudgeon,* and *Dace* also received Ultras about carriers plying the route, but none of them could score.

On the morning of the day of sailing, *Skate* was also alerted by an Ultra. She waited off Truk and sent three torpedoes at *Zuiho*. There was a large geyser of water and the carrier heeled to port, but it was only a premature torpedo explosion. Farther north, off Iwo Jima, the *Gunnel* had an opportunity, but an inopportune zigzag forced the sub deep to avoid a collision. It appeared that the last submarine to have a chance before the carriers reached Japan was *Sailfish*.[42]

The sub had been in Pearl Harbor undergoing refit early in November. Edwin Keller had hoped to get on *Sailfish,* but because there were no openings, he signed aboard *Sculpin*. Now, ironically, Keller was a prisoner aboard a carrier that was being stalked by the submarine to which he had wanted to be assigned.

Making her tenth patrol, *Sailfish* was skippered by Lt. Cdr. R. E. M. "Bob" Ward. Almost all the officers were new to the boat, including the executive officer, Lt. George F. Richardson, the radar officer, Lt. William Bruckart, and the torpedo officer, Lt. Walter P. Murphy. On the way to the patrol area off Honshu, the torpedo in the number eight tube made a hot run, and Murphy went over the side in rough seas to inspect the outer doors. The torpedo had safely ejected, but one tube was out of commission.

A full-fledged typhoon was in the making when Ward received the Ultra about the approaching carriers. Murphy, who also ran the TDC, was not privy to the secret source of the message, which was known only to Ward and Richardson. He was told the contact came from another submarine. But, said Murphy, "I remember course 320, speed 18 being given to us, and it was exactly what I used in the first estimate in the TDC."

The waves had become huge, with forty- to fifty-knot winds and no visibility beyond five hundred yards. Late on 3 December, *Sailfish* made radar contact on the convoy at ninety-five hundred yards: course 320 and speed eighteen knots, just as predicted by Ultra. They built up speed to twelve knots. Ward logged, "The seas are mountainous with a driving rain. Can't see a thing but blackness and water with the water mostly in my face." At midnight a ship turned on a green-tinged searchlight. Ward took *Sailfish* down to forty feet and readied a bow shot at the largest radar pip. At 0012, four torpedoes set at twelve feet were on a twenty-one-hundred-yard run toward the target.

Aboard *Chuyo*, the *Sculpin* prisoners had suffered through three miserable days. The only opening in their compartment was a small hatch above, through which inadequate amounts of food and water were passed. Wounded motor machinist's mate George Rocek, who had made all nine of *Sculpin*'s patrols, said, "Every time we would bang on the hatch for water, the guard would open it, spit on us, and slam the hatch closed. That was it."

The weather turned so bad that even the carriers rolled heavily in the seas. Because the convoy was approaching Honshu, and the poor weather seemed to preclude any submarine attack, *Maya*'s commander suspended evasive maneuvers. *Sailfish* had a straight shot. Just after midnight on 4 December, Ward heard two timed explosions. He took the boat down and for the next hour and a half reloaded torpedoes while counting nineteen depth charges, none very close.

One torpedo hit in the port bow magazine, but it did not catch fire. However, the hull plates were torn open and the forward section of the flight deck collapsed. In order to proceed, Capt. Okura Tomasaborou reversed direction and continued on at half speed. In their small cell, the prisoners were jolted by two explosions, one in the side and one in the propellers. Fires broke out, filling the passageways with smoke. The prisoners undogged the compartment door, but found it was locked from the outside. No one came to let them out. They could hear damage control parties hollering, hammering, and trying to shore up the hull, but the tossing seas made it hopeless. Water seeped into the compartment. They freed a pipe from the toilet and wedged it between the door and wall, prying it open a little. Then, pushing with all their strength, they sprung the door open. The men scrambled into the smoky passageway, stumbling their way left and right in the darkness, assisting the two amputees, trying to find a way out. *Chuyo* radioed a distress signal, but it wasn't acted upon. The convoy sailed on. It was about 0215.

Sailfish surfaced and was running up *Chuyo*'s track for another attack. It appeared to be heading northwest at two to five knots, and for the next two hours Ward tried to maneuver *Sailfish* into another attack position. The bad weather allowed time for the prisoners to get topside. They had spent two hours below decks, with frenzied Japanese crewmen running past, completely ignoring them. They found a room with life jackets, and a small galley with bottles of soda water, which they opened and thirstily guzzled. Meanwhile, the approaching dawn and improved visibility forced Ward to quickly line up another shot. At 0552 he fired three more torpedoes at a range of thirty-two hundred yards, and five minutes later heard two hits and saw a puff of smoke and fire. Two torpedoes had hit the port engine room. The ship went dead in the water. Guns began firing to all points of the compass, but even with the illumination, Ward still could not visibly make out his target.

Chuyo's prisoners finally made it to the flight deck, where they saw Japanese sailors lashing logs together to make rafts. The prisoners were rounded up in the center of the deck, stripped of their life jackets, and tied up. *Chuyo* had been frantically sending out distress signals, and finally *Maya* and *Urakaze* turned back. It was not until 0748 that Ward could make out his target. "Finally see something," he logged. "Aircraft Carrier, range about 10,000 yards, dead in water. . . . Nothing else in sight." Two hours passed before *Maya* and *Urakaze* hove into view, long enough to distract the Japanese crew, and the prisoners began to untie themselves. By this time *Sailfish* had readied another salvo, and at 0940 three more torpedoes were speeding toward the stricken carrier. Two of them connected, once again in the port side.

"She just shuddered and shook," said George Rocek. "You could feel the vibration. She had a slight list to port. But after that torpedo hit, she started getting a more pronounced list and the bow started going downward." The crew scrambled to the high starboard side, followed by the prisoners, who had freed themselves from their bonds. The carrier tilted up at a 45-degree angle, and the men slid down the deck into the raging ocean.

Those aboard *Sailfish* could hear the sound of *Chuyo* breaking up, and at 0951, Ward raised the scope to find the carrier had disappeared. In her place, however, was a heavy cruiser bearing down on him, and *Sailfish* went down for the next three and a half hours. When her periscope next poked the surface, no ships could be seen. Ward cleared the area and recorded, "One full day's work completed."

All was not so serene in the boiling ocean where *Chuyo* had disappeared. Captain Okura and 1,250 officers, men, and passengers went down with her. Rocek was sucked down in the vortex, then blown back to the surface in a rising bubble of air. Some of the prisoners survived the sinking. Rocek saw Ensign Smith and the mess cook, Maxiso Barrera, but the sea eliminated them one by one. The *Urakaze* bobbed in the ocean like a cork, rescuing the Japanese survivors. Rocek floated on a raft with some Japanese for four hours before the destroyer came by again. He grabbed for a line hanging over the side, but a Japanese officer stepped on him, forcing him underwater. When he came to the surface he managed to grab the line and was pulled to the deck. He fell face downward and was left there, mistaken for a *Chuyo* crew member. When it was discovered he was an American, some destroyer crewmen hoisted him up and carried him aft to throw him into the ocean before they were ordered to desist. Rocek was placed in a tiny compartment off the main deck. *Urakaze* had rescued 160 Japanese crewmen and 1 American submariner.

Rocek shivered in his locker all day, unattended, until a sailor, cautioning him to keep quiet, handed him a few crackers to eat. Rocek was so dehydrated, he couldn't work up any saliva to eat them. His next visitor was a drunken petty officer, who "yelled and laughed and then slugged the hell out of me with both hands." Rocek's tormentor returned every half hour to repeat the routine. When they pulled into Yokohama, Rocek was tied up and blindfolded and taken to Ofuna Camp, where he was placed with the twenty *Sculpin* prisoners who had been on *Unyo*. The camp was a repository for many captured U.S. submariners. There were men from *Perch*, many of *Grenadier*'s crew, and two survivors from S-44, which was sunk in the Kuriles in October. Rocek was the only surviving prisoner from *Chuyo*. The *Sailfish* had killed half of *Sculpin*'s survivors. Ultra information and a persistent submarine attack had finally resulted in the sinking of a Japanese capital ship, but the attack

showed that intelligence gleaned from intercepted messages could be a double-edged sword.[43]

1943 CURRENTS

In December 1943, many of the remaining Canadians were removed from
Hong Kong. Compared with other camps, those in Hong Kong were not bad.
With the exception of Lt. Col. J. L. R. Sutcliffe, commander of the Winnepeg
Grenadiers, all the Canadian officers survived the war. On 15 December, 504
prisoners were taken from Shamshuipo Camp to embark on SS *Soong Cheong*.
The ship was carrying a scrap-iron ballast. It had been overhauled by the
Chinese in Kowloon, but other than emptying the forward and aft holds, there
were no preparations made to accommodate passengers.

A member of the Hong Kong Volunteer Defense Corps, Gunner V. G. H.
Upton, climbed aboard and immediately saw that the galley was filthy. There
was one steam boiler with which to heat water for tea or cook rice and vegetables. First the rusty, grimy boiler had to be scraped and cleaned, but the
men had no tools. They volunteered to wipe it clean with their own clothes.
There was neither room to stretch fully out nor to lay fully flat without over-
lapping legs across shoulders.

All lights were turned off from sunset to sunrise, and visits to the latrine
had to be made by crawling through the dark on all fours. It was impossible
to sleep, and the ship was so small and rolled so badly in the heavy seas that
seasickness was rampant. Soon, the decks and prisoners were soaked with
vomit. The thoroughness of the overhaul *Soong Cheong* had received was
quickly evident. Said Upton, "Water spurted through the sides each time she
rolled and poured in from the leaky decks overhead. The Chinese had just put
red lead and paint over huge cracks and holes and fear was added to other discomforts. We had to bail every half hour to lay down for half an hour." They
hoped they wouldn't simply break apart and sink.

To add to the prisoners' woes, interpreter Niimori was back. The man who
had made the British prisoners' lives a hell on the *Lisbon Maru* was also in
charge of this contingent. Before sailing, Niimori had participated in the beating and torture of two Canadian hospital patients, A. Archibald and J. T. F.
Murray, all for the alleged theft of some personal belongings. They were hung
from their wrists for hours, their toes barely touching the floor, savagely
beaten across their backs, and starved for four days.

It took five days to get to Formosa, where *Soong Cheong*'s engines finally quit. They chugged into Takao on 20 December and were transferred to *Toyama Maru*, a 7,089-ton, Army-controlled cargo ship built by Mitsubishi in 1915. Although nearly destitute to start with, the hungry prisoners began selling their clothes and personal belongings to the crew in exchange for an increase in the rice ration, which only amounted to about two hundred grams a day per man. The *Toyama Maru* sailed away carrying a cargo of prisoners and ammunition.

On 1 January 1944, they anchored in Beal Harbor, near Shanghai, where the prisoners were ordered off the ship to parade on the wharf so the Japanese could see their winter clothes. They were supposed to hand the POWs over to the authorities in Japan, complete with all the clothes they had been issued in Hong Kong. When it was discovered that some of the men had sold their clothes for food, Niimori and a Sergeant Kato flew into a rage, beating many of the culprits. A Canadian named Peter Doucett was singled out and attacked so savagely that he later died. His rage over, Niimori seemed to calm down, and *Toyama Maru* continued on to Moji, where it unloaded on 5 January. About two hundred men, including Upton, were ferried across to Honshu, where they were sent to Narumi Camp. Some of them were in such bad shape they were finally "hospitalized" at a medical center run, incredibly, by a lowly Japanese soldier. Private Asakura was not overly concerned about his patients' health. While the men deteriorated from vitamin deficiencies, Asakura distinguished himself by sucking off all the sugar coating from the vitamin tablets supplied by the Red Cross then spitting what remained of the tablets into the stove.[44]

There were few territorial gains for the Allies in the Pacific in 1943, in spite of many hard-fought battles, including land campaigns on New Georgia and Bougainville and many clashes at sea. Little by little, islands in the Solomons were recaptured on the road to Rabaul, but Operation Cartwheel, the drive against New Britain, was a protracted and costly endeavor. From the capture of Guadalcanal to the invasion of Bougainville, ten months had elapsed, and the Allies were only four hundred miles closer to Japan, with three thousand miles to go.

A two-pronged advance, one of the routes to cross the central Pacific, was decided upon. MacArthur was opposed to the plan, for his line of advance, through New Guinea to the Philippines, would be a secondary show. His pride was at stake. He had made promises to the people of the Philippines and to his former Army, now all prisoners of war, that he would return. Nevertheless, it was finally decided that both lines of advance would be followed. Bougainville was invaded in November 1943, and so were the Gilbert Islands, in Admiral Nimitz's first major central Pacific offensive. Both campaigns were bloody affairs. If there was to be any swifter progress in 1944, many Japanese bases would have to be bypassed.

At the end of 1943 Japan had one million tons less shipping than at the end of 1942. There were fewer hellship voyages in 1943. For the most part, the captive work forces were employed where they were needed. Whereas the majority of shipments in 1942 were on a north-south axis, the voyages of 1943 were split about evenly between north-south and east-west. There were about the same number of trips to the empire as there were among the islands of the East Indies or between Malaya and Borneo. Once again, the Japanese shifted prisoners on a contingency basis, without much apparent planning. Enlisted men, officers, and civilians were moved up and down the Borneo coast from Kuching to Jesselton, Labuan, Sandakan, and back. Prisoners and native laborers were removed from Ceram, Ambon, and Timor to Java and Singapore, and later returned to Ceram, Ambon, and Haruku.

Again, there were losses. The *Moji Maru* and *Nichimei Maru* were bombed, and the latter was sunk. *Suez Maru* was torpedoed with a loss of POWs, as was the escort carrier *Chuyo*. However, 1943 was not as disastrous to captives at sea as was 1942.[45] About forty-one hellships plied the ocean, carrying approximately 23,343 prisoners—down by thirteen ships and more than 26,000 men. The average voyage took 9.8 days, not significantly different from 1942. There were 964 deaths, about 1,266 fewer than the year before. The death rate was 4.1 percent. Had anyone been keeping statistics, he might have concluded that things were looking brighter for transported prisoners. It was not to be. As the situation deteriorated for the Japanese, so it did for the prisoners. Nineteen forty-four would be Hell Year.

1944

FLEEING FROM THE ALLIES

As the new year began, Japanese soldiers, sailors, and civilians, as well as prisoners of war, were forced to pay a higher price for increased U.S. submarine efficiency. The *Ikoma Maru,* a 3,156-ton transport owned by the NYK Line, had made several trips between Kyushu, Palau, and New Guinea. It was in Hollandia, New Guinea, on 8 January, and sailed back to Palau, arriving on the thirteenth. On the twentieth the *Ikoma Maru, Yasukuni Maru,* subchaser 32, and auxiliary subchaser 47 were heading back to New Guinea in what was designated the No. 8 Wewak Convoy.

SEAS OF DEATH

The *Ikoma Maru* was carrying 611 men of an "Independent Brigade," along with gasoline, provisions, ammunition, and mail. This "brigade," in fact, was composed of former Indian soldiers who had been inducted into the Japanese Army against their wishes. Some had been working in the Palaus for the past six months since being carried there on *Thames Maru.*

The weather was bad, and *Seahorse,* plying the lanes south of Palau, was having a tough time maintaining efficient surface watch. Cdr. Slade D. Cutter, on his third patrol in *Seahorse,* was not unduly worried, however, for on 21 January, he received an Ultra: a convoy would be traveling from Palau through his area. Sure enough, shortly after noon, the *Seahorse* made contact, and Cutter called for an end around, to get in front of the convoy and wait. It was a long run, and several hours later approaching darkness made Cutter opt for a night surface attack. He hoped to get both ships at the same time. In the waning light, he could see crates piled high on the decks.

Both ships appeared to be zigzagging independently, so Cutter dropped the idea of a simultaneous attack. At 2137, at a distance of about twenty-eight hundred yards, he fired three torpedoes at the near freighter. The second ship was in line of bearing just to the left of the first, at thirty-six hundred yards. Two minutes after firing, an explosion thundered from the first freighter. The *Seahorse* was coming around to fire at the second ship, when, to everyone's surprise, the third torpedo, which had missed the near ship, slammed into the far one. Cutter had inadvertently hit both ships with one attack.

The *Ikoma Maru,* hit in the port engine room, slowed and took on water. *Seahorse*'s "miss" slammed into the 3,021-ton *Yasukuni Maru,* which sank in twenty minutes, taking with her sixty-eight men. On *Ikoma Maru,* damage control was making progress. Cutter pulled away to reload, this time firing four torpedoes, all of which missed. The fire control party realized that the bridge target bearing transmitter (TBT) was out of alignment by a few degrees. After adjustments to the TBT, Cutter fired two Mark 18 electrics from the stern tubes at 2324. While the *Seahorse* put on speed to clear the area, one fish struck *Ikoma Maru*'s number three hold, which contained gasoline, and the ship erupted in brilliant flames. *Ikoma Maru* lasted only two more minutes before its burst seams drank in enough seawater to send it down stern first.

The *Seahorse*'s crew was treated to a spectacular show on the nighttime sea as oil from the ship's bunkers blazed on the ocean surface and bobbing drums of gasoline cooked and exploded one by one. Cutter allowed all the below-deck men topside to see the results of their handiwork. The two subchasers hovered in the rough seas, picking up only Japanese survivors. Only when all the Japanese were safely aboard did the subchasers begin to pick up the Indians. Khudadah Khan, Mohammed Niwaz, Mir Ali, and Abdul Shah were among those rescued, and they, along with many others, were beaten by the Japanese, as if they were at fault for the attack. They would survive to name Captains Hamana and Inouye and Lieutenant Yamashita as their tormentors. It was slight compensation, though, for 43 crewmen and 418 Indian prisoners were killed or drowned.[1]

The waters of the Java Sea continued to be dangerous for Allied sailors and soldiers. Late in December 1943, the *Kunishima Maru,* a 4,083-ton freighter built in 1937, stopped at Ambon Island. As *Suez Maru* had done the month before, it picked up a number of prisoners who were too sick to work. Unescorted, it sailed to Kolaka, Celebes, where it loaded a cargo of nickel ore, then proceeded to Kabaena Island off the south coast of Celebes, where it was to rendezvous with the *Kyoko Maru*. There would be no meeting, however, for *Kyoko Maru*, a 5,800-ton vessel recently loaded with 7,500 tons of fuel oil at Ceram, was torpedoed off Kabaena on 27 December by the submarine *Ray*. When her erstwhile convoy mate went down, *Kunishima Maru* altered course and headed directly to Makassar, dropping off its patients. This group of POWs survived.

Another group of POWs traveling through the area in February 1944 would not be so lucky. The high death and sickness rates of POWs forced to work on Ambon and Haruku necessitated replacing them with "healthy" prisoners from Java. On 24 February, about thirty-five hundred laborers—the majority native Javanese, with a few hundred prisoners of war—were assembled in Surabaya to travel to Ambon on the 6,200-ton *Tango Maru*. Formerly the German ship *Rendsberg*, it was seized by the Dutch in Tanjong Priok in October 1940, renamed *Toendjoek,* and scuttled as a block ship in Tanjong Priok's harbor in March 1942. The Japanese raised it in August and renamed it *Tango Maru*. Joining the laborers were sixty-six hundred Japanese soldiers from various army units, packed even more tightly aboard the 4,805-ton cargo ship *Ryusei Maru*. The convoy pulled out, accompanied by minesweeper 8, minesweeper 11, and auxiliary subchaser *No. 5 Takunan Maru*.

On the day of sailing, two submarines in the area received Ultra messages. The *Raton,* under Lt. Cdr. James W. Davis, and *Rasher,* under Lt. Cdr. Willard R. Laughon, were directed to converge in the Bali Sea for a sweep of Rass Strait. A two-ship convoy was expected to enter the area between 1800 and 2000 on 25 February. Both boats coursed through Lombok Strait, and twenty miles north of Bali, heavy squalls blew in. Late in the afternoon they established voice radio contact, and during a break in the rain pulled side by side so that the two captains could decide on a rough search plan. They patrolled on nearly parallel courses, with *Rasher* about six miles north of *Raton*. At 1730, *Raton* had a radar contact and *Rasher* had a visual. Laughon turned away to pull ahead of the convoy's projected track and radioed to Davis his intentions.

The sun had set before Laughon drew his boat into position. The twilight and rough seas were ideal for a surface attack. One of the escorts had apparently dropped out of the convoy, because the two cargo ships were guarded by only

BURMA

Rangoon

Moulmein

Ye

Nichimei Maru
15 Jan. 43

Tavoy

THAILAND

Bangkok

Mergui

HAINAN

Yulin

INDO
CHINA

Phnom Penh

Saigon

South

China

Sea

Montevid
1 July

O

Victoria Pt.

Gulf of
Thailand

Andaman

Sea

Balaba

Penang

Jesselton

Harugiku Maru
25 June 44

Belawan

Medan

MALAYA

Kuala
Lumpur

Str. of Malacca

Brunei

Miri

Singapore

Kuching

BORNEO

SUMATRA

Pakanbaroe

Balikpapa

Padang

BANGKA

Muntok

Junyo Maru
18 Sept. 44

Palembang

Bandjarmasin

Java Sea

Suez Maru
29 Nov. 43

Tanjong Priok

KANGEAN

Sunda Str.

Batavia

Surabaya

JAVA

BALI

LON

Lombok Str.

Locations of sunken hellships in the southwestern Pacific.

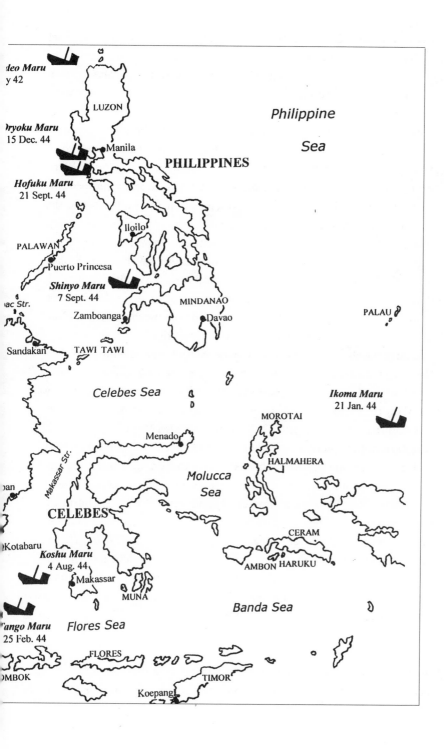

deo Maru
y 42

LUZON

Philippine

Sea

Oryoku Maru
15 Dec. 44

●Manila

PHILIPPINES

Hofuku Maru
21 Sept. 44

Iloilo●

PALAWAN

●Puerto Princesa

Shinyo Maru
7 Sept. 44

MINDANAO

ac Str.

Zamboanga●

Davao

PALAU

Sandakan●

TAWI TAWI

Celebes Sea

Ikoma Maru
21 Jan. 44

MOROTAI

Menado●

HALMAHERA

Makassar Str.

Molucca

Sea

an

CELEBES

CERAM

)Kotabaru

Koshu Maru
4 Aug. 44

AMBON HARUKU

●Makassar

MUNA

Banda Sea

'ango Maru
25 Feb. 44

Flores Sea

FLORES

)MBOK

TIMOR

Koepang●

two escorts. Because it was a captured ship, Laughon could not find the larger *Tango Maru* in his identification manual. Nevertheless, he very accurately estimated its tonnage at sixty-five hundred. The smaller ship, trailing about fifteen hundred yards on the starboard quarter, was so heavily laden that the Plimsoll line was below water. The two escorts looked ragged and badly in need of paint. The convoy was zigzagging, currently on course 135, speed about seven knots.

While plotting the attack, the port escort moved ahead of *Tango Maru*'s beam and pulled thirty-eight hundred yards ahead. With that opening, *Rasher* bored in one thousand yards astern of the escort and, at 1943, fired four torpedoes with a zero gyro angle, straight to the target about one thousand yards away. As the sub pulled away to reload, three torpedoes connected and ripped the maru apart. Laughon descended to the conning tower to watch the radar screen. The other ship and one escort were fleeing. The near escort made a sweep toward *Rasher,* then returned to assist the torpedoed ship. It was useless. Within five minutes of the torpedo hits, *Tango Maru* disappeared beneath the waves. Ten minutes later, three great underwater explosions were heard from the ship's boilers. More than three thousand native laborers and POWs were killed.

The large number of troops aboard *Ryusei Maru* were suddenly awakened to the dire predicament they were in. Submarines were out there, they were guarded by ineffective escorts, were overloaded, and were moving at slow speed. Only the rain squalls and poor visibility gave them temporary respite. It took *Rasher* another hour and a half to line up *Ryusei Maru*. The *Raton* was boring in from the opposite side, but she was troubled by the escort on that side. Again *Rasher* had the better shot. At 2127, Laughon fired four more torpedoes at the maru laboriously trying to steam away at 7.5 knots. Three of them walked along her length, bow, stack, and stern. Within six minutes, *Ryusei Maru* was gone. The *Rasher* hauled away into the darkness, and Laughon radioed Davis, apologizing for "hogging the show."[2]

Unknowingly, *Rasher* had eliminated 4,998 soldiers and crewmen. The two successive attacks, resulting in the deaths of about 8,000 people, may have been the highest casualty total at sea in history. Once again, Ultra and submarines proved to be a deadly combination.

ACTION IN THE INDIAN OCEAN

If Japan had its own Pearl Harbor, it was at Truk on 17 February 1944. U.S. carriers hit the atoll with a devastating blow, sinking about two hundred thousand tons of warships and merchant ships. Two light cruisers and four destroyers were lost, but luckily for the Japanese, they had just shifted the bulk of their fleet to bases farther west, including Singapore and Penang. Perhaps smarting from the inability to stop the Americans in the Pacific, they turned to try their luck in the Indian Ocean.

The 16th Squadron of the Southwest Area Fleet, consisting of the heavy cruisers *Aoba, Chikuma,* and *Tone,* set sail from Penang on 26 February under Vice Adm. Sakonju Naomasa. They rounded southern Sumatra through Sunda Strait and slipped into the Indian Ocean, where British forces were thinly spread. Orders were to capture enemy ships. Should it become necessary to sink a ship, prisoners could be taken, but "only the minimum needed for interrogation." No orders were given to take other survivors.

Sakonju's cruisers conducted a fruitless sweep about five hundred miles south of the Cocos Islands, and Sakonju was about to clear the area when, on 9 March, *Tone* spotted a ship on the horizon and moved in to investigate. It was the British-built 7,840-ton passenger-cargo ship *Behar* hauling a load of zinc from Australia to Bombay. The *Tone* closed and signaled for *Behar* to heave-to. When *Behar*'s wireless began sending out a distress signal instead, *Tone* opened fire with her 8-inch guns, blasting huge holes in her and sending her to the bottom in twenty minutes. Surprisingly, of the 111 persons aboard, only 3 failed to make it to the lifeboats. *Tone* steamed up close, a line of armed men at her rails, and her crew began hauling the survivors, including two women passengers, on deck, handling them roughly. CO William Phillips protested, receiving a beating with a bat for his efforts. They were taken below, tied, and stuffed into a small storeroom, where guards systematically beat them with bamboo batons.

After a time they were taken to a slightly larger room and untied, but they remained at close quarters in a place that felt like a sauna. For six days they were left in their box, given little food and water, and only allowed out twice a day to use the latrine hanging over the side of the ship. Finally, on 15 March, they reached land. The prisoners learned they were at Tanjong Priok, the port of Batavia, but they remained blissfully unaware that an argument was raging over their fate. *Tone*'s Capt. Mayazumi Haruo, a rare Japanese Christian, had been berated by Sakonju when the admiral learned of the sinking of *Behar.* Sakonju pointed out that they had orders to capture enemy ships, not sink them, and he grew angrier when he learned that Mayazumi had picked up 108 prisoners. Mayazumi apologized, then asked what he was supposed to do with the captives.

"Dispose of them," Sakonju ordered. Mayazumi signaled to Sakonju, who was on the *Aoba,* that he wished to land his prisoners on Java. "Dispose of the prisoners immediately," Sakonju ordered again. Yet when *Tone* reached anchorage, the captives were still alive.

Mayazumi took a launch to the *Aoba* and pleaded for the lives of the prisoners, but Sakonju was unmoved. Mayazumi returned to his ship, and that same morning, the selection was made. Capt. Maurice Symonds, Chief Officer Phillips, six other crewmen, twenty-one Indian ratings, and seven passengers, including the two women, were sent to the *Aoba,* where they were questioned and later placed in prison camps in Batavia. The *Tone* pulled out to sea. That evening, Mayazumi instructed his executive, Commander Mii, to execute the prisoners. Mii refused. Mayazumi then issued direct orders for Lieutenants Ishihara, Tani, and others to carry out the executions. The seventy-two captives were lined up on the deck and butchered like animals. First they were felled with a blow to the stomach, then beheaded. It took some time to wash the blood out through the scuppers into the Java Sea.[3]

TO BUILD ANOTHER RAILROAD

There were two small prisoner shipments out of the Philippines in March 1944.The first resulted from a need for medical personnel to care for the thousands of ill POWs in Japan. Realizing that sick or dead captives would not help the war effort, the Japanese initiated a draft for doctors and dentists from Cabanatuan and Bilibid. Lt. Stanley W. Smith, a dentist in the Naval Medical Corps had strong thoughts about the call: "No one in his right mind wanted to be included." They had heard rumors about camps in Japan and Manchuria, and although the Philippine camps were no picnic, they didn't want to freeze to death in the north either. Besides, moving north would put them farther from the Allied troops they hoped would arrive. Those selected spent the next weeks preparing for the northern winter by buying or bartering for whatever warm clothing or extra food they could get.

Forty medical doctors, 10 dentists, and 150 enlisted medical corpsmen left Cabanatuan for Bilibid. During the trip to Manila and the stay at Bilibid, the captives received more food than they were accustomed to: bananas, peanuts, fish, and coconuts. When they finally went to the docks on 6 March, they found "an old, ratty-looking tramp merchantman." *Kenwa Maru* had just arrived the day before from Halmahera in the Moluccas. Hurriedly, 378 Japanese civilians went into the forward part of the ship, while the 200 medical personnel went down a ladder into a quadrangle lined with two-tiered bays about six feet wide and four feet high.

To keep up with the rest of the convoy, the freighter took on no other cargo and thus rode high in the water. The rolling and pitching of the light ship made almost everyone seasick. Lt. John R. Bumgarner of the Fifth Medical Battalion, counted twelve other ships and a cruiser escort. After they got underway, he became concerned about being torpedoed. There was no possible way that two hundred men could climb one ladder and get out in time if the hold was flooding fast. Lieutenant Smith prayed that Allied planes and submarines would not find them. "A gnawing feeling of uncertainty gripped us," he said, "overshadowing any optimistic outlook we were sharing with each other down in the ship's black, foul-smelling hold."

On the way to Formosa there was a submarine alarm, and the hatch above them was slammed shut, leaving them for what seemed like an eternity in the pitch darkness, while depth charges boomed in the distance. When the hatch cover was thrown back, the Japanese claimed it was only an exercise, yet one of the other freighters seemed to be missing. Bumgarner spent the night slapping away rats that scurried across his face. He was somewhat mollified knowing that accommodations were not much better for the Japanese civilians, who were leaving the Philippines by any means possible. Some of the American doctors were called upon to treat sick Japanese children, using American Red Cross medicines.

Bad weather and low visibility hindered further submarine attacks, and one week's travel brought them to Takao. The *Kenwa Maru* was loaded with hundreds of bags of sugar. One dark night the resourceful and hungry prisoners found a small trap door into a forward hold, where they were able to squeeze through and load up every available pocket, sock, or mess kit with as much of the sweet cargo as possible. By slitting open only the corners of the sacks and pouring out a small portion from each, none of the Japanese were ever any wiser. The captives gorged themselves on as much unrefined sugar as their constitution would allow. Later, Lieutenant Smith would call the freighter the "sugar ship."

The voyage resumed on 15 March, this time with Convoy TAMO-11, consisting of twenty-two ships and five escorts. They carried oil, rice, ore, bauxite, and miscellaneous cargo. Three ships carried sugar and seven carried passengers. Thankfully for all the nineteen hundred civilians aboard, the convoy made its way safely to Moji, where it docked on 22 March.[4]

On the same day *Kenwa Maru* was sailing from Luzon, 188 Army, 80 Navy, and 40 Marine POWs were leaving Cabanatuan for Manila. They spent more than two weeks in Bilibid Prison, where, to everyone's surprise, they received new blue uniforms. "Rather unusual," said 4th Marine George B. Nelson. The 308 Americans looked rather swank on 24 March as they boarded *Taikoku Maru*, a 2,633-ton steamer heading for Japan. Their uniforms were soon filthy as they went in a forty-by-sixty-foot hold filled with ore to within eight feet of the top. Aside from being crowded, however, the extremely harsh treatment of many other voyages was absent.

"I have never considered the *Taikoku Maru* a 'hellship,'" said 4th Marine Martin Christie. "It was not a pleasure cruise by any means, [but] we lost no personnel to sickness or disease during the voyage." Nelson too, thought that the journey "was one of the better trips to Japan, if there was such a trip." Another 4th Marine, Woodrow W. Bennie, was not so sanguine. He complained about using toilets fastened outboard of the hull, because when the waves splashed in the rough weather, a man would get a bath at the same time. The cooking was done on the fantail in a cast-iron barrel, and when it rained, which was often, the rice would only get partially cooked, giving the men more stomach ailments. Said Bennie, "Imagine three hundred men in one hold, with one ladder out—three hundred men with the shits!"

Taikoku Maru made a speedy dash across Luzon Strait, reaching Formosa on 27 March. There, a trough with running water was installed on deck to facilitate the men's toileting. They remained in Takao's harbor for six days. A few kind Japanese officers invited some of the Americans on deck and saw that they were fed bananas and canned fruit. They were unhappy about the war situation, but thought it made sense to treat their captives well. *Taikoku Maru* left Takao in Convoy TAMO 15 on 2 April, with five other marus, escorted by CDV *Kurahashi*. As they went north the weather got rougher, and Woodrow Bennie gave up trying to keep his diary. They reached Moji on 8 April, and Osaka on the tenth, Easter Sunday. There they boarded trains for the copper mines at Hitachi.[5]

Laborers were streaming into Japan from places other than Southeast Asia and the Philippines. There was a never-ending demand for workers in a land where production had always been labor-intensive. As battle casualties mounted and supply lines were severed, the use of foreigners or prisoners could free up more Japanese for the front lines and ease the civilian workload at home. For that purpose, many Chinese and Koreans had been brought to Japan, where they were worked hard and treated with contempt. Seven hundred Chinese from the Peking Internment Camp were selected to sail to Japan to work for the Hazama Company. The first consignment of four hundred were assembled in Tangku on 20 April, where they boarded *No. 6 Kotobuki Maru*. The Shipping Board duly made out the paperwork, assigned lodging, issued work certificates, arranged railway transportation, and made ship bookings—all the trappings of a legal, contracted work crew. The remaining three hundred Chinese followed on a second ship, and another Japanese business had been subsidized with free foreign labor.[6]

Until this time, Sumatra had not seen much prisoner traffic. The Dutch were the largest group to surrender there, the other Allied units being air crews, sailors, or scattered ground units trapped at the surrender or caught trying to escape to Ceylon or Australia. Many had gotten to Padang on the south coast, where they were finally rounded up by the Japanese. Some captives were sent north to Burma via Medan in 1942. The remainder were imprisoned in northern Sumatra, where they languished for nearly two years. In 1944, conditions became markedly harsher when they were trucked back to central Sumatra to begin laying a narrow-gauge railway across the island. The 140-mile line was planned to connect Muara, which linked with Padang on the south coast, to Pakanbaroe, near the Kampar River, which led to the north coast. The rails would cut off much dangerous sea traffic around the west end of Sumatra, which was within striking distance of Allied aircraft based in Ceylon and India. As with the Burma Railway, the idea of constructing a cross-Sumatra track was researched by the Dutch but abandoned as impractical. The Japanese thought a line would expedite coal shipments from Sawahloento in the south, cross-country to the north coast, then by water to Singapore. Once again, construction was haphazard and amateurish, with tracks built on poor foundations in swampy soil, and with bridges of insufficient strength to withstand flash floods.

Prisoners and internees from Sumatra began the project, but as usual, manpower demands were greater than could be supplied locally. Lolke Talsma was in the KNIL when Java surrendered and spent time in camps in Bandung, Tjilatjap, and Batavia. In May 1944, Talsma and a mixed group of Dutch and British prisoners, along with a handful of Americans, were gathered in Batavia for the trip to Sumatra. Some of the Americans had quite an experience getting to this point. They had been on the merchant ship SS *American Leader* when it was sunk by the German raider *Michel* west of the Cape of Good Hope on 10 September 1942. Already aboard were three Americans from the tanker SS *William F. Humphrey,* which the *Michel* had sunk on 16 July, and twenty-two British survivors from *Empire Dawn,* sunk two days later. In early October, the raider transferred the prisoners to the German supply vessel *Uckermarck,* which in turn took them to Batavia and turned them over to the Japanese in November. The *American Leader*'s captain, Haakon A. Pederson, was sent to Manchuria, but most of the merchant mariners remained on Java for a year or more.

On 19 May 1944, a contingent of 777 prisoners, including 18 *American Leader* mariners, went from Batavia to Singapore on a small coastal steamer for eventual shipment to Japan. Five days earlier another party had left Batavia for work on the railroad in Sumatra. The small *Chuka Maru* carried about 1,200 prisoners, with 6 more of the *American Leader*'s crew, including 3d Officer George W. Duffy. Also boarding was Lolke Talsma, who was forced down into a coal bin, "loaded in like sardines in a can." For two days they sat with knees pulled up under their chins. The sick were never able to get out to use the latrines. There was no food, and only a sip or two of brackish water was allowed. Men became black with sweat and coal dust. Some, said Talsma, "went stark crazy," and several died.

Chuka Maru arrived at Padang on 17 May. When the prisoners stepped off the ship they were greeted with a tropical rainstorm; they cheered, opened their mouths to catch the fresh water, and washed themselves clean. They could face the rest of the trip with more courage. Trucked to Muara, they were then distributed among fourteen camps along the proposed railroad line, and joined the others already at work. They were placed in units, each with a special task: rail carriers, sleeper carriers, rail joiners, hammer men, repair men, and even tea brewers to try to prevent dehydration.

Australian Frank Robinson said that he and his countrymen knew more about felling trees and squaring timbers for bridges and sleepers. While they did the cutting, said Robinson, the "poor old Englishmen and the Dutchmen were used more or less as animals to pull logs into position on the bridge." Talsma thought the worst part was trudging through swamp and jungle, carrying steel rails on his shoulders. However, much of the heaviest work went to the Javanese *romusha,* who had been lured out of their villages with promises of good paying jobs.

As sections of rail were completed, the Japanese sent locomotives along to test the track's durability. One engine crept out along a dike built over a swamp when the rain-softened embankment gave way and the engine nose-dived deep into the muck. The workers burst out laughing, which drove the Japanese wild. They were beaten until the guards were hot and tired, and for extra punishment they were made to stand out in the sun for two days. Many collapsed, and some died. Said Talsma, "Such incidents were commonplace and a terror to think back on." Several small and large prisoner shipments over land and sea followed, bringing in more than six thousand POWs and thirty thousand *romusha* to work on the railway. Talsma called the track "the death railroad of Pakan Baru." More than seven hundred Allied prisoners and perhaps twenty thousand or more *romusha* died building it. It was all for no purpose, for the railroad was never used.[7]

Work on the Burma Railway left an indelible mark on tens of thousands of Allied captives and native laborers. In Thailand, F Force suffered most, losing 33 percent of its original strength, while H Force lost 20 percent. The death rate was not as bad in Burma, with the small Branch Party Five losing about 21 percent and the large A Force, on the job the longest, losing 13 percent. The survivors of F and H Forces were moved back to Singapore by December 1943, with the exception of seven hundred sick, who were left in hospitals in Kanchanaburi. The other parties slowly moved out of Burma and down the rails to camps at Chungkai, Tamarkan, Tamuang, and Non Pladuk. Food and medicine were more readily available at these camps, and the hungry and dying prisoners viewed the supplies as manna from heaven. For the cynical however, the suddenly available shelters, swimming facilities, and well-stocked kitchens meant that the Japanese were up to something. Were these simply fattening pens, prior to more work details?

Regardless, December 1943 to the spring of 1944 were some of the "best" days for the POWs remaining in Indochina. Men recovered from illness, put on weight, and optimistically began to think that they just might survive the war. In March 1944, Ken Williams was sent east. At 105 Kilo Camp the men were given clean clothes and fruit and were forced to sing for what Williams called "a propaganda farce." The Japanese filmed them, whistling while they worked. But as the cameras rolled, the defiant Aussies sang what Williams called "an unprintable parody of 'Bless 'em All.'" When the Japanese learned what was being sung, they beat the men and forced them to sing the more recognizable "Tipperary." Williams found his time spent at Kanchanaburi was actually idyllic compared to what he had been through.

The manpower shortage in Japan was so acute that the military was granting conscription deferments for many workers, and the domestic labor force was to be supplemented with 381,000 Koreans, a number of university students, and even middle-school pupils. Furthermore, with the war situation deteriorating, the Japanese thought it would be smart to hold POWs in Japan as bargaining chips. Another ten thousand prisoners were ordered to Japan.

In Chungkai in March, recruiting began for the first group of 750 men. In April, Ken Williams was drafted into a Japan Party and sent to Saigon for eventual shipment to the empire. In Tamuang in May, F. W. G. Power, a sapper in 2/12 Field Company RAE, heard the rumor that men were being selected to dig a canal across the Isthmus of Kra, the narrow neck of the Malay Peninsula. He decided he would get a better deal by going to Japan. The parties were given "new" clothing—a ragtag assortment of multicolored shirts and shorts, straw hats, and rubber shoes. Catcalls likened them to a "women's army" as they marched to the trains that would carry them to Singapore. Nevertheless, the first parties left their camps somewhat optimistically in the spring of 1944, traveling along the same railway they helped build. The Britons, who played a major role in building the famous Kwai bridge near Kanchanaburi, left their camp as defiantly as they had arrived. After much bowing and official ceremony, they marched off, singing the insultingly obscene words of Colonel Bogey's March to the uncomprehending Japanese.[8]

JAPAN PARTY ONE

JICPOA knew something big was in the offing, for it had been intercepting Japanese radio messages since April about upcoming POW shipments to Japan. There were messages about sending prisoners via NYK Line ships, with cautions that there should be no contingents of more than 300 prisoners per ship. A 7 April message from Kanchanaburi indicated that there were 42,840 prisoners on hand but 23,350 of them were ill. An intercept on 10 May complained that it was impossible to get good coolies to load ships. A 16 May intercept indicated that 10,000 prisoners would be sailing north, with discussion about the efficacy of shipping some from Singapore and others from Saigon. "You see," read the message, "we can use prisoners who are being loaded at Saigon for stevedoring while they are waiting to embark." The initial idea was to send 3,000 prisoners from Saigon and 7,000 from Singapore, but in the end it was decided that all should sail from Singapore. On 17 May a message said that the first 2,000 prisoners would embark from Singapore during the last ten days of May. The intercept concluded, "Furthermore, foodstuffs, approximately three months rations, for their consumption en route will be taken along without fail." As usual the timetable was not kept, for Kanchanaburi radioed that 2,000 captives would not be ready until 31 May.

While these preparations were being made, the ships that were to compose Convoy HO-02 formed in Singapore's Keppel Harbor. It was a very large convoy: about nineteen ships and five escorts. The 777-man contingent that had arrived on 22 May from Batavia had waited in River Valley Road Camp for almost two weeks, losing several men to illnesses. The night before loading, a friendly Korean guard named Minni San smuggled five Aussie officers out of the camp for a night of brandy drinking. Suffering tremendous hangovers, they just made it back to camp before marching to the docks. Crammed aboard *Miyo Maru*, bound for Osaka, were 267 Aussies from 2/2 Pioneers, 2/3 Machine Gun Battalion, and 2/40 Battalion; 190 Brits; 266 Dutch POWs; 18 *American Leader* seamen; and 25 men of the 131st Field Artillery who had missed the earlier journey to Burma. About 450 more POWs boarded *Hiyoki Maru*, which was also loaded with bauxite. The 5,494-ton *Kokusei Maru* carried bauxite and 456 prisoners, and the *Hozan Maru* carried 451 prisoners. Other ships included the *Shonan Maru*, with a load of bauxite, *Seishin Maru*, with aviation gasoline for Manila, *Celebes Maru*, also with aviation gasoline, and the *Teihoku Maru*, *Nichiwa Maru*, *Nasusan Maru*, *Tainan Maru*, *Kennichi Maru*, *No.* 1 *Konan Maru*, and *Tamahoko Maru*. Escorts were CDVs 1, 8, 15, and 20, and CM *Wakataka*.[9]

Besides knowing the convoy's composition and cargo, Allied intelligence was privy to the convoy's daily noontime positions as it traversed the South China Sea from Singapore to Manila. HO-02 sailed on 3 June. The next day, another intercept gave details of the convoy's composition. The decoder added his own comments to the message, repeating that HO-02 consisted of eleven or more ships, "several carrying American prisoners." On 6 June, the first sub-marine contact came about two hundred miles southeast of Cape St. Jacques. The *Raton,* on her fourth patrol, put two torpedoes into CDV 15. The explo-sion snapped the eight-hundred-ton escort in two, killing 104 crewmen. All the prisoners were battened down below decks until the danger had passed. While the convoy hurried on, CDVs 8 and 20 remained behind to rescue 34 survivors. On the seventh, yet another intercept indicated that HO-02 carried 900 or more prisoners. Although the convoy's itinerary was known, no other submarines managed to make an attack, and it reached Manila on 11 June.

Convoy HO-02 spent the next three days in Manila while the 6,780-ton *Tamahoko Maru* loaded 7,500 tons of copper ore. When it sailed on the four-teenth, several ships had left the convoy's ranks. One day out, said Aussie Norm Segal on *Miyo Maru,* they "ran slap-bang into a typhoon." The pris-oners were battened below as waves thirty feet high crashed over the decks. The cold water cascading on the decks above made the hot atmosphere in the holds condense and fall back on them like rain. No one could get out to use the *benjos,* which in any case had been washed away, so they relieved them-selves where they sat. One of the engines broke down and the outside cook-house also washed overboard. No one ate for four days until they struggled into Takao.

The *Miyo Maru* was a wreck. While the other prisoner-bearing ships in the convoy continued, taking their bauxite and human cargo safely to Japan, *Miyo Maru* would have to be offloaded. Even with its copper ore, *Tamahoko Maru* had the most remaining space, so on the eighteenth, the prisoners were trans-ferred to her. They were given two holds to spread out in, and living conditions were much more bearable. In addition, there was a small consignment of sugar in one of the lower holds. Thanks to a sympathetic Formosan, the hatch was left unlocked, and the prisoners stole and ate all the sugar they could.

The remaining six ships of HO-02, accompanied by numerous escorts, left Takao on 20 June, called at Keelung on the twenty-first, and headed north across the East China Sea. As they neared Kyushu, the guards celebrated their deliverance from harm, drinking, singing, and telling the prisoners, "Tomorrow, I'll be home."[10]

So often do such words set the stage for a tragedy. On the night of 24 June, the *Tang* eased ahead at five knots, waiting for an approaching radar contact

SYUNKO MARU.
TAMAHOKO MARU.
TYOKO MARU.
YAE MARU.
YURI MARU.

Gross tonnage: 6,780.

Length: (w. l.) 425'.

Beam: 53½'.

Draft: (loaded) 28⅜' (light) 8⅜'.

Speeds:
Normal cruising—10 knots.
Maximum—12½ knots.

Built: 1919–20.

Machinery: Reciprocating, single screw, 555–580 NHP.

Fuel:
Type—coal.*
Capacity—2,300 tons.*

Radius: 15,000 miles at 10 knots.

Complement: (crew) 60 (pass.) 2.

Owners:
**See "Remarks".

Potential naval value: AP, AK.

Remarks:
*The TYOKO is fitted for fuel oil and has a bunker capacity of 1,570 tons and a deep tank capacity of 936 tons.
**YURI, YAE—Kokusai Kisenō Kaisha, TYOKO, TAMAHOKO—Yamashita Kisen K. K. SYUNKO—Osaka Syosen Kaisha.

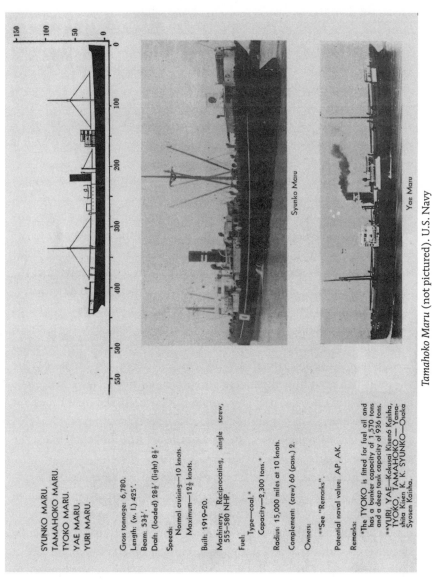

Syunko Maru

Yae Maru

Tamahoko Maru (not pictured). U.S. Navy

at twenty thousand yards. It was an Ultra that brought *Tang* to the spot, not far from the lights of Nagasaki. Intelligence had tracked the convoy's progress up from Singapore. On 19 June it picked up another message from Takao, which, the decoders noted, "is probably the schedule for the HO-02 Convoy from that point north to Moji." Also tacked to the bottom of the intercept were the words, "The Convoy appears to consist of 11 ships, several of them carrying American prisoners." Despite this knowledge, submarines were sent toward the approaching targets.

The *Tinosa* and *Sealion II* also waited, at thirty-mile intervals to the west, but *Tang*'s skipper, Cdr. Richard H. O'Kane, wanted the position closest inshore. "The Japanese had to run ships up this coast to Nagasaki or call it quits," he figured. And here they were.

"A mess of ships," came the word from the conning tower. The convoy was zigzagging on a base course of 340, speed twelve knots. As O'Kane bored in, he saw six ships in two columns, surrounded by what he figured to be two circles of escorts. The *Tang* sneaked across the stern of the leading port escort of the outer circle, paralleled the convoy's course for a time, then cut inside the inner circle, between two other escorts. She slid across the stern of the convoy, and turned, trailing in its wake. The submariners held their breath as their boat steamed between the two rear escorts, both about twelve hundred yards off either beam. If she remained undetected, *Tang,* at sixteen knots, would slowly pull ahead of the escorts and catch up to the convoy. They had been in taut situations before, said O'Kane, "but never before in one where all words had been in whispers for nearly two hours." It was a dangerous maneuver, and one that probably would not have worked nine times out of ten. However, an aggressive, skillful, and lucky submarine captain, plus perhaps a lack of vigilance on the part of the escorts' lookouts, made the approach successful.

Finally, dead ahead were the fat sterns of six ships. O'Kane decided to target the two largest ships in the port column, but a heretofore unnoticed patrol boat in that sector caused him to head to starboard to target the right-hand column from shoreward. The convoy commander had conveniently steadied on course zero and slowed to ten knots, apparently feeling safe in the home stretch. Close in, the ships became clearer; the trailer appeared to be an engine-aft tanker or freighter, while the next ship ahead was a large four-mast freighter with a high composite superstructure. O'Kane readied all six bow tubes. Just minutes before midnight, three torpedoes were fired to walk along the length of the trailing ship, and a spread of three more were fired at the leader. *Tang* put all four engines on full speed and cleared out, while the submariners counted down the torpedo run of one minute and forty eight seconds.[11]

Lt. Lance Gibson of 2/3 Battalion was sleeping in the forward hold when he heard an explosion. He reached for his shorts and shirt, but a tremendous blast knocked him back to the deck. Next to him, Maj. John D. Morris hesitated momentarily, then tried to put on his clothes. Gibson never saw him again. That quickly, said Gibson, "the water just came in and we were knocking against the top of the hold." The hatch cover had been blown off, and he kicked along the roof, desperately trying to reach the opening. Sgt. Jim Barnes, in the RAAF, was also in the number one hold. He tried to reach the coaming at the hold's edge but was not tall enough. Within seconds, the water rose and floated him out, only to entangle him with the cables and winches. Barnes had slept on the hatch covers on deck every night on *Miyo Maru,* but he decided to sleep below on *Tamahoko Maru.* His friends slept on the hatch covers and were blown over the side.

One torpedo hit directly under the forward hatch; the second hit midships. Gunner Allan Pollock was topside when he saw a vivid orange flash. The concussion sent him through the air and right back into the hold. Just as quickly the rising water flushed him back out again. Sgt. Peter McGrath-Kerr of 2/40 Battalion was roused by an explosion of a ship in the starboard column. Some men ran to that side in time to see a torpedo track approaching. McGrath-Kerr only remembered the one great explosion as the torpedo hit directly beneath the bridge. He saw men on a hatch cover blown into the air, flying either into the ocean or back into the hold. "Down in the hold, there was pandemonium," he said. "Where the explosion had smashed the side of the ship men sleeping there had been killed, including most of the Japanese guards. Water poured into the hold and in a little over a minute after the explosion the ship went down, carrying hundreds of men with her."

Lieutenant Gibson thought he was going down but struggled with all his might and finally popped to the surface, terribly sick from all the water he had swallowed. Three ships had been torpedoed, and a fourth one blew up as he paddled in the darkness looking for something to hold on to. He found a part of the bridge superstructure and joined a number of Dutch prisoners on it. Pollock was luckier. He came up out of the water right next to an empty raft, which he climbed aboard and had all to himself for the next twelve hours. Pvt. William C. Atkinson of 2/40 Battalion found a raft with seven prisoners and one Japanese crewman hanging on to it. Atkinson wanted to drown him, but the others dissuaded him. "The raft can't support any others," they said. "What happens if one our mates comes along? He'll have to go then." But no one else was found, and the lucky man survived.

A. E. Long thought it was about ten in the morning when the first Japanese vessels arrived to pick them up. They rescued thirty prisoners, but after half an hour, when it appeared there were still many Japanese soldiers and crewmen to pick up, they made the prisoners jump back overboard. Soldiers were picked up first, then women and children. One Aussie, thinking he would get rescued sooner, swam to a Japanese child on a raft and cradled her; he was one of the last to be rescued. Long was finally picked up by what he thought was a whaling ship. He could barely walk, and was greeted with a kick in the ribs for being too slow.

At first, no one was being picked up. Lieutenant Gibson saw men who grabbed for the boats getting booted back into the water. Gibson believed that when the friendly Korean interpreter Minni San was rescued, he talked the Japanese into saving the POWs. On the rescue ship, Gibson saw a young Japanese woman cradling a baby. When one of the Japanese sailors realized the baby was dead, "he took it from her and heaved it over."

The violence of the explosion, the rapid sinking, and the lack of life belts and rafts accounted for the loss of 560 out of the 772 POWs on *Tamahoko Maru*. Fifteen American soldiers and sailors were killed, as well as 13 merchant mariners from *American Leader*. Incredibly, *Tang*'s six torpedoes sank four ships, the two targeted and two more that were struck by the torpedoes that missed the first two. Down went the 4,399-ton *Nasusan Maru*, the 3,175-ton *Tainan Maru*, and the 1,937-ton *Kennichi Maru*. On the afternoon of 25 June, the 212 survivors of *Tamahoko Maru* entered Nagasaki's harbor. They were made to face inboard, as if they might see something of vital military importance in the bay. As they pulled up to the wharf, the prisoners and the decks were hosed down. One Japanese doctor and one nurse came aboard, but their only medicine was a bottle of mercurochrome. From there, the survivors were taken to Fukuoka 13, a Dutch camp in the middle of Nagasaki. There, in

August 1945, a number of them would face another big surprise, as the city became the target of the second atomic bomb.[12]

While HO-02 was sailing north, a single ship sailed from Singapore with two hundred Australians and three hundred Dutch, many of them survivors from D Force. Albert Drager, a twenty-one-year-old Dutch soldier who would emigrate to Canada after the war, had just come down from Non Pladuk, which he called a "rotten camp." Shipped by boxcar on 28 May, he reached Singapore and waited. On 5 June, they boarded *Teia Maru*, the ex-French *Aramis*, a 17,537-ton transport captured in Saigon in April 1942 and subsequently used for prisoner repatriation and ferrying Red Cross supplies. Although the ship still had French trimmings, there were no Folies Bergère floor shows or French chefs. The cuisine consisted of the standard two mugs of sticky rice per day and an occasional watery soup. Accommodations were also standard: men jammed aboard with the aid of rifle butts. Able to cruise at seventeen knots, *Teia Maru* sailed without escort and reached Moji on 19 June without incident.[13]

On the twenty-fifth, the same day *Tamahoko Maru*'s survivors were pulling into Nagasaki, a mixed force of 720 Dutch, British, and Australian prisoners, with 54 prison staff, boarded *Harugiku Maru*, formerly the 3,040-ton Dutch steamer SS *Van Waerwijck*, which was scuttled 3 March 1942 in Tanjong Priok but salvaged by the Japanese. The ship left Belawan, the port city of Medan, heading for Pakanbaroe with more workers for the Sumatra railroad. British officer Major Campbell was in charge of the prisoners, with the entire expedition under the command of Japanese lieutenant Doi. The POWs were forced into the holds by means of rope ladders, where there was standing room only, and the only latrine was a bucket being passed around. Late in the day, *Harugiku Maru* left Belawan and moved off shore.

The next morning, a convoy of two tankers and several cargo ships joined up and sailed through the narrow Malacca Strait. This confined area was dangerous to shipping, as well as to submarines, for the shallow water did not leave much space for a sub to hide in. It did, however, facilitate the laying of mines. On just such a mission that June was HMS *Truculent* on its fourth patrol, under Lt. Cdr. R. L. Alexander. On 24 June, *Truculent* had been near the Malayan shore, dodging junks and laying mines in Klang Strait. In midafternoon, she grounded in only thirty-two feet of water but managed to work herself free. "Screwed our way out of the mud," Alexander recorded. "It is regretted that having laid eggs it was thought fit to try and hatch them out!"

Having finished the operation, Alexander took his boat across Malacca Strait to the Sumatra side. At 0958 on 26 June, about one hundred miles southeast of Belawan, he sighted the smoke of a convoy guarded by a circling airplane. It was cloudy and the sea was calm and flat. As the convoy neared, Alexander counted three small ships of about fifteen hundred tons each and a larger ship of about four thousand tons. There were two subchasers and a minelayer as escorts. Alexander set his sights on the larger ship, a "two-deck old passenger type, painted light greenish gray" and looking "like a depot ship of some kind." At 1112 Alexander fired four torpedoes, and two minutes later he succinctly recorded: "Two hits. Consider target sunk."

Truculent turned away from the escorts only to hit the bottom mud at fifty-eight feet. It should have been the end. The subchasers sped overhead, dropping a string of six depth charges, but they were off the mark. The *Truculent* gunned the motor while two more very close charges near her stern "assisted the submarine on her way." Alexander slowly pulled away, barely below the surface of the sea, at only fifty feet. The charges knocked the asdic (sonar) out of commission for three-quarters of an hour. When repaired, the subchasers were still heard in the vicinity, but they seemed to be unable to zero in on the submarine, which was so shallow that an overhead pass might have scraped against the periscope shears. Alexander guessed that the chasers had no anti-submarine sound equipment. When he chanced to take a periscope look, he saw two planes and two subchasers, well astern. By 1300, *Truculent* had drawn clear to the north.

The two hits on *Harugiku Maru* were more than enough to do her in. She broke in two, her stern half lying on its side in the shallow water. The prisoners were quickly allowed out and over the side, and even though the ship went down in fifteen minutes, there was not a large loss of life, for the sea was calm and this time the Japanese were inclined to pick them up. Even so, Captain Miyasaki and Lieutenant Ishie were later accused by survivors of not having enough life-saving equipment and not providing treatment for the wounded. Thirty crew and civilian employees were killed, along with 180 POWs. The trip to Pakanbaroe was over. About 540 survivors were delivered to Singapore's River Valley Road Camp on 28 June, but their broken bones, burns, and other injuries prevented them from going to the Sumatra railroad.

Instead they would remain in Singapore, possibly to ship out with another party destined for Japan.[14]

While the need for laborers in Japan was the catalyst for the June prisoner shipments from Count Terauchi Hisaichi's Southern Command, the concern about approaching Allied forces was the catalyst for prisoner shifts in the Philippines. In May, the U.S. Army landed on Biak, off the western end of New Guinea and only eight hundred miles southeast of Mindanao. To prevent a possible recapture of the prisoners in Mindanao, they would have to be moved north, either back to Luzon or all the way to Japan.

Early in June 1944, the word was sent around Dapecol that the prisoners would be sent back to Luzon. Although Dapecol had been no picnic, the thought of more marching, a ship ride, and the starvation conditions at Cabanatuan was even less appealing. Nevertheless, on 6 June, the day the Allies stormed ashore in Normandy, France, the captives began their journey. After a big meal of rice, squash, sorghum, and a bit of carabao meat, they were jammed into trucks for the drive to the harbor at Lasang. To prevent any escapes, they had to remove their shoes, were blindfolded, and tied together with ropes secured to the sides of the trucks. The Japanese were not happy, for there had been too many escapes in the past. In April 1943, a group of ten, under Cdr. Melvin H. McCoy, successfully got away while on a work detail. In July, McCoy, Capt. Ed Dyess, and Maj. Steve Mellnik were taken by the submarine *Trout* to Australia. Their stories about prisoner treatment gave MacArthur all the more resolve to retake the Philippines. In October 1943, three more men escaped from a dike repair job after having split open the head of Japanese guard with an ax. In March 1944, another bloody escape attempt by eleven men resulted in the deaths of five guards, the recapture of three prisoners, and the eventual killing of two more. The attempts only served to make security tighter and punishments more severe for the others.[15]

About 1,240 prisoners were taken on barges out to the *Yashu Maru*, a small, "dirty, greasy cargo freighter." Carl Nordin, who had been on Mindanao since his capture, said they were all placed in the forward holds, where "it was as bad as the proverbial slave ships. Included were the sick, the paralytics, and the insane. Water was limited, many men had diarrhea, and there were few toilets. We were terribly crowded" and "it was as hot as hell." They suffered in the harbor for six days. The only high point came when they were issued the rest of the Red Cross parcels delivered by the *Gripsholm*.

The *Yashu Maru* finally left Davao Gulf on 12 June. About one thousand Japanese soldiers also boarded and were placed in the after well deck. The prisoners were watched by guards with machine guns and rifles. There were so many captives that they had to sleep in shifts, about one-third of them at a time rotating above and below. The convoy of two ships and two gunboats crossed Moro Gulf and anchored at Zamboanga, on the southwest tip of Mindanao, on 14 June. Shortly after midnight on the fifteenth, the prisoners topside heard a splash, then rifle shots. Lt. Col. John H. McGee had arranged for a friend to throw his barracks bag over the side. When the guards rushed to the spot and began shooting at the bag, McGee dove off the other side. He swam to shore and eventually joined the guerrillas.

The Japanese were furious. Everyone was forced into the holds and the hatches were battened down. It was hot and crowded, and, not knowing if the Japanese would take reprisals, the tension was unbearable. Nordin called it "a veritable nightmare." Lt. Donald H. Wills of the 26th Cavalry Scouts could take no more. He was sorry he did not join the escape attempt back in April 1943 and vowed he would also get away.

In the morning, the Japanese called for prisoners to help build a fence around the perimeter of the well deck, using six-foot wooden rafts for the barriers. Wills volunteered, and as he was working, he made his escape plans. There were places near the outboard *benjos* where the rafts wouldn't fit, and Wills piled up boxes in those spots to fill in the gaps. He noted that they made nice steps right to the top of the fence. That evening, Wills packed himself a survival kit, including a small knife, sulfa tablets, quinine, Atabrine, vitamins, a syringe, needles, compass, and chocolate bars. Meanwhile, *Yashu Maru* sailed north, slowly traveling up Mindanao's west coast. Wills figured that by nightfall they would pass the point where the coastline swings eastward, so he would have to make his attempt soon. Although he was a good swimmer, he hoped they would not be more than five miles from the shore when he made his jump.

Wills went topside just after sunset, ostensibly to use the *benjo*. It was raining, so the guards were bundled up and didn't appear alert. Wills asked one for permission to use the latrine in his best broken Japanese, and the guard answered in words he had picked up from the Americans: "Okay, okay." Wills passed him, and just before the *benjo,* he dashed to the boxes, rushed up to the top railing, and leapt. The guard screamed and lunged at him, but he was gone. Wills hit the water and went deep. When he came to the surface, bullets were slapping the water, and even a few grenades exploded behind him, but he was off the ship.

He swam around the stern and headed for shore, only to see the second ship in the convoy bearing down on him. More shots were fired, and two red flares went off, but Wills kept swimming. He discarded his clothes except for his underwear and his survival bag. Fighting thirst, cold, cramps, and exhaustion, he swam for about five hours, and when he finally touched a sandy bottom he was too weak to drag himself completely out of the surf. Eventually, Wills found friendly natives and joined the guerrillas, fighting with them until he reached U.S. forces on Leyte in April 1945.[16]

For this escape, beatings increased, and food and water rations were reduced. On 17 June, the prisoners arrived at Cebu City, disembarked, and marched to old Fort San Pedro. About a thousand men were crowded into a metal warehouse, while the rest were left outside in a wire stockade. After three days, they went back to the docks, where they worked loading the next ship that would take them to Manila. No one knew its name. Nordin believed it was an ex-German ship; its number was "824," and some of the men came to call it the *Singoto Maru, singoto* meaning "work" in Japanese.[17]

After working as stevedores, the prisoners climbed aboard, and the ship set sail on 21 June. The *Singoto Maru* had not been converted to carry passengers, with the usual wooden tiers built along the hull, and the crowding was worse than on *Yashu Maru.* Lt. M. L. Daman of the 12th Quartermaster Regiment said the "conditions aboard that ship were the worst you could possible think about—filth of all kinds. They didn't build latrines of any kind, and they didn't let us on deck at any time because earlier two men had escaped."

Some prisoners were found with matches—a serious offense—and for punishment they were fed only once that day. Capt. Russell Hutchison of the 200th Coast Artillery was frantic. He had parts of a radio secreted away in his kit, but the baggage was stored in a separate hold. He managed to find his kit, but looters had broken it open, stolen some food, and left the radio pieces lying about. With a little Yankee ingenuity, Hutchison hollowed out several bars of Red Cross soap, packed the parts inside, reformed the bars, and urinated on them to glue them together. The soap passed inspection.

It was a four-day trip to Manila, and conditions were the worst since they had left Davao. The rice ration was cut, and what little they had was lowered into the hold in buckets. One man, said Lieutenant Daman, went berserk. "He went stark raving mad. They finally had to chain him to a post there to keep him from hurting any of the other prisoners. Altogether, we lost fifty-six men, and they were simply lifted up to the main deck by ropes and then thrown over the side." On 24 June they docked at Pier Seven, the point from which most of them had departed on their trip to Mindanao eighteen months earlier. Some went to Bilibid Prison, others to Cabanatuan. Those at Bilibid would soon go back to the bay to board yet another hellship.[18]

SUBMARINE CONNECTION

During the Pacific war a unique connection developed between prisoners and the submarine force—a dichotomous relationship with the submariners either acting as killers or saviors. Submarines had been used for special missions since early in the war; they acted as lifeguards for aircraft carrier operations, laid mines, sent weather reports, evacuated civilians, did photoreconnaissance, supplied guerrillas, bombarded islands, landed special agents and coast watchers, and rescued prisoners. There were forty-three special missions in 1942, ninety-five in 1943, and ninety-nine in 1944.[19]

Submarines were intimately involved with the POW situation in Borneo. The Australian group that escaped from Sandakan in June 1943 went to Tawi Tawi and Mindanao. They connected with the guerrillas and passed on information about the prisoners at Sandakan. The result was Operation Python I. A party of six Australians with five thousand pounds of supplies and equipment were taken from Fremantle to Borneo on the *Kingfish*, and, on 6 October 1943, under Capt. F. G. Chester, they landed at Labian Point, about one hundred miles southeast of Sandakan, to establish observation posts along the coast from Sandakan to Tarakan. They were to coordinate efforts with Captain Hamner on Tawi Tawi and report Japanese activities, especially ship movements through the Sulu Archipelago. It was Hamner's group that was first reached by the escapees from Sandakan. These covert operations helped target Japanese tankers running through the area, but they were no help to the POWs at Sandakan. In fact, they were seen as a threat—one that finally resulted in a tragic denouement.

Chester's party successfully operated alone until January 1944, when Python II entered the picture. Agents under Maj. William Jinkins, who had escaped from

Ambon in 1942, were dropped off at Labian Point by *Tinosa*. From the start, everything began to go wrong. Sgt. W. Brandis got lost in the jungle and the natives reported him to the Japanese. He was captured and handed over to the Kempeitai. Under torture, Brandis revealed much about the Python operations. Soon after, Japanese patrols were hot on the trail of the agents, who were harassed constantly and kept moving between jungle hideouts. Sgt. Donald G. McKenzie and Lt. Alfred J. Rudwick were caught, and it was decided that the remaining men should be evacuated. In March, the survivors reached Tawi Tawi, where they met *Narwhal*, which had just been to Mindanao gathering up Sandakan escapees Major Steele, Walter Wallace, and Jim Kennedy. At Tawi Tawi, *Narwhal* took aboard the Python evacuees with Major Jinkins and Captain Hamner and headed for Australia. They painted a grim picture of Australian suffering in Japanese prisons on Borneo, much as had the escapees from Mindanao told of the conditions of American prisoners in the Philippines.[20]

The increased submarine activity, clandestine operations along Borneo's shores, the 10 October uprising, and the killing of Japanese seamen by escaped prisoners caused the Japanese to resort to even harsher treatment. An extra battalion of soldiers was brought in from Manchuria to guard the Sandakan airfield. More machine-gun emplacements were set up. The remaining prisoners were put on starvation rations—about seven ounces of rice a day. The captured Python operatives were hanged as spies at Jesselton in December 1944. Late in February 1944, those arrested in the Matthews purge the previous summer were given trials in Kuching. Australian doctor James Taylor and Lt. Rod Wells were given sentences in Outram Road Jail. Eight civilians were shot. Capt. Lionel C. Matthews, having been found guilty, was executed by firing squad on 2 March 1944. As he was driven away he showed that he had lost none of his courage.

"Keep your chins up boys," he shouted. "What the Japs do to me doesn't matter. They can't win."

Constant Japanese harassment meant that the remaining Python agents would have to be evacuated. In April 1944, *Haddo* waited offshore for two hours, not knowing the commandos had no boat, and no rendezvous was made. The next month, *Redfin* attempted a pickup, but the nighttime meeting was ruined when *Redfin* was attacked by a Japanese patrol boat and almost lost its own landing party of sailors. When a Japanese patrol approached, the commandos were again forced to hide in the jungle. Their whereabouts were known, they were being tracked by bloodhounds, traitors, airplanes, and natives, and it was only a matter of time before either the Allies or Japanese found them.

The *Harder*, under Cdr. Samuel D. Dealey, was the next sub to attempt a rescue. When she left Fremantle, she took Major Jinkins, who came along to help effect the rescue of Chester's group. Off Tawi Tawi, *Harder* treated the Aussie to a show when Dealey sank two destroyers on successive nights. On the night of 8 June, *Harder* surfaced offshore and two boats went in, beaching right between two Japanese patrols a mile and a half on either side. Light signals were sent ashore and, finally, a torch flickered in response. Jinkins called out to shadowy figures on the shore.

"Who are you?"

"Gort," came the reply—which was Chester's nickname.

"Is Alex with you?" Jinkins asked.

"Yes," replied the voice of Alexander Chew, another mate of Jinkins.

Confident that they had the right men, the pickup was made, and they hurriedly paddled back to the sub. The last six men of Python had been saved. While *Harder* sped for deep water, they spent the night talking nonstop, while trying to wolf down as much good submarine chow as they could eat. The coast watching operation had mixed reviews. They reported eighty-eight Japanese shipping movements through the area, some of which resulted in sinkings. However, they lost some men, and the Japanese tightened the screws on the Sandakan prisoners. Plans were made for their rescue, possibly by 1 Battalion Australian Paratroops, but eventually the idea was scrapped. No advantage was found in taking Sandakan—it had but twenty-three miles of roads, could only be supplied by sea, and had a water-logged airfield. Additionally, extremely poor planning and many foul-ups had delayed action until the window of opportunity had long passed. Politically, had it been taken, it would have put pressure on MacArthur to attempt a rescue of Americans in the Philippines, and, after American POWs were rescued in 1945, it was too late for a similar operation in Borneo. In addition, it probably would have caused a spate of massacres throughout the other POW camps in Asia. The Sandakan captives were left to their fate. Prisoners of war, whether on land or at sea, were expendable. In Australia, the story was concealed for years.[21]

THE SUMMER SHIPS

The threat of the approaching Americans made the tropical Philippine atmosphere even more feverish in the summer of 1944. Prisoners were shifted among the islands and from camp to camp with abandon. As is true with most military operations, however, it was a case of hurry up and wait. The GI term "snafu" certainly applied to Japanese military planning. Of the more than eleven hundred men who arrived from Mindanao on *Yashu Maru* and *Singoto Maru*, about six hundred in poor health were taken north to Cabanatuan, while five hundred of both the sickest and healthiest men made the short march to Bilibid Prison in Manila. There, the sickest would remain behind and the healthiest would form up for Japan. Meanwhile, another five hundred relatively healthy men were brought from Cabanatuan down to Bilibid. Somewhere along the road passed two parties of five hundred, heading in opposite directions. Carl Nordin, waiting in Bilibid after getting off the *Singoto Maru*, thought it was great to get a bath, to be able to stretch out, to get three meals a day, plus be issued cigarettes and be allowed to buy coconuts and peanuts. On the other hand, Sgt. James D. Gautier Jr. of the 27th Bomb Group, who had been in a camp in Baguio for many months, thought Bilibid was "a hellhole of filth and disease." He only got one cup of rice and water, while cockroaches and other vermin filled the cells, and, he complained, "the whole place smelled of excreta."

On 2 July, the five hundred from Cabanatuan and the five hundred healthiest from Mindanao were placed aboard what Nordin called "an ailing and miserable old tug" and what Sgt. Neal Harrington of the 200th Coast Artillery called "an old freighter of dubious seaworthiness." The *Canadian Inventor* was a captured freighter, but this time she would be laden with nothing but prisoners. About six hundred went into the forward hold and four hundred into the aft hold. Conditions varied according to point of view. Gautier said it was so crowded that a man couldn't sit down unless he put his legs over someone else, and that a few men were trampled in the crush. The holds smelled of manure and urine, and rats and lice abounded. To Nordin, however, the two meals a day of rice and vegetables on the first day were pleasing, and compared to the previous voyage, there was more room.

The *Canadian Inventor* sailed from Manila on 4 July, and everyone was forced to go below while passing Corregidor, ostensibly to prevent them from seeing the island's defenses. The next day the old freighter developed boiler trouble and returned to Manila for repairs. There it sat for eleven days, and there it took on the characteristics of a true hellship from all points of view. Sanitary facilities consisted of buckets placed in the hold and hauled up by ropes when full. At times the "honey buckets" and rice buckets made the trip side by side. The hold was like an oven, and water was obtained by gathering drops of condensation off the steam pipes.

Gautier believed that a man had to have a great will to live to force himself to eat in such conditions. While some starved, staring dumbly at their meager rations, others fought like animals over morsels of food. "Men stole from each other and a few were murdered," Gautier said. "Crazed individuals tried to slash other men to drink their blood." Sometimes men died and no one even knew until the body started swelling. "Of course," said Gautier, "when men died that meant more space, more rice to eat and water to drink for the rest of us."

While they waited in the bay, they saw several damaged Japanese warships. Said Capt. Benson Guyton of the 200th Coast Artillery, "They had huge holes. One large ship with its forward, three-gun turret muzzles leaning over the side splashing water. A beautiful sight." There was also another freighter nearby being loaded with gasoline. To the prisoners' joy and consternation it blew up and burned, but the resultant flames and smoke only made their condition more unbearable.

With boiler repaired, *Canadian Inventor* again sailed on 16 July. Some men were allowed topside, but the Japanese kept them on tenterhooks. They were allowed to smoke, but only at designated times. One prisoner who smoked at a forbidden hour was made to kneel for hours on the hot steel deck in the sunshine. When he was pulled up, the skin from both of his knees stuck to the deck. He later died. Once outside the calm waters of Manila Bay, they were beset by a typhoon, and the light load of prisoners meant the ship rode high, rolling like a cork in the waves. Men became seasick and vomited, and latrine buckets overturned, adding to the horrible smells. "The mess and the stench almost defy description," wrote Nordin. "The incidence of men losing it all and screaming in the darkness of that hell hole was increasing now."

With the rain came some respite, for the water pouring in the open hatches allowed the men to drink and wash. Then, to add to the roller coaster of hope and despair, the change in weather brought about colds and flu. When the boiler began acting up again and the ship's speed dropped, the convoy left them behind to limp toward Formosa alone. By this time, *Canadian Inventor* was dubbed "Mati Mati Maru," *mati mati* meaning "wait wait." One night, Neal Harrington heard a few officers discussing the possibility of taking over the ship. They outnumbered the guards, and there were prisoners aboard who could navigate. The problem was that the food supply was low, and their fuel and speed were not sufficient to get them to any Allied base before they would be overtaken. The idea was dropped, and the "Mati Mati Maru" finally pulled into Takao on 23 July.

The reason for loading only prisoners in Manila now became apparent, for the ship took on a large cargo of salt. The men were able to surmount the bulkhead separating them from the salt, and climbed into it to find clean places to rest. They now had an unlimited source of seasoning for their rice—at least until they decided to use the salt as a latrine. Again there were ups and downs. They were allowed to buy commissary products, such as canned fruit, bananas, onions, and garlic, and they were fed rice, camotes (sweet potatoes), squash, and even some pork. It filled their stomachs, but it also brought on a spate of diarrhea. In time, the POWs contaminated nearly the entire cargo of salt. Nordin called it a deliberate act of sabotage.

During the last few days of July, more ships pulled into Takao's harbor. One of them, the *Hakushika Maru,* may have been damaged in the typhoon, for it had a big hole in the hull above the water line. It also carried prisoners, these coming north from Singapore. Gautier could see them waving—comrades in misery.

Canadian Inventor pulled out on 4 August, creeping north through Formosa Strait. She only made it as far as Keelung, on Formosa's north coast, when she put in to the harbor for another twelve-day wait. Nordin complained of the "big dealing," of crap games, con games, and hard trading, run mostly by men from Cabanatuan. It often led to fights. "We were sorry we picked them up in Manila," he wrote in his diary. On the seventeenth they were on their way once more, this time escorted by several subchasers. Halfway through the Ryukyu Islands, the need for repairs sent them ashore for the third time. They were in and out of Naha, Okinawa, for the next six days, unable to overcome their boiler problems. During one of these sorties, the prisoners heard explosions of what they guessed were torpedoes and depth charges. The escorts speeding past dropped their tin cans so close by that rust chips flaked off the hull and rained down on them. The noise and vibration made it seem like the sides and bottom of the old tub would collapse.

Canadian Inventor was lucky, for that night a larger target was selected by the attacking U.S. submarine. Late on 22 August, Cdr. John Corbus in *Bowfin* had put two torpedoes into the 6,754-ton *Tsushima Maru.* Its cargo had been determined in the mood of hysteria that spread after the U.S. invasion of the Marianas. General Tojo had been forced to resign as prime minister. American prisoners were to be moved north. Okinawa was to be fortified, and Japanese civilians were to be evacuated to the homeland. Aboard *Tsushima Maru* that night were 1,788 evacuees, many of them schoolchildren, teachers, and parents. Some of the survivors remembered being packed in like sardines on what they called a "slave ship." They did not get far, for *Bowfin*'s torpedoes broke the ship in half. Teachers tried to round up the children and get them aboard life rafts, but there were not enough rafts and not enough time. The rest of the convoy sped off, and the escorts did not stop to give aid. Some survivors hung on to wreckage for three days before passing vessels stopped to pick them up. In all, about 1,529 people were killed. Of the 741 children, only 59 were rescued. The *Canadian Inventor,* unaware of the drama being played out in the ocean nearby, hid inside a cove on a small island the rest of the night.

The last few days of the voyage were spent coasting along Kyushu's western shore. To cap off the ordeal, Dr. Thomas H. Hewlett had to perform an emergency appendectomy with only a razor blade. They laid the man down on a straw mat and Hewlett cut him open. "No anesthetic. Nothing," he said. "Sewed him up with an old piece of string. And he lived." *Canadian Inventor* reached Moji on 1 September, and the captives debarked the next day. After marching to an abandoned stable, they got their first fresh water in nine weeks. Accounts differ on the number of men who died aboard ship, from only one to a dozen. Considering what they had been through, the death toll was surprisingly low. Carl Nordin, who had come all the way up from Mindanao in the bowels of three hellships, had been at sea almost constantly since 6 June, nearly the entire summer. The trip on *Canadian Inventor* had lasted sixty-two days. No trip, Nordin believed, "exceeded our length of time in hell." He was wrong.[22]

The next ship out of Manila carried sixteen hundred prisoners from camps all across Luzon. The *Nissyo Maru* was a 6,527-ton passenger-cargo auxiliary, built in 1939 and owned by Nanyo Kaiun Company. It was 420 feet in length, and its oil-fueled, steam turbines gave it a cruising speed of fifteen knots. Although structurally sound, its appearance gave the prisoners a sense of foreboding. Seaman Virgil V. Vining had served on the minelayers *Bittern* and *Finch,* and after both of them had been bombed and sunk, he had fought as a soldier on

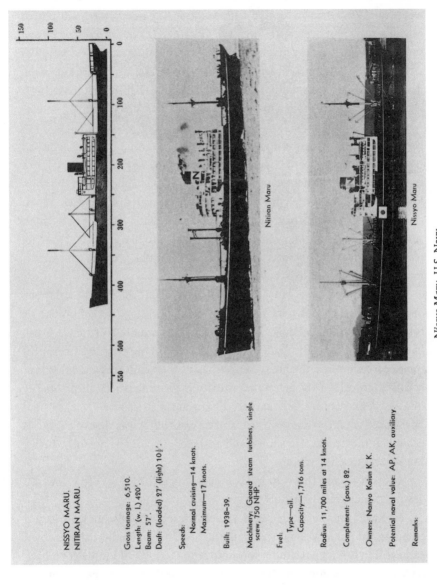

NISSYO MARU.
NITIRAN MARU.

Gross tonnage: 6,510.
Length: (w. l.) 420'.
Beam: 57'.
Draft: (loaded) 27' (light) 10½'.

Speeds:
    Normal cruising—14 knots.
    Maximum—17 knots.

Built: 1938–39.

Machinery: Geared steam turbines, single
    screw, 750 NHP.

Fuel:
    Type—oil.
    Capacity—1,716 tons.

Radius: 11,700 miles at 14 knots.

Complement: (pass.) 82.

Owners: Nanyo Kaiun K. K.

Potential naval value: AP, AK, auxiliary

Remarks:

Nitiran Maru

Nissyo Maru

Nissyo Maru. U.S. Navy

Fort Hughes in Manila Bay. He had spent much of his captivity working at Nichol's Field under a cruel Imperial Japanese Navy officer known as the "White Angel" and worked later as a stevedore on the Manila docks. On the waterfront Vining heard "secret" information. "We were always well-posted on ship-convoy movements," he said. On the morning of 17 July, Vining tramped up the gangway of what he called "an old dilapidated, rusty hull of a Nippon ship." A similar observation was made by Preston J. Hubbard, of the 409th Signal Corps: the ship was "a rusty, decrepit freighter that looked as if it had been retrieved from a maritime junkyard."

Not everyone had recently arrived at the pier. One group from Cabanatuan had been waiting to board *Nissyo Maru* since 11 July. Bernard T. Fitzpatrick of the 194th Tank Battalion watched as stevedores loaded horses on the ship. Each was carefully hoisted in a sling and gently deposited on the deck. When the POWs' turn came, they were forced up by gun butts and bayonets. Later, a prisoner was asked if they had been loaded aboard like animals. "No," he responded, "we were not loaded like animals. They took good care of the animals. We were loaded like coal down a coal chute."[23]

Once up the gangway, Hubbard had what he called "the most brutal shock of my life." Peering down into the dark hold, a hot, stagnant column of air rose to envelop him. Below was a writhing mass of hundreds of men. A plank had been lifted from the deck, and guards were forcing everyone to drop all their possession into the hole, everything but their canteens and mess kits. Fourth Marine Don Versaw saw a Cabanatuan guard the men called "Mickey Mouse" because of his large ears screaming at the prisoners. "Mickey" had once asked what the name meant, and he was told it was that of a famous American movie star. He smiled and accepted his name gracefully. Today, Mickey was in a foul mood.

"Take off shoes! Throw in hold! *Hyaku* [hurry]! All bags too! Now. Go down ladder. Speedo, speedo!"

"Air Raid," another camp guard, joined Mickey in confiscating goods and clubbing the men. Versaw was reminded of how one might shake down garbage in a bag to make room for more at the top. Virgil Vining got a hobnailed boot in the stomach when he tripped to the deck. When he looked over the edge, he could not believe they would try to force so many men into such a small place. He thought the hold was no larger than sixty feet square—a very good guess, for *Nissyo Maru*'s beam was fifty-seven feet. Already the main deck near the hatch was strewn with about with the limp bodies of fifty men who had passed out and were hoisted over the heads of the men below and taken topside. It was so unbelievably tight that as Versaw helped pass up unconscious bodies, Vining was likewise passed down into a small gap in the corner. "My feet never touched the deck for several minutes," he said.[24]

There was no more space in the wooden tiers built along the sides, yet the bodies kept coming. Preston Hubbard, a country boy from Tennessee, never could stand closed-in spaces. Movement occurred only in waves, "like jelly in slow motion," he said. His arms were pinned to his sides. "I panicked. The stifling, foul air had become virtually unbreathable. I was suffocating. . . . All around me men were screaming—some praying, some cursing. I lost consciousness." Before being trampled, Hubbard was luckily grabbed and passed up the stairway to the deck.

PFC Andrew D. Carson of the 59th Coast Artillery was one of the first few hundred men in the hold. He selected an upper tier, about halfway back in the hold, but within minutes he realized it was a mistake. By then, however, he had no choice, for the men coming in after him pinned him in his place. The steel deck was only inches above his head and heat radiated down on his face "like the blast from an open oven door." He sat with his knees pressed against his chin, arms wrapped around his legs. "At first it was remarkably quiet," Carson said. "At first there was no panic. But here and there, especially among those in the very back of the press, a man broke and began screaming and cursing, cursing the bodies pressed against him, cursing the Japs who had put him there, cursing the God who had abandoned him." The panic spread. "Fights broke out. Eyes were gouged, cheeks ripped, and bodies lacerated as men pushed and tore at each other in their struggle for the breath of life." The physical pressure was bad, but, said Carson, "the psychological pressure was incredible."

As Robert J. Dow, 27th Bomb Group, listened to the screaming, panic began to grab at his gut. He was about to crack when someone passed a canteen to him, telling him to take a drink and pass it on. It would keep him from fainting, the man said. Dow took a big swallow, then the man next to him grabbed it and drank too. It was urine. At first Dow was so angry he could have killed someone, but almost immediately fear took the place of anger. What would happen to him now?[25]

The tropical sun was already dipping down over the Bataan Peninsula, and the guards still had a few hundred men to force below. Hubbard had revived, but he remained sprawled out on the deck, faking unconsciousness so he would not be sent back below. A guard came by and gave him a bruising kick in the ribs, but Hubbard successfully played dead. Finally, the Japanese decided they could not fit sixteen hundred men into one hold, and over the next hour, about half of the men struggled back up the ladder to find a new home in number two hold, just forward of the bridge. It was larger than the first, giving the prisoners there a bit more room to move.

Don Versaw was one of the men transferred to the number two hold. His new home had no sleeping tiers, just a solid iron deck, and with no territorial divisions, the men seethed back and forth in constant motion. Versaw finally sat down in a spot only about two feet square. Back in the first hold, there was still no room for those crushed to the insides of the tiers. Andrew Carson felt the tension increase as daylight faded. Soon the darkness was absolute, and even breathing seemed to be more difficult. Finally, the ship's engines began to vibrate and *Nissyo Maru* loosed her moorings and slipped farther out into the bay, only to anchor for the night. The moonlight allowed Carson to make out faces nearby. He saw a prisoner with a rag, sopping up condensation from the sides of the hull and squeezing the liquid into his mouth. Men next to him told him to stop, but he kept sucking on the dirty rag. Half an hour later, said Carson, the "stupid bastard vomited all over himself and the two or three guys crowded around him. He was told in no uncertain terms that he was a no good son of a bitch and to go ahead and die." The man retched all night.

Carson had his own problems. He could not move an inch and his entire body ached. He wanted so badly to stretch his legs, that a wave of terror came over him. "It was the same panicky feeling I remembered from childhood," he said, "when I had foolishly dived deep into a lake, stayed down too long, and had run out of breath before I got back to the surface." His body trembled. He had seen so much of death over the past two years of captivity that he thought he could stoically face the possibility of his own demise. However, he said, "this time it was different. I didn't want to die here in this total blackness. . . . Not like some animal sealed below decks in the bowels of the ship." He pressed his head against his knees and tried to calm himself. Men needed to believe in something, he thought. In desperate times, they will cling to any ray of hope. Surely it would get better.

It didn't. In his misery, Carson now felt the hot trickle of urine coursing under him. Men with diarrhea let go, and a warm slop coated the shelf. Bodies pressed in on him, holding him immobile. His chest was constricted and he gasped for breath. Cursing and weeping filled the night. Here were hundreds of tough American fighting men, Carson thought. They were battle-tested veterans, yet "underneath this veneer of toughness were typical American kids, who, in their pain, their suffering, still cried out in the dark for their mothers."

It was the worst night of Carson's life.[26]

After that ordeal, the remainder of the voyage contained few new surprises. The *Nissyo Maru* moved out into Manila Bay on the seventeenth, the day after *Canadian Inventor* sailed, but she was to remain anchored there for another week, soaking up the sun's heat. Every morning the planks would be removed from the hatches and the men would see broad Japanese grins as they amused themselves over the misery of their charges. "How easy it was," Vining observed, "for eight or ten guards to control nine hundred prisoners."

About thirty hours passed before the Japanese allowed the prisoners their first water, about half a canteen each. Rice was lowered to them in wooden buckets, but if a man wasn't in the right spot, he might never get his portion. Some didn't care. They had given up. Preston Hubbard, after being booted into consciousness on the deck, was placed in the forward hold. Someone found a trap door that led to a smaller hold below, and Hubbard, Robert Dow, and others climbed down the ladder to their new sanctuary. The air was somewhat better there, and a man could grab a few puffs from a cigarette without the Japanese finding out. The deck above them had numerous cracks, however, and, said Hubbard, "we had to endure a constant rain of excrement." Dow left his refuge to go above to sleep during the second night. The man next to him told Dow that his canteen was jabbing into him, and asked him to move it. Dow complied. When he awoke in the morning, Dow took a sip from it. Urine again! It was the second time he had been tricked. The man had somehow gotten Dow's canteen, drank the water, and filled it with urine. He felt like killing the man, but the culprit vehemently denied everything. Suddenly Dow's strength drained from him, and he slumped to the deck in despair.[27]

On 24 July, *Nissyo Maru* joined Convoy HI-68, which had sailed from Singapore on the fourteenth. The convoy consisted of thirteen ships, including *Aki Maru,* which had carried the top officials of the Dutch East Indies to

Formosa. The large convoy was protected by CDVs *Hirado, Kurahashi, Ishigaki,* 11, 20, torpedo boat *Hiyodori,* and escort carrier *Taiyo.* As it rounded Corregidor and headed north at eleven knots, Vining hoped that the Japanese had done a good job at sweeping the channel, for he had sown mines in those very waters. "I didn't care to get shot in the feet by one of my own guns," he said.

Surprisingly, after they were underway, more food was available for the prisoners. They were fed cups of steamed barley. The first day, when sea breezes and clouds cooled things down, the men ate hungrily. The next day, under a burning sun, they all lost their appetite. The problem was dehydration. There was just not enough water, and the barley went dry in their mouths. Unable to swallow, men gave up eating and fell back in a stupor. Hubbard did not know how any of them survived. He ate so little that he only had to use the *benjo* three times in seventeen days. Hubbard believed that besides outright torture and murder, the greatest crime the Japanese committed was to deny helpless prisoners adequate drinking water. The guards on deck played horrible games. They brought out containers of water, showed them to the captives, drank from them, then washed their feet in them. They flung the rinsings into the hold and laughed uproariously.

"Terrible things happened in the blackness of night," said Andy Carson. "Men were found dead with their throats torn open and we knew at least one of us had sustained his own life by drinking the blood of another. The crazy one, the blood drinker, was never caught, but the killing stopped." Carson assumed the demented man had died in his own private hell.

Having to endure an unbearable thirst was perhaps the worst physical torture, yet Hubbard's nightmares were of men living in each other's excrement. During the entire voyage, one or two inches of semifluid waste coated the floor of the hold—a mixture of bloody, dysentery-induced diarrhea, urine, vomit, and rainwater. It coated everything "like a thick beige soup." Hubbard had hallucinations about tubs of excrement, which would grow until they took on the size of backyard swimming pools. His clothing was soaked in it; he could feel it squishing in his socks. For more than forty years he was haunted by visions of emaciated, dead men splattered with excrement. However, he said, Mother Nature must provide some protection for men undergoing such traumatic experiences: the entire time on board he could not smell the odor that emanated from the hold. Only when he saw the Japanese don masks every time they approached the open pits did he realize that the stench must have been horrific.[28]

As if they didn't have enough to worry about, in the early morning hours of the twenty-sixth they were awakened by a bump and a vibration that ran through the steel hull. Seconds later came explosions. Flames filled the sky, and even deep in the holds the prisoners could see a red glow filtering in. Off the northwest coast of Luzon, the convoy had run smack into a wolfpack of three submarines, the *Flasher, Angler,* and *Crevalle,* which had been ordered to that point to await the convoy. The wolfpack tracked HI-68 throughout the twenty-fifth, but only *Crevalle* managed an unsuccessful attack. Early the next morning, in quick succession, *Aki Maru* and *Tosan Maru* were hit, and in the same column as *Nissyo Maru,* the 5,280-ton tanker *Otorisan Maru* went up in a sheet of flame. A quick course change allowed *Nissyo Maru* to avoid the stricken ship, but she passed so closely that smoke from the tanker billowed into her. Hysteria broke out in the holds and men scrambled for the hatch, thinking they had been torpedoed. The Japanese set up machine guns and prepared to start shooting. Still trapped in his hole, Carson could not move no matter how hard he struggled. Then and there he smelled fear; he knew firsthand it was a tangible thing. "I have smelled it. Fear has a sharp pungent odor all its own, different from any other smell. Dogs can recognize it instantly and in this instance, so could I, and once having smelled fear you can never forget its odor." All you can do, he said, "is tighten your ass and wait for the final shock."

But it didn't come. A priest, Father Stanley Reilly, climbed a pole near the center of the hold and tried to calm the men. He continuously repeated the Hail Mary in a firm yet gentle voice until his words had the desired effect.

"Holy Mary, Mother of God, Pray for us sinners, now and at the hour of our death." With each repetition his voice lowered, and the men quieted down accordingly. It became so quiet that the noise of the far off depth charges were heard, but they brought no more fear.

When the tension had eased, Father Reilly offered another suggestion. "Let's pray for the men in the submarines—they want to go home too." He started the Rosary, and in the red glow of the burning ships, many of the men joined in supplication.[29]

The rest of the voyage was anticlimactic. The U.S. submarines also sank the *Kiyokawa Maru,* but, somehow, *Nissyo Maru* steamed unharmed into Takao on the twenty-seventh. The prisoners were allowed on deck, where much of the sewage was hosed off them. Don Versaw leaned over the railing with his mind in a turmoil. Should he jump? Shore was not far away. He would be insane to do it, but he would be insane to go back into the hold again. Without knowing how, his feet led him down the ladder. His tortured mind told him that it was futile to resist. He had stopped fighting back. Later, someone suggested that they try to take over the ship. An argument ensued, and the consensus was that no one would be able to operate the ship anyway. It was an agreeable resolution. They had all just about given up.

Nissyo Maru sailed again on the twenty-eighth, but the rest of the voyage was routine. Men ate, argued, fought, became ill, went crazy, died, and were hauled topside and thrown overboard. Andy Carson had lost all track of time. He believed he must have been aboard for five or six weeks. As he lay with his companions he finally noticed how horrible they looked, then realized he must look the same. Bony, emaciated skeletons in G-strings, all a "dirty streaky brown color." Finally one of them snickered and another laughed. One said that if the folks at home could see them marching down Main Street, "they'd run like hell." The thought of their horrid, frightening appearance got them all chuckling. Soon, said Carson, "we were like a bunch of little kids at the dinner table with the giggles." Men were laughing throughout the hold, not having any idea as to what they were laughing about. They didn't give a damn anymore.

The days dragged on without variation, but a noticeable change had come over them. The first days were pure hell, the following days were lesser hell, and soon, hell was the norm. They had learned to adjust to Hell. "By God," affirmed Carson, "we were going to survive."

Nissyo Maru reached Moji on 3 August. The Japanese gave all the baggage to the men in the number three hold, while those in the forward hold only got their shoes back. As they stumbled down the gangway they were sprayed with disinfectant, then marched to a large concrete loading dock and allowed to sit down. The concrete was almost heaven. For the first time in almost three weeks they could stretch out to full length, and they thankfully collapsed into a blissful sleep.[30]

More prisoners were to leave the Philippines that summer. The next contingent gathered in Manila in late August: 150 from Bilibid, 517 from Cabanatuan,

345 from Clark Field, and 150 from Camp Murphy (Nielson Field), for a total of 1,162. In the days before sailing, there were a number of personnel changes, as some were too sick to make the journey; others "traded" places. Bill Garleb of the 31st Infantry thought MacArthur would rescue them first, so he swapped with a sergeant who wanted to go to Japan. Dr. Dan Golenternek was slated to go to Japan but stuck with the hand that had been dealt him. The man who wanted to trade places with him ended up on *Oryoku Maru*, which left in December. Eventually, 1,035 men sailed—most of them Army POWs, with 196 Navy POWs, and 11 civilians—aboard *Noto Maru*, a 7,191-ton Army-controlled cargo ship.

Pvt. Ernest Norquist recorded in his diary that on 25 August they were all crowded into one forty-by-sixty-foot hold. No one had room to sit, and twelve men fainted from the heat in the first hour. The latrine had three "holes" and one urinal, but only one man was allowed there at a time. For supper they had rice-and-radish-fish soup. Robert Johnston likened the below-decks scene to "a can full of slimy earthworms." He was not far from wrong, for some men folded up soft burlap bags to sit on only to discover the reason for the softness: they were full of maggots. Once it was found that the hold would accommodate all of them, they were ordered to sit down. In order to do so, a man had to rest against the folded up knees of the man behind him. Thus they sat for two days.

Convoy MAMO-02 consisted of the *Kashii Maru*, *Mayasan Maru*, *Nissho Maru*, and *Noto Maru*. It was protected by CDVs *Shimushu*, *Etorofu*, *Shonan*, 7, and 28; SC 41; patrol boat 102; and destroyers *Hatsushimo* and *Wakaba*. So many escorts meant it was an important convoy, originally part of the Singapore-bound HI-71 but detached for Manila. While biding his time on *Noto Maru*, Capt. E. Pearce Fleming hoped his warning would get through. Fleming had been with the Philippine Scouts, and when Bataan surrendered, many of his men escaped back to their villages or were later paroled by the Japanese. Because they needed work, some took jobs with the Japanese while continuing to pass information to the guerrilla forces and the American prisoners. Fleming traded information with Clare Phillips, known as "High Pockets," a Manila operative who was instrumental in getting life-saving supplies and useful information to the prisoners at Cabanatuan. Phillips, said Fleming, knew of POW ship sailings a week to ten days in advance. Fleming received information about the upcoming voyage of *Noto Maru*, and he passed it to a trusted former scout, Felippe Maningo. Before prisoners even boarded, word was passed to Allied intelligence about the voyage. Somewhat naïvely, Fleming hoped that the information would be passed to U.S. submarines so they would not fire on *Noto Maru* on its way to Japan. He had no way of knowing that such information never was a deterrent. Fleming assumed his message never got through to the submarines, because, he said, "several of the ships in our convoy were sunk on the way up there."

MAMO-02 pulled out on the twenty-seventh but spent the night in Subic Bay on the northwest side of the Bataan Peninsula. The next day, the high-speed convoy raced north across the South China Sea. Down in the torrid hold, the scene was similar to that which had been played out on the other hellships. Those who had eaten coconuts and garlic stolen aboard by friendly Filipinos got severe diarrhea. One man in a G-string was seen climbing up the ladder with one hand, "his other hand over his rectum, but human waste was squirting from him." Some men passed out and some died. They were carried out, bodies over heads, and hoisted topside. Robert Johnston felt so horrible that he faked passing out and was carried to the deck where he was able to stretch out and get some air.

Before sailing, the Japanese had given each man a blanket and about three feet of rope. When it was realized that the blankets could be tied to the I-beams, scores of hammocks were suddenly swinging above, easing the crowding. Even with more room, the tropical sun baking the iron holds could not be avoided. As the heat drove some men out of their minds, Lt. George Sense found a way to keep them quiet. He was a large man, about six feet two inches, and still in good shape. He molded a ball of soap and stuffed it in the toe of a sock. When a man would get out of line, Sense would "wop" him with the sock to get him to calm down. It worked. Said Captain Fleming, "It was something you wouldn't normally do, but under the circumstances I think it was appropriate."

Before reaching Formosa, the inevitable submarine scare occurred. The hatch covers were left open, and the prisoners could hear planes buzzing overhead, along with the Japanese shouting excitedly. One nearby depth-charge blast shook the hull. Pvt. James C. McCormick of the 200th Coast Artillery thought the ship had blown up. "The hatch was open, for once, and everybody started up the ladder," he said. "But they ran three or four machine guns in and started to fire. That quieted people down." Some men had had enough.

Said Brownell Cole, "Believe it or not, I hoped to hell we got hit. Kill us all. Blow us sky high." When the action ended, the Japanese told them that they had sunk a U.S. sub, but no one believed them. The convoy pulled into Takao late on 30 August.

There was no offloading. The next day, after detaching four escorts, they hurried north. The Noto Maru could make sixteen knots. According to one prisoner, "That sucker could really fly." The entire convoy was fast. At Keelung, Oryoku Maru joined them, and they raced across the East China Sea, reaching Moji on 4 September, after only a nine-day voyage. The inevitable glass-rod treatment followed, and the men stumbled off the ship to be grouped for their various destinations. About half of them were dropped off at various camps along the railroad from Shimonoseki to Tokyo; the remaining five hundred were taken to Hanawa, in far northern Honshu. All things being relative, the trip on Noto Maru was one of the better hellship voyages.[31]

Native laborers were still being shuffled among the islands of the East Indies that summer. The airfield at Makassar was in need of repair, and 1,513 Javanese were induced to sail to Celebes to work on it. In Batavia, on 29 July, they boarded the 2,295-ton cargo ship Koshu Maru. The vessel, owned by the Chosen Yusen Company but under Army control, also loaded air base supplies and 540 additional passengers. It was joined by Shinai Maru, and with the auxiliary minesweeper Keinan Maru and the netlayer Hayabusa Maru as escorts, they sailed across the Java Sea.

The slow-moving convoy arrived at Kotabaru, Laut Island, off the southeastern tip of Borneo, on 2 August. They continued east the following day, with the torpedo-boat Kisasagi replacing Hayabusa Maru. The small convoy did not escape the attention of William T. Kinsella, commanding Ray on its fifth patrol. Just before dawn on 4 August, in the middle of Makassar Strait, Kinsella lined up Koshu Maru in his sights. Four torpedoes were on their way for deadly effect. The first missile struck the engine room amidships on the starboard side, and two more smashed into the forward part of the number three hold. The Javanese laborers didn't have a chance, for the little ship broke in two and sank in minutes. The Ray went deeper to evade, counting nine depth charges, but the sub stole away undamaged. Going down with Koshu Maru were 273 passengers, 28 gunners and crewmen, and

1,239 of the laborers. The confined waters of the Java Sea remained a dangerous place for both sides.[32]

JAPAN PARTY TWO

One month after the sailing of Japan Party One, the second party was ready to depart. From upcountry railway camps and from Changi, the captives gathered in Singapore's River Valley Road, unaware that as they were being assembled, members of the first party were being torpedoed in the East China Sea. Japanese plans to send more than five thousand POWs in this contingent would make it the largest group shipped during the entire war.

The Japanese asked for volunteers, and Sapper Bill Power weighed his chances. On the plus side there would be no more jungle, he would probably get better food, medical treatment, clothing, and shelter, and he wouldn't have to dig the canal that was rumored to be built across the Kra Isthmus. The winters, however, would be cold, there would be bombing raids, and the ship might be sunk at sea. In the end, the grass seemed greener over the fence, and Power opted for Japan.

Before they left River Valley Road, they were issued sand boots, a cotton shirt, and a pair of gaudy cotton shorts, a "present," they were told, from "a benevolent emperor." The POWs thought it was more likely that the authorities were just too embarrassed to have the populace see them wandering the streets of Japan in nothing but G-strings. Nevertheless, the footwear was welcome on the hot steel decks.

Convoy SHIMI-05 was a large one, consisting of ten ships escorted by the torpedo-boat *Sagi* and minesweepers 17 and 18. The *Mexico Maru, Olympia Maru, Shirahato Maru, Kurogane Maru,* and *No. 6 Kyoei Maru* sailed with five prisoner-laden ships: 609 on the 8,151-ton cargo ship *Hakushika Maru,* 738 British POWs on the 7,399-ton armed merchant cruiser *Asaka Maru,* 1,024 prisoners on *Sekiho Maru,* 1,065 on the 5,462-ton cargo ship *Rashin Maru,* and 1,287 POWs on the 5,825-ton cargo ship *Hofuku Maru.*[33]

The Australian contingent was under Maj. Reginald W. J. Newton, called "Roaring Reggie," a man of strong will and big voice. Six hundred Australian, 300 Dutch, and 165 British prisoners boarded *Rashin Maru,* a captured freighter that had seen better days. It was a Blue Funnel ship, first called *Potomac,* then *Canadian Prince,* before being taken by the Japanese. The *Perth* sailor Ray Parkin gave it his assessment. It had been bombed out and burned.

The bridge was gone and the deck had dropped down fifteen inches because of the fire. Somehow it was still afloat, but, said Parkin, "this thing, she was virtually a derelict." A man beside Power nudged him and said, "Get a load of that big wooden wheel down at the stern; don't tell me they steer this thing with that!"

Before embarking, each man had to grab a block of rubber eighteen inches square and seven inches thick. Major Newton approached Lieutenant Tanaka and asked gruffly, "What the hell are these things for?"

"They are your life preservers," Tanaka answered. "You will carry them on board with you and look after them."

While going up the gangway, a prisoner near Newton tested the buoyancy of the "life preservers" by dropping one into the harbor. "It went straight to the bottom," said Newton.

On board, Parkin noticed that on the poop deck they had jury-rigged a bridge. They were armed with an old brass cannon with cannonballs piled alongside, "just like you'd see in old fashioned pictures of battlefields." There were no hatch covers on the first two holds; the ship was open right down to the bottom, which could be very risky in a rough ocean. Said Parkin, "We reckoned we were the terror of the China seas."

Nevertheless, *Rashin Maru* managed to get up steam and left with the convoy on 4 July. Power remembered the date because it was Independence Day. An intercepted message sent to Tokyo from the Southern Area Army indicated that there were 5,727 Allied prisoners sailing with the convoy, a slightly higher total than sent in a previous message giving the individual ship totals.

The accommodations were even more primitive than on most hellships. The prisoners had never seen anything like it. "It's *byoki*," said one. "It's a bloody sick ship." Between decks there was only one thin shelf, incapable of holding many men. For the remainder, it was standing room only until they managed to wrestle themselves into awkward sitting positions. When feeding time came, it was nearly impossible to untangle to form up a queue. The cuisine was not worth the effort to reach it: rice pap with rotten fish that tasted like herring, liberally sprinkled with maggots. "And it stunk," said Sgt. Frank Baker. "You were sick from it, but you got over that and you ate it again because there was nothing else."

"The toilets," said 2/4 Machine Gunner Des Colevas, "were the usual 'man on the flying trapeze' contraptions hanging over the side and ablutions meant a tin on a rope over the side if you weren't caught; if you were, you were lucky you didn't follow the tin over the side. You could be a week await-ing your turn for a wash, by which time you stunk to high heaven—you and five hundred others."

There was no toilet paper and they had to make do with what they could find, even if one's favorite book had to be used for "bum fodder." Herb Mc-Namara had a book of Shakespeare's plays and was trying to memorize one as a mental exercise to keep himself sane. While lying on deck one afternoon he came to a place with one page missing. Dismayed at being unable to fin-ish, McNamara was about to give up when a gust of wind blew a piece of paper past him. As he grabbed it, he couldn't believe his luck, for it was exactly the page he needed. When he turned it over, however, "here was a very nasty big brown smear on the back of the page!"

When Bill Power and others complained of having no toilet paper, a Japanese guard suggested a remedy. "Nippon understand," said the guard. "All men do *summa summa* [same as] Dutch." Then he filled a bottle with sea water, squatted over, and mimicked a man holding the inverted bottle with one hand and splashing his backside with the other. "*Wakarami* [under-stand]?" he asked.

"We *wakarami*ed," said Power. Later in the day, Power saw a mate called Curly vigorously washing his hands in a pool of rainwater that had accumu-lated in a hollow on the warped deck.

"What's wrong, Curly, did you miss?" someone asked him.

"Ah, these yeller bastards an' their bloody boong ideas. I got a boot full of water, a hand full o' shit, an' I *still* got a dirty arse!"[34]

Convoy SHIMI-05 successfully reached Miri, Borneo, on 8 July. During the next two days the convoy reorganized as MI-08 and left for Manila on the tenth. The *Shirahato Maru* and *Hofuku Maru* dropped out to wait in Miri for another convoy, while eight new ships joined in, including two new escorts, the torpedo boat *Hiyodori* and CDV *Mikura*. The weather was good on the way north, but the dysentery problem got worse. Major Newton asked the Jap-anese for disinfectant, explaining that it would help kill the flies, which would alleviate the dysentery. Of course, there was no disinfectant, but Newton was ordered to have each of the men kill one hundred flies per day. The men made a good show, considering their condition, and in the first few days, flies were plentiful enough that every man easily killed his quota. Counting them was another problem. They dutifully brought their catch to Korean guards, who would sit with a tally book and count off, *ichi, ni, san, shi.* Inevitably they would lose count and have to start over, usually after being distracted by laughing prisoners. As a remedy, the flies thereafter had to be properly lined up in ranks of ten. As the flies became scarce, a racket soon developed, and businessmen could be found going through the prisoners shortly before fly-counting time, selling their wares: "A hundred flies—ten cents." As ludicrous as it might appear, the flies eventually disappeared.

Convoy MI-08 safely reached Manila on 16 July, but now followed a period of interminable waiting for many of the prisoners. Instead of flies, they fought heat, thirst, and lice. The lice bred like mad in between the bales of latex and in the men's kits. Few could sleep because of the constant biting. A louse is fairly transparent, said Ray Parkin, "but once he's had his breakfast you can see the little blood spot in his stomach, and that gives him away." They would sit in little lice-catching circles topside and pick the critters off each other. "That," said Parkin, "was just part of the deck sports we had on board."

The convoy was reorganized again, and more vessels carrying Japan Party Two were split up. MI-08, now consisting of twelve ships and seven escorts, pulled out on 23 July, heading for Formosa at eight knots. The *Sekiho Maru* and *Hakushika Maru* sailed with it. Conditions were "appalling" aboard the latter, and Lance Cpl. L. E. Keens named Sgt. Hiramatsu Aitaro ("Scarface") as one of the prisoners' chief tormentors. They reached Takao unmolested on the twenty-seventh, and again MI-08 was reorganized. Sixteen ships departed three days later, escorted by CDVs 1 and 18, minesweeper 17, the torpedo boat *Sagi,* and the auxiliary netlayer *Kishin Maru.* They reached Keelung and sat until 4 August, finally making their last run across the East China Sea. The slow, seven-knot convoy was waylaid on 9 August by the U.S. sub *Barbel.* Down went the 1,937-ton *Yagi Maru* and the 2,333-ton captured ship *Boko Maru,* which carried a load of sugar. *Barbel* counted twenty-one depth charges dropped by the frustrated escorts, but the sub escaped unharmed. The convoy sought shelter at Amami O Shima in the Ryukyus. Finally, on 13 August, the prisoners were delivered to Moji.[35]

On the same day MI-08 was being torpedoed, MATA-26 was ready to leave Manila Bay. The *Rashin Maru* and *Asaka Maru* joined the convoy after spending almost a month in Manila with their POWs detailed to work parties. The *Hofuku Maru* had come up from Miri on 19 July but remained behind, its 1,287

British and Dutch POWs languishing in Manila Bay until mid-September. The convoy rounded the Bataan Peninsula and started north when it was attacked by submarines. Bill Power was sitting contentedly in one of the outboard *benjos* when he saw a splash in the water.

"Look," he said to the chap in the box in front of him, "flying fish, don't they keep a nice, straight formation?"

The POW glanced to the spot Power pointed to and said, "That's not a flying fish, it's a bloody torpedo!"

Power helplessly watched it approach, thinking how ironic it would be to killed by his own side—if not blasted by the explosion, perhaps drowned or eaten by a shark. Fortunately, the Japanese had seen the torpedo and the helm was thrown hard over. Power thought it would hit, but the deadly fish passed by thirty yards from *Rashin Maru*'s stern, only to plow into another freighter. Its mast lazily went up in the air, slowly turning, and then crashed into the sea. The guards hustled them below, and Power wondered if the torpedo had been meant for them. He figured a sub captain would not waste a torpedo on "such a pile of trash" as *Rashin Maru*.

Hugh Clarke, who was in D Force on the railroad with Major Newton, thought they were barely a mile out of the harbor when there was an enormous explosion. A tanker that was said to have been carrying Japanese nurses completely vanished. When the smoke cleared there was only floating oil and debris, with no sign of people in the water. Below, a bugler who had managed to keep his instrument began to play "Rule Britannia," and almost everyone began singing. "The Japs were going crook on top," said Clarke. "But we wouldn't shut up, we finished it." The guards found the man with the bugle and brought him topside for a severe beating. They broke his arm and threw the bugle overboard. Major Newton went up to protest, but was beaten for his efforts.[36]

After that crisis the convoy ran in to a typhoon south of Formosa. The balmy weather of the past month was gone. Said Bill Power, "The ship was being tossed about like a cork and the wind had risen to a shriek." Parkin said they retched so much there was nothing left to get rid of. "I think some of them were in fear of disemboweling themselves through the mouth," he said. With all the guards just as ill as the prisoners, one man suggested that this was the time to take over the ship. Power heard a response: "For Christ's sake, go away and drown yer bloody self."

Rashin Maru had two large girders running the length of the ship, spot-welded to the deck. A crack developed amidships, where the old superstructure had been. Frank Baker was amazed that she didn't break apart. The waves were more than fifty feet high, and from the bow, one minute he would be looking directly down at the stern, then directly up at it, as *Rashin Maru* bobbed up and down in the huge troughs. Bangs were heard—nearly as loud as rifle shots—as the spot welds snapped apart. The open hatches shipped a lot of water, but, said Parkin, the thing that saved her was the high freeboard, for there was little cargo besides prisoners and rubber. With the weight deep in the holds, the rolling was exaggerated. "It goes like a pendulum," said Parkin. "It swings about very violently." He was lying on his back on deck when one roll actually lifted him to his feet from a prone position. "I just grabbed a stanchion and saved myself from being chucked down into the middle of the hold."

A broken beam dangled down in the hold, swinging like the Sword of Damocles above the bundles of latex, occasionally knocking into them and scattering them about. As Parkin watched, one chap was being chased by the swinging beam, which weighed about two tons. If he had stepped into one of the broken bundles and slowed down, the beam would have caught him and cut him in half.

With welds popping and loose girders crashing about, *Rashin Maru*'s captain pulled out of the convoy and sheltered among some small islands north of the Philippines. Without hatch covers and with water coming through every crack, their survival was a mystery to Major Newton. "That ship did have a soul," he said. "There was something there that nobody could ever fathom."

Although newer and sounder, built in 1937 by Mitsubishi for the NYK Line, *Asaka Maru* was also having troubles. It took on water through a staved-in coal hatch, and the hull developed cracks, flooding the lower holds. It had been torpedoed and damaged near Halmahera in March, and the typhoon of 13–14 August reopened her poorly repaired seams. With the drainage pump damaged and unable to keep up with the leaking, *Asaka Maru* left the convoy and gently ran itself ashore near Takao on the fourteenth. The ship was aided by CDVs 6 and 16, and over the next few days, its cargo of bauxite and manganese was successfully unloaded. The *Asaka Maru* was refloated and safely made it into Takao's harbor for repairs. Under the harsh control of Lt. Ino Takeo, and with insufficient food and medicine, about 31 British POWs had died since they left Singapore.

The remainder, about 707 men, were transferred to the 4,351-ton, Japan Sea Steamship Company vessel, *Hakusan Maru*. It had just come south from Moji in MOTA-22 and had been waiting at Saei, a few miles north of Takao, for the typhoon to blow over. Besides picking up the British POWs, *Hakusan Maru* loaded men of the Japanese 60th Air Regiment, plus survivors from several other shipwrecked vessels. It sailed on 22 August and reached Japan on the thirtieth. Meanwhile, *Rashin Maru* waited until the typhoon passed then continued on to Takao. The Korean guards were allowed to go ashore in shifts, where they purchased food from the local shopkeepers. When back aboard, they discovered some of their purchases had been lifted by two light-fingered Dutchmen. They caught the culprits and made them kneel on the hot deck. When they didn't kneel as erectly as ordered, glass bottles were placed behind their knees, and pressure exerted downwards until the bottles shattered. The Dutchmen were made to kneel for another hour, with shards of glass piercing their flesh and blood coursing down their legs.

On the last days across the East China Sea, another hole was found in the ship's bottom, but instead of informing the Japanese, the prisoners decided to enlarge it into a nice fountain for a seawater bath. Inevitably the bilge pumps could not handle the water, and the leak was discovered. The ship's carpenter fashioned a large tapered plug, drove it into the hole with a hammer, and the leak was stopped. At least many of them had a nice bath. Actually, the crew was not bad—the Korean guards were the problem. "We had no complaints about the crew or the captain," Hugh Clarke said. He was a "very humane sort of fellow." In fact, "when people died he always slowed the engines and there was a ceremony as the body went overboard." Just two days before reaching Moji, the last man died. The body of WO Ned Turner was wrapped in a blanket, weighted, and slid out under a flag—another offering to the fish of the China Seas.

They reached Moji on 8 September. Some had been aboard since 1 July, and although the voyage had been broken up by a three-week delay in Manila, they had spent seventy days on the old tub. Before unloading, white-coated Japanese came aboard, armed with their glass rods and slides. After taking their samples, the crate was being lowered to the launch by a crane. A heavy swell lifted the launch at the wrong moment, and the POWs heard a great crash, followed by the noise of hundreds of pieces of glass breaking. Glass slivers lay scattered across the deck. The head of the white-coated brigade shrugged his shoulders as if to say, "so what," and the prisoners were allowed to debark. Extraordinarily, *Rashin Maru*'s merchant mariners, not nearly as patriotic as the guards or the Imperial Japanese Navy sailors, lined the deck and waved farewell to the departing POWs.[37]

JAPAN PARTY THREE

While the last ships of Japan Party Two were nearing Kyushu, the third group was readying to sail. Because of the rapidly disappearing merchant marine, many prisoners from the railway worked on the Singapore waterfront for the next few months. It was not until September that sufficient shipping was available to take the third party to Japan.

The orders, "All fit men go Nippon," had finally come to pass. Although "fit" was obviously a relative word. While awaiting shipment, old railway plagues had returned in the forms of beriberi, pellagra, cholera, dengue and blackwater fevers, malaria, and tropical ulcers. Some of the POWs in Singapore who were in better physical condition were late arrivals who had spent months in Saigon. They had been befriended by the Vichy French and could buy luxuries such as soap, toothpaste, cigarettes, fruit, and occasionally a bottle of rice wine. M. Robert "Bob" Farrands, a corporal in 2/19 Battalion and a participant in the "Melbourne Cup" race in Tavoy in 1942, thought they would all be shipped to Japan, but a friendly guard told him that their column was too large and "too many ships were being sunk as they left Saigon." Instead, they would all have to be sent by rail back to Singapore.[38]

In June 1944, the "good life" was over. On the returning train in Phnom Penh, Sgt. William D. Cuneen, 13th Battalion, 4th Antitank Regiment, made tense, unwanted contact with an Allied agent. He was approached by the man right under the watchful eyes of the Japanese guards. The agent passed him medicine and war news: Normandy and Saipan had been invaded. The agent wanted to know who was in the POW party and where they were headed. Cuneen and Brigadier Varley passed the man a list of the POWs, written on a roll of toilet paper. The agent moved away, and the train continued on its journey. As it passed through Bangkok and down the Malay Peninsula, they learned that the country had been devastated economically and the natives were nearly as destitute as the POWs.

Singapore was a poor place compared to Saigon, and the newcomers only exacerbated a bad situation. Chinese and Malay coolies indicated that few ships were available because the "Americana boom-boom" destroyed them at sea. Sailing arrangements were not finalized until 4 September. Roy Cornford saw thousands of Red Cross parcels on the dock; the Japanese distributed a portion of them. They got their first mail in years, and Cornford was thrilled to get five letters. They were to embark on some of the same ships they had been loading with tin, rubber, copra, and scrap iron the past few days. "Soon you all be fish food," taunted the Japanese as the POWs tramped up the gangways.

Sgt. Harry Jones of the Royal Signal Corps was told that he should live for today, for tomorrow he would be dead. Strangely enough, Jones was encouraged by the talk of doom, for he believed it implied the Allies had intelligence on the convoy, that they would try to destroy it, and it would open a way for him to escape. As on *Rashin Maru,* each POW was given a "life preserver" in the form of a block of rubber. "I was lucky enough to find a life jacket that I wore all the time," said Bob Farrands.[39]

Convoy HI-72 consisted of seven ships and six escorts. Back at sea again after being repaired in Takao was the *Asaka Maru,* with a cargo of bauxite and 593 passengers. The *Shincho Maru* carried 573 passengers and a load of fuel oil. The *Nankai Maru,* an 8,416-ton transport, was loaded with 6,500 tons of bauxite and 4,000 drums of aviation gas. The *Zuiho Maru* was a civilian-owned oiler of 5,135 tons, loaded with 8,000 tons of oil. The 6,863-ton seaplane tender *Kimikawa Maru* carried bauxite, aviation gas, and 273 passengers. Two large passenger-cargo vessels awaited the prisoners. The *Rakuyo Maru,* built in 1921 by the Mitsubishi Shipbuilding Company in Nagasaki, was 477 feet long and displaced 9,418 tons. In addition to bauxite, 601 British, 716 Australian, and several American prisoners, including Col. Harry R. Melton Jr. of the U.S. Army Air Corps, were loaded aboard. Its destination was Yokohama. Cliff Farlow, a corporal in the 2/19 Battalion, called it "a dirty, disgraceful looking ship."[40]

The 10,509-ton *Kachidoki Maru* had a more storied past. She had also been built in 1921, but at the Camden, New Jersey, yard of the New York Shipbuilding Company. Originally named *Wolverine State,* she made only a few trips for the Pacific Mail Steamship Company when she was sold in 1923 to the Dollar Line and renamed *President Harrison.* In 1930, she was reconfigured to her present design, a 524-foot ship with well decks, masts and cranes fore and aft, and a central passenger area with a single stack. In 1938, *President*

Rakuyo Maru. U.S. Naval Historical Center

Harrison was on a mission to Chinwangtao in north China to evacuate about two hundred embassy guards from Peking and Tientsin, as well as an important archaeological discovery, the bones of "Peking Man." The Japanese found her on 8 December 1941, but rather than surrender, the ship's master ran her aground on a small island near Shanghai. She was towed to Shanghai, and two months later *President Harrison* became *Kakko Maru,* the largest U.S. ship ever to fall into enemy hands. Later renamed *Kachidoki Maru,* she flew the red and white ensign of the Japanese merchant fleet. Now in Singapore on 4 September 1944, she was the flagship of the number sixteen maritime transportation commander and carried 6,000 tons of bauxite, 900 British POWs, and the ashes of 582 Japanese soldiers.

Providing escort for these valuable ships and cargoes were the destroyer *Shikinami,* the frigate *Hirado,* flagship of the number six escort commander, Rear Adm. Kajioka Sadamichi, frigates *Mikura* and *Kurahashi,* CDV 11, and auxiliary subchaser 19.[41]

The 2,218 POWs on *Kachidoki Maru* and *Rakuyo Maru* suffered another thirty-six hours down in the hot bowels of the ships before finally getting underway. The Australians would not stand for the cramped quarters. Bob Farrands read a sign in English that said the space was designed for 180 third-class passengers. "They wanted to put 1,315 of us in the hold," he said. Men broke into open revolt and forced their way topside. In order to prevent a deadly confrontation, the Japanese captain agreed to allow about 200 on deck at a time. Farrands remembered the captain's admonishment, spoken in English: "All persons will no longer be treated as guests of the Nipponese Government but from now on will be treated as prisoners of war." The POWs got a kick out of that. The captain told them there was nothing to worry about, for he had already made eighteen successful trips from Singapore to Japan. At that point, Farrands said, "Some wag amongst us yelled out that Ajax, a successful Sydney racehorse, won eighteen straight and went down on the nineteenth." The men on deck roared in laughter, but the captain was not amused. On 6 September the convoy sailed. Soon, the prisoners were no longer amused either; the *Rakuyo Maru* carried only six small wooden *benjos*.

By noon of 7 September, convoy HI-72 was about 150 miles east of Kota Bharu on the Malay Peninsula. On *Rakuyo Maru*, Bill Cuneen was selected as a cook and worked in a shack on the stern. For security reasons, they could only cook during the daylight hours and they had only two pots. It was nearly impossible for him to make even a cupful of rice for each of the prisoners. Billeted aft, nearby Cuneen was a covey of prostitutes, called "jig-a-jig" girls. Cuneen kept his distance, but could authoritatively tell the men that the girls "wore no underpants."

In the middle of the mouth of the Gulf of Siam, HI-72 altered course to the northeast, so that by noon on 8 September, it was off the southern tip of French Indochina. After several days at sea, the men became so gamy they could barely stand their own stench. They pleaded to be allowed to wash, and permission was granted for them to hose down with the topside salt water pumps. As hundreds of them washed naked on the open deck, the "jig-a-jig" girls watched, giggled, and teased. Roy Cornford, trying to scrub away his grime, noticed some of the girls laughing, "with some holding their hands apart to show what size they saw." To the men, deprived of so many "necessities" over the past few years, the teasing women were another torture.

On 10 September, one problem was temporarily alleviated as an afternoon thunderstorm dumped rain on the convoy, now two hundred miles from shore and angling northeast into the vastness of the South China Sea. The men on decks danced for joy, holding their mouths and canteens wide open. But even this was short-lived. After dark, the rain turned to a cold drizzle, and those topside shivered in a chilled, wet misery.[42]

On 11 September, about a hundred miles northeast of the Paracel Islands, they were joined by Convoy MAMO-03 from Manila: *Kagu Maru,* a sixty-eight-hundred-ton seaplane tender, *Kibitsu Maru, Gokoku Maru,* and three escorts, CDVs 10 and 20 and minesweeper 21. When the two convoys united, the three escorts were released to return to Manila.[43]

The enlarged HI-72 reconfigured, with the tankers moving to the center of three columns. The *Rakuyo Maru* shifted to the rear of the starboard column, *Shikinami* was in the van, and the frigates and patrol boats took position on the flanks. Curly Martin thought there were fifteen ships in three columns of five. The tension rose aboard all the ships, for the convoy was now out of effective range of land-based air cover. On *Kachidoki Maru,* men heard one Japanese soldier joke, "This is the day we sink."

By midnight the POWs had fallen into a fitful sleep. At about 0200 on 12 September, however, their sleep was shattered by a flash and an explosion as the frigate *Hirado* was torpedoed by the *Growler.* Harry Pickett, a signalman in 2/4 Battalion, was dozing under a pile of bags near *Rakuyo Maru's* bow. When he heard the explosion he ran to the rail to see what looked like a destroyer on fire. Suddenly Pickett was grabbed by a Japanese guard. He thought the guard might lose his head and throw him over the side, yet, strangely enough, the man just tightened Pickett's life jacket and walked away. Harry Jones was with another group of men standing at the railing, cheering the sinking as if they were at a football game. On *Kachidoki Maru,* most of the men were sealed below decks and could not see the sinking. Yet they knew something was happening, for their ship made a radical course change. Zigzagging wildly in the darkness, *Kachidoki Maru* struck another ship almost bow to bow. They scraped and rumbled along their full lengths before separating. The men in the hold felt like they had heeled over 45 degrees before righting. They never knew exactly what happened, and it was another hour before they calmed down enough to fall back to sleep.[44]

The sun was just rising and the POWs assumed they had made it safely through the night when *Sealion II's* torpedoes struck *Nankai Maru* and *Rakuyo Maru.* Those who had been cheering when *Hirado* blew up quickly changed their tune. The *Nankai Maru* was hit first, waking the prisoners on *Rakuyo Maru* so they were fully aware before the torpedoes smashed into their own ship. The first hit in the bow penetrated the number one hold, which was filled with rubber, and the second one smashed directly into the engine room. The bow hit bent the plates so severely that the front end dug into the sea like a snow plow, cascading water across the decks and into the forward hatches. There was instant hysteria. The POWs tore at each other to be the first up the ladders.

Harry Pickett saw a Japanese gun crew get blown over the side, then fought against a wave of water that came up on deck as deep as his chest. Down in the hold, John R. Hocking, a corporal in the 2/2 Pioneers, felt the ship tilt forward and smelled a strong odor of cordite. Had the torpedo hit about thirty feet farther aft, it would have entered the number two hold and killed hundreds of POWs.[45]

Immediately the Japanese took to the lifeboats, kicking out any prisoners who attempted to join them. Many jumped into the sea. Some POWs took revenge on their guards. A dozen men attacked and killed the bow deck gun crew. Bill Cuneen saw a man bashing some Japanese crewmen with a two-by-four piece of timber. He applauded as a few other mates tossed the semiconscious men over the side. Reginald S. Stewart of the 13th Antitank Battery was looking for a life jacket when he saw three Japanese soldiers steal the life jackets from a like number of prostitutes. Stewart and other prisoners quickly found some metal angle irons, beat the soldiers, and took the jackets themselves. Cliff Farlow remembered a man named McGregor who was about to go over the side but decided he would go back and kill some Japanese first. He picked up an iron bar and headed toward the bridge. Farlow never saw him again.

Bob Farrands found a wooden "raft" about six feet square and eight inches thick with rope hooks around the circumference. He threw it overboard and jumped behind it. "Down I went," he said. "I thought I would never come up." Pvt. Frank J. Coombes found a hatch cover to climb on, which he paddled about "like a surfboard." He joined another group of rafts when a Japanese officer try to climb aboard. "One of the blokes," said Coombes, "called him over and pushed him under and held him down." F. E. "Curly" Wiles, a former prize fighter from London and now a private in the 5th Battalion, Bedfordshire and Hertfordshire Regiment, teamed up with a few mates. They found one of the portable *benjos* floating by and climbed aboard, sailing the China Sea on an outhouse.

About one thousand men abandoned ship before *Growler* came back for a second attack. Her torpedoes struck *Shikinami* about 0700, and those in lifeboats gave a hearty cheer when the destroyer exploded. Those in the water were not so lucky. The *Shikinami*'s tremendous disintegration, quickly followed by its depth charges going off, caused brutal shock waves through the sea. "It was like someone kicking you in the stomach," said Reginald J. Harris, a gunner in 2/10 RAE. The results ranged from internal injuries to death. Don McArdle felt a whack in his guts and then a strange trickling inside, as blood vessels burst in his stomach. Roy Cornford, who had drunk as much water as he could before going overboard, now lost it all when the concussion squeezed it all back out of his stomach.[46]

The Japanese were too busy saving themselves to be concerned about the prisoners, although there were instances of murder on each side. In the water, some POWs were allowed into the boats with the Japanese but were forced to row. Other boats refused to allow any POWs on board. Since the Japanese had abandoned the ship first, the remaining men on board saw no reason to rush to judgment. About 1820, thirteen hours after she was torpedoed, *Rakuyo Maru* finally slid to the bottom more than one mile below. There were about twelve hundred British and Australian POWs in the water.

After *Kurahashi* had finished picking up *Hirado*'s survivors, it sped to the scene of the next attacks. The *Mikura* and *Kagu Maru* were also separated from the convoy to help rescue survivors. One of *Mikura*'s officers called in English to the POWs that they must not come near the ship or they would be shot. The Japanese, said Ken Williams, "had the cheek to wave as they left us behind." On one raft, when the men realized the escorts were not rescuing any prisoners, they sat on a lone Japanese soldier and held his mouth shut. When the frigates left, the POWs beat their captive to death. A British prisoner commented, "Some of the men were already dying of thirst. They drank his blood. It was horrible."

By 1900 on 12 September, the Japanese had rescued everyone they were going to rescue. They then carried out one last act of vitriolic meanness: the frigates tore back through the center of the floating survivors, chopping up some in their propellers and drowning others. It was the last straw for many men; they started dying about an hour after the ships left. It was as if they had lost the will to live. Some succumbed to their injuries, others just gave up hope and slid off their rafts and disappeared. Yet when darkness fell that first night, there were still a number of men with spirit enough to sing out a throaty chorus of "Rule Britannia."[47]

On the night of 12 September, the remnants of HI-72 must have thought they were out of harm's way. In the confusion of *Sealion II*'s and *Growler*'s attacks,

Asaka Maru, Kibitsu Maru, and *Gokoku Maru* headed off on a different tangent, first making for Takao, then changing course for Hainan. The main body of HI-72 now consisted of *Kachidoki Maru, Zuiho Maru, Shincho Maru, Kimikawa Maru,* CDV 11, and SC 19. The convoy reached its rendezvous point at 19N-112E and made a turn to the north to confuse any stalking submarines. It was about to turn toward Yulin, Hainan, when more ships began exploding left and right, this time victims of the *Pampanito.*

The *Zuiho Maru* was able to send off a message: "Submarine certain. Torpedo attack, damage at 2250, 12th, in position 19-23 North, 111-50 East." *Zuiho Maru* suffered no casualties, but eight thousand tons of oil would be lost with her.

On *Kachidoki Maru,* things happened fast. Three torpedo tracks were seen coming from the port side. A hard turn avoided all but one torpedo, which struck the number seven hold. Split seams along the water line quickly filled other holds, and by 2310 the engines had flooded and stopped. Most of the 900 British POWs were in the number two hold. The Japanese were on deck launching lifeboats and letting the POWs fend for themselves. The captain ordered abandon ship at 2315, and in twenty minutes she was three-fourths underwater with a 40-degree list. At 2337, *Kachidoki Maru* heeled over to 80 degrees and slid beneath the waves. Only twelve crewmen were lost, but 476 POWs and other passengers died.[48]

The POWs who survived the sinkings now had to face the sea. The few lifeboats the POWs had managed to secure were dangerously overcrowded. One contained sixty people, with another seventy-five hanging on the sides. Men that swam up had to be kicked and punched away, left to drown. One boat holding perhaps thirty to thirty-five men sailed away from the crowd, heading east toward the Philippines. They were never seen again.

Ken Williams waited on *Rakuyo Maru* until the last minute. When the starboard deck was going awash, he took some planking and dropped into the water. "Off I went on my four-day sail," he said. He teamed up with Curly Martin, Frank Farmer, and several others. As the sun grew hotter, the suffering increased. Heads and faces were burned. Lips cracked and swelled. They became thirsty, ravenous, and exhausted from hanging on to their pitiful bits of flotsam. Roy Cornford considered himself lucky to have a hat and a Japanese t-shirt, and only his arms were badly burned. He saw a dead Japanese soldier floating by with a canteen bobbing around his neck and went after it.

Kachidoki Maru (ex-President Harrison). U.S. Marine Corps

He got the canteen, but the cork was gone and it was full of seawater. Then he realized he was too weak to swim back to the raft and almost drowned.

At dawn on 13 September, the survivors tried to even the odds against them. Boats and rafts were tied together when possible, water and food was distributed, token sails were made, oars patched together, and canvas stretched out to hopefully catch a few drops of rain. The daily rations for one group measured one billiard-ball-sized lump of rice and two cigarette tins of water. Some men tried to catch fish by wiggling their toes in the water as bait, and they actually caught a few. Unfortunately, the fish were so salty it only made them thirstier. Others gulped down seawater and began to go crazy, killing themselves or having to be killed by their comrades to prevent them from harming others.

It was dreadful to hear men talking to nonexistent parents, wives, and children, then watch as they "walked" off to pay them a visit and disappeared under the waves. But at least there were no sharks. For some strange reason, perhaps because of the thick, jellylike pools of oil, the sharks stayed away.

Fights between English and Australian POWs broke out over who was to have use of a better piece of floating debris. Aussie Bob Farrands had a set-to with Brit Curly Wiles over space on a raft. They punched, kicked, and choked each other before coming to the mutual agreement that there was room enough for everyone.

Kachidoki Maru survivors were the first to be rescued. On the morning of the thirteenth, Japanese craft from Hainan, including the *Niishio Maru*, *Kasuga Maru*, CDV 11, and SC 19, were on the scene. Several fishing trawlers assisted by towing lines of lifeboats and rafts behind them. On the frigates, the oil-covered prisoners were hosed down and given rice and water. Some, however, were beaten by the surviving crew of *Kachidoki Maru*. Finally, the POWs were left to fall into a fitful sleep on the decks.

After the 12 September debacle, the three escorts of MAMO-03 were directed to turn around and proceed to the point where HI-72 had been attacked. They arrived in the vicinity of the *Rakuyo Maru* sinking on the morning of 14 September, and, to the surprise of the desperate survivors, began to pick them up. CDV 10 hauled 157 men aboard, among them CPO Victor R. Duncan, off *Perth*, and Capt. Rowland Richards, plus nine 2/2 Pioneers, including George Carroll, Bill Mayne, and Harold Ramsey. As Carroll climbed up, he was hit in the back of the head with a rifle butt and knocked back into the lifeboat. When he climbed back he got another whack but managed to stay on deck. The others were also knocked in the head by rifles or batons, but were finally allowed to sit huddled on the bow. In spite of the initial treatment, they were fed some hot biscuits with a sweet, brandy-flavored liquid. They were the last of the POWs rescued by the Japanese. Another group of survivor boats nearby, containing Australian Brigadier Varley and American Colonel Melton, were never seen or heard from again. The captains of CDV 20 and minesweeper 21 were apparently not so kind-hearted.

By the third and fourth day in the water the survivors began to die by the hundreds, thirst and despair being the main killers. Those still clinging to life were terribly burned and blinded by sun and oil. Grasping at any hope of relief, some tried urinating into each other's mouths. Don McArdle and Harry Jones watched to see its effects; it only seemed to make them go insane. Harry Pickett tried it and said "it was horrible." McArdle and Reg Stewart tried to poke holes in dead men's necks to get some blood, but nothing came out. Two other men used penknives to cut into their own veins for blood and died for their efforts. Cannibalism was mentioned, but never confirmed. There were perhaps three hundred prisoners still alive.[49]

The submarines that caused havoc with HI-72 were *Growler*, *Sealion II*, and *Pampanito*, a wolfpack nicknamed "Ben's Busters," after the pack leader, T. B.

"Ben" Oakley Jr., commander of the *Growler*. The wolfpack had come from Pearl Harbor and assembled in Luzon Strait on 29 August, just missing *Noto Maru* as it crossed through the area. Not so lucky was Convoy MI-15, on its way from Moji to Miri, Borneo. On the thirtieth, an Ultra was sent to Ben's Busters, as well as to another pack nearby, "Ed's Eradicators," consisting of *Barb, Queenfish,* and *Tunny*. The two packs jumped the convoy as it left Takao and sank or damaged five ships. After that, it was slim pickings for the Busters until they received another Ultra on 10 September. A large convoy was making its way north from Singapore and would be at a point about 250 miles south of Hong Kong on 12 September. The Busters raced for the interception point.

The three subs met late on the eleventh and planned their search pattern, heading southwest into the convoy's projected path. Sure enough, early on 12 September, just as indicated by Ultra, along came HI-72. The *Growler* struck first, then *Sealion II,* then, pursuing doggedly until late that night, the *Pampanito* scored. Although Ultra did not disclose the cargoes of the ships to the submarine commanders, JICPOA knew. As early as 5 September the names of the ships, cargoes, destinations, and daily noontime positions of the convoy had been intercepted and translated. Stopping thousands of tons of gas, oil, and bauxite from reaching the empire was imperative. Aircraft production required tons of aluminum, which was found in bauxite ore. In July 1943, a twenty-eight-page diplomatic summary constructed from decrypts revealed the shortage. Japan imported 77 percent of its bauxite, and Allied planners realized that stopping the imports would seriously curtail Japanese airplane production.[50] On 10 September, word went out to the Busters and Eradicators to stop that convoy. In the grand scheme of things, 2,218 Allied lives were worth less than several ships carrying gasoline, oil, and tons of bauxite ore.

RESCUE

After the 12 September attacks, *Growler* had been detached from the wolfpack and *Pampanito* and *Sealion II* patrolled for a few days near Hainan, before heading east across the South China Sea. On the afternoon of the fifteenth, *Pampanito* discovered wreckage in her path and closed to investigate. There were men out there, men floating on rafts—alive! Said Cdr. Paul E. Summers, "It was naturally believed that these would be Japanese, so small arms were broken out and preparations made for taking prisoners."

Officially, Summers was out to take prisoners, and a party of men was armed for its own safety. There was no set policy for this situation. If a skipper could capture useful equipment from a ship, or gain information from a prisoner, all the better. If he saw fit to destroy the ship along with the survivors, it was up to him. It was not ostensibly condoned or disapproved. Submarine skippers had always acted inconsistently in this situation. In the Atlantic and Mediterranean, British submarines and German U-boats in rare instances had shot floating survivors. On one occasion, German commander Werner Hartenstein in the U-156 sank the British liner *Laconia*, which was carrying 1,800 Italian POWs. The date was 12 September 1942, exactly two years before the sinking of *Rakuyo Maru* and *Kachidoki Maru*. Rather than do further harm, Hartenstein packed 236 survivors aboard his small boat and towed a number of full lifeboats along behind him. Hartenstein even broadcast uncoded radio messages to the Allies, telling them where he was and what he was doing, in the hopes that he would not be attacked while carrying out his mission of mercy. Two more U-boats, an Italian submarine, and Italian and French surface ships were called in to help in the rescue. Regardless of his precautions, which included showing a large Red Cross flag on his deck, Hartenstein was bombed by a U.S. Liberator which killed people in the lifeboats and damaged the U-boat. Hartenstein cut the boats loose and played no more part in the rescue. The bombing infuriated German admiral Karl Dönitz, and he responded with the so-called Laconia Order: No attempt of any kind will ever be made to rescue any survivors from sunken ships.[51]

Not restricted by such decrees, Summers on *Pampanito* had his options: leave them, pick them up, or kill them. If Summers officially was looking to pick up prisoners, unofficially he may have had other thoughts in mind. Lt. Richard Sherlock heard Summers order them to break open the gun locker. "Anyone who wants to shoot Japs, get yourself a Tommy gun and come out on deck," Summers called out. Shortly after, said Sherlock, "a whole bunch of guys came out from the Gun Access hatch under the Conning Tower with Tommy guns, all set to have a ball." Gunner's Mate Tony Hauptman emerged carrying a 12-gauge double-barrel shotgun. He was followed by Torpedoman Jim Behney with a Thompson submachine-gun. Motor Machinist's Mate Mike Carmody and half a dozen others followed suit. "We were not going to pick them up," said Hauptman. "The captain told me to do away with them.

Pampanito (SS 383). U.S. Naval Institute

I was going to shoot them." Tony walked forward to the bullnose and stood there waiting, shotgun leveled at the approaching life rafts.

Seaman Gordon Hopper's conscience was bothering him. He manned the 20-mm gun, and the order he heard given to all the topside gunners was that "we would sweep past the rafts and shoot the survivors upon the captain's command." As Hopper loaded and adjusted the gun, many thoughts raced through his mind. If they were Japanese they were still human beings and they represented no threat to him. He couldn't kill them. He was "appalled at the prospect of shooting helpless men on rafts in the middle of the South China Sea." But this was war. He had to obey orders. "Waiting for the captain's word," Hopper explained, "I was debating what to do, knowing that if I refused to fire or fired wildly I could be court-martialed or even shot on the spot for disobeying an order during combat."

The sub moved closer to the waving men. Hopper could almost make out their individual faces. He lined up the gunsight on the nearest one. A burst from a 20-mm could cut the man in half. Hopper set the sights on the man's chest and waited for the word from Summers that he hoped would never come. Hopper's finger tightened on the trigger, when a man called out from the waves below.[52]

On one large raft closest to the sub, former schoolteacher Francis Farmer and Curly Martin, both privates in 2/10 Battalion, had been discussing their likely fate when Martin thought he heard the sound of engines. It appeared to be a submarine. At first it went by, and Martin thought it must have been a U-boat. Farmer stood up and waved his hat, and the submarine closed in. Farmer could see men on the deck with guns. Martin waved too. "I, fortunately," he said, "had a lot of fair, curly hair at the time, and they knew I wasn't Japanese and they came back to have another look."

The *Pampanito* had approached a group of about fifteen men on several rafts. Some had Australian "Digger" hats, and a few wore Japanese-style caps. They were waving frantically and shouting all at once so that no words could be distinguished. Most of the crew on deck were startled when they heard an obviously English voice angrily call out, "First you bloody Yanks sink us. Now you're bloody well going to shoot us." On the bullnose, Tony Hauptman lowered his shotgun and called back, "Who are you?"

"Prisoners of war," one yelled. "Australians. British. Prisoners of war. Pick us up, *please*."

Several men moved to assist them, but Summers was not yet sure. Just one, he cautioned, then yelled out, "Get the one that speaks English."

The reply was defiant: "You dumb bastards. We all speak English."

Hauptman put down his shotgun, held up one finger and said, "One man. One man only." A rope was thrown across and several men jumped in the water and began swimming for the submarine. Hauptman shouted for them to stay put, while Jim Behney raised his machine gun. Farmer was the first to reach out. "I grasped the rope," he said, "and was hauled across the intervening water to the sub's side, up which I was assisted by two crewmen. When I thanked them in English, they were incredulous." He was escorted to the conning tower where he quickly told his story.

"Take them aboard!" Summers ordered, and Frank Farmer became the first survivor of the "Railway of Death" to return to Allied control. Harold Martin and Ken Williams followed close behind. "They threw us a line," said Williams, "and the three of us were soon on board. After hearing our story, they immediately started searching for more."

Word passed through *Pampanito* like a flash, and almost everyone not on duty tried to come up to help. Fire controlman William E. Yagemann climbed on the side of the hull. He saw that the men were so weak that they couldn't even grab the lines; they'd reach out and fall off the rafts. They were almost impossible to haul up. "It was like trying to capture a greased pig," Yage-

The first three men rescued from the Burma Railway after their return home to Australia. *Left to right:* Harold "Curly" Martin, Frank Farmer, and Ken Williams. *Courtesy* Ken Williams

mann said. Crouched on the side tanks he cut his knees on barnacles and had his back wrenched by someone using his leg as a ladder. Hopper breathed a great sigh of relief, slid down from his gun, and jumped in the water. On deck and along the tanks a dozen more eager submariners assisted in the rescues.

Yeoman Charles "Red" McGuire heard the order, "Stand by to pick up prisoners," but he assumed they were Japanese. One survivor managed to climb down the ladder under his own power. McGuire saw a short, oil-covered man who barely came up to his chin. Coming from behind, McGuire grabbed him in a headlock and banged his head into the ladder.

"Blimey!" the fellow yelled out. McGuire wiped some oil off his face with a rag and asked, "Who the hell are you?"

"I'm a British prisoner of his Imperial Majesty, the emperor of Japan," the man smartly answered.

"No you're not," McGuire countered. "Now you're a free man on a United States submarine." The man's eyes lit up, and an embarrassed McGuire said, "I'm sorry. Does your head hurt?"

"Oh, no," the man answered. "I'm just fine." And he walked away, McGuire said, "as happy as a lark."

Pampanito combed her way through the wreckage, searching for more survivors. In the patrol report, Summers recorded, "A pitiful sight none of us will ever forget." He broke radio silence and sent out a message to *Sealion II* asking

The crew of *Pampanito* helping POW survivors of *Rakuyo Maru*, 15 September 1944. U.S. Navy

for help. About twenty-eight miles to the northeast, Cdr. Eli T. Reich got the word and swung his boat back to the scene at four-engine speed.

Cliff Farlow was having hallucinations from heat and thirst. "I looked out and saw my mother and father milking cows under palm trees in the South China Sea," he said. "Obviously I was getting pretty delirious." One of his mates saw something that looked like a submarine, then they heard the thunder of the engines, but they figured it was "a bloody Jap sub." When it neared, Farlow saw "blokes come out on the deck with machine guns and we thought we were going to be done over." However, one of them called out, "They're Australians!" Two sailors jumped in, swam over, and helped Farlow and his mates aboard.

Bob Farrands's raft was thoroughly waterlogged and he sat in water up to his chest. He was "thirst crazy," he said. "I would shut my eyes and see the soda fountain running in a shop back in my home town, but no one would give me a drink. We always had a water bag on the verandah at my home. Water was running out of it, but still I could not drink." Others on the raft said they could see ships, but Bob's oil-blinded eyes could see nothing. He heard an engine, and finally rubbed enough oil out so that he could distinguish what appeared to be "a Yank sub."

"A sailor dived in and put a rope around my chest," Bob said. "I was pulled and assisted on to the deck. There I stood stark naked, covered in emulsified oil. A sailor said, 'Are you all right, Aussie?' and I said, 'As good as gold.' Then he let go of me and I fell flat on my face." Farrands was given a water-soaked cloth to suck on and hauled below.

The third and fourth rafts were picked up by 1730. Then another small raft was seen with one man lying motionless on his back. A sailor dived in with a line and swam out to him. When he reached him, the survivor bolted upright and tried to jump off, perhaps thinking that the Japanese had found him again. He was persuaded to calm down and stay on the raft until he could be helped aboard. This was John Campbell, 2d Battalion, Gordon Highlanders. The strain of the rescue was almost too much for him. He was nearly blind, and he collapsed while being hauled on deck and remained semiconscious while taken below.

At 1753 they found another large raft with eleven men. While they were hauling this group aboard there must have been fifty men on deck at one time—a dangerous situation. Suddenly, one of the lookouts called out, "A flight of low-flying Jap planes!"

Summers shouted to clear the deck. In moments, crewmen, as well as survivors who could hardly walk, somehow came to life and dashed for the open hatches. Then almost immediately, the crisis passed. "Never mind. It's a bird!" came the shout. Summers sarcastically recorded: "Fortunately one of the planes was seen to flap its wings, proving the formation to be large birds gliding in perfect order."

At 1835, *Pampanito* sent a message to ComSubPac explaining the situation. They continued the search until dark and were about to call it off when looming up out of the black sea was another group of about one dozen men. When they were taken aboard, a head count was made. They had rescued seventy-three men, almost doubling *Pampanito*'s crew. Being "cramped for living space" and unable to sight anyone else in the tropical night, Summers broke off the operation.

One of the last men brought aboard was Harry Pickett. He had been on his own for quite awhile. "It was darkish," he said. "I could feel the regular pulse of a motor through the water. Then I saw a sort of shape." Pickett heard what he called "a good old American accent" call out, "Can you catch a rope, buddy?" It was Floridian Jim Behney. Pickett grabbed a line and was lifted bodily in the big man's arms. Behney's name, said Pickett, "I will never forget. He carried me below." Gordon Hopper didn't return to the 20-mm gun. "All the rest of my life," he said, "I have thanked God that I didn't have to make the decision to fire or not to fire. All the rest of my life I have treasured the memory of helping save lives rather than terminate them."[53]

In the meantime, Eli Reich conned *Sealion II* through the debris-filled waters until darkness closed in. He picked up fifty-four men and believed no more could be safely taken aboard. Even with others close by and calling for help, he pulled away. "It was heartbreaking to leave so many dying men behind," Reich wrote. Some of his crew who were still on deck in the darkness had recurrent memories of the scene for years afterward, especially at the plaintive cry of "Over here! Over here!" fading out in the night.

Sealion II also radioed Pearl, and ComSubPac gave both boats permission to head for the nearest Allied base at Saipan, about 1,800 miles away. Since Reich reported that many men were still in the water, Vice Adm. Charles Lockwood ordered *Barb* and *Queenfish* to head immediately to the scene of the rescue. They came to lend a hand, but about 150 miles away they ran into another convoy. This one, HI-74, had left Singapore on 11 September. It consisted of the *Harima Maru, Omuroyama Maru, Otowayama Maru, Hakko Maru*, and the big tanker *Azusa Maru*, filled with 100,600 barrels of oil. It was escorted by the frigate *Chiburi*, the training cruiser *Kashii*, and CDVs 13, 19, 21, and 27. Guarding them all was the twenty-thousand-ton escort carrier *Unyo*. On 12 September, while moving north in the wake of HI-72, HI-74 received word of an attack on its sister convoy. The convoy commander, Rear Adm. Eizo Yoshitomi, ordered them to swing about 60 miles to the east to bypass the attack area. They succeeded in avoiding the "Busters," but late on the sixteenth, ran smack into the "Eradicators."

Barb's torpedoes sent down *Azusa Maru* and *Unyo*. When the carrier sank about 0700 on 17 September, again the code breakers knew. Back at Pearl Harbor, Capt. Wilfred J. Holmes, a liaison officer between the Submarine Force and the cryptographers, was looking through a batch of the latest Japanese naval messages. He picked up a garbled one about a vice admiral shifting his flag from one ship to another, and another one that commented about the imperial portrait being safe. Holmes knew right away that a carrier had gone down, even before the men on the submarine that had sunk it. The *Barb* and *Queenfish*, however, had lost a few more hours in their race to pick up the last survivors.[54]

By 17 September, the remaining POWs had been in the water for about five days, and they were in terrible shape. Finally, after noon, *Barb* and *Queenfish* began to find them. Now, however, the rescues were made exceedingly difficult because of an approaching typhoon. The submarines nosed amid the wreckage, pitching in the heavy seas, trying to rescue the few surviving men without running them over. Scenes played out on *Pampanito* and *Sealion II* were reenacted on *Barb* and *Queenfish* as the dazed, incredulous survivors were hauled below and kindly cared for by men-of-war suddenly become angels of mercy.

Among the last picked up were from the well-organized raft of "Blood" Bancroft, who had already survived the *Perth*, *Maebashi Maru*, *Yamagata Maru*, and the Burma Railway. Their worst problem was fresh water, which was somewhat solved on the fifth day when the rains came. The men opened their mouths to the heavens. The rain was a life saver, but with the change in weather came the high seas of the typhoon. The raft bobbed like a cork, and only on the high crests of the waves could they see what looked like an approaching submarine. At long last, the raft was pulled up alongside. In contrast to the emaciated, weak survivors barely clinging to life, Bancroft smartly stood up on the raft and saluted *Queenfish*'s executive officer, Lt. Jack Bennett.

"HMAS *Perth*. What ship, sailor?" Bancroft asked.

"American submarine," Bennett answered, somewhat startled. Then Bancroft bounded aboard, shook his fist in the air and exclaimed, "I knew you bloody Yanks would rescue us!"

The rest of that day and into the eighteenth, the two subs combed the area. Charles E. Loughlin's *Queenfish* had picked up eighteen men. Cdr. Fluckey, having rescued fourteen men, contended that he would have forgone the pleasure of an attack on a Japanese task force to rescue any one of them. "There is little room for sentiment in submarine warfare," he wrote, "but the measure of saving one Allied life against sinking a Japanese ship is one that leaves no question, once experienced." One can only speculate about Fluckey's reaction had he known everything the code breakers had known. By dawn, with high winds and "skyscraper waves," the rescue was all but over. All that could be seen were dead, bloated bodies bobbing grotesquely in the seas. Had there been anyone left alive by that time, Nature would soon eliminate him. The *Barb* and *Queenfish* broke off and headed for Saipan.[55]

The crews of all four submarines were shocked at the former POWs' condition. On *Pampanito*, Pharmacist's Mate Maurice Demers was overwhelmed, and crewmembers volunteered to be nurses. Almost every man took a corresponding survivor to care for, helping to wash off the oil, administering medicines, feeding, and donating clothing. It was a most moving experience, hardened soldiers and sailors weeping together in sorrow and joy. Most of the survivors were in shock. Demers gave fifteen of them morphine shots. The next thing he noticed was their eyes, gray from vitamin deficiencies. He worked on their eyes, cleaning out the oil and dirt, then moved to the ears, noses and mouths. Some had globs of oil like chaws of tobacco, but they were too weak to even spit them out. After treating the most obvious physical symptoms, Demers retreated for a few minutes to his medical books, diagnosing a few of the diseases, such as beriberi and pellagra. They should have been quarantined, but that was impossible on a submarine. The crew resigned themselves to the situation and went about their new jobs as nurses with a passion. "You didn't have to ask anybody to help," Demers said. "They just did it."

After their thirsts were quenched, the former POWs were soon asking for something more substantial. Harry Jones got a large mug of hot vegetable soup, and even though his lips and tongue were cracked and swollen, he was happy that he could still taste the wonderful brew—"something good and wholesome, the like of which I had not partaken of for the last two-and-a-half years." Jones and some of the more fit ones just sipped their soup in silence, unable to restrain the tears of joy that came to their eyes.

Bob Farrands was quartered in the after torpedo room. He perked up rapidly. "The poor bloke that looked after me must have got sick of my voice," he said, "as I never shut up." Farrands was given plenty of hot soup and tea, he said, "but the best meal was a slice of bread and butter; it was beautiful." Try as Demers might to ease them back into a regular diet, many of them overdid it. About twelve hours after he was taken aboard, Pvt. Walter V. Winter, 2/4 Machine Gun Battalion, decided he wanted a good old American hamburger and a Coke, and he sneaked into the galley. The cooks fried him a big burger, complete with onions, relish, and ketchup. Winter wolfed it down and about an hour later was as sick as a dog. Demers could only say, "I told you so."

Almost everyone responded well to their treatment. The only one in serious trouble was John Campbell. Try as he might, Demers was unable to find a vein substantial enough to insert a needle. It was as if the man didn't have any blood. In one foot, there was a hole the size of a silver dollar, going clean through. They speculated that fish had been gnawing on him. Campbell could barely drink, and they only succeeded in trickling some water down his throat.

While heading back through Bashi Channel, Campbell died, despite the crew's best efforts to save him. He was stitched into a canvas bag and taken topside. Under a beautiful, star-filled night, a ceremony was conducted and Campbell's body was committed to the deep. There were more deaths on the other boats. They had rescued 159 men: the *Pampanito* had saved 73, with 1 death; *Sealion II* saved 54, but 4 died; *Queenfish* collected 18, but 2 died; and *Barb* saved 14. Hospital records later indicated that the survivors were sixteen pounds underweight, 95 percent had malaria, 67 percent had recurrent dysentery, and 61 percent had tropical ulcers. All had vitamin deficiencies, malnutrition, and skin lesions. Five had scarred corneas from the oil, 20 percent had acute bronchitis, nine had bronchopneumonia, and one had tuberculosis.[56]

Regardless of the loss of life, almost every prisoner was glad the hellships they had been on were destroyed and they were free again. The men recovered from *Rakuyo Maru* gave firsthand information about the conditions on the Burma Railway, and Blood Bancroft was able to supply news about the fates of *Perth* and *Houston*. Commander Summers thought he was the first to learn that the ship he sank was the ex-*President Harrison*, but the code breakers had known it before he did.[57] The practice of sending Ultra information to submarine skippers placed them in the position of unwittingly attacking friends. Submarines were acting in the disconsonant capacity of having to sink ships and kill passengers, and then pluck them from the ocean. Nevertheless, the bonds that grew among rescued prisoners of war and the submarine crews were heartfelt, emotional, and lasting.

THE LAST OF JAPAN PARTY THREE

The survivors of HI-72 were taken to Hainan. The Vic Duncan and Rowley Richards group off *Rakuyo Maru,* picked up by CDV 10, passed close by the scene of the *Kachidoki Maru* and *Zuiho Maru* sinking. As it passed by the still-burning remnants of *Zuiho Maru*, it slowed as if looking for more survivors and the POWs were worried, lest they be sitting ducks for another torpedo

Happy POW survivors on the *Pampanito,* at Saipan on 20 September 1944. U.S. Naval Institute

attack. They were rightly concerned, for *Pampanito* had been watching the same wreck earlier in the day, only moving out when Summers noticed wispy smoke trails on the western horizon. While heading for the new targets on the afternoon of the fourteenth, *Pampanito* saw lifeboats, and assuming they were Japanese, continued on. The long chase ended at nightfall with disappointment, when Summers discovered the "freighters" he had been chasing were only two small trawlers with high masts, belching a lot of black smoke. He figured they were too small to waste torpedoes on. The *Kachidoki Maru* survivors didn't realize how close they came to being attacked once again.

The POWs were collected at Samah, Hainan, and placed aboard *Shincho Maru.* The *Rakuyo Maru* men were appalled at the condition of the *Kachidoki Maru* survivors, many of whom were injured in the explosion of the ship or badly burned while escaping. Most were covered in oil and blinded. Many had broken bones. Vic Duncan had never seen a group of men so demoralized and was ashamed for them. "They just lay there in their filth and didn't try to do anything. A lot of them were cringing and scared. They'd had it," he said. Dr. Richards knew they had a reason for their despair, because the fractured limbs and burns were dreadful. "It was horrible," he said. "Equaled only by the worst 'death huts' on the railway." Richards tried to set limbs and clean and dress the burns, but the smell of burned flesh was overpowering. "I went to look at a few of these guys and had to throw up," he said.

There was an air raid that night, but none of the ships were hit. The next morning they saw *benjos* being rigged up and learned they were going to be sent to Japan on the open deck of a loaded tanker. It was the last straw. They had seen what happens when a tanker is torpedoed, and they were not going to have any part of it. They would swim ashore. The Japanese told them they would be shot, but the prisoners defied them, for they would "rather be machine-gunned than roasted." It was the closest many prisoners had ever come to rebelling.

The protest worked. On 15 September, they were removed from *Shincho Maru* and transferred to the 9,574-ton *Kibitsu Maru*, a converted dock land-ing ship with stern doors and double side-by-side funnels. The ship's peculiar appearance led some POWs to believe it was an ex-whaler.[58] Although it was not a tanker, it was still carrying fuel oil and was as potentially dangerous as a tanker. About 157 POWs from *Rakuyo Maru*, 520 POWs from *Kachidoki Maru*, and a thousand Japanese survivors from those ships and the *Nankai Maru*, *Hirado*, and *Shikinami*, were loaded on her.

On 15 September, *Kibitsu Maru* sailed to Yulin, where the remnants of HI-72 was reorganized. Slated for Takao was *Shincho Maru*, with SC 19 and auxiliary netlayer *Kainan Maru* as escorts. Scheduled for Moji were the *Asaka Maru*, *Gokoku Maru*, *Kagu Maru*, and *Kibitsu Maru*, with escorts *Mikura*, *Etorofu*, and CDVs 10, 18, and 26. They sortied late on the sixteenth. The typhoon that troubled the submarine rescue operations also caused the two convoy echelons to become separated. The rolling seas were miserable, but the POWs did have more room in the landing ship's cavernous hold. The guards avoided the sick men, fearing that they would catch something. They would call into the hold, "Two men, *mishi!*" which was the signal for two prisoners to go topside to collect the meager rations: rice and stew, plums, or a rice cake. They had no utensils, but they found sheets of zinc that they bent and shaped into plates. They drank water from buckets and slept on straw strewn on the deck. There were no open hatches as on a conventional cargo ship, and one could not tell night from day. Dysentery spread rapidly, and men could not find their way to the *benjos* in the darkness. One or two men died each day.

As the ship pitched in the storm, the creaking and clanging noises boomed inside the hollow vessel and sounded like explosions. Every heavy wave that slapped into them sounded like a torpedo. They were nervous and frightened. No one could sleep. It was like living in a constant nightmare. As if this wasn't enough, on 20 September, south of the Pescadore Islands, the convoy was attacked by B-24s. The *Gokoku Maru* took a hit that damaged its rudder. The *Asaka Maru, Kagu Maru,* and *Mikura* were all damaged by near-misses. The *Kagu Maru* headed for Takao, while the others received aid from the Bako port authorities. CDV 20, which had been at the scene of the *Rakuyo Maru* rescues, took over as escort for *Kibitsu Maru,* and they both raced for Keelung, Formosa.

After hull repairs, *Kagu Maru* left Takao, with CDVs 10 and 11. They met up with *Kibitsu Maru* in Keelung on the twenty-fifth, and the two ships and three escorts finally continued on to Japan. The prisoners below decks could not shake their uneasiness. Unexpected noises still made them jump, and they tried to secure any loose gear they could find. The ordeal was not over, for near Amami O Shima, they were being stalked by another submarine, this time *Plaice,* on her second patrol, skippered by Clyde B. Stevens Jr.

Plaice got radar contact on the zigzagging five-ship convoy at twenty thousand yards. One escort was ahead, and two on the flanks, ranging up and down. Early on 27 September, Stevens fired four bow torpedoes at the largest target, which appeared to be a transport. Just at that moment, CDV 10 began dropping back and overlapped the torpedo run to *Kibitsu Maru.* The night was shattered by four great explosions. Stevens believed he hit both the escort and the transport, but 10 caught one or two of the torpedoes while the others may have exploded in the wreckage. It immediately split in two, bow and stern sections angling into the air. In three minutes it was gone. Smoke and fire obscured the other ships. The captain of 10, who had rescued the Duncan-Richards group, was not paid back in kind by his enemies.

The explosions of torpedoes and subsequent depth charges were enough to drive the prisoners to the edge of insanity. The *Kibitsu Maru* rang like a bell. There was a rush for the one ladder that led topside, leaving a crush of men fighting in the darkness. Richards was on deck when he saw the escort blow apart, seemingly only one hundred yards away. It was so close that the windows on *Kibitsu Maru's* bridge blew out. The two marus and CDV 20 sped off. The *Plaice* chased them for an hour and a half, but they were moving at over fifteen knots and Stevens gave up. At the scene of the sinking, CDV 11 could find only eight survivors.

On the twenty-eighth, the two remaining marus pulled into Moji. Because *Shincho Maru*, in the second echelon, had also been bombed on 21 September, they were the only two ships of the combined HI-72 and MAMO-03 convoys to reach Japan. The Japanese regretted that they sent both convoys together. In spite of some hard-learned lessons that well-protected, large convoys were theoretically safer, they felt that by routing them separately, more of them might have gotten through. Convoy tactics more often would degenerate into small groups or single ships sneaking along in shallow coastal waters by day, and hiding in harbors at night. Richards estimated that eight men had died since leaving Hainan. The prisoners unloading from *Kibitsu Maru* kneeled down and touched the earth, thankful to reach land—any land.[59]

HELL MONTH

In terms of prisoner casualties at sea, September 1944 was the worst month of the war. It started out inauspiciously enough. B-24 Liberators had been flying bombing missions over the Palau Islands from New Guinea and Biak the preceding few months, and U.S. carrier task forces had made several raids. It was only a matter of time before some planes would be shot down. Two Army sergeants, Reynold B. Mooney and Hilary Gilbert, were downed and captured. On 19 August, they were placed on the cruiser *Kinu* at Palau, which carried them to Manila, via Cebu and Palawan. WO Howard L. Roeder, CPO John C. MacMahon, and CPO Robert A. Black were placed aboard special subchaser *Uruppu Maru* on 2 September. Lt. Grant Roy and Sgt. Earl Curry of the U.S. Army bailed out of a Liberator over Palau on 25 August and were also placed on the subchaser. Lt. Arthur Shumaker and Sgts. John Moore and Alexander Bick of the Army bailed out of a B-24 over Koror on 1 September, were captured on the fifth, and were placed aboard the 4,806-ton *Nanshin Maru*, an ex-British ship built in 1914. All ten pilots were to be sent to Manila for interrogation. They all disappeared.[60]

On Mindanao, Dapecol was being closed down. In June 1944, many of its occupants had shipped out on *Yashu Maru*. Before that, in March, 600 men had been detailed to a work party to build an airfield at Lasang, on Davao Gulf. In August, they were still there, and the airfield was ready for operation. The 5th Air Force in New Guinea also knew it was ready to accommodate planes and paid it a visit the same month. When the first raid came over, the Japanese realized that the field was untenable, and the project was abandoned. The prisoners were put on reduced rations for three weeks, when, abruptly on 20 August, they were hobbled with ropes and marched off to the gulf. About 750 Americans were crowded into the holds of a Japanese freighter. No one seemed to know the vessel's name, but some had seen the number "86" on its side. Pvt. Victor Mapes of the 14th Bomb Group thought it was about 120 degrees below decks. The ship slowly sailed south for several days, then back north, hugging the erratic Mindanao coastline.

The holds were unbearable. Men passed out and others screamed enough that the Japanese opened the hatches and pointed machine guns down at them. Once a day, five-gallon cans of water were lowered down, but they weren't nearly enough to go around. Mapes saw a man drain the canteen of a buddy who had fainted, then refill the canteen with his own urine. The man awoke, drank the urine, and immediately tried to murder his "friend." One man went crazy and began shouting biblical phrases so loudly that they thought he would draw the guards down on them. They tied him up, and when he persisted, they beat him with canteens. Mapes tried to build a tolerance for seawater, by adding a little of it to his rice ration. He believed it helped. There were no outside *benjos*, just "honey buckets," but they stank so badly that the Japanese would not haul them outside to dump them.

After about two weeks, the "86" came to a halt in Zamboanga, barely two hundred miles from Lasang. After a two-day wait the POWs, under cover of a drenching rain, were ordered topside and made to walk over a plank that crossed to a ship tied up alongside. The ship switch was ostensibly made to confuse the guerrillas, who were passing ship information to American intelligence operatives. This time the POWs were closed in the holds of the 2,634-ton captured transport, *Shinyo Maru,* while Japanese soldiers vacated *Shinyo Maru* to board "86." The switch would not prevent an attack.

During the transfer, Capt. Bert Schwarz of the 27th Bomb Group remained behind so as not to be first into the hold. When they forced him over, he was one of last in and thus got a spot right under the hatch cover. Even so, there was enough lime dust in the air that he couldn't breathe. About 500 men went into the after hold and 250 in the forward hold. Disconcertingly, the prisoners watched as the Japanese practiced drills to kill them if they were attacked by submarines.

Paddle (SS 263). U.S. Naval Institute

The convoy consisted of the *Shinyo Maru, Miho Maru, No. 2 Eiyo Maru, Jintsu Maru,* and *Ryuka Maru,* along with the escorts, auxiliary gunboat *Kiso Maru,* and SC 55. It left Zamboanga on 7 September, hugging Mindanao's west coast. It was here that prisoners had jumped overboard previously, so all the captives were battened down below.[61]

The *Paddle* was prowling the same waters, on her fifth patrol, and skippered by Lt. Cdr. Byron H. Nowell. She had come through the Molucca Sea from Fremantle and across the Celebes Sea to Tawi Tawi. In transit, *Paddle* received a change of area assignment to move into the Sulu Sea and patrol the west coast of Mindanao, where a convoy was expected. Nowell reached his station on the sixth, but was plagued by plane contacts, which seemed to hover about regardless of whether or not a convoy was traveling up the coast. He figured *Paddle*'s light gray, peeling paint was easy to spot in the calm, clear water. He surfaced and headed straight for Sindangan Point, about one hundred miles north of Zamboanga.

At daybreak, *Paddle* submerged ten miles off the coast and settled in to wait. She was early, for smoke didn't appear in the southwest until late in the afternoon. Nowell spotted a float plane, then ships' masts. A tanker was leading two medium and two small freighters. Nowell estimated that they would pass as close as 500 yards off Sindangan Point. He lined up the tanker, the 5,061-ton *No. 2 Eiyo Maru,* and at 1651 fired four torpedoes with a torpedo run of

1,875 yards. Quickly shifting to the freighter next in line, Nowell sent his two remaining bow fish on a torpedo run of only 1,350 yards. Only three seconds after firing the last torpedo, the first one struck the tanker. Nowell watched the last tracks arrowing toward the freighter, but he had to shift his periscope quickly to the right, since the starboard escort was charging in. All available personnel were rushed into the forward torpedo room to compensate for the weight loss and keep the bow from broaching. They went deep, and the scope dipped beneath the sea before Nowell could witness the damage. Nevertheless, he recorded, "Loud, characteristic, breaking up noises were heard almost immediately, however, and continued for some time after depth charging began." He believed that the freighter went down, and possibly the oiler.

Nowell's guess was good. The *Eiyo Maru* turned to run herself aground in shallow water off Sindangan Point. The freighter, *Shinyo Maru,* blew apart. The *Paddle* went down to three hundred feet and counted forty-five depth charges, some of which jarred the boat but caused no damage.

On *Shinyo Maru,* events unfolded with terrifying speed. The Japanese saw the torpedo tracks approaching, and immediately a bugler began blowing general quarters, reminding Vic Mapes of "Gunga Din." Fourth Marine Cpl. Onnie Clem said the bugler blew, missed some notes, then "pooped out." The hatches were torn off and the guards went into their kill drill, tossing in grenades and opening up with machine guns. Clem heard a great explosion, saw a flash, and everything turned orange-red. He didn't know if the grenades or the torpedo hit first. "The next thing I knew," he said, "I was kind of flying, just twisting and turning, and there were clouds of smoke all around me. I couldn't see anything but these billowy forms like pillows. I thought I was dead."

Pvt. Cletis Overton heard two explosions. One torpedo hit forward of the bridge and a second between the aft hold and rear superstructure. Almost immediately, another explosion, perhaps from the boilers, shattered the hull. The bow section split apart, and within seconds five hundred men were beneath the water. Overton kicked and fought to reach the surface. As soon as he did, a drowning man latched onto him and tried to pull him under. He struggled in the rising water under the hatch when the bow dipped under and more water came in from the deck above. He floated through the opening in time to see the Japanese still firing their machine guns at prisoners on the deck.

When Onnie Clem opened his eyes he realized he was underwater, and that the "pillows" around him were floating bodies, some dead, some trying to swim. He thought the ship had already gone down and he was about to drown himself when his head bobbed to the surface. He was still in the hold, but there was light coming from an opening, and he fought his way to it. "You'd pull one person out of the way to get a little closer to the hatch." It was "survival of the fittest," he said.

Captain Schwarz thought the entire bottom had blown out of the ship, and within seconds, he was in thirty feet of water. He got out on deck and swam over the railing as the bow went under. Disoriented from the blast and confusion, Schwarz swam in a circle. He was heading back to the ship where the Japanese were lowering lifeboats and shooting men in the water when he was grabbed by Dr. George Colvard. The "Doc" pointed Schwarz toward shore. Colvard had been helping wounded men on deck before Japanese gunfire drove them into the water. He swam from raft to raft, assisting all he could.

Vic Mapes popped to the surface amid floating barracks bags, bodies, and debris. "You could hear the ship's whistle blowing constantly," he said, "like a wounded animal." At the edge of the deck, Mapes caught his leg under a steel beam. When the ship lurched sideways, "I heard the crunch of solid bone breaking." He was free, but his leg dangled uselessly in the water. Trying to swim with his arms only, he came to a lifeboat with Japanese soldiers in it. One raised his rifle to fire. Mapes didn't want to see himself shot, so he turned away, only to see the swimmer next to him take the bullet instead. Mapes ducked under and swam with all his might.

Pvt. Hayes H. Bolitho found a different way off *Shinyo Maru*. Underwater, he pushed against a number of dead bodies that reminded him of nothing more than sponges. When he came to the surface, he knew he could not reach the hatch, and the guards were dropping grenades in. The great hole torn by the torpedo was closer. With the hold nearly filled, Bolitho swam for the opening. He shot out through the hole but was immediately slammed back against the side of the ship by the swirling water. By that time the deck was awash, and the water dragged him back aboard. His jaw, right arm, and ribs were broken. Dazed, Bolitho calmly walked across the deck while machine gun bullets buzzed around his head. Untouched, he reached the other side and jumped in. Back in the water, Bolitho found the strength to team up with another American to fight a Japanese for a piece of floating debris. They killed the soldier, but Bolitho suffered a bayonet wound in the process.

Most of the 750 prisoners were killed in the explosions of the torpedoes or drowned in the ship. Almost all of those who escaped either were shot by the Japanese, succumbed to their wounds, or drowned while swimming to shore. Mapes met up with Mike Pulice, a friend of his from the 200th Coast Artillery, who also had a broken leg. With two good left legs between them, they grabbed a wooden spar and kicked for the shore. They went past Colvard and asked him to join them, but he had business helping the maimed on another raft. Ten minutes after Mapes and Pulice kicked away, the grounded *Eiyo Maru* put a shell directly onto the raft, obliterating it.

About thirty prisoners who swam near *Eiyo Maru* were "saved" by the Japanese and taken aboard while guns crews continued to blast the water with machine gun and artillery fire. Float planes swept low, strafing all the swimmers they could find, and motor launches combed the wreckage, pulling surviving Japanese from the water and shooting the Americans. At nightfall, the prisoners on *Eiyo Maru* were tied by the wrists, hung up, and shot, one by one. One man hid in the anchor compartment, climbed down the chain, and escaped to shore.

Once on land, the prisoners were still not safe, for gunfire from the beached oiler and motor launches sweeping in near the beach continued to blast the shoreline. Some made it to shore that night, while others floated until the next morning. Filipino natives were shocked to find the shore littered with wreckage and bodies of dead Americans and Japanese. They began rounding up the Americans, who were scattered for miles along the coast. Only eighty-two Americans made it to land, and one died soon thereafter. The Filipinos took them to the guerrillas in the vicinity. One of them, Lieutenant Colonel McGee, who had escaped from *Yashu Maru* in June, would try to evacuate the American survivors.[62]

After the attack, *Paddle* moved off northwest. The last escort left at 1800 and *Paddle* returned for another look. At 1912, she was shaken by two aerial bombs that exploded astern, and Nowell took her down for another hour. Coming to periscope depth after dark, he found two small ships still in the area, one of them conducting a sonic search. Nowell decided to surface and head north toward Cebu to look for the rest of the convoy. He had no further luck, but the submarine *Bashaw* found the convoy on 8 September, and sank the 2,813-ton *Ryuka Maru*. *No. 2 Eiyo Maru* managed to float free and make her way to Cebu, where she was finished off by an air raid on the twelfth.

The guerrillas contacted Australia, and the *Narwhal,* under Cdr. Jack C. Titus, was selected to attempt a pickup. Unsure as to how many men the submarine could take, the freed prisoners drew numbers. Cletis Overton was disappointed because he picked number seventy-two and figured there wouldn't be enough room for him. Vic Mapes, on the other hand, drew number one. But before he could get down the sub's small hatch, he would need his leg straightened. Said Mapes, "Six men got hold of me and pulled that leg. I yelled. You could hear me for miles." But they straightened his leg. They assembled in Sindangan Bay and on the night of 29 September, *Narwhal* surfaced offshore, looking, according to Mapes, "like a battleship."

A yellow rubber dinghy came to shore and the first load was gathered up. With Mapes anxious to get away, one big submariner in shorts jumped to the beach and stood for a minute, wiggling his toes in the sand, saying how good it felt to be on solid ground. After several loads were taken, a submariner asked how many men there were. "Eighty-one," was the answer. A signalman flashed the sub and back came the response. It was no problem, said the submariner on the beach. They could take everyone. Overton breathed a sigh of relief.

Once they were all safely aboard, Narwhal backed off into deeper water and the journey home began. The first thing on men's minds was food. Mapes was asked what he wanted, but he couldn't think of anything. Finally he blurted out, "A peanut butter sandwich and tomato soup." Mapes could not eat much. He was ill, and his leg swelled and grew gangrenous.

On 30 September, the novice submariners were treated to an unexpected ride when *Narwhal* sighted a Japanese plane. Overton heard the diving alarm, which he likened to a Model T horn. The sub started down at a steep angle. Overton almost slid out of his bunk and Mapes was thrown against the bulkhead. When he saw a sailor crossing himself, Mapes thought, "Oh oh, this is apparently not normal."

The stern planes were set at a 20-degree angle when, suddenly, all power was lost and the planes could not be operated manually. They were nearly at two hundred feet when Titus ordered the main ballast blown and all back emergency. The dive was halted, but now the process was reversed, and *Narwhal* went shooting back to the surface stern first. With the plane only a mile off, Titus again ordered her down to ninety feet. Luckily, no bombs fell.

While heading to New Guinea, *Narwhal* crossed paths with the Japanese hospital ship *Hikawa Maru*. Titus took photographs and watched the untouchable target slide past his sights. On the night of 2 October, a cracked liner put the number one main engine out of commission. Then Titus picked up radar interference from another submarine, which he thought must be from either *Paddle* or *Seawolf*. To liven up things for his passengers, as if they needed entertainment, Titus threw an equator-crossing party on 4 October, initiating the "pollywog" former POWs into seasoned "shellbacks." They successfully landed at Mios Woendi, off the New Guinea coast, on 5 October. After being administered the new wonder drug penicillin, Mapes's leg got better, but it would take several years of operations and skin grafts for it to fully heal. If *Narwhal* had truly crossed paths with *Seawolf* during the night, it was the last boat to see her. The *Seawolf* was en route from the Admiralties to Samar in the Philippines with seventeen Army agents when attacked by the "friendly" destroyer *Richard M. Rowell*. The *Seawolf* was lost with all hands. Guerrilla submarine operations were no safer than offensive combat operations, and to prisoners of war or submariners, friend could be as deadly as foe.[63]

For the prisoners on Haruku, the past year and a half had been a horror. Hundreds had died from overwork, starvation, and disease, and those who were evacuated died at sea. The airfield, constructed at such a cost, was abandoned when the Allies controlled the sky. The POWs were sent to the neighboring island of Ambon, where they helped finish the airfield at Liang. By mid-August, when it became apparent that this field too would be untenable, the prisoners were shipped again.

During a light raid over the town of Ambon, leaflets were dropped warning that the place would be destroyed. It was blasted by Liberators from late August on. Don Peacock, the RAF man, injured his ankle diving into a latrine to escape strafing P-38 Lightnings. When two small Army transports came into Ambon's bay, about 500 POWs, half of them stretcher cases, including Peacock, were taken aboard. They, and 115 Japanese passengers, were split between the 950-ton *Kenzan Maru* and the 443-ton *Sugi Maru*. Empty fifty-gallon drums in the hold served as platforms for the stretchers. Most of the prisoners were forced to remain below, but Arthur Stock, an RAF maintenance man who had come to Ambon on *Cho Saki Maru*, was given a Red Cross arm band and enlisted as a nurse, had access to the deck. The little convoy, escorted by a small gunboat, sailed on 31 August. More than once the Japanese had the prisoners rush on deck and wave, showing off the remnants of their British uniforms as Allied planes buzzed overhead. "No longer," said Peacock, were the Japanese "blustering conquerors."

They pulled in to the Celebes coast for a few days, camouflaging the ships with tree branches. The prisoners were allowed to trade with the natives, and the fruit, eggs, and vegetables they got were the best they had eaten in years. Peacock actually had a piece of fried chicken and thought he was in heaven. Next stop, on 12 September, was at Makassar. Due to Allied air strikes, the docks seemed deserted, and the skipper was reluctant to wait around. After taking on the bare minimum of supplies, they crossed the Strait to Kotabaru, Laut Island, docking there on 15 September. At that time, communications broke down, and no escorts or orders followed. The *Kenzan Maru* and *Sugi Maru* were seemingly stranded, and the sick prisoners began to die. Every morning, burial at sea was the first order of business. The death toll hit double figures and continued to rise. Allied decoders picked up distress messages from the ships on 25 September, complaining that they had been told to wait for escorts that never arrived. After ten days they were short of provisions, water, and fuel, and if they could not sail within three days, they would be unable to continue for lack of fuel.

Finally orders came from Balikpapan: *Kenzan Maru* and *Sugi Maru* were to proceed independently from Laut. They pulled out on 27 September, crossed the Java Sea, and reached Surabaya on the twenty-ninth—where the prisoners had started their journey eighteen months earlier. The voyage took almost one month. Fifty-five men perished on *Sugi Maru*. Grateful for the small favor of being allowed to purchase fresh food, Art Stock sardonically commented that on his ship "no more than 25 people had died."[64]

As the air raids increased, the Japanese hurriedly ran their captives out of the Moluccas. At Ambon on 17 September, *Maros Maru* was loaded with five hundred British and Dutch prisoners. This six-hundred-ton ship was formerly a Dutch vessel, scuttled at Batavia in 1942 and refloated by the Japanese in 1943. After waiting in the rain and mud for three hours, the men were taken on barges to the ship. Flt. Lt. W. M. Blackwood, RAF, couldn't believe they would all fit below decks—and they didn't. The holds were filled, and the remainder of the prisoners were expected to travel as deck passengers. The sick and wounded, including stretcher cases, were jammed in any available space on a deck only thirty feet across and forty-five feet long from the after bulkhead to amidships. Firewood was then packed in, and the deck was full to the gunwales. "The effect was like a London tube train in the rush hour," said Blackwood.

The first night at sea was rough, and *Maros Maru* shipped seas across her decks, tossing the men like driftwood. One man died before morning. Beriberi was the curse on the voyage, and thirty more men died under the pitiless sun before an awning was provided to give a bit of shade. They were given less than half a pint of water per day, while laughing Korean guards bathed in the drums of drinking water. Prisoners died so fast that they were simply tied to sandbags and dumped overboard.

On 21 September they arrived at Raha, Muna Island, off the Celebes coast. They were greeted by a sailing junk that deposited another 150 British and Dutch prisoners aboard, the survivors of a small transport that had been sunk by a Liberator. Now, with the additional wounded, starving, and naked men, the deck of *Maros Maru* became a hellish inferno. Blackwood saw men blister and turn black in the tropical sun. There were only two *benjos*. Delirious men drank out of bed pans. "The night air was filled with the yells and screams of the dying, the curses of the worn-out trying to get some sleep, and the chronic hiccoughing that afflicts a man about to die of beri-beri." Prowling the night, disturbed by a hiccupping Dutch prisoner, Gunso Mori ordered him to be given an injection to keep him quiet. It didn't work and Mori ordered another injection. A half hour later, with little improvement, Mori ordered a third injection, or he would come and beat the man senseless. Either remedy would have worked, for after the third shot the man died.

In Bone Bay the engines broke down, and neither the Japanese masters nor their Javanese crew had the expertise to fix them. With deaths averaging about eight per day, the British realized that the longer the voyage lasted, the more of them would die. They agreed to repair the engines and maintain them for the rest of the trip.

Maros Maru reached Makassar about 9 October and waited for forty excruciating days. The prisoners unloaded her cargo and finally had room to move below out of the hot sun. Fresh fruit was allowed aboard, but now blackwater fever struck. While anchored, 159 bodies were thrown into the harbor from this floating charnel house, as sharks waited hungrily at the ship's hull for their daily meal. Prisoners saw corpses being torn apart before they had time to sink.

All the while, Gunso Mori, interpreter Kasiyama, and the Japanese commander, Lieutenant Kurishima, did nothing to alleviate the horrid conditions; they seemed to revel in human torment. A sigh of relief went up as the hellship finally sailed from Makassar. Another few days brought her across the Java Sea, anchoring in Surabaya about 22 November, after a sixty-seven-day voyage. Only half of the POWs, about 325, were still alive, if one could call the diseased and starved wrecks of humanity alive.[65]

What began as a routine voyage from Java of another hellship developed into the greatest single ship disaster of the Pacific war. The initial surrender on Java had placed about thirty-two thousand Allies in Japanese custody. As POWs left Java in 1942 for work on the Burma Railway, they were partially replaced by POWs from the outer islands of Timor and Ambon. In 1944, there were still thousands of prisoners to tap for projects such as the Sumatra railroad. Even with all the movement, there were still men on Java who had been there since the beginning; most of them were Dutch and British, but there were also a few Australians and Americans.

Sgt. Gordon R. Miller of the 131st Field Artillery had missed several shipments that had carried his unit to the corners of Asia. A back injury received while working on a Javanese railroad kept him out of the October 1942 drafts. Back problems and a persistent tropical foot fungus kept him at Bicycle Camp for two more years, where he became good friends with Stanley Gorski, a boatswain's mate off the *American Leader*. Gorski, too, had missed the shipments that took his mates to Sumatra, Singapore, or Japan only to be sunk on *Tamahoko Maru*. When the Japanese found that Gorski could operate a teletype machine, they used him in their communications units. He not only had access to much war information that the Japanese tried so hard to keep secret, he also confiscated mail and distributed it to the Allied officers. He and Miller were both big fellows, more than six feet tall and still strong, hence, said Gorski, the Japanese usually left the two of them alone.

By September 1944, Miller was anxious to get off Java, if only to get to wherever the rest of his outfit had been sent. Gorski volunteered for the same draft so they could stay together. Neither knew that their destination was Sumatra, to work on a railroad. In the second week of September, about 1,700 Allied prisoners gathered in Tanjong Priok, most of them Dutch, but including 14 Americans. In addition, there were 506 Ambonese and Menadonese prisoners and 4,320 Javanese native conscripts. Incredibly, they were all to be placed aboard one boat, the 5,065-ton freighter *Junyo Maru*.

Most of the Dutch had come from the 10th Infantry Battalion, KNIL, in Batavia, plus a number from the Stadswacht (City Guards). After having trekked along many dusty roads, Hans Luning of the 10th Infantry was glad to take a train from Batavia to the harbor. His group was allowed to rest by the roadside as four thousand or more *romusha* were herded into the forward holds. Luning pitied "all these poor devils struggling along looking like skeletons." As the ship loaded, Luning noticed the shambles that had become of the harbor: iron, pipes, tubing, boilers, rails, sheeting, ships' masts, all haphazardly scattered, awaiting shipment but going nowhere. Willem Wanrooy, a nineteen-year-old Dutch POW, also felt sorry for the Javanese. After a ten-hour wait before boarding, his group of twenty-two hundred men would have no picnic either. They could not all fit in the after hold, and Wanrooy was left on deck with the last two hundred men.

"The ship was in a state of complete neglect," said Luning, "everywhere the rust had set in and much of the metal had rusted through completely." In the hold, a bamboo scaffolding had been built to accommodate the passengers. Even so, it was standing room only, which led the optimists to conclude that the journey would take only a few hours. Painted on the funnel was the number "652," and on a brass plaque they discovered the inscription "Liverpool 1908."[66] Luning found himself on a tarpaulin covered with a black, gluey substance that might have been sugar at one time. Soon, they all became blackened. Above them, only every other hatch cover was removed, and the air below was unbearably hot.

Junyo Maru sailed on 16 September, accompanied by two small gunboats. The guards donned life jackets; the prisoners had none. There were only two small lifeboats hanging outboard and a few life rafts against the railings, buried under the prisoners' baggage. Only a short distance out of the harbor they dropped anchor and waited a full twenty-four hours, while the men topside blistered in the sun and those below decks baked. An English prisoner could take it no longer and jumped overboard. The guards thought it funny until he appeared to be striking out strongly for the shore. He was picked up in one of the lifeboats, brought back, and beaten senseless, with the warning that the next escape attempt would mean death. That same day in number four hold the scaffolding collapsed and several men were seriously wounded—but at least they were taken topside.

Surprisingly, the food was better than expected. Cucumbers and other vegetables were in heaps on the well deck, where the galley was located. The cooking was done by POWs, in boilers connected to a steam pipe. They ate rice, vegetable soup, and pickled pork. As they sailed west, the men fell into a restless routine, subdued and quiet, hardly speaking because it took too much energy. The night breezes hardly cooled down the sweltering holds.

At daybreak they figured they were somewhere in Sunda Strait. Luning recognized the shattered volcanic island of Krakatoa. Obviously they were not going to Singapore, but into the Indian Ocean. They turned northwest, traveling fifteen miles off the Sumatran coast, and guessed their destination was Padang. The gunboats patrolled in circles around them, accompanied by two planes overhead. On the night of the seventeenth, a cool drizzle began, which turned into a rain storm, and in no time, all those on deck were soaked and freezing in the cold wind. On the eighteenth, the sun appeared and dried them out. Late in the afternoon the escort planes disappeared. About half past five, Luning felt a dull thud and the ship trembled. He thought the boiler had exploded. Men jumped up and scrambled for the ladders. A few seconds later there was another bang, much louder and more severe than the first, and smoke began billowing into the after holds. Sirens started blaring.

The British submarine *Tradewind,* skippered by Lt. Cdr. H. L. C. Maydon, had left Trincomalee, Ceylon, on 8 September for its third Far East patrol. Maydon encountered only sampans and coastal barges, blasting them with demolition charges and his Oerlikons, but sinking nothing but cargoes of cement, cinnamon bark, coconuts, and nutmeg. It appeared to be a relatively unproductive patrol. The high power periscope was out, and the radar was defective. Maydon figured he'd never sight a good target. In midafternoon on 18 September, however, Lt. P. C. Daley sighted a small plume of smoke to the south at 13,500 yards. Maydon decided to run at full speed on the surface, to get in as close as possible before submerging and having to rely on the low power scope. The target was zigzagging on a west to northwest course, covered by escorts on both port and starboard. Getting within 3,000 yards, Maydon was able to make out the primary target: an old-fashioned merchantman, with three islands, two masts, and a single, tall funnel. Counting the prop revolutions on the sound gear, he estimated the speed at eight knots. Maydon did not have a great firing angle, approaching somewhat bow to bow. However, at 1548 the ship obligingly zigzagged to course 295, setting him up with a near 90-degree track and a range of about 1,800 yards.

Three minutes later *Tradewind* was four torpedoes lighter. The fish were spread at six hundred feet, about one and a half times the target's length. Maydon lowered the scope, and within two minutes, two distinct explosions were heard. *Tradewind* didn't wait around, for Maydon took her deep and retired away from the Sumatra coast. Several minutes later, only three faint depth charges were heard.

The quiet aboard the retiring submarine was in great contrast to the pandemonium on *Junyo Maru*. Luning was in the middle of the hold and figured he'd never get up the ladder in time. He ran to the scaffolding and climbed up. From there he could almost reach a lower beam on which the hatch planks were resting. Someone gave him a boost, and he pulled himself to the beam and sprang topside. Wanrooy had been on deck when the torpedo hit. Something caught his eye. "As I looked up," he said, "I saw human bodies and pieces of wood, metal and other debris blown high in the sky from somewhere midship."

"Be calm. Break down engines," a Japanese voice called over the loudspeaker.

The second jolt brought a trembling blast beneath Wanrooy's feet. Strangely, there were a few moments of silence. Then chaos, howls, and screams.

"Torpedoes! Abandon ship!" people were calling out. Panic swept the deck. Men jumped overboard, while others tried to dig out the life rafts. Wanrooy tried to help men climb up the single iron ladder. "Scratched, beaten and bloody, some reached the deck," he said. "The bowels of the ship were belching up. It was horrible." Numbed by the tragedy unfolding, Wanrooy sat down, took off his boots and outer clothing, and jumped into the ocean.

Still on deck, Luning saw men tearing at the covered-up rafts. Some frightened Japanese guards ran past, jumping into the sea while still carrying their rifles, while others on the center deck were busy getting the lifeboats ready. The siren was still blaring. Although the ship was still high in the water, Luning went to the railing and jumped. He popped to the surface near a large raft with about fifteen men already clinging to it. He grabbed a rope noose and

hung on, and they paddled away to escape the shower of debris and the suction of a sinking ship.

An excellent swimmer, Wanrooy pulled away on his own. The two Americans, Miller and Gorski, managed to stick together. They found a raft, but it
was already crowded, so they had to look elsewhere. Gorski, from Wisconsin,
had swum in the Great Lakes many times and figured he could make it to shore,
which he estimated at four miles away. Not so the Texan, Miller, who had little swimming experience. Gorski decided to stay next to his buddy. Nearby, the
Japanese who commandeered the lifeboats were being surrounded by desperate men. As they tried to grab the gunwales, one guard used an ax to chop the
hands or split the skulls of anyone who tried to climb aboard.

"Oh my God, what an awful sight," exclaimed Wanrooy. There were bodies everywhere. The *Junyo Maru*'s stern went deeper and the bow rose into the
air. There were hundreds of people still clinging to the sides and decks. The
stricken vessel lurched over and two holes could be seen in its side, one below
the foremast and another near the stern, both about twenty-five feet wide. On
the high bow, the remaining native laborers huddled in a compact mass, as
if they were numbed by fear or resigned to their fate. A few tried climbing the
mast, as if that would save them. When the angle got too steep, many tum-
bled down the deck, crashing into the bridge or falling into the sea. Wanrooy
thought they "dropped off like ants from a sugar loaf." *Junyo Maru* stood up
almost vertically, and, said Wanrooy, "the ship disappeared against a sunset
sky burning with yellows and oranges. Foam and water bells churned madly
in a maelstrom of death and destruction. More than five thousand souls perished before my eyes." When the ship went down, many of those remaining
were ready to give up. "I looked at death and saw a friend," said Wanrooy, but
he decided to fight with all his strength to stay alive.

By 1700, Maydon brought *Tradewind* back to within three miles of the sinking, but saw only one escort, presumably in a rescue operation. "It might have
been profitable," he said, "to have waited until they were well laden with survivors and then to have surfaced and gunned them." Fortunately for the survivors, the lack of a high-power periscope denied Maydon the ability to see
how heavily armed the gunboat was. Instead, *Tradewind* left the area for good.
By 4 October, she was back in Ceylon.

The gunboats picked up the Japanese first and then went back to get the
remaining prisoners. When darkness fell, Luning was able to get his bearings

by the stars, but it soon became overcast and the wind and seas picked up. It grew cold. There were seventeen men clinging to his raft. One more would surely sink them. Every time they heard a call for help, they would purposely paddle away. Luning could hear men calling out all around him. "I will never forget those cries in the pitch dark night, especially the 'talung, talung' of the *romusha*."

Luning made it through the night, and at daybreak, a Japanese corvette loomed up out of the mist. He swam to it, clutched at the ropes hanging from the side and was hauled aboard. "I forgot all about those people sitting or hanging on the raft," he said. "I never once looked back, or even for one moment gave them a single thought." He was a survivor. Wanrooy too passed the night clinging to a hatch cover with several others. A few died, one after giggling uncontrollably, and then drowning himself. Wanrooy vowed he would live. At daybreak he saw a far-off ship and he kicked with all his might, pushing the hatch cover with two men for five long hours. The ship appeared no nearer. His head throbbed, his throat was burned dry, and his body ached. "I had reached the edge of madness," he said.

When he could take it no longer, Wanrooy let the hatch go "and swam like a maniac, arms and legs grinding through the water. A race against death, death the ocean. I left the two men on the hatch behind." Finally the ship neared and dropped a rope. He grabbed it and was pulled aboard, dropping exhausted to the deck. Someone poured cool water down his throat. He thought about the men he left behind. "Yet," he said, "the importance of my own life took precedence over compassion. . . . I survived the nightmare on the ocean, but the ordeal of it all is engraved forever in my memory."

During the night Miller and Gorski found a small raft. There was not enough room for both of them, and Gorski, still thinking he could make shore, said good-bye to his friend and struck out on his own. At daybreak, Gorski was still far from shore when he was luckily sighted by the Japanese corvette and hauled aboard. Miller clung to the raft for a time, but during the night more men were encountered, some wounded and unable to swim any longer. Miller got off the raft to let a weaker man have his place. When the sun arose, Miller was gone.

Of the 2,200 Allied and Indonesian prisoners, 1,520 died. Of the 4,320 Javanese laborers, 4,120 died. The 5,640 deaths were the most in any single ship sinking in the Pacific. The 880 survivors were taken to Padang, and in two weeks' time were put to work building the Sumatra railroad. Only 96 POWs were alive when the war ended. As for Japanese thoughts about the rescue operation, an intercepted radio message of 22 September read: "In the future we do not anticipate saving any such personnel."[67]

Back in the Philippines, the consolidation of POWs to Luzon for eventual shipment to Japan continued. On Palawan, POWs had been working on the airfield near Puerto Princesa for two years. Completion of the strip and the approaching Allies meant the Japanese could send a portion of the POWs back to Luzon. About fifty men had died, leaving three hundred, and of these, half would be sent back and half would remain as a contingency labor force. Two sheets of paper were passed out, labeled "A" and "B," and the POWs were told to sign one. They didn't know what they were for. Don Thomas decided to sign sheet "B," simply because his buddy signed it. On 14 August they were lined up in two ranks, and the "B" people were told to pack their gear; they were returning to Manila.

At least four POWs would not be returning. Floyd G. Laughlin, Wallace K. Martin, Mason C. Poston, and Samuel L. Tucker, sole survivors of the submarine *Robalo*, were locked in a cell in the Puerto Princesa jail. The sub had left Fremantle in June for its third patrol, under Lt. Cdr. Manning M. Kimmel, son of Adm. Husband E. Kimmel, who was blamed for the Pearl Harbor disaster. On 3 July, an Ultra sent *Robalo* through Balabac Strait, south of Palawan, and into the South China Sea, looking for a *Fuso*-class battleship that was to be in the area. The contact was unproductive, and *Robalo* finished her patrol off the Indochina coast. While returning through Balabac Strait on 26 July, *Robalo* struck a mine. Six men survived the explosion and sinking, swimming to Comiran Island. Two were shot by the Japanese and the last four were taken to Puerto Princesa. On 2 August, the sailors wrote out a brief note explaining their situation—they were being held as spies, not prisoners—and dropped it out of the jail window. A passing POW picked up the note and secreted it away, eventually getting it to the guerrillas, who passed word along to Admiral Christie in Australia.

They would not be joining the 150 POWs going to Manila. Henry Henderson said they were marched to a small transport ship but did not sail for nearly a month. They slept aboard, but every day they went to the docks or the airfield to work. Finally, on 15 September, *Maru Hachi* (eight) got underway.

After an uneventful three-day trip, they reached Manila and were taken to Bilibid Prison.

About two weeks after *Robalo* sank in Balabac Strait, *Flier* crossed through, also responding to an Ultra. On 13 August, she too was blown apart by a mine. Fifteen men, including Cdr. John D. Crowley, survived the explosion and swam toward shore. After fifteen hours in the water, only eight crawled ashore on Manatangule Island. They lived like castaways for six days, until found by friendly natives and taken to a U.S. Army–Filipino coastwatcher unit. The unit had been dropped off in June by the submarine *Redfin*. Radio contact was made with Australia, and on the night of 30–31 August, *Redfin*, under Lt. Cdr. Marshal H. "Cy" Austin, attempted the rescue. Joining the *Flier* men were nine other passengers, including a British missionary, his wife, and two children. Two were soldiers who had escaped when Bataan surrendered in 1942, and had made their way to Palawan. Another was Seaman Charles Watkins, who had come down with the POWs on *Sanko Maru* in August 1942. He had escaped shortly after reaching Palawan, and lived the last two years with friendly natives and guerrillas until this escape opportunity arose.

Austin looked for the signal of three white lights from the lighthouse at Brooke's Point, but approaching the rendezvous point, he found a small cargo ship instead. After interminable delays, Austin took *Redfin* within four thousand yards of the ship and flashed signals to the coast watchers. When the boats finally appeared, Austin recognized Crowley's voice and the pickup was made. The *Redfin* fired sixty rounds of 4-inch shells at the cargo ship on the way out. She reached Darwin on 6 September. Thus a handful of sailors and soldiers reached home safely. The remaining *Robalo* men and POWs in Puerto Princesa would not be so lucky.[68]

Hell Month was not quite over. Convoy HI-72 with Japan Party Three had been torpedoed by submarines and bombed by Liberators. While its last ships were fleeing to Formosa, incredibly, one ship left from Japan Party Two was still waiting to sail. The *Hofuku Maru* had separated from SHIMI-05 in Miri, and she waited in Manila Bay for a month while the wretched prisoners slowly died of starvation and disease. Sickness was more prevalent than on *Rashin Maru* or *Asaka Maru* and the Japanese were reluctant to let the ship continue, fearing to bring any tropical maladies to the homeland. Without proper nutrition and medical care the prisoners tried to treat their own ailments. When the dehydration that accompanied dysentery became severe, they found some thin, hollow wheel spokes that they sharpened and used as needles. They condensed steam from pipes in the engine room and used the water to drip down into the sharp spokes, which had been stuck into the patients' arms. The intravenous fluids, full of pyrogens, gave them fevers, but probably saved some lives. Nonetheless, since leaving Singapore, deaths were estimated at 94 to 184. Finally, on 24 August, a number of prisoners were removed and sent to Bilibid, while a similar number replaced them.

The already overtaxed medical facilities of the prison were not equipped to deal with them. Dr. Paul Ashton said they were "dropped like orphans on our doorstep." He received an additional sixty-six British and five Dutch patients in his Communicable Disease section of the prison. The Japanese suspected they had cholera and would transport them no farther. The days were hectic for Ashton; he got little outside help. "I suppose the name 'cholera' scared them off," he said. Ashton treated cases of dry beriberi, edema, scurvy, optic nerve degeneration, pulmonary congestion, enlarged hearts, vocal chord paralysis, and a virulent form of dysentery. "They were collectively the sorriest seventy–one men—absolutely frightening," Ashton said. "To this day I cannot think of a reason why the Japanese had not thrown them all overboard, such was their fear of contagion." Despite the rudimentary medical care, nine British prisoners died.

Convoy MATA-27 gathered in Manila Bay. Finally the *Hofuku Maru* would attempt to finish its journey. Joining it was *No. 1 Ogura Maru, Surakaruta Maru, Yuki Maru, Shichiyo Maru,* and *Nansei Maru*. The escorts were CDVs 1, 3, 5, and 7, and CM *Enoshima*. They left late on 20 September and anchored in Subic Bay for the night. The next morning they headed for Takao. It was their bad luck to be sailing up the Luzon coast when swarms of U.S. carrier aircraft struck. Prisoners still in the Philippine camps remembered the day well, for 21 September was the first time in two and a half years they had seen U.S. planes attacking the Japanese at Luzon. Prisoners cheered as a U.S. Navy Hellcat downed a Japanese plane in a dogfight in the skies over Cabanatuan. They cheered at Bilibid and Nichol's Field as planes from the *Intrepid, Bunker Hill,* and *Lexington,* in Vice Adm. Marc A. Mitscher's Task Force 38, soared overhead while planes from the *Hornet* and *Wasp* blasted dozens of Japanese ships in Manila Bay.

MATA-27 did not escape their attention. While nearing Masinloc, about eighty miles north of Corregidor, it was jumped by several flights of dive bombers and torpedo bombers. The 213 Dutch and 1,076 British POWs on board had mixed feelings about the attack, but their feelings mattered not one iota. At 1035, forty planes singled out the ten-knot, twenty-six-year-old *Hofuku Maru* and blasted it to pieces. Twenty minutes later, sixty more planes came in. An intercepted radio message gave the code breakers up-to-the-minute information: "*Hofuku Maru* sank. *No.* 1 *Ogura Maru* is on fire and unable to make way. *Surakaruta Maru* in danger of sinking." A third and fourth raid by upwards of one hundred planes destroyed the rest of the convoy, along with CDV 5. MATA-27 was gone. Of the 1,289 POWs aboard, about 100 Dutch and 100 British prisoners either swam to shore or were picked up, then taken either to Cabanatuan or Bilibid. Some would ride more hellships. Only 42 other POWs were rescued by the CDVs and continued the journey, reaching Takao on 25 September.[69]

The last of the 1944 Japan parties had met their fates. Hell Month was over. More than 9,300 prisoners and laborers had been killed at sea—all but about 400 by "friendly fire." It was the worst month of the war for numbers of deaths, but not perhaps, for unsurpassed suffering and horror.

THE OCTOBER SHIPS

The survivors of *Hofuku Maru* had little respite. About 165 of the fittest British and Dutch barely got ashore when they were back at Manila Bay, joining 1,000 Americans for another attempt to sail to Japan. There were at least two sailings scheduled for late September to early October. Capt. William N. Donovan, in the U.S. Army Medical Corps, was a physician at Bilibid. He was selected to go on the first ship but asked Bilibid's commandant if he could go on the next one. He was denied because it was too much trouble to change the lists. Another doctor, Alvin C. Poweleit, was scheduled for the second ship but was scratched from the list and put about the first ship when another doctor developed amoebic dysentery. "This was just another example of how much is a matter of chance," Donovan said. "In all of these experiences it seems that a lot of people were killed just by chance—one person would be killed if he were a couple of feet ahead of you, or if he got on the wrong ship."

On 1 October, the prisoners marched to Pier Seven, which was in shambles after the recent air raids. A convoy was forming up, and scaffolds hung over the sides where the names of a few of the ships were being painted out. This was disconcerting to the prisoners, as there would be no markings to distinguish their ship from any other. Julien M. Goodman, a doctor, saw a red cross and the number "2" painted on the funnel. Before sailing, the red cross was painted over and the number was changed to "8." Goodman thought the ship weighed about 1,500 tons. No one knew its name. Some called it "Benjo Maru"; others nicknamed it "Horror Maru." From the latter appellation, the name "Haro Maru" has been adopted by a number of prisoners and authors, though there was no actual "Haro Maru." The ship was likely the *Hokusen Maru*, a 2,256-ton freighter.[70]

About seven hundred men were pushed into the forward hold and four hundred into the smaller aft hold. Right away, Sgt. Forrest Knox of the 192d Tank Battalion knew he had made a mistake. They were issued winter clothes and shoes for the northern climate, and Knox and many others got overheated on the docks. He drank up his water. "Somehow it never crossed our minds what was going to happen to us," he said. They moved into the harbor and moored to a buoy. Immediately men passed out from the heat. There were no attempts to get them topside: "They just slid down out of sight, where men just stepped or stood on them."

"It was hot—oh, God, it was hot!" exclaimed Captain Donovan. In the larger forward hold, which was only twenty by twenty-five yards, he thought it must have been 120 degrees. He spent the first night with two men piled on top of him. The next day, a search was made for a couple of doctors to go to the aft hold. "Jesus, it can't be any worse than this," Donovan said to Al Poweleit, and both men volunteered. Pvt. William R. Evans of the 200th Coast Artillery heard the Japanese say that they would be down there for twelve days.

"No way we can live down here for twelve days," Evans protested. They were, in fact, down there for thirty-nine days.

The deck of the forward hold was covered with coal, and the after hold, once used as a stable, was littered with manure. It was nearly impossible to breathe. Only a few prisoners were allowed topside, and their jobs were to raise and lower the "honey buckets" and food buckets, which soon became almost indistinguishable. Donovan, in helping to pass up a pail of urine, inadvertently dumped some of it on the chaplain's head. George Burlage, who had come north with the contingent of 150 men from Palawan, thought the coal was useful, for the men "started going in it" and it absorbed some of the waste matter.

The worst torture was the lack of water, and men began to go mad. The complaining and cursing turned into pushing, screaming, trampling, clawing and biting. The Japanese threatened to fire into the holds and then cover the tops completely if the commotion wasn't stopped. Fourth Marine corporal Alton C. Halbrook heard an interpreter say, "I don't need to take you to Japan. I've got the numbers. Either sit down, or I'm going to make a bunch of numbers." The threat wasn't sufficient to calm the half-crazed men. Forrest Knox found an officer and faced him down.

"What are you going to do?" he demanded. The officer wouldn't answer, but just stared blankly. He searched out other officers. "They were all the same—zombies," said Knox. He went back to his group and said they were on their own. The officers had lost control. The screaming and the bedlam increased. A prisoner topside called down, "They're going to do it. They're going to cover you with canvas!"

That would be everyone's death sentence. Immediately, vigilante groups formed to "quiet" the men who had gone mad. Knox wore a small towel wrapped around his head and a man who had worked in a mental institution showed him how to use it to strangle a screaming man. "As a guy goes crazy he starts to scream," said Knox, "not like a woman, more like the howl of a dog." The crazy ones howled because they were afraid to die. But, said Knox, "now the ground rules changed. If they howled, they died." Some were strangled, others were beaten to death with canteens. "They'd bang on his head," said Donovan. "When you hit a person with that it's a real blow. They beat them to death. They killed about seven of them that way. Then they'd just take them and throw them over the side."

Spero Dardaris of the 228th Signal Corps said that the only physical violence between Americans that resulted in deaths that he ever saw was on this ship. "We all needed water desperately," he said. "Some men became delirious and began roaming about, stumbling and falling over men who were dozing. One man falls and another man pushes him off. He falls across two other men who promptly kick him off onto two others who do the same. It is so dark you can't even see who it is. This poor man, out of his mind, is kicked from pillar to post, not knowing what he's doing. By daybreak he's dead." Said Dardaris, "Few of us were 'normal.' It was like a page out of 'Dante's Inferno,' if you have ever seen illustrations from that book. Only those people were full-figured. We definitely were not."

One of the dead men was a fellow named Ed Lewis. Bill Evans had managed to tie up a hammock to raise himself above the chaos below. He awoke one morning to look beneath him. There he saw Lewis, "all hunkered over with his head beat in. I don't know what crime he'd committed," said Evans, "but the guys near him must have killed him. No one was ever punished for these deaths, and the Japs didn't give a shit."[71]

Captain Donovan went topside in a fruitless attempt to get the men more water, leaving his canteen in the safekeeping of Dr. Poweleit. It was stolen. Poweleit verbally thrashed the men for their shameful behavior, and, surprisingly, the canteen reappeared. As the deaths increased, the Japanese realized they had to have a doctor to sign the death certificates. Donovan and another medical officer went topside. They asked the other officer what a particular prisoner died of.

"Lack of air and water," he said.

"Jesus, you can't say that," said the English-speaking interpreter. "We've got to send this in to Tokyo."

The Japanese turned to Donovan and asked him the cause of death.

"He died of anoxia and dehydration," answered Donovan, which of course, meant the same thing, but apparently sounded more innocuous to the untutored Japanese record keeper. "That's what they sent in to Tokyo," said Donovan.

After three days of hell, the convoy finally pulled out. MATA-28 consisted of the *Hishigata Maru, Kohoku Maru, Kokurei Maru, Bunzan Maru, No. 8 Shinyo Maru, Shoei Maru, Hokurei Maru, Terukuni Maru,* and *Hokusen Maru.* It was escorted by minesweeper 20, minesweeper 41, and SC 41. After a stop at Cabcaben on the Bataan Peninsula, it traveled along the coast to Santa Cruz, and reached San Fernando la Union on 5 October. There it absorbed Convoy MIMA-11, consisting of the 6,515-ton tanker *Tachibana Maru,* fleet tanker *Kamoi, No. 2 Yamamizu Maru, Omine Maru,* and five escorts.

Hugging the coast did not prevent submarine attacks, for on the sixth, the *Cabrilla* got in close enough to dispatch *Hokurei Maru* and *No. 2 Yamamizu Maru.* The torpedoes passed right by *Hokusen Maru.* "In the quiet you could hear it coming," said Knox. "Sounded like a motor boat." He quickly uncapped his canteen and drank all but a swallow of water, because he "didn't want to die thirsty." Cpl. Louis B. Read of the 31st Infantry heard sailors saying that they could hear submarine sonar echoing off the hull and "this caused more people to go off their rocker." Some prayed they would be torpedoed.

The convoy pulled into Lappoc Bay, where on the seventh it received word that U.S. carriers had been spotted east of Formosa. The convoy broke up, with some ships remaining, some forging ahead, and some heading west toward Hainan in the hope of avoiding an air attack. On the eighth, the air raid warning was canceled and the convoy veered toward Formosa, but the next day, another warning of a Formosa air raid sent it heading toward Hong Kong. Instead of planes, the convoy ran into more submarines, and down went the *Kohoku Maru,* victim of *Hoe,* and the *Tachibana Maru,* victim of *Sawfish.* Below decks, things were getting worse. Goodman wrote in his diary, "Hatred among the men is becoming more and more bitter in the hold. . . . Good Lord, how long? How long?" On 11 October, only four ships were left to arrive in Hong Kong: *Kokurei Maru, Bunzan Maru, Hishigata Maru,* and *Hokusen Maru.*[72]

In Hong Kong, Allied aircraft finally caught up with them. On the sixteenth, bombers and fighters from China bases hit them. About fifty men were topside when the attacks began, and Spero Dardaris was caught sitting in an outside *benjo.* They were ordered below, but Dardaris had to finish his business. He watched bombs hit the freighter moored next to them while all the ships opened up with machine-gun fire. Finally a Captain Compton rousted Dardaris out and tried to force him below. Spero ran away and was chased in circles around the winch while the attack continued. There was no way he would go below to be killed in an iron tomb. Finally, when the last planes buzzed away, Dardaris sheepishly gave himself up. "Okay," he said, "I'll go below now."

Conditions deteriorated during the five-day wait at Hong Kong. It was the worst experience of Corporal Burlage's life. "Maybe you don't believe this," he said, "but people just tried to bite your throat to get blood. You know, they were thirsty, just going out of their minds." A doctor nearby opened his kit and took out some morphine capsules. He offered one to Burlage, telling him to take it if he wanted to end it all. "I'm not going to put up with it," the doctor said. "We aren't getting through." Burlage watched him swallow the capsules. "He took all of his," he said. "He killed himself. People were doing that."

While some gave up, others tried to survive at any cost. Sergeant Knox's canteen was stolen when he fell asleep. They were passed topside for filling, and Knox watched as they were lowered down in a bunch. He had etched a design into his and would recognize it anywhere. As the full canteens were claimed, Knox saw his being taken by a stranger.

"That's my canteen," Knox confronted him.

"Oh," the man said, "I thought it was mine."

"No!" growled Knox, expecting a fight. The most common way of killing a man was clubbing him with a full canteen, but, said Knox, "I was ready for him; by then I was a tiger. If he tried to hit me, I was going to do my best to kill him first. I mean, on this ship, in this place, there was no mercy." Instead of fighting, the stranger handed the canteen back.

On the twenty-first, they left Hong Kong and ran for Formosa. One man, on the edge of insanity, kept scratching at the steel bulkhead, hour after hour. The scraping infuriated Knox.

"What the hell are you doing?" Knox thundered.

"I'm trying to make a hole," the man answered.

"A *hole?* For what?"

"There's water out there," the half-demented prisoner answered. "I can hear it."

Several insane prisoners were taken topside and tied to hatch covers lashed to the deck. Another man died but had no dog tags, so the Japanese could not record his name. The prisoners couldn't recognize him either. To Knox, seeing the corpse's gaping mouth and emaciated body, it hardly looked human. "Looked like a mummy," he said.

A three-day trip finally brought *Hokusen Maru* to Takao, where it tied up on 24 October. Again the prisoners waited on board, this time until 8 November. When they finally debarked, Goodman wrote, "We are on land again and nothing else matters; no matter where they send us, or what they do to us, nothing except death by burning can equal the torture of the last month." Death estimates ranged from twenty to fifty each day, but the most often repeated number was thirty-nine deaths for thirty-nine days. Before they debarked, the prisoners would be visited by an even sorrier lot of survivors from yet another October hellship.[73]

Those who did not sail on *Hokusen Maru* were destined to board another vessel in the next convoy forming up in Manila Bay. On the afternoon of 11 October, 1,782 POWs boarded the 6,886-ton civilian-controlled cargo ship *Arisan Maru*. She carried no freight other than passengers. The Philippines were being emptied of foreigners, and this contingent came from camps all across Luzon. In addition to the U.S. Army, Navy, and Marine personnel, there were a hundred civilians of various nationalities. About 600 of the POWs were destined for the Kwantung Army in Manchuria. More frequent air raids made it imperative that ships delay no longer than necessary, and after a quick loading, *Arisan Maru* pulled out.

Once clear of the harbor, however, the ship turned south and headed for the west coast of Palawan, where it waited for several days while the expected air attacks did roar through the Manila area from 15 to 18 October. While anchored off Palawan, Maj. Robert B. Lothrop attempted to escape. Lieutenant Yamaji and his forty guards were vigilant, and Lothrop was caught and shot. Four other POWs died of illnesses. On 20 October, *Arisan Maru* returned to Manila.

This time, Convoy MATA-30 quickly formed up and was ready to sail on the twenty-first. It consisted of the *Kokuryu Maru*, *Kikusui Maru*, *Ryofu Maru*, *Shikisan Maru*, *Taiten Maru*, *Eiko Maru*, *No. 1 Shinsei Maru*, *Arisan Maru*, *Tenshin Maru*, *No. 3 Toyo Maru*, *Eikai Maru*, and *Kimikawa Maru*. It was escorted by the destroyers *Harukaze*, *Kuretake*, and *Take*, fleet supply ship *Kurasaki*, and SC 20. The *Kimikawa Maru* joined this relatively slow convoy because on the eighth it had been damaged by a submarine torpedo. It and *Arisan Maru* were the two slowest ships, able to travel at no more than seven knots. They hoped to reach Takao on the twenty-fourth.

Plans, of course, have a way of coming unraveled, especially in wartime. At 0600 of the twenty-third, the Japanese destroyers picked up radio signals: enemy submarines. Three hours later *Harukaze* picked up more signals. How many were out there? In fact, MATA-30 had stumbled into one of the largest concentrations of submarines assembled in the Pacific to date. The area between Luzon and Formosa was called "Convoy College" because of its usual profusion of good targets. MATA-30 was about two hundred miles west of Cape Bojeador on Luzon's northwest coast, when plans were made to break up the convoy and send the fastest ships off to try and make Takao on their own. It was nearly hopeless, for nine submarines were fully alert and waiting. *Snook* and *Cobia* were in one pack; *Sawfish*, *Icefish*, and *Drum*, called "Banister's Beagles" and under Cdr. A. B. Banister in *Sawfish*, were another pack; *Shark II*, *Blackfish*, and *Seadragon*, called "Blakely's Behemoths" and under Cdr. E. N. Blakely in *Shark*, were a third pack; and *Tang* operated alone, farther north in Formosa Strait. The convoy avoided the Luzon air raid but could not dodge the submarines.

Shark II (SS 314). U.S. Naval Institute

At 1730 on 23 October, the torpedoes began striking home. First sunk was *Kimikawa Maru,* a victim of *Sawfish.* She went down in under three minutes. Just after midnight on the twenty-fourth, a dud torpedo slammed into *No. 1 Shinsei Maru,* damaging it enough that it had to slow down. At 0100, torpedoes from *Snook* crashed into *Kokuryu Maru,* and the convoy began to break apart—every ship for itself. By 0315, *Snook* closed in again and sank *Kikusui Maru.* Not yet satisfied, *Snook* bored in again, and at 0605, put down *Tenshin Maru.* With the morning sun, more subs were able to get into action, and at 0758, *Drum* put three torpedoes into *Shikisan Maru,* sinking it in less than two minutes. *Seadragon* got into the picture at 1100, blowing apart *Taiten Maru,* and a subsequent attack at 1225 finished off the damaged *No. 1 Shinsei Maru.* Many of its crew and passengers were saved by *Eiko Maru,* but to no avail, for at 1405, just as the rescue was ending, *Seadragon* torpedoed and sank *Eiko Maru.* The remaining ships had scattered—all except the slow-moving *Arisan Maru.*

Ed Blakely on *Shark* had spent much of the day trying to get his pack into position, but was unable to make his own attack. Finally, a single freighter with a couple of escorts presented itself in *Shark*'s periscope. Blakely sent his torpedoes racing toward the ship and at 1730, two hit the starboard number three hold and one hit the stern. On *Arisan Maru*, they were expecting it.

The usual conditions were present in the bowels of the hellship, and many prayed that a bomb or torpedo would end their miserable existence. They got their wish. "Dinner" was being served, and Sgt. Philip Brodsky, who had survived two years on Palawan, was just robbed of his supper. While one man distracted him, another grabbed his rice. Enraged, Brodsky swung with all his might and smashed the thief in the face. Of course it was too late, for the man had already gobbled down the small portion, and all Brodsky did was break his hand. While trying to repair the injury, he felt three quick explosions. Torpedoes!

Sgt. Calvin Graef of the 200th Coast Artillery had already survived two hellship rides, going to and from Mindanao. He didn't want to leave Luzon because scuttlebutt had it that MacArthur would be returning at any time. Yet there he was again, on a third hellship. At least Graef was allowed out of the hellish holds while on cooking duty. The torpedoes struck while he was topside. Immediately, the guards pointed machine guns at them and forced them below, and the hatch cover was slammed shut. The torpedoes had hit in the empty hold, and, surprisingly, there was no panic. Said Graef, "There wasn't any hysteria, in fact, if anything, it was more or less that if the ship were sunk, it could be that some people would get out and that would be better than what we had been going through."

In the number one hold, the Japanese cut the rope ladders, but even then there was no panic. The men waited. The ship seemed to be staying on an even keel, and no water appeared. In another hold, the Japanese left the hatch open but stood guard with weapons ready, looking down at them. After half an hour the guards disappeared and the prisoners crept out. Cpl. Donald L. Meyer was with about six hundred men in the forward hold. He and a few others climbed a stanchion to the top, where they could hoist themselves out. They found more rope, which they lowered down for the men below to fasten to the cut ladders. With the rope ladders repaired, the men scrambled topside. Meyer found a canteen full of water, threw some planks overboard, and slid down a cable into the ocean.

The Japanese did not fire at the prisoners because they were too busy saving themselves, getting into the few available lifeboats, or swimming to the nearby destroyers. By the time the prisoners had freed themselves, the ship was nearly empty of Japanese. Those who had remained behind soon wished they hadn't, for several enraged prisoners took out their frustrations on any Japanese they could find. The *Arisan Maru*'s stern broke off and floated away, but, surprisingly, both halves were still afloat. Graef headed for the galley to find some food, which he gobbled down, and he also found two canteens of water. Regaining his strength, Graef rounded a corner to come face to face with a bewildered, weaponless guard. In a second, Graef pounced on him, strangling him with one hand and pounding his head on the steel deck with the other. When the man stopped struggling, Graef let go. He was trembling, but he felt avenged. He saw other stranded Japanese men receive the same treatment. "There were no Japanese guards that I know of that managed to get off that ship alive," he said.

Civilian Robert S. Overbeck worked his way over to the gaping hole in the ship's side. He stepped into the current and was swept out into the ocean. Overbeck caught one of the lifeboats but received a bad cut on the arm as one of the Japanese clubbed him back into the water. About thirty-five men swam toward a destroyer, only to be beaten off. Witnessing that, most of the others decided to remain on board. While some looked for rafts or life preservers, many took Graef's course and headed to the galley. Sergeant Brodsky thought "it was just comical to watch some of the guys drinking bottles of ketchup and eating all this sugar" while "smoking two cigarettes at a time." Pvt. Anton Cichy of the 194th Tank Battalion made sure he chowed down on all the food he could find, plus he packed up more food and water, even before he looked for a life preserver. Hundreds more either could not swim or had given up. They ate as much food as they could find and simply sat on the deck while the ship settled, resigned to their fate.

While many aboard *Arisan Maru* prepared for death, the sailors aboard *Shark* had little chance for prayers. Blakely lowered his periscope and listened to three torpedo explosions echoing through the hull, but there was no time for rejoicing as high-speed screws quickly took their place. The *Harukaze* got an underwater contact fifteen hundred yards off her port beam and quickly closed in. Dropping seventeen depth charges, *Harukaze* sliced across the spot and circled back for another run. *Take* joined her, in what the Japanese described as a "splendid attack." *Harukaze* regained contact at sixteen hundred yards to starboard and bored in again. Another series of depth charges blasted *Shark*. During the following hours, *Snook* and *Seadragon* both tried unsuccessfully to contact the pack leader. Blakely and his crew were gone.[74]

Arisan Maru did not sink as Brodsky thought it would. There was no spraying and spouting and whirlpools of foam. The water slowly rose to the deck, and "it just floated right under so peacefully." Brodsky stepped off the ship and swam away in icy cold water. They had been in a storm the past few days, and the waves were still fifteen feet high, making it very difficult for even the good swimmers to remain afloat. Many hundreds that didn't die in the explosion or go down with the ship died that first night, abandoned in the cold, turbulent ocean. The Japanese had left them behind.

Over the next few days, the POWs' numbers dwindled rapidly. In the hot sun they hoped for darkness, and in the cold night they wished for the sun. Many drowned. Others held on, only to drink seawater and go crazy, or refrain from drinking and die of thirst. For many, their emaciated, starved condition did not provide them the strength to fight the waves. The survivors would be those blessed with pure, blind luck.

Brodsky found a floating hatch cover and climbed on it. The next morning a destroyer approached. He waved and pleaded, but the Japanese stared impassively at him as their ship sped by. He was losing hope when he saw another man floating nearby. Cpl. Glenn Oliver had found two hatch covers that were tied together with some other wreckage. They joined up and tied their hatches into a triangle, but later, four empty rafts came floating by, and they quickly shifted to the rafts. For the first time in thirty-six hours they were able to get out of the water and rest.

After Bob Overbeck was clubbed on the arm while trying to get into a Japanese lifeboat, his fortune changed. The Japanese had simply abandoned the lifeboat after they climbed aboard the destroyer. Overbeck saw it, maybe a mile away. He took off his life jacket and swam with all his strength, reaching the prize at nightfall. It was partially filled with water, but he found a keg and tested its contents. It held about three gallons of fresh water. After dark, a box bumped into the side of his boat. Overbeck grabbed it, opened it, and discovered a sail. He wondered what else fortune would bring him.

Pvt. Avery E. Wilbur had stepped off the stern section of the ship when it went under. He had a life preserver and was prepared to swim, but he was shocked by how cold the water was, and how high the white capped waves looked from deep down in the troughs. He could see no other survivors, even though he was sure there were enough life preservers for everyone. He found a piece of wood and floated on it until he saw the lifeboat. In a few minutes he was on board with Overbeck.

Tony Cichy saw the Japanese beating men who tried to get on their ship, so he swam in the opposite direction. Soon it was almost dark and he was all alone. In the gloom he thought he saw a lifeboat with a man standing up, but he didn't want to shout, for he thought the man was Japanese. Yet as they drifted apart, Cichy could keep quiet no longer and he called out. An American voice answered, and Cichy began swimming with all his might, but could not make any headway in the wind and waves. "Swim fast if you want to make it," Overbeck shouted. He had no oars and could not help. When about to give up, a four-foot plank floated near Tony and he grabbed it. Lying on it like a surfboard he paddled again and rapidly closed the distance. Now there were three on board.

Calvin Graef also tried to board the destroyer. When he got to the hull he was clubbed in the head by a blow that nearly severed his ear. When he backed off he saw that the long poles were not rescue devices, but were being used to swat the Americans or push them under water. He swam away and happened across two bamboo poles, which he tied together with his only piece of clothing, his G-string. With his poor raft he floated through the night. In the darkness, Graef bumped against a body. He reached and grabbed the man by the arm. It was Don Meyer.

"Come on and join me," Graef said.

"I'm finished," Meyer sputtered. "Let me go on and die."

"Oh no!" Graef exclaimed. "You're not leaving me out here all alone."

Together they hung on to the bamboo through the night, until morning brought sight of a distant lifeboat. Kicking with their remaining strength, they reached it, but did not have enough strength to climb up its side. Suddenly, three heads popped up.

"Where did you characters come from?" asked Avery Wilbur.

"Don't ask stupid questions," said Meyer, and the two were hauled aboard.

A short while later something else bumped the boat, and a sturdy pole was fished out of the ocean. It might make a mast. While they tried to rig a sail, over the horizon returned the Japanese destroyer that had refused to help them the day before. The five men decided to play dead and slumped down, lying across each other haphazardly. The destroyer, probably the *Harukaze,* as the *Take* had already departed carrying 347 survivors from various sunken ships, circled them at two hundred yards. The survivors peeked through half-closed eyes to see the crewmen break out machine guns. The destroyer circled them for agonizingly endless seconds, then finally put on a burst of speed and peeled away.

When the five men were able to breathe again, good fortune sent them another gift. This time a box was fished out of the sea which contained an actual mast—the very one that was designed to fit their boat—plus ropes and a pulley. It was fortunate also that they had not found and rigged the mast and sail before the destroyer appeared. The next task was to fix the broken rudder, and as one man banged on the hull, seeking to loosen a plank, he dislodged a sealed tin from a compartment. Inside was a supply of hardtack! Now they had food, water, a mast and sail. With a little more luck, and with Overbeck's knowledge of astronomy, they could use the sun and stars to sail for the Chinese coast, which they estimated to be more than two hundred miles to the northwest.

Their luck held through this remarkable odyssey, for the wind took them three hundred miles west. Near the coast they were found by a Chinese junk and guided to land. The five naked wrecks walked down the main street of town, stared at by the incredulous Chinese, until a guerrilla reached them, gave them blankets and took them to a shelter. He told them that they had landed on the only five-mile area on the whole Chinese coast that the Japanese didn't control. Given clothing, food, weapons, and a guide, the five men walked, drove, and bicycled their way through Japanese, bandits, and wild dogs until they reached a U.S. outpost at Anlung. Next they boarded a DC-3, which carried them to Kunming, then Casablanca, Bermuda, and finally Washington, D.C. Wilbur and Cichy were able to supply information on the Japanese defenses around Lingayen Gulf, which MacArthur planned to use as an invasion site. The five men thought they were the only survivors of *Arisan Maru*.[75]

While the lifeboat was swept to the China coast, Sergeant Brodsky and Corporal Oliver floated on their rafts. Once Brodsky swam out to a floating body to see if it had a canteen. It had none, but he took the life jacket back to the raft to use as a pillow. They looked for corpses.

"We didn't say much about it," said Brodsky, "but each of us was thinking if we found one we would eat it." It had been three days since they had food or water. Crazy things were going through their minds. Said Brodsky,

"We came to an agreement that no matter how tough it got one wouldn't try anything on the other; wouldn't shove the other over and eat him."

One morning, Oliver found a dead minnow on the raft. He took the head and gave Brodsky the tail. They sucked on it for an hour. Early on the fourth morning Brodsky saw the smoke of a six-ship convoy. He fastened his shorts to a stick and began waving. One of the escorts pulled toward them and threw out a line. They grabbed the ropes, but they were so weak they could not climb. Hanging there, Brodsky was sure they would be thrown back into the sea, but finally they were hauled up, scraping themselves on the hull. Brodsky said, "I was like one big burn from the sun. There were big scabs all over me. When they pulled me up along these barnacles they pulled all the scabs off. I was bleeding and pussy. It was awful."

He asked for *mizu* (water), but the Japanese insisted on questioning them first. They said that they were survivors from a prison ship, but the Japanese insisted they were really sailors from a sunken U.S. submarine. Finally they were given clothing, water, and hot *lugao,* a watery rice. It burned all the way down, but it was delicious. The two recaptured prisoners remained on the deck for another day and a half.

One of the Japanese freighters also found a water-logged prize. Boatswain's Mate Martin Binder, from the sub-tender *Canopus,* had gone into the water, clinging to a raft with ten other men. After three days, all but Binder and one man were gone. The fourth day, Binder's companion drank seawater, went crazy, and swam away. Shortly after, the convoy came by and pulled Binder from the sea. They treated him roughly at first, also convinced that he was an American submariner. The convoy reached Formosa on the thirtieth.[76]

In Takao, Brodsky and Oliver were turned over to the Army and questioned again. However, threats of beheading could not change their stories about being prisoners on a sunken ship, and they were finally thrown in another room where they found Binder, who had undergone his own interrogation. The three were blindfolded and removed to another room where they heard the clicking of rifle bolts. It was another psychological ploy to make them confess, and it had the same results as before. Finally tiring of the game, the Japanese threw them into a truck and drove them to a jail cell, where they met a fourth American, Pvt. Charles Hughes, also an *Arisan Maru* survivor. Another few days of questioning and beating passed before they were removed once again, taken to the harbor, and ferried out to a freighter. The ship looked familiar to Brodsky. It was the one he had not gone on when it sailed from Manila on 1 October: *Hokusen Maru*.

They were not allowed to talk to the prisoners on board, but Brodsky recognized a few of his mates from Palawan. They nodded acknowledgments, and later, saw to it that they got some rice. The ship sailed but returned one day later, evidently considering the passage too dangerous at the moment. On 8 November, the prisoners were all unloaded, sprayed with disinfectant, given showers, new clothing, divided into three groups, and sent by train to camps at Shirakawa, Taihoku, and Inran. It would be two months before they would finish their journey to the empire. Only nine POWs survived *Arisan Maru*'s sinking. It was the largest loss of American lives in a single disaster at sea.[77]

THE DECEMBER SHIPS

The rush to evacuate all POWs from the Philippines was at its climax. The remaining able-bodied men were cleaned out of Cabanatuan and Bilibid, leaving behind either the sickest or those who were serving "special" sentences, such as for escape attempts or smuggling. All but 30 of the 1,619 men gathered at Pier Seven on 13 December were Americans. About 1,100 were officers. They were under the control of Lt. Toshino Junsaburo and his interpreter, Wada Shunusuke, both merciless in their dealings with the POWs. They boarded the 7,362-ton passenger-cargo ship *Oryoku Maru*, following 1,500 Japanese troops, 547 Japanese women and children, 1,127 crewmen and passengers from other shipwrecked Japanese vessels, and the ashes of 728 war dead. Some women and children laughed as they passed the sorry-looking prisoners. Also loaded aboard were items looted from the Philippines, including General MacArthur's Packard.[78]

The prisoners were distributed among three holds, with about six hundred in the first, two hundred in the second, and eight hundred in the third. Some thought that the Filipino operatives in the harbor area would get word to MacArthur about the sailing, so no attacks would be made on them. Clandestine radios did send out alerts to U.S. carrier forces in the area, but to no avail. During the night, the number from the ship's funnel was exchanged with that of another ship in the harbor, in the hope of confusing the Allied eavesdroppers, but again to no avail. Late on the thirteenth, Ultra messages went out to submarines *Flasher, Hawkbill,* and *Becuna* "to patrol off Manila Bay north of Lubang Island to watch for combatant ships coming out." The

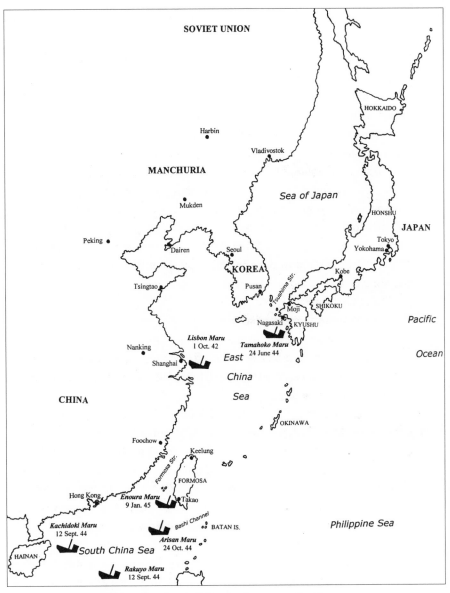

Locations of sunken hellships in the western Pacific.

only "combatant" ships to come out with Convoy MATA-37 were a few escorts, including *Momo* and SC 60.[79]

Conditions in the holds matched or exceeded the worst of the hellships. The *Oryoku Maru* moved out into the bay, but dropped anchor. The heat built up to intolerable levels and the men yelled and begged for water. The hunch-backed interpreter, inevitably called "Running" Wada, shouted into the holds, "There is no water for you. If you do not remain quiet, I will close the hatch!"

His threat brought no halt to the cries, and Wada ordered the hatches closed, bringing the POWs close to panic. Wada called down again, "You are disturbing the Japanese women and children. If you do not shut up I will order the guards to shoot into the hold!" Finally, several officers managed to restore some semblance of order. Cdr. Frank Bridget, a Navy pilot, climbed the ladder and, under the muzzles of the guards, pleaded with Wada for relief. His entreaties worked, and Wada opened the hatches, nevertheless allowing only four men at a time on deck. It was enough to prevent large-scale deaths. At about 1900, a dinner of rice and seaweed was passed below. Throughout the night in the pitch black pit, haunting cries, moans, curses, and threats were heard

"Don't touch me!"

"Keep away from me, you bastard!"

"Somebody help me! He's going to kill me! Oh, God, no!"

The heat, thirst, and lack of oxygen drove men mad. There were deaths from suffocation and deaths from being trampled. As on a few other hellships, men turned into vampires.

At about 0300 on 14 December, *Oryoku Maru* got underway, and with first light, about fifty dead men were removed from below. By 0800, the men quickly learned that their status as POWs would not save them, as carrier planes from Task Force 38's *Hornet* and *Hancock* found them heading north, west of the Bataan Peninsula. No bombs scored, but the ship was strafed several times during the day. After the attacks, American medical personnel were called on deck to treat wounded Japanese, after which they were severely beaten as punishment for the air attack.

Planes returned twice more during the day, sinking and damaging other ships in the convoy, and prisoners saw for the first time a frightening new weapon, as rockets slashed into the ships, killing and injuring prisoners as well as Japanese. The damaged *Oryoku Maru* turned into the dubious shelter of Subic Bay, where the Japanese civilians were offloaded. The prisoners spent another horrible night suffering from thirst and wounds. Screaming became commonplace, and there was a complete lack of discipline. Men drank their own urine and sipped the sewage running in the open drains along the hull. Said Loren E. Stamp, a Pharmacist's Mate off *Canopus*, "More men were killed to keep them from killing others in their frenzy. Still more tried to kill themselves." The prisoners were sure that the Japanese knew they would be bombed again at daylight, and they were purposely left there to die by the hands of their own countrymen.

As expected, *Hornet*'s planes showed up after dawn, and when the attack ended, *Oryoku Maru* had taken six rocket hits and at least one 500-pound bomb hit directly in the aft hold. Finally, Wada told them they could leave the ship but would have to swim to shore. The ship was sinking about three hundred yards off Olongapo Point, the location of the ex–U.S. Naval Station. While swarming on deck, more aircraft appeared, but the desperately waving prisoners with their naked white skins caused the pilots to hold fire. Finally one of the planes wagged its wings in recognition and flew off. While the majority of prisoners splashed into the water and struck out for shore, some starving men looked for food. Lieutenant Toshino found a man eating in the galley, promptly drew his pistol, and shot him. Other Japanese soldiers fired down at men who had jumped ship on the seaward side, apparently figuring they were escaping. Yet it was perhaps more a case of target practice, for even the men who had promptly swam to shore were greeted with a surprise on the beach. The Japanese had set up machine guns and blasted away at swimmers who did not come to shore directly within certain boundaries.

The survivors were herded onto a one-hundred-foot cement-paved square, surrounded by a fifteen-foot-high chicken wire fence. It was once a tennis court, now a torture slab where the POWs would spend the next five days. There were 1,333 prisoners left, and more would die of wounds and exposure. One Marine's gangrenous, wounded arm was amputated with nothing but a mess-kit knife. Not surprisingly, the man died. They baked in the day and froze in the night. Capt. Manny Lawton found it incredible that their captors could be so cruel.

On 20 and 21 December, trucks came to carry the men to San Fernando, Pampanga, a road junction east of Bataan, where many had passed through on the Death March two and a half years earlier. They were placed in a jail and in a movie house, while transportation was being arranged to carry them north to Lingayen Gulf. Wada explained that they must select 15 of their sickest men to return to Manila for hospitalization. Instead, the victims were taken to a cemetery by a death squad led by Cpl. Aihara Kazutane, where they were bayoneted and decapitated, one by one.

Trains took the remaining prisoners to San Fernando, La Union, where they arrived on Christmas morning. They marched to the beach and waited for two days until being loaded on two ships: 1,070 on *Enoura Maru* and the last 236 on *Brazil Maru*. They pulled out on the twenty-seventh. On 30 December, the men heard guns fire and depth charges explode, but they were not hit. Not so lucky was the destroyer *Kuretake*, sunk by the torpedoes of *Razorback*. By the time they reached Takao, 16 prisoners had died on *Enoura Maru* and 5 more on *Brazil Maru*.

"New Year's Eve," recorded Cecil J. Peart, a Navy pharmacist's mate serving with the 4th Marines, "and what a horrible one!"[80]

1945

LAST OF THE HELLSHIPS

As the new year began, all but the most diehard Japanese military men must have realized that the end was near. They had lost 3,823,000 tons of shipping in 1944; 2,388,000 tons had been sunk by submarines. The merchant fleet had been reduced to 2,564,000 tons, 40 percent of the tonnage available at war's start. About fifty-three hellships carrying 47,057 men sailed in 1944. Casualties were about 17,383. About the same number of hellships and prisoners sailed in 1942, but in that year only two ships carrying prisoners were lost, for a death rate of under 5 percent. In 1944, with voyages averaging 11.7 days, thirteen hellships went down, and the death rate was an incredible 37 percent.

FORMOSA TO JAPAN

The suffering was not over for those on the *Enoura Maru* and *Brazil Maru*. They waited several more days at Takao, locked in the holds. Even on the 5,860-ton *Brazil Maru*, with only about 230 remaining captives, men continued to die. On 4 January, Cecil Peart wrote, "Sixth American died this A.M. Few were sorry since he was a thief and had degenerated mentally more than the rest of us. Oh yes, it's obvious that we're all degenerating under these terrible circumstances."

On 6 January, all the POWs were moved to the *Enoura Maru*, but the next day, the last thirty-seven British and Dutch prisoners who had survived

Hofuku Maru's sinking were taken ashore. "Never saw or heard of them again," said Peart. On the eighth, a load of sugar was placed aboard, and the prisoners immediately found a way to steal some of it, despite Wada's warnings. The ships in Takao's harbor would not remain unmolested, for on 9 January another carrier raid blasted them. At least one bomb exploded just outside *Enoura Maru's* forward hold, instantly killing three hundred men. In the number two hold a hatch cover dropped, crushing several men. Cecil Peart was injured, but his best friend lay mortally wounded. Peart called that night "the loneliest in my life." A Catholic priest, Father William Cummings, made an unusually effective, calming speech. "Whatever the talk and prayer," said Peart, "everyone seemed thankful someone had mentioned God's name. For all we knew, we were existing in Hell."

No aid was offered by the Japanese for three days. Finally, on 12 January, permission was granted to remove the dead bodies and assist the wounded. About four hundred corpses were taken to shore on barges, stacked with wood, and set on fire. The prisoners on this grisly detail did not want to talk about what they saw, for they wondered if they too would share the same fate. The next day, all of them were moved back to *Brazil Maru*. There were about nine hundred men left.

Also in the harbor was the *Melbourne Maru*, a 5,423-ton passenger-cargo ship that had come south from Moji, depositing soldiers of the 19th Infantry Division in Takao. The name was covered over, but "Melbourne" was still legible beneath the paint. Going aboard were survivors of the *Arisan Maru* and *Hokusen Maru*. After his ordeal on the latter ship, Forrest Knox never cared much if he lived or died. He stood upright at the rail while U.S. dive bombers blasted the ships all around him. Only one other man stood with him—Martin Binder, a survivor off *Arisan Maru*. Both braved the bombs in a contest of one-upmanship. Knox watched to see who would flinch first. "I was sure that bugger wouldn't last," said Knox. "But he stood right there and never turned a hair." Both men apparently believed that life could not possibly hold further terrors for them.

About five hundred more prisoners from *Hokusen Maru* boarded *Melbourne Maru*. Spero Dardaris, who had spent the past two months in camp at Inran, got off the train on 13 January. The city, he could tell, had been bombed recently; its warehouses smoldered, and the air smelled of burned sugar. His heart sank when he saw the ship. He believed that the only reason he survived the trip from Manila was that *Hokusen Maru* was too small and shabby to be attacked. *Melbourne Maru* was too large for comfort.

They finally got underway on the fourteenth. Convoy TAMO-37 included the *Melbourne Maru,* with more than 500 prisoners, 1,000 tons of sugar, and 1,500 tons of salt; *Brazil Maru,* with more than 900 prisoners and 12,100 bags of sugar; *Oei Maru,* with 3,000 bags of sugar; and *No.* 11 *Hoshi Maru,* with 1,800 bags of sugar, scrap metal, motor parts, hemp, and cattle. The night before sailing, 15 more men died on *Brazil Maru,* a rate that got progressively worse as they neared Japan. The weather grew colder, and the men huddled together for warmth. The convoy took a roundabout course along the Chinese coast into the Yellow Sea before heading east to Korea. The trip was made even slower as on the seventeenth and eighteenth, as *Brazil Maru* slowed to tow another crippled vessel. Men were giving up and dying by the dozens. Father Cummings, who on Bataan was credited with the saying "There are no atheists in fox holes," had been getting weaker as he gave his food to other starving men. He could not last, but as he wanted to give a final prayer, another man lifted him up.

"Our Father Who art in Heaven, hallowed be Thy Name." Once more, his prayers seemed to dispel the men's cries. "Thy will be done, on earth, as it is in Heaven." Cummings trembled, and his eyelids began to close.

"Give us this day . . ." Cummings shook once more, then relaxed.

Another man was gone.

No one seemed frightened anymore. Many wished for one big explosion to end it all.

"Come on, Navy. Send Mr. Wada to hell," someone cried out.

An entry in Maj. Roy L. Bodine's diary illustrates the desperate situation: "27 January, Saturday. . . . Coldest night we've had. No chow or water in AM. . . . Suffered agony all night. Soiled pants moderately two times. No control due to lost fat. Father Cummings died. Kowalski gone; I'm the only one left from my foot locker. About 40 died. Not buried today. Hope it ends soon."

Melbourne Maru reached Moji on 23 January, with only 1 recorded death. The *Brazil Maru* reached Moji on 29 January. The next day, only 450 men could march down the gangway into the bitter cold Japanese winter. About 1,169 had not survived the voyage from Luzon. Out of 20,000 U.S. soldiers and sailors who had been captured with the fall of the Philippines, only 1,300 remained to be liberated in General MacArthur's long-awaited return.[1]

LAST OF THE HELLSHIPS

There were still prisoners of war on Formosa. Not all who had left earlier went by boat. In October 1944, General Wainwright and several other high-ranking officers were flown to Japan, then later took a ship to Pusan, Korea, and a train to Mukden. The rest would face sea voyages. Not all those who had come from Manila on *Hokusen Maru* sailed on *Melbourne Maru*. About half were still scattered in camps in northern Formosa. Others, such as Henry Henderson, worked in a sugar mill in Takao until 24 January, when he took a train to Shirakawa. On the trip, said Henderson, "as luck would have it, one of the POWs died. He was Pvt. Hughes, one of the survivors of the large ship [*Arisan Maru*] that was sunk by torpedoes." Hughes's body was taken along so the numbers would always tally up during *tenko* (roll call). "We carried him on the train until arriving at Shirakawa where he was cremated," said Henderson. "Whooee! What a stinker he had become."

Promptly on the twenty-fifth, Henderson's group boarded the *Enoshima Maru*, which had been in Keelung, loading the remaining high-ranking officers from other camps. Six hundred and five men were ready to sail when Japanese doctors, suspecting cases of spinal meningitis among the prisoners, halted the voyage. Forty-one men were removed and *Enoshima Maru* successfully made the voyage to Moji.

One month later, Convoy TAMO-46 left Keelung. It included the *Juzan Maru*, with 900 troops bound for Shanghai; *Brazil Maru*, with 3,000 tons of sugar and 370 troops bound for Moji; *Taifu Maru*, with 3,000 tons of sugar and 374 passengers bound for Moji; *Tenryu Maru*, with 200 tons of salt and 60 passengers bound for Moji; and *Taiko Maru*, an Army-controlled cargo ship, with three thousand tons of sugar and 700 prisoners. The *Taiko Maru* sailed on 27 February and successfully reached Moji.[2]

In the south, the last of the hellships were less bothered by rampaging carrier aircraft, but submarines and minefields were still a menace. Aircraft- and submarine-laid fields off Rangoon, Moulmein, Tavoy, Penang, Bangkok, and Saigon, plus the sub threat and lack of shipping, forced the Japanese to concentrate convoys in and out of Singapore. These obstacles and the need to use most of the available shipping to send precious oil and other raw materials to the empire precluded the evacuation of all the POWs from Indochina. After Japan Party Three sailed in September 1944, it was not until December that available shipping could be found for a fourth group.

Even so, it was not a large contingent. About 525 British, American, and Australian POWs, including 21 men from the *Perth,* boarded *Awa Maru* on 16 December 1944. The 11,249-ton passenger-cargo ship, now converted to a hospital ship, was one of the newest and fastest liners still sailing. *Houston* survivor James Gee had already ridden *Kenkon Maru, Maebashi Maru,* and *Yamagata Maru.* He was waiting to board *Rakuyo Maru* in September, when the Japanese cut the queue and told Gee and about 35 others that there was no more room. Now, with Japan Party Four, Gee would board his fourth hellship. He didn't like the odds.

"We knew that our people were retaking the Philippines about this time," said Gee. "We knew that they were bombing and sinking almost every Japanese ship that went through. We'd had some pretty direct stories from natives and others. So we figured our chances of getting to Japan were pretty darn small." Aussies William "Buzzer" Bee and Val Savage also missed *Rakuyo Maru.* They heard about its sinking and mourned the loss of their mate, Blood Bancroft, not knowing that he had been rescued by a submarine and was at that time on his honeymoon in Fremantle.

The prisoners sat in the holds for ten days before sailing. On 26 December, Convoy HI-84 pulled out. It consisted of eight ships, including *Awa Maru,* which also carried 475 other passengers and a load of tin and rubber; *Miri Maru,* with fuel oil; *Toa Maru,* with aviation gasoline; *Akashi Maru,* with fuel oil and 100 passengers; and *Amato Maru,* with fuel oil, machine oil, and 200 passengers. It was guarded by the escort carrier *Kaiyo,* CDV *Okinawa,* CDV 63, and patrol boat 102.

As hellships went, *Awa Maru* was one of the lesser evils. It was crowded, and only a few men at a time were allowed to use the latrines on deck ("boy," said Gee, "they'd be standing there with that rifle really watching you"), but the merchant seamen were fairly decent fellows, and the food was "a better grade of stuff than what we had been used to."

The trip north followed the coastline as much as possible, so close that the liner scraped bottom a few times. The weather was cloudy and rainy almost the entire trip, which Gee figured is what saved them from air attack. On the thirtieth, off the eastern bulge of Indochina, *Kaiyo* was unsuccessfully attacked by a submarine, possibly *Dace,* but the eleven-knot convoy kept going. "You talk about being as nervous as cats on a hot tin roof," said Gee. "We could just feel those subs and airplanes bearing down on us."

Their fears were justified, but the agent was not a sub or plane. On 1 January 1945, south of Hainan, *Miri Maru* struck a mine and was left behind. Convoy HI-84 sped on, reaching Hong Kong on the fifth. It made a stop near Shanghai on the ninth and reached Moji on the thirteenth in the midst of a snowstorm. In his summer-green Dutch uniform, Gee almost froze. They stood in formation on a parade ground until late at night. "It was a bitter, cold, humiliating experience," Gee said. Then they were marched to their new camps in the mountains above Nagasaki.[3]

The *Awa Maru* departed Moji for the southern territories on 17 February. Japanese authorities had contacted the United States to arrange safe conduct, for on this trip *Awa Maru* was transporting Red Cross relief supplies to prisoner of war camps. Its markings were to be clearly visible: white crosses on each side of the funnel, white crosses on each side of the ship, and all navigation lights on. Its sailing schedule was sent to all the submarines, along with an admonition to leave it alone. The message was broadcast three times on three successive nights in February. Nevertheless, while crossing the Gulf of Siam, it narrowly missed an attack by *Pampanito* and *Sealion II,* some of the same submarines that had been the nemesis of Japan Party Three.

Awa Maru unloaded relief supplies in Hong Kong, Saigon, and Singapore. All that remained was to ferry the last of the supplies to Batavia, but on the last leg of the journey, five hundred Indian prisoners were placed aboard. On 8 March she sailed for Java, made the deliveries, sailed north to Muntok, Bangka Island, took on twenty-five hundred tons of oil, and returned to Singapore. The *Awa Maru* had dodged a few more bullets, but her charmed life was almost over. She sailed for home on 28 March, due at Tsuruga, Honshu, on 5 April. She got as far as the Formosa Straits on the first when spotted by *Queenfish.* Cdr. Elliot Loughlin had received an encoded message about a hospital ship, but the message gave no details of course, speed, or route. The *Queenfish* made radar contact on a foggy night. The target, traveling at seventeen knots, seemed to have too small a pip for a large liner. Four torpedoes were fired, and four explosions flashed through the fog. The *Awa Maru* went down in two hundred feet of water about ten miles off the China coast, killing more than two thousand soldiers and civilians.

The target disappeared from radar and Loughlin headed in. He picked up one survivor, and only then learned what he had done. Loughlin reported his error and was immediately ordered back to Guam. Before leaving, he searched the area for evidence of what type of cargo the ship was carrying. He picked up some crude rubber and tins of an unidentified black substance, hopefully to help in his defense that the ship was carrying contraband.

Regardless, Loughlin faced a court-martial. U.S. submarines could not go around sinking ships that the government had guaranteed safe conduct to, no matter what they were carrying. In fact, Ultra already knew that on the outward passage, *Awa Maru* carried five hundred tons of ammunition, two 155-mm cannons, about two thousand bombs, and twenty crated planes. On the return she carried a cargo of rubber, lead, tin, tungsten, sugar, and about seventeen hundred passengers. Vice Admiral Lockwood had even requested to be allowed to sink *Awa Maru* because of this breach of agreement, but was refused. Of course, the United States could not deny safe passage to the ship because it was carrying war material without also giving away the secret that the Japanese codes had been cracked. Loughlin's defense would have to rest on what he fished out of the sea. Nevertheless, the military court ruled that he could not have known of the cargo before the sinking, and he received a Letter of Admonition from the secretary of the Navy.[4] Even though he was a courageous skipper with a fine record, Loughlin was indirectly sacrificed to maintain the secret of Ultra.

The *Awa Maru* did not carry the last of the POWs out of Singapore. A trickle of captives kept flowing in from the Burma Railway camps, as well as from the East Indies. In June 1944, the Imperial Navy issued an order that all Allied prisoners in the East Indies were to be sent to Surabaya. Small interisland steamers and ferry boats of all sizes brought them to Java. In September, Don Peacock reached Surabaya on the *Sugi Maru,* and Art Stock arrived on *Kenzan Maru.* They took trains to Batavia, where they arrived on 1 October. They stayed at Makasura Camp for the next three months, a place Peacock described as a "POW Hilton" compared to what he had experienced on Haruku and Ambon. After Christmas they were ordered to provide a draft of men to go north to Saigon, but the idea of another sea voyage appealed to no one. A few men hacked their feet with *chunkels* (spades), injuring themselves enough to be scratched from the list, but on 8 January 1945, one thousand prisoners, mostly Brits with a sprinkling of Aussies, boarded what Peacock called "a respectable-looking OSK ferry." A four-day ride brought them to Singapore, where they happily debarked and were marched to River Valley Road Camp.

Most of them hoped it was the end of their travels, even though Singapore was being bombed by the Allies. Peacock and Stock met fellow British prisoners who had worked on the Burma Railway, quickly learning that privation, starvation, and suffering are relative terms. "They came running to greet us as soon as our guards had left," said Peacock, "and gave us an instant inferiority complex. They looked disgustingly fit, apparently never shorn of their hair; they had a reasonable amount of flesh on their bones, and generally made us look like scarecrows." Of course, Peacock was describing men who had had more than a year to recover from the rigors of the railway. Both groups disdained those who had never left the relative luxury of Changi, dubbing them the "Changi pensioners."

They spent a few weeks watching Allied planes blast the city, when they learned that River Valley Road was to be emptied and its prisoners sent to Saigon. There were 3,000 POWs, but the ship that was to take them could fit only 2,500. Happily for Peacock, he was one of the lucky 500 not selected in what he termed the "lottery of misery."

Convoy HI-88D consisted of *Engen Maru, Taigyo Maru,* with a load of fuel oil and rubber, and *Haruyasa Maru,* a thirty-five-hundred-ton cargo ship with its 2,500 prisoners and internees, including 406 Aussies, 500 Brits, and 700 Javanese laborers. The ships, escorted by CDVs *Yashiro,* 13, and 31, pulled out on 4 February.

AIF machine-gunner Donald Stuart had been captured on Java, had worked on the railway, and was now on a ship that he said was like the Yank Liberty Ships, "thrown together out of sardine tins and welded with chewing gum." On the voyage Stuart said the men prayed for night so the planes wouldn't find them, then prayed for daylight so the submarines wouldn't get them.

Perhaps their prayers had some effect. Early in the morning of 6 February, *Engen Maru* was struck by *Pampanito*'s torpedoes. It went down quickly, its stern settling on the shallow bottom and its bow high in the air. The next day, the second ship in the wolfpack, *Guavina,* got in her licks on *Taigyo Maru,* and that ship went down bow first into the shallow sea.

"Oh Jesus, that's good!" said a prisoner on *Haruyasa Maru.*

"Good?" came the reply. "If those bastards are about, the Yanks or who-ever they are knocking them off, they could knock us off too!"

"Shut up," said a third voice in the darkness of the hold. "All those Japs on that ship have gone down. That's good."

Stuart was delighted when a magazine on *Taigyo Maru* apparently blew up, setting off "a real bloody Guy Fawkes show." *Haruyasa Maru* was running out of coal, however, and the Japanese were frantically rushing about, breaking off interior wooden fittings and feeding them into the boilers, trying to coax out every knot of steam. Sparks and smoke poured from the stack. "You could see half of the China Sea . . . with our bloody flare from the funnel," said Stuart. "But we got through."

The *Guavina* and *Pampanito,* the latter of which had already sunk hellship *Kachidoki Maru,* had come within a hair of knocking off another one. The sub-marines went after the two slightly larger ships. By the time they could break free of the escorts, *Haruyasa Maru* was out of range. Belching smoke, it chugged to Cape St. Jacques on 8 February, then up the Mekong River. The convoy was dissolved and the POWs went no farther than Saigon.[5]

Some of the POWs coming from the East Indies never made it as far as Singapore. In October 1944, a wooden trading vessel took Tony Cowling and about 450 men, "the last and fittest" of the Haruku labor force, to Ambon, then to Kendari, Celebes, then to Muna Island, arriving on the eleventh. One month later they were at the docks again, loading on a one-hundred-ton coastal craft, this time headed for Makassar with 100 men. The next day the little craft was strafed by two P-38s. The Japanese jumped in the lifeboats, the ship went down, and once again there were POWs in the water. They swam to a nearby island but were promptly recaptured. The next day they were back at Muna, after losing 27 men in their fruitless excursion.

They were stuck there for the next five months in what Cowling called a "death camp," where 178 men died between October and April. Many had lost faith. "If there really was a God directing operations could this kind of thing happen?" Cowling wondered. It was evident to him that "the king-dom of heaven is in the individual will to survive." On 13 April, 50 more prisoners were placed aboard an eighty-ton coastal craft, and a six-day trip finally brought them to Makassar. They were put in the camp with men who had been there since the Java Sea battles in 1942, and there they waited until July.

Cowling had less to complain about in Makassar. He received clothing, soap, cigarettes, books, and food, and he wondered why his captors had changed so much for the good. Was the attitude of the Imperial Navy, who ran the camp at Makassar, so different from the administration on Ambon, or did they all finally realize the war was nearly over and it might be a good idea to treat the prisoners better?

On 26 July, Sergeant Major Yamamoto and nine guards were in charge of loading 416 "healthy" prisoners from Makassar on the 834-ton *No. 17 Nanshin Maru,* which, according to Cowling, was a "tanker with a heavy list to port." A white line was painted down the ship's center, and the prisoners were made to stay on the high side of the line, ostensibly to prevent the lopsided ship from capsizing. They sailed the same day, accompanied by AM 8 and SC 4. Rations consisted of rice, fish, sugar, and biscuit—better than what they had been subsisting on for the past two years. Water, however, was strictly rationed. The men baked under the sun while their feet burned on the steel deck. Said Cowling, "The constant breeze sucked sweat out of us until we were dehydrated skeletons." On 29 July, they arrived safely at Surabaya. Surprisingly, only one man had died.

On 6 August, Cowling's group entrained for Batavia. In Bicycle Camp they were the pariahs, separated from their fellow prisoners with barbed wire. Cowling believed the Japanese did not want the other POWs to know what conditions were like on Haruku, Ambon, and Muna. Once again, the newcomers thought the old residents were in relatively good health. "At least they had some meat on their bones," said Cowling. "Not too much, but considerably more than we had." Four days later, said Cowling, a miracle occurred: "We were given three Red Cross parcels to divide amongst the fifty of us." Cowling also received seventeen letters, most of them more than two years old. Something definitely was up. On 15 August they officially got the word: the Japanese had surrendered. The war was over.[6]

THE PRISONERS' FATE

Although many POWs had been moved to Japan, the end of hostilities still found them scattered throughout the remnants of the Japanese "Greater East Asia Co-Prosperity Sphere." Luck had played a large part in their transportation, treatment, and ultimate fate. Most of the 150 men who signed list "B" and left Palawan in September 1944 reached Manila only to suffer or die on

Hokusen Maru or *Arisan Maru*. Those left behind faced worse odds. The Japanese made them dig three trenches, each 150 feet long and 4 feet deep. The POWs were told they were air raid shelters, and they practiced scurrying into them during drills. On 14 December 1944, a U.S. convoy was sighted. It was heading for Mindoro, but the Japanese on Palawan thought it was coming to invade their island. An air raid was announced, the Americans were sent into the trenches, and the Japanese poured gasoline in and set them on fire with torches and grenades. Any POWs who climbed out were bayoneted or shot. Even so, thirty to forty Americans escaped the massacre. Most were hunted down by the Japanese along the shore or in the jungle, but ten men survived by swimming across the bay and finding shelter with the inmates of Palawan's penal colony. They were then passed to the guerrillas and eventually evacuated by Navy seaplane. The *Robalo*'s four survivors did not make it.[7]

Soldiers and sailors were not the only ones roughly handled. Pilots seemed to draw extreme ire, especially near the end of the war. Still, luck had a great bearing on one's ultimate fate. Famed Marine aviator Maj. Gregory "Pappy" Boyington was shot down in the sea near New Ireland in January 1944 and plucked out of the water by a Japanese submarine. While some captains murdered captives they had just "rescued," Boyington was given tea, cookies, and cigarettes and carried safely to Rabaul. With the assistance of a friendly interpreter who claimed Boyington had important information to divulge, he was flown to Tokyo, thus avoiding the Tunnel Hill Incident. In March 1944, in retaliation for an Allied bombing attack, up to forty pilots and other POWs were removed from their shelter at Tunnel Hill on New Britain, taken to a place southeast of Rabaul called Matupi, anesthetized with injections of experimental drugs, then buried alive. The Imperial Navy, in charge in that theater, had been given instructions that no more prisoners should be sent to Japan after being interrogated.[8]

In the Moluccas, captured fliers were at great risk. On Ambon, those rounded up by the Tokkeitai, the Navy counterpart to the Kempeitai, were systematically killed. Nogi Harumichi, a Navy ensign working with the Tokkeitai said, "Those who fell from the sky at the front all got killed." When he questioned his superiors about this practice, he was told to be silent and "process them." Nogi believed it was done because the commanders did not want the troops or prisoners to know the Japanese forces were collapsing. In October 1944, a PBY crashed off the Celebes coast. Nine airmen were captured and taken on *Daikeku Maru* to Kendari. They were interrogated by the Tokkeitai and beheaded; *shobun* was the word. In June 1945, four Army airmen in Makassar were executed. At a trial held after the war, the accused Japanese explained that the airmen were killed because they could not be sent to Surabaya, since there were no planes or ships left to transport them. The Graves Registration team found more than a hundred bodies in the Kendari area alone.[9]

Elsewhere, pilots met similar, or worse, fates. Some of Lt. Col. James H. Doolittle's B-25 pilots who were captured after their April 1942 raid on Tokyo were officially executed, while a number of B-29 pilots downed over Japan late in the war were mobbed and killed by irate civilians. On Chichi-Jima, some American airmen were used for bayonet practice. Maj. Matoba Sueo had the bodies butchered, cooked, and fed to his unwitting subordinates as a big joke. In the Philippines, Imperial Army units scattered to the hills, shooting and eating natives or stragglers from other units. On a larger scale, the hungry Japanese on New Guinea killed and ate not only Allied pilots but also Indian prisoners, natives, and dead soldiers of both sides. It was not an isolated occurrence, but a systematic and organized military strategy deemed necessary for the bypassed, starving garrisons.[10]

Few, if any, prisoners from large camps met a worse fate then those men unlucky enough to have been sent to north Borneo. After the Python operations and resulting executions, rations were cut to the starvation point in Sandakan. In June 1944, 100 British prisoners under Flight Lieutenant Black-ledge, RAF, were removed and taken to Labuan Island off Brunei Bay to build an airfield. They were joined in August by a party of 200 British POWs from Kuching under Captain Campbell. By March 1945, there were 112 left. They were taken to the mainland, and by June, the last of them were killed "while escaping."

The 1,700 men left in the main camp at Sandakan faced a series of death marches. With the Allies closing in and no roads connecting the east and west coasts of Borneo, the Japanese planned to move the prisoners 250 miles across a primitive jungle track to Jesselton, where it would be easier to evacuate them if necessary. The first group of about 450 left in January 1945, in sections of about 50 men each, traveling 164 miles to Ranau, where they stopped near an incomplete fighter strip. Many did not survive the trip. The track was constructed by natives under Japanese orders, and they purposely hacked a trail through the worst terrain possible. POWs died of exhaustion or were shot by the Japanese as they faltered. Only 300 reached Ranau. They were not meant to go any farther, as one by one, they began starving to death.

In Sandakan the remaining 1,250 men were further reduced by disease, starvation, maltreatment, and execution, until by May, only 900 were left. In late May, a second march left Sandakan, with 536 ambulatory men. Only 183 of them reached Ranau in late June, where they found only 6 men alive out of the first group. On 9 June, the third march left Sandakan with all the remaining POWs who could stumble along; they all died or were killed before they had gone fifty miles. By 1 August, there were only 32 POWs left at Ranau. They were all executed. When the third march departed, there were 185 POWs left in Sandakan. In July, only 23 of the remaining 53 could walk, and on the thirteenth they were executed. In August there were 5 remaining POWs. The last was beheaded on 15 August, one day after the Japanese agreed to surrender. There were rumors that one of the last men was crucified. Of the 2,400 captives at Sandakan, only 6 survived the camps or the death marches, all by escaping from Ranau or along the trail.[11] The Sandakan Death Marches were a first magnitude tragedy, the number of deaths four times greater than the number of Americans who died on the Bataan Death March. Yet more than twice as many men died in the sinking of *Junyo Maru*.

Although the location of almost every POW camp in Japan was known, it was not known if there were any POWs in the Hiroshima area, and that was one of the reasons it was selected as an atomic bomb target. In fact, there were about one dozen downed airmen in the city. Some survived the blast, but three were killed afterward by civilians; two were beaten to death and one tied to a stake and stoned. It was known that there were POWs held in the Nagasaki area, but that did not prevent the city from being bombed. About 80 POWs were killed in the blast. Even after the war ended, it was the fate of some prisoners to be dogged with bad luck. The attack transport *Colbert* was ferrying 631 former POWs out of Dairen, Manchuria, when, on 17 September 1945 in a storm near Okinawa, she hit a mine. Luckily, there were only 3 casualties. Some planes carrying former POWs in and out of Okinawa crashed. A bizarre accident occurred while American planes were flying former POWs out of Japan. The bomb bay door swung open in one crowded bomber, and several newly liberated prisoners were dropped thousands of feet into the Pacific. In an even more bizarre series of accidents, a number of POWs in Japan were killed as American planes flew over their camps, dropping much-needed food supplies to the hungry men. The ecstatic men ran after the parachute-dropped crates, and several were killed when some chutes failed to open. To have survived prison camp and hellship only to be killed by cans of flying tomatoes was supreme irony. The last Wake Marine to die in prison camp was killed by cans of Spam.[12]

Had the war not ended when it did, the prisoners' fate was likely to be a swift death, à la the Palawan massacre. From Java, Malaya, Borneo, and Thailand to northern Honshu, plans were being made to kill the POWs when the Allies closed in. Trenches were dug as air raid shelters, camps were surrounded by extra barbed wire and machine guns, and explosives and gun emplacements were set up at coal mine entrances. The prisoners would not be retaken. They would be killed. There is probably not a former POW alive who is not thankful for the atomic bombs.

HOW MANY MORE?

Although the existence of more than 150 hellships has been confirmed, research into this subject is not complete. The majority of hellships involved in this study carried white men of European ancestry. There were also many shipments of Indians, Chinese, Koreans, and East Indians. During the drive up New Guinea's north coast in 1944 and 1945 the Australians and Americans found perhaps 8,000 or more Indian soldiers who had been shipped there from Malaya. When the war ended, the Australians returning to Rabaul were surprised to find great numbers of people they had never expected: 5,463 Indians, 1,397 Chinese, 688 Malayans, and 607 Indonesians. Thousands of Javanese were moved throughout the East Indies. About 4,000 of them worked on the Sandakan airstrip. If it was a tragedy that only 6 Australians survived out of 2,400, who speaks for the 3 Javanese that survived out of the 4,000?[13] How many were transported, when, and in which ships? A number of considerations limit our knowledge: the language barrier for an English-speaking researcher makes it nigh impossible to locate and translate source material from those nations; much of what could have been written about those voyages may never have been recorded in the first place; and the Japanese destroyed numerous records of hellship voyages at the end of the war.

Even so, there are tantalizing bits of radio intercepts that indicate additional ships carried POWs. The *Anami Maru* departed Singapore in May 1943 with Indian prisoners. The destroyer *Akitsuki* carried POWs from Truk to Roi, Kwajalein Atoll, in November 1943. In January 1944, several American planes attacked a Japanese convoy near New Ireland. One PBY was shot down by the gunfire of *Kenshin Maru* and destroyer *Oite*. Five airmen were captured, but two died. The survivors were taken on *Oite* to Rabaul. In January 1944, an intercepted message from Kobe to Rabaul indicated that *Ikuta Maru* would be carrying POWs, but how many and to where is unknown. On 12 February 1944, *Toka Maru* carried six prisoners from Cape Jacquinot, New Britain, to Rabaul. In March 1944, prisoners on Palau were to have been sent to Ofuna on *Wakatake*, however the destroyer was sunk by aircraft on 30 March. It is not known if POWs were aboard at the time. The *Wakatake*, however, was likely the escort that picked up Gunner's Mate C. W. Kuykendall on the twenty-seventh and took him to Palau. Kuykendall was the only survivor of the submarine *Tullibee*, which was sunk by a circular run of one of her own torpedoes. Ofuna Naval Interrogation Center and Omori Camp held many submariners, and Kuykendall eventually arrived there on another ship.

A radio intercept from Surabaya on 15 July 1944 indicated that another 500 men were being sent to Ambon, but whether prisoners or laborers was not specified. On 6 August 1944, a message from Surabaya said that a ship, possibly *Taian Maru*, was unloading 570 white prisoners and their baggage. A 10 August message from Peking to Tokyo, said that arrangements were completed for sending and supplying 2,000 prisoners to work in Japanese harbors. An intercept dated 5 September 1944, sent from Batavia to Ambon, stated, "The first special contingent of 600 prisoners (27 of whom have died), escorted by 16 guards arrived safely on September 3rd." The name of the transport was not given. In July 1945, three bombers attacked a small convoy returning from Indochina to Singapore. One was shot down and 8 airmen were picked up by the destroyer *Kamikaze*.[14]

In February 1942, sixty-five British nursing sisters left Singapore on the *Kuala*. It was bombed and sunk, and the survivors swam to Pompong Island, where they were picked up by the *Tanjong Penang*, which was also sunk. This time some of the survivors were picked up by the Japanese and taken to Muntok, where they met survivors of the *Vyner Brooke*. The sisters were then sent to Palembang, where Japanese officers tried to persuade them to staff a brothel for their use. In October 1944, they were moved back to Muntok on a small riverboat with two hundred other women, and in April 1945, shipped once more to Sumatra, to Loebok Linggau Camp. Eight nurses died on the last trip, and at war's end only twenty-four were still alive.[15]

In September 1942, civilian photojournalists for *Life* magazine who were captured in Manila were taken on *Maya Maru* to Shanghai and were ultimately repatriated on *Gripsholm*'s second trip. At least three times, in November 1942, August 1943, and May 1945, captive Marines in China were sent to Japan. The 1943 "technician" shipment of 500 POWs included merchant mariners from the captured *President Harrison*. Generals Wainwright and Percival joined 353 other high-ranking officers and civilians in Japan, a few days after being flown out of Formosa. On 9 October 1944, they sailed from Moji to Pusan on *Fukuji Maru*. From there, they took trains to various Manchurian camps. More officers left from several camps on Kyushu in May 1945. Lieutenant Michel, off the *Pope*, Lieutenant Blain, off the *Exeter*, and 1,000 others gathered in Fukuoka for the journey. Two packet boats sailed each day for Pusan, and Michel and the others gathered aboard them for the dash across the Straits of Tsushima. In Pusan, they entrained for Mukden. On 10 October 1944, a ship carrying 500 conscripted Okinawan laborers who had been building an airfield in the southern Ryukus, was supposedly torpedoed and sunk while returning to Okinawa.[16]

After the war it was the job of the International Military Tribunal Far East (IMTFE) to investigate and prosecute Japanese war criminals. Former prisoners were called upon to give sworn testimony of the treatment they received on land and at sea, and many of their statements referenced other hellships. In August 1942, the *Tufuku Maru* was said to have carried 500 prisoners from Batavia to Singapore, with 29 men dying of dysentery. The *Tojuku Maru*, carrying 1,200 POWs, was to have sailed from Singapore to Japan on 30 October 1942, and 27 died on the trip. Also in October 1942, *Oyo Maru* was said to have taken captives from Batavia to Singapore. The *Matsu Maru* was said to have carried POWs in July 1943, from Java to Singapore. The *Ussuri Maru* was to have taken POWs from Java to Japan in October 1943.[17]

There are also a number of vessels mentioned as being hellships in other publications, but corroborating references cannot be found. Among them are: *Coral Maru*, supposedly leaving Manila for Japan in October 1943, with 800 POWs; *Umeda Maru*, to have departed Manila with 1,400 POWs in November 1942; *Ryukyu Maru*, supposedly sunk near Timor in November 1943, with 42 casualties but about which nothing else is known; *Hokko* (possibly *Hioki*)

Maru, said to have carried POWs from Manila in October 1942 and from Singapore to Japan in July 1944; *Shoun Maru* and *Tenshin Maru,* carrying 50 prisoners each from the Philippines to Osaka in 1942; and *Kohho Maru,* said to have taken 883 POWs from the Philippines to Fukuoka in 1943.

Some of these may be corruptions of other names, or phonetic guesses of ship names by POWs whose memories may have dimmed over the years. Other hellships listed in various publications are clearly misspellings of actual hellships: Oryoki (*Oryoku*), Enuri (*Enoura*), King Kong (*Kenkon*), Rokyo (*Rakuyo*), Tomohoku (*Tamahoko*), Weills (*Wales*), Yinagata (*Yamagata*), Toyofuku (*Hofuku*), and Tattori (*Tottori*). Another mysterious "October Ship" or "Unknown Maru" appears from time to time. This ship supposedly took 1,100 or 1,800 POWs from Manila in October 1944, only to be torpedoed at an unknown time and place by an unknown submarine. It is simply a composite of incorrect recollections about *Arisan Maru.*

A sordid chapter that is inevitably omitted from sea transportation accounts is that of the "comfort women," a euphemism for the prostitutes forced to serve Japanese troops. There may have been 139,000 comfort women, 80 percent of them Koreans and most of them taken from their homelands against their will and sent to the far corners of the Pacific. Javanese, Indians, and Chinese women were taken from Surabaya to the Lesser Sunda Islands. There were Formosan women taken to Sarawak, Rabaul, and Timor. Javanese women were sent to Singapore, Malaya, and even Sandakan. More than 700 Korean women were sent on one ship from Pusan to Rangoon in July 1942. At one time, 2,800 of the 3,200 comfort women in Burma were Korean. At sea they were treated like cattle and were not even listed as human beings but as "munitions" or "canteen supplies." These women sailed, suffered, and died on their own hellships. They died on torpedoed ships bringing them to the front lines at Guadalcanal, and they died on torpedoed ships returning them to Japan from the Marianas and Okinawa. Most of the "jig-a-jig" girls who died on *Rakuyo Maru* were Koreans. And, in a fate similar to some POWs, the Japanese killed a number of their own comfort women to keep them from being captured by the Allies.[18]

Radio intercepts and IMTFE testimony indicate there were other hellship voyages, but unfortunately, there often was not enough corroborating information to develop a complete itinerary. In addition to more than 100,000 comfort women, thousands of Korean laborers were moved to Japan, and perhaps thousands of Chinese were likewise transported. Indian prisoners were moved to New Guinea and the Bismarcks, voyages of which we know very little. How many thousands of native laborers were moved among the islands of the East Indies? How many scores of small craft ferried prisoners along the coasts of Malaya, Java, Borneo, or the Moluccas?

Even if the majority of ships listed above prove to be nonexistent, or duplicate listings for actual hellships, there are enough documented voyages to illustrate the magnitude of these episodes. More than 126,000 men and women were forced to ride in floating jail cells under horrible conditions. More than 21,000 died. If the full truth is ever uncovered, these numbers may pale in comparison. Regardless, the sheer numbers involved are much higher than previous studies have indicated. The enormity of this sordid chapter of the Pacific war has not been adequately exposed.

CONCLUSION

By August 1945, the Japanese merchant marine had nearly been swept from the sea. Hard-pressed shipyards had added 465,000 tons to the fleet, but losses of 1,809,000 tons caused the total tonnage afloat to drop to 1,466,000 tons, only 23 percent of what Japan had started the war with. Submarines accounted for 420,000 tons, the first time they had been surpassed by other agents.[1] During the waning months of the war, aircraft and aircraft-laid mines were the best means to sink the few remaining ships furtively traveling the coast, in the Inland Sea, or anchored in harbors because of insufficient fuel. Fewer than a dozen hellships attempted to sail, and only the *Enoura Maru* was sunk—bombed while at anchor. The Japanese war effort had been drowned.

DEATH RATES

War means killing. That may be an obvious statement, but it was never truer than in World War II. We may have the perception that combatants pay the ultimate price of war, yet in World War II, civilian deaths outnumbered combatant deaths by more than two to one, fifty-five million civilians to twenty-two million combatants.[2] Perhaps we also have the perception that captives were moved out of harm's way, adequately housed and fed, and treated fairly. Here it depends on who did the capturing and who was the captive. Only about 4 percent of the American, British, and Australian prisoners of war captured by the Germans or Italians died in POW camps. Forty-five percent of

Germans captured by the Russians died, and 60 percent of Russians imprisoned by the Germans died.[3]

Statistics vary, but Allied prisoners had a much greater chance of surviving under the Germans than under the Japanese. Gavan Daws claims that
about 27 percent of prisoners captured during the Pacific war died in Japanese
hands. The American death rate was about 34 percent; Australian, 33 percent;
British, 32 percent; and Dutch, 20 percent. Were the Dutch better survivors
because many of them had lived in the tropical Indies and were better adjusted
to the climate, flora, fauna, diseases, and germs? Perhaps. But fewer of them
were transported on hellships also, and fewer were sunk. Gavan McCormack
claims that 22,000 Australians were captured and 36 percent died. E. Bartlett
Kerr and Robert LaForte say that 40 percent of 25,000 American prisoners
died. Author and former POW Paul Ashton claims that more than half, or
54 percent, of 24,000 American servicemen captured in the Philippines died
as prisoners.[4]

Estimates for death rates on the hellships vary also. Gavan Daws states that
50,000 Allied prisoners were transported on hellships and that 10,800 died, a
rate of 21 percent. Daws argues that the number of deaths on hellships reveals
a sustained Japanese atrocity second only to deaths of prisoners completing
the Burma Railway, which left nearly 12,000 dead. Van Waterford found a
much higher hellship death rate; he claims that 35 percent, or 22,000 of 62,000
POWs, died at sea. His death count is high, however, because he double-
counted some hellships (the *Hofuku Maru* and *Arisan Maru*, for example).[5]

The total number of men transported in hellships is difficult to determine.
If we simply add total prisoners carried on each hellship, we find that the ships
carried about 126,000 prisoners (see appendix). That number is deceptive,
however, because many of these men sailed in hellships two, three, or four
times. For example, some *Erie Maru* passengers also sailed on the *Yashu Maru,
Singoto Maru, Shinyo Maru,* or *Arisan Maru.* Men on the *Kenkon Maru* were
also on *Maebashi Maru, Yamagata Maru,* and *Awa Maru.* Some men rode
Celebes Maru, Rakuyo Maru, and *Kibitsu Maru.* Some *Hofuku Maru* survivors
also rode *Hokusen Maru* and *Melbourne Maru.* There were many such instances, which inflate the numbers. If a prisoner traveled on a hellship, do we
count him once, or do we count him each time he sailed? If we subtract mul-
tiple sailings out of our 126,000, we may be closer to Daws's 50,000 individuals who journeyed on hellships. If we take the total number of prisoner

deaths from the table in the appendix, however, we find that 21,000 men died on those ships, almost twice Daws's count. Our death rate, then, is greater than 40 percent, a staggering figure.

To help put this death rate into perspective, we need some figures for comparison. During the American Civil War, 28 percent or 13,000 Union soldiers died at Andersonville Prison Camp. During World War II, about 40 percent of all Japanese merchant mariners died. Twenty-two percent of American submariners were killed—the highest percentage loss of any branch of service. Nine thousand more prisoners died on hellships than died working on the Burma Railway, which was, according to Gavan Daws, the worst sustained Japanese atrocity of the war. The U.S. Army suffered 16,000 deaths in the Normandy campaign, and 19,000 were killed during the Battle of the Bulge. During the entire Pacific war, about 20,000 Marines died. Clearly, it was deadlier to be a POW on a Japanese ship than to be a U.S. Marine fighting them.[6]

PRISONER TREATMENT

Japanese authorities were aware of the poor treatment of prisoners. The December 1942 Order No. 1504, detailed in chapter 1, expressed concern over the poor physical condition of POWs reaching Japan. The few Allies who escaped told stories of horrible treatment, and little by little, a sordid picture evolved. The United States, Britain, and Australia faced the dilemma of lodging formal protests with the Japanese, not knowing whether it would help or hurt the captives. Would Japan let more relief ships in, or would they tighten the screws for punishment? President Roosevelt thought it best to withhold atrocity information, but General MacArthur issued his own warning to Southern Area commander Count Terauchi, saying he would hold Japanese leaders personally responsible for improper POW treatment.

Apparently press leaks and warnings had some effect, for in December 1943, the Japanese Prisoner of War Bureau issued an order to all camps: "Care should be taken to avoid issuing twisted reports of our fair attitude which might give the enemy food for evil propaganda and bring harm to our interned brothers" (a reference to the Japanese nationals held in the United States).

In January 1944, after having learned that at least some Red Cross supplies had reached the POWs, the okay was given, and the stories of escapees Dyess, Mellnik, McCoy, and others went out in hundreds of newspapers. Secretary of State Cordell Hull lodged a formal protest, but one month later, the only

Japanese response was to deny some of the allegations and state that others were being investigated. By March 1944, possibly becoming more sensitive to world opinion, the Prisoner of War Bureau issued an admonishment to the camp commanders, stating that "enemy propaganda" was adding to the hostile feelings toward Japan. If poor POW treatment continued, it would hinder Japan's "prosecution of moral warfare." In addition, prisoners were to be given their full allowance of food, medicine, and clothing, for those in poor health would not "increase our fighting strength."

Official announcements were one thing, but intercepted messages from Tokyo to the foreign office in Berne, Switzerland, revealed a different attitude. They complained that the Japanese interned in America were being badly treated, that the Allies were attacking their hospital ships, and that plans to ship more Red Cross supplies would meet with little enthusiasm. Although Japan would publicly make concessions about treatment and relief, the message concluded, "we wish that you would remain silent and treat with secrecy the fact that we do not at present intend to carry on any positive campaign ourselves."[7] The POWs remained at the mercy of the local commanders of prison camps and hellships.

Crowding and lack of water, food, and sanitary facilities were among Allied POWs' most cited complaints. However, sailing on any troopship during wartime was not a pleasant experience. Similar complaints were voiced by Allied soldiers on the *Empress of Asia, Hugh L. Scott, Tasker Bliss, Republic,* and *President Harrison.* The *President Coolidge* shipped twenty-five hundred men to the Philippines, while *Empire Star* took twenty-five hundred escaping men from Singapore. The Dutch ship *Kota Gede* fled Java with twenty-one hundred RAF escapees packed in the holds like sardines. Granted, situations such as these were not punctuated with deliberate starvation, but crowding and sanitary facilities were serious problems.

The Japanese often maintained that prisoners were treated no differently than their own troops, and that is a valid point. The rough scaffolding, tiers, bunks, or shelves so often described by POWs on hellships were the very same accommodations that Japanese troops squeezed into. Such crowding was experienced by the Japanese soldier from the first days of the war, even when the Japanese merchant marine was at full strength. As the eighty-four-ship invasion convoy sailed into Lingayen Gulf in 1942, seaman Masuda Reiji was in awe of the crushing numbers of two thousand soldiers, hundreds of horses, and tons of supplies that were crammed aboard his ship, the 9,683-ton *Arizona Maru*. Treatment and regimen of the Japanese soldier was harsh, and there was concern over conditions aboard ships in tropical climates. The Japanese tested their endurance by jamming thousands of men aboard ships, three men to a three-by-six-foot mat. They were left aboard for a week in 100-degree temperatures, while water was rationed and soldiers were physically beaten for the slightest improprieties. Even so, they successfully carried out landings. Such conditions did not appear to have too adverse an effect, and Japanese troops went to battle under similar terms for the rest of the war.[8] Perhaps it should not be surprising that POWs were treated so badly.

Prisoners on hellships observed that they shared much the same lot as the Japanese soldier. On *Tottori Maru*, POWs mixed with Japanese soldiers in the holds, sharing similar fare, trading, and haltingly communicating at times about home and family. On *Aki Maru*, Japanese soldiers slept in two tiers on one level of the hold while prisoners slept in two tiers on the next level. All were cramped. Wrote one officer, "Japanese soldiers were in the same situation. No angry mood. Food the same for everybody: rice, three times a day. Latrines were a joke. . . . Stinking mess." Seldon Reese on the *Dainichi Maru* said that conditions were pure hell for both Japanese and Americans. The accommodations, food, water, and smell affected everyone. "Again," said Reese, "their own men, as well as ours, were treated this way."

We have related many hellship stories, but perhaps one more will serve to illustrate a point. Incredibly, this 7,089-ton cargo ship held six thousand men, more than were aboard *Junyo Maru*. The "agony of transport ship life" was a great burden, said one soldier. "We were worse than caged animals. . . . [We were] like criminals, ready to be tortured." The *benjos* "were hung like birdcages on the side of the ship," he observed. "I couldn't believe this at first. Rows and rows of boxes with a hole in the middle swayed like swings in the wind. We had no choice. There was no other place to do it. We hung on to the swing's rope and did it directly into the ocean." They noticed yellow streaks trailing in the ship's wake, the result of the droppings from scores of latrines. One of the maru's engines conked out, and half a dozen ships in the convoy adjusted their speed down to match. Men got sick from the rolling seas and heat, and the steel decks baked the vomit. They were stuffed in what they called "silkworm shelves," eleven men in each six-by-twelve-foot area. There was no room to sit up, and they feared suffocation. Some of the men returned from the latrines with feces on their clothes or shoes, spreading the mess into their berths. Illness swept the ship, and two men died before they had gone two days from port.

"It was a life for beasts," one private observed, but he could not say such a thing out loud for fear of a beating. One former health service clerk went on deck from the stinking inferno below but couldn't stomach any breakfast even in the fresh air. He was contemplating his fate when he heard the shout, "Torpedoes!"

Four fish from the *Sturgeon* plowed into the maru's port side. Great holes were torn, and thousands of drums of gasoline turned the holds into crematedtoria. Many who survived the explosions drowned when the ship sank almost immediately. About fifty-six hundred men were lost.[9]

This story sounds familiar, for similar episodes occurred on scores of hellships. The ship in the above scenario was the *Toyama Maru*, which had taken Canadian prisoners from Formosa to Japan in December 1943. On this occasion, 29 June 1944, she was not carrying POWs, but Japanese soldiers of the 44th Independent Brigade, from Kyushu to Okinawa. This was the Japanese version of hell—not far different from the Allied version. It does not justify Japanese treatment of Allied prisoners, but it does open a window to their perspective. At his trial after the war, General Tojo said that there had been no intention of cruel or inhumane behavior: "It was unfortunate that standards which a Japanese soldier would not find unbearable had apparently proved to be inadequate for western prisoners."[10]

Hell is relative.

VOYAGE DURATION

How long did hellship voyages last? Did they get worse and longer as the war progressed? Previous studies seem to indicate so. Lionel Wigmore, in his Australian military history, said that ten-day voyages in 1942 were common, twenty- to thirty-day voyages occurred in 1943, and in 1944, voyages took up to seventy days. Author James Burfitt agreed that in 1942, voyages were quick, but they got successively slower in 1943 and 1944. As examples he used the *Kamakura Maru*, which took C Force from Singapore to Japan in nine days in 1942, *Wales Maru*, which took J Force to Japan in twenty-three days in 1943, and "Newton Force," which was seventy days at sea on the *Rashin Maru* in 1944. Gavan Daws echoed the appraisal, stating that in 1942, prisoners might only be several days on the water, and that 1943 was worse than 1942, and 1944 worse than 1943.[11]

We have seen that 1943 was not worse than 1942 in numbers of hellship voyages, prisoners transported, or in total deaths. In fact, there were about the same number of hellship voyages and prisoners shipped in 1942 and 1944. However, most deaths occurred in 1944. Voyage duration is more difficult to assess. How does one compare ships that sailed directly with ships that made several layovers? Ships that sailed at different speeds? Ships that sailed alone or sailed in convoys? Should the hellship that went from Singapore to Manila, stopped for a week, then continued to Japan be counted as one or two voyages? One cannot draw conclusions by taking a short voyage in 1942 and comparing it to a long voyage in 1944. Generalizations are not so easy. Voyage length did not necessarily get longer as the war progressed.

In 1942, a Singapore-to-empire voyage of three thousand miles averaged twenty-five days. The *Kamakura Maru*, a fast liner, made the trip in nine days, but *Fukkai Maru* took forty-one days. Strangely enough, a 1942 trip from Manila to Japan, only a fifteen-hundred-mile journey, averaged twenty-seven days. Clearly there were numerous factors involved in voyage times. In 1943, Singapore-to-empire voyages averaged twenty-three days, faster than in 1942, and Manila-to-empire voyages only took fifteen days. Contrary to previous estimations, Singapore-to-empire voyages in 1944 only averaged nineteen days, faster than in any year. Singapore-to-Manila trips took thirteen days. Manila-to-empire voyages took twenty-five days. Formosa-to-empire trips took nine days. Some of the discrepancies with other appraisals stem from treating multilayover voyages as one trip. *Rashin Maru* went from Singapore, to Miri, to Manila, to Takao, to Moji. It spent more than three weeks in Manila with its POWs on work details, and it was not really one seventy-day voyage. However, if we wish to count the ships of Japan Party Two—*Rashin Maru, Asaka Maru, Hofuku Maru, Sekiho Maru,* and *Hakushika Maru*—as if they were on one continuous voyage, we find that 1944 voyages from Singapore to the empire averaged nearly thirty days, marginally higher than in 1942. If we consider time that POWs spent on board ship, regardless of layovers, the four longest trips occurred in 1944: *Canadian Inventor,* sixty-two days; *Maros Maru,* sixty-seven days; *Rashin Maru,* seventy days; and *Hofuku Maru,* seventy-nine days. Because of the severed long-distance sea routes, travel in 1945 was the fastest of any year, with voyages averaging only eight days.

Perhaps at first glance it appears that hellship voyages got worse as the war progressed. As the Japanese lost battles, territory, and supplies, they may also have lost what little tolerance they had of POWs. Did standards deteriorate in 1944? Author Donald Knox wrote that in 1942 and 1943, "shipments of prisoners took place relatively without incident," a grossly inaccurate statement. He believed that only after the fall of Saipan in the summer of 1944 were the Japanese "forced to take extreme measures," and only the vessels sailing in the second half of 1944 earned the name hellships.[12]

Preston Hubbard took exception with Knox's evaluation. Hubbard claimed that the Japanese never changed. The standard of POW treatment was low to begin with, and stayed low. Effects of treatment varied somewhat with surrounding conditions, but standards did not change. Hubbard wrote that "Japanese treatment of POWs issued from an attitude unaltered by time, place, or strategy." From surrender to liberation, "the brutality suffered by prisoners was rooted in the moral and ethical standards of the Japanese military."[13]

Once again, generalizations are difficult. POWs described their voyages in horrific terms from the first journeys of 1942. Yet we do see a yearly increase in on-board deaths not attributable to Allied attacks or Japanese atrocities. In 1942, 234 died, in 1943, 274 died, in 1944, there were 674 deaths, and in 1945, 453 died. Overall, conditions appeared to deteriorate in 1944, due to either a change in Japanese attitude or external causes—or, perhaps, a combination of the two. One barometer that shows the deterioration is in the increase in on-board murders.

HOMICIDE ON THE HELLSHIPS

In his book, Gavan Daws stirred up quite a controversy when he concluded that of all the nationalities who were Japanese POWs, only Americans killed each other in the holds of the hellships. Although Daws used sources from several countries, he conceded that he chose only Americans to follow in detail.[14] Absolutes can give historians fits, but one must admire Daws for going out on the limb with his statement that "only Americans" killed each other. It is not quite accurate, but this study finds much cogency with his evaluation— with some caveats.

Among Americans, there was one attempted suicide on the *Tottori Maru* in 1942. Not until 1944 were more suicides, murders, or attempted murders recorded. On *Singoto Maru*, one man went berserk, but instead of being killed, he was tied up to prevent him from hurting himself or others. On *Canadian Inventor,* one POW reported that a few men were murdered, and others witnessed men going crazy, with some slashing their wrists to drink blood. On *Nissyo Maru* there were fights, with men killed, and veins torn open for the blood. On *Noto Maru* an officer bashed men with a soap sock to maintain order. On *Hokusen Maru* men were killed with canteens, there was fighting, people were beaten to death, there were suicides, and throats were bitten. On *Oryoku Maru,* men killed each other, some drank urine, and others turned into vampires. The great majority of POWs on these ships were Americans, but there were other nationalities aboard, particularly on *Hokusen Maru,* with upward of two hundred British and Dutch prisoners.

However, on *Dainichi Maru* in 1942, a vessel carrying twelve hundred British and Dutch POWs, similar scenes of horror filled the night. Flight Lieutenant Cooke said that prisoners fell "into depravities of which I, for one, did not realise the human race was capable." Men drank each other's urine, cut open their own veins to drink blood, or killed other men for their blood. Some gave up and committed suicide. Cooke could not bring himself to relate all the horrible things he had seen. On the *Maros Maru*—carrying mostly British prisoners—screaming, cursing, and fighting is detailed, and murder is posited but not specified. Homicides occurred on ships not carrying Americans, and one might speculate how many times it transpired but was left unmentioned by nationalities perhaps not so candid as Americans seem to be.

There were murders among the British on *Dainichi Maru* in 1942, but only in the latter half of 1944, on ships carrying Americans, did homicides become commonplace. Were conditions on these ships worse than on almost all of the others, forcing men to resort to murder to survive? It appears so, at least for the Americans. There were dozens of other ships that sailed in 1944, however, and reports of murders among British, Dutch, and Australian prisoners are nonexistent. Was there something about national character that enabled one group to more successfully overcome adversity, or just something about it that precluded admission of guilt?

SURVIVAL

How well a group survives in combat is dependent on a number of external factors, such as planning, strategy, tactics, logistics, equipment, supplies, weaponry, and the overall preparedness of your side versus the enemy. On another level, survival also depends on physical condition, training, leadership, group cohesion, camaraderie, and even national character. There have been strong points made in recent studies that national character, or tribalism, was one of the chief determinants in POW survival.[15]

How much did the above factors contribute to survival? Were any of them more important than others? There were good and bad prison camps, but two of the most important criteria that made a camp good or bad were location and commander. A camp on the outlying edges of the communication and supply lines might receive a fraction of the supplies that a closer camp might get. Some camps were in healthier climates. Some were closer to the front lines and were bombed more often. All camps were under the reign of the local commander, who might treat his charges with compassion or contempt. Zentsuji Camp in Japan was a model camp, and prisoners sent there had it relatively good. The China Marines received decent food and shelter and were not subject to overly harsh treatment. Dapecol on Mindanao was better than Cabanatuan on Luzon, which was better than O'Donnell. Hong Kong camps were relatively innocuous. Saigon was better than Singapore. Bicycle Camp in Java and Changi in Singapore were tolerable to decent, and the Burma Railway camps were almost all terrible. While camps on Haruku and Ambon had among the worst death rates of all, assignment to Sandakan meant almost certain death.

How did small units fare? Of the 360 American sailors and Marines captured after the sinking of the *Houston*, 75, or 21 percent, died as POWs. Of the 327 Australians captured after the sinking of *Perth*, 89 died, for a death rate of 27 percent. In the 2d "Lost Battalion" of the 131st Field Artillery, about 544 were taken prisoner, and 91 men, or 20 percent, died in captivity. In the 200th Coast Artillery, about 1,428 men were captured, and 605 died as prisoners, a rate of 42 percent. In Company B of the 192d Tank Battalion, 69, or 44 percent, of the 154 taken prisoner died. There were 47 merchant mariners captured off *American Leader,* and 18 died in captivity, for a 38 percent death rate. Of the 1,593 Americans and Guamanians captured on Wake Island, 244 died in Japanese custody, a low rate of 15 percent. Only 6 percent of the soldiers, sailors, and Marines captured on Wake died: 27 out of 474. In the Australian 2/2 Pioneers, 865 men were captured, and 258, or 30 percent, died. Of the 2/21 Battalion men on Ambon who did not get sent to Hainan, 405 out of 528 died, for a death rate of 77 percent. In Fitzsimmons's Force on the Burma Railway, only 13 out of 194 men died, for a 7 percent death rate.[16]

One can argue that a man's nationality was the most important survival factor, or that small-unit cohesiveness was the prime element, or training, or will to live, or friendship, or any number of ingredients were the most significant. Australian prisoner Russell Braddon, half-jokingly suggested that the way to survive as a captive was to be an entrepreneur, have a Parker pen, fingers full of rings, a couple of Rolex watches, and a mouth full of gold teeth.[17] In spite of all the above verbiage, the most significant survival factors on land were camp locations and who ran them; at sea, it depended upon whether or not one rode a hellship that was attacked. Australians were said to be better survivors than Americans because of their tribal cohesiveness and sharing, while Americans were more capitalistic, traders, and loners. If so, why did *Houston* men have a better survival rate than *Perth* men? Simply because more *Perth* men were on sunken hellships. *American Leader*'s men had a worse rate still, again because a greater percentage of them rode torpedoed hellships. The Texans of the 131st Artillery had half the death rate of the New Mexican 200th Coast Artillery. Were Texans more cohesive or better trained and led than the New Mexicans? No. The New Mexicans simply had the misfortune to lose 18 men on *Oryoku Maru*, 41 on *Shinyo Maru*, and 117 on *Arisan Maru*. Company B of the 192d Tank Battalion was certainly a small, cohesive unit. Why did it have 44 percent casualties as prisoners? Because its men experienced O'Donnell, Cabanatuan, and several hellships. Why did the Wake Marines have such a low death rate in captivity? They were in a camp with sufficient food, shelter, and clothing, without sadistic overseers, and they rode no attacked hellships. On the Burma Railway, about 15 percent of the prisoners died in Burma as opposed to perhaps 40 percent in Thailand. The Americans in Fitzsimmons's group only lost 7 percent, but F Force lost 45 percent. Was it because of national character? Hardly. The Americans were cared for by a doctor, Henri Hekking, who had lived in the Indies for years and had experience with jungle herbs and remedies. F Force was composed of many sick British and Dutch POWs, who happened to have walked right into a cholera epidemic. Why did the Dutch have a significantly lower death rate as prisoners? Daws ascribes it to having a more adaptable constitution. They also rode less torpedoed hellships.

One might also compare female nurses. The Australian and British sisters who were captured after the fall of Singapore faced shipwreck, massacre, and hellship travel between several camps on Banka Island and Sumatra.

Thirty-seven percent of the British nurses died. The American nurses captured with the fall of the Philippines stayed in the relative shelter and security of Manila for the entire war. None died. It was argued that unit cohesiveness and being a part of a group saved their lives. However, all three nationalities of nurses were in small, cohesive units. Were American nurses that much better adapted for survival? That is highly unlikely. The answers lie in location and luck. To survive as prisoners of the Japanese in World War II, what a unit was made of was not as important as where it was sent.

Although some POWs thanked God for their survival, there were many poor fellows who prayed just as fervently, but were killed nevertheless. The man who survived the torpedo explosion when falling beams formed a safe pocket for him, was surrounded by those crushed by the same beams. One man's miracle was another man's death. Just being a survivor meant that a man had to think about his place in the universe. Did he make it because of some grand cosmic scheme, or was he alive by pure, blind luck? The implications were frightening. If all external and internal factors were exactly alike for two units of different nationalities, and they still had different survival rates, perhaps a case could be made for tribalism or character as factors influencing survival. Since those conditions would be nearly impossible to manufacture even in a controlled experiment, let alone in prison camps or on hellships, what we are left with is chance, the luck of the draw, the roll of the dice. The fates of thousands were as predetermined as straws in the wind.

FRIENDLY FIRE

If POW survival depended for the most part on luck, what part did "friendly fire" play in making that luck just a little bit worse? On land, POW camps were hit by Allied bombs many times. At Tan Tooey, Ambon, one raid killed 37 prisoners; at Mukden, a raid killed 20; in Tokyo, a May 1945 raid burned 62 captives; and at Non Pladuk, Thailand, nearly 500 prisoners became casualties. At sea, friendly fire was much more serious. Only 1,540 deaths can be attributable to disease, starvation, thirst, suffocation, suicides, beatings, and murder—deaths that ultimately stemmed from intolerable treatment. On the other hand, more than 19,000 deaths were the direct result of Allied bullets, bombs, or torpedoes. About 93 percent of POW deaths at sea were caused by friendly fire. The Allies killed as many of their own men on Japanese ships as the Germans killed of Allied forces during the Battle of the Bulge. The Allies killed 7,000 more prisoners at sea than the combined American Army, Navy, and Marine Corps deaths on Okinawa, the bloodiest campaign of the Pacific war.

As if these figures aren't shocking enough, a number of those Japanese ships were sunk with full knowledge that there were Allied captives aboard. We not only killed our own, we often knew we were doing it. As I have illustrated, radio intelligence was a key factor in providing information about convoys, cargoes, and routes traveled. How often did the Japanese send news of POWs sailing in convoys? If they followed their own orders—always. Japanese Army Instruction No. 22, regulations for handling POWs, contained more than two dozen articles. Articles 15, 16, and 17 specifically ordered that prisoners of war being sent to the rear must be reported to General Headquarters. The number of prisoners, the points of embarkation and debarkation, the dates of arrival and methods of communication and transportation had to be promptly passed from the sender to the receiver.[18]

The intercepted messages and the Ultras that followed spelled death for thousands of POWs. The sinkings of POW ships in 1942 were most likely not Ultra-related. By late 1943, *Bonefish*'s sinking of *Suez Maru* was probably the result of an Ultra, and *Sailfish*'s sinking of *Chuyo* definitely was. By 1944, there was hardly a submarine operation conducted without Ultra aid. Early in the year, messages were being read within hours, and by the summer, they were being intercepted and translated within minutes. Ultra was very effective. Intelligence gave the submarines their marching orders, and W. J. Holmes, who was a key figure at JICPOA, said that on some nights every submarine in the Pacific was working on Ultra contacts. Either the Military Intelligence Service in the Pentagon, JICPOA at Pearl Harbor, or MacArthur's intelligence staff in the Southwest Pacific Area knew virtually all about the makeup of the Japanese convoys.[19]

Information missed by radio intelligence could sometimes be gathered by "old-fashioned" sleuthing and spying. The larger cities of the Far East were full of anti-Japanese locals or Allied operatives who reported on ship movements. Spies in Singapore often passed along word of ships and cargoes. Intelligence learned in June of 1942 that the Japanese were planning to build a railway to Burma, and they knew in January 1943 that British and Australians were building it, contrary to the story that submarine-rescued POWs first exposed the episode to the rest of the world. The Allies even learned about the planned move of the Aussie POWs out of Sandakan. It was said that the guerrillas knew more about the POW camps than the Japanese did.[20]

In the Philippines, the underground network was working well, keeping MacArthur informed of Japanese activity. Frank and Helen Jones were Allied Intelligence Bureau (AIB) agents, operating in Manila the entire war, radioing information to other Philippine operatives, who would get the news to Australia. Col. Courtney Whitney had a network of operatives in Manila, supplied by submarines and sending him information in Brisbane, which he passed to MacArthur. Double-agent and AIB spy Mario Bansen worked as a clerk in Japanese headquarters and passed much important information to American guerrilla leader Col. Russell Volckmann, who forwarded it to Whitney. Manila Harbor officials slipped word of Japanese ship movements, cargoes, and tonnages to AIB monitors, who passed it to MacArthur. Even unassuming Filipina mothers such as Josefina Guerrero could be successful agents, keeping a special eye on the Manila waterfront and passing word about ship and troop movements. Claire Phillips catered to Japanese officials at Manila's Club Tsubaki, and although despised by many locals, she was really a master spy. On one occasion, as she entertained ships' crews, her Filipino boys rummaged through the ships, bringing back proof that at least some Japanese vessels painted with red crosses were carrying ammunition. Japanese American Richard Sakakida worked in Manila with Japanese officials where he was able to assist some captured guerrillas to break out of prison, as well as copy and forward many important documents. Sakakida helped one judge advocate general pack to ship out on a convoy in April 1944, then passed information about the convoy's sailing. Ultra confirmed it, and submarines were vectored out to meet it. The important *Take* (Bamboo) convoy was subsequently waylaid by *Jack* and *Gurnard*, which sent four troop-laden transports and 3,565 soldiers to the bottom of the sea. Manila was so thoroughly wired with Allied operatives that in September 1943, when Count Terauchi flew in and took a room at the swank Manila Hotel, MacArthur knew about it two hours later. Terauchi was in the same suite that the general and his wife had lived in before fleeing the Philippines.[21] It appears certain that the Allies knew which convoys were carrying prisoners.

In 1944, many more hellship sinkings were Ultra-directed, including *Seahorse*'s sinking of *Ikoma Maru*, *Rasher*'s sinking of *Tango Maru*, and *Tang*'s destruction of *Tamahoko Maru*. Intelligence knew there were POWs sailing in HO-02 as it was tracked from Singapore all the way to Nagasaki. *Koshu Maru's* torpedoing by *Ray* may have been Ultra-directed, while *Sealion, Pampanito,* and *Paddle* definitely had alerts about the prisoner-laden *Rakuyo Maru, Kachidoki Maru,* and *Shinyo Maru.* Very much was known about HI-72. The daily intelligence summary of 12 September even indicated that the number 16 maritime commander, under his "secret" code name KO KE A MI, was sailing on the *Kachidoki Maru,* and that *Kachidoki Maru* was in fact the "Ex Pres. Harrison." Prisoners of war were known to be aboard *Hofuku Maru,* but submarines did not get to her in time; planes blasted her to the bottom. Ultra-directed wolfpacks decimated MATA-30 and *Arisan Maru.* Aircraft destroyed *Oryoku Maru* and *Enoura Maru.* The fact that submarines received these Ultras, however, is difficult to glean from their patrol reports, for captains were not allowed to mention them. In July 1943, ComSubPac issued a stern warning: "Neither actually nor by implication should reference be made to Ultra messages sent by this command x same rule applies for writing up patrol reports."[22]

Japanese ships carrying POWs were unmarked, and many a complaint was made of that fact. However, since these ships almost always carried troops or war materials in addition to POWs, marking them as hospital ships would also have been illegal. It was a no-win situation for both sides. The Allies often knew the names of the ships carrying POWs, but even so, the submarines could not identify individual ships in a convoy. There were no flags saying "POWs Here," and since subs could not get close enough to see ship names, even if not painted out, there was no way to distinguish one from another. They were ordered to go after a convoy. It would not be prudent to mention POWs; it would be counterproductive, would perhaps make the sub captains tentative in their attacks, would raise ethical and moral arguments, and it would open up avenues for possible legal actions by victims seeking reparations.

Ultra itself remained a secret until 1974, but finally, between 1978 and 1988, the National Security Agency released more than half a million decrypted Japanese signals. Why were they withheld for so long? Wartime codebreaker Alan Stripp understood the process, but could not fathom the reason for the continued withholding of records. Stripp reasoned that "the Japanese knew their contents because they sent and received them, and we knew because we broke and read them. Who was there left to hide them from, and why?"[23] Perhaps the answer lies in the just indignation of thousands of surviving kinfolk who would not take kindly to knowing that the lives of their lost loved ones were played with so cavalierly. Friendly fire was not so friendly, nor inadvertent.

In a March 1945 memorandum, Capt. Harry L. Pence listed fourteen Japanese ships sunk by Allied forces while carrying POWs. This study has found twenty-one ships attacked for damage and nineteen sunk. Vice Admiral Lockwood said, "The sinkings of Japanese merchant ships resulting from Communication Intelligence ran into hundreds of ships and probably amounted to fifty percent of the total of all merchantmen sunk by submarines."[24]

One may rightly condemn the Japanese treatment of POWs during World War II. But Allied treatment was not always exemplary. Should one be surprised that so many POWs went to their doom on hellships? Probably not. The purpose of this book is not to debate the morality of war. Every commander expects to take losses in order to accomplish his objective. If the prison vessels were left unmolested, the ships, personnel, and cargo that reached Japan had the potential to do more harm in the future. America and Japan were in a bloody death struggle, and any means taken to gain victory were justifiable at the time. Both sides had been dehumanized. The psychological distancing that facilitates killing was in evidence not only on the battlefield, but in the plans of the strategists and tacticians. The Pacific war was a Manichaean struggle between completely incompatible antagonists. It was a war without mercy.[25] If any innocent parties got in the way they would have to suffer. It is harsh, and indubitably heartless, especially when looked at through a fifty-year cushion of time. War is hell, and hell is relative. The fatal Ultras were sent. Axis and Allies died together.

HELLSHIPS / SLAVE SHIPS

It does not take a great stretch of the imagination to find many similarities between the Atlantic slave trade of the fifteenth to nineteenth century, and transportation of Allied prisoners in the twentieth century. Numerous examples show the resemblance. In 1510, Spain's King Ferdinand first approved sending black slaves to the West Indies to work the mines. It was thought that humane treatment would be the best policy because starving, weak, or injured slaves would not be productive workers. They were to be rested and fed well before embarking on their journeys. While at work, they were to be given a day of rest every two weeks. Regardless, slaves generally began the trip exhausted, hungry, or hurt. On-board treatment depended on the slave ship's captain and officers. At times the crew was treated almost as badly as the slaves.

In the late 1600s, the Royal African Company shipped 5,000 slaves per year, and about 4,000 arrived, for a death rate of 20 percent. Ships were small; in the seventeenth century each carried on average between 230 and 400 slaves. The *Prince of Wales,* however, carried 600 slaves in 1771, and by the 1850s, steamships could haul up to 1,000 slaves at a time. In the 1780s, Britain used ninety ships to carry about 35,000 slaves per year. Journeys averaged between thirty-five and eighty days, but larger vessels under good conditions could make a trip in thirty days. Shorter trips between West Africa and Portugal might only take twenty days.

Slaves were jammed in the holds "like herrings in a barrel." They had to sleep laying on top of each other. "Bilge places" were hung over the sides of the ships for the slaves to relieve themselves, but their numbers meant that many had to relieve themselves where they sat. One of the few surviving slaves who recorded his experiences wrote, "The stench of the hold while we were on the coast was so intolerably loathsome that it was dangerous to remain there for any time." He stayed on deck for air but was forced below when the cargo was loaded: "The closeness of the place, and the heat of the climate, added to the number in the ship . . . almost suffocated us." The air was unfit for breathing, and it "brought on a sickness among the slaves, of which many died, thus falling victims to the improvident avarice, as I may call it, of their purchasers."[26]

On voyages during the 1780s to the 1820s, space per individual averaged out to about four by five feet, but a 1799 law only required eight square feet per slave. On some ships, second tiers were built to allow more room, but that only reduced space for water casks and supplies. Sailcloth funnels were rigged up to channel air below decks. Crew and passengers often were accommodated below in similar conditions. Hammocks, when available, were slung in every corner. Food staples depended on the nationality of the slaver: cassava, maize, oats, or rice. Supplements included beans, yams, potatoes, coconuts, or oranges, and occasionally flour or biscuits, salt beef, or dried turtles—about the same fare eaten by the crew.

Through the years, numerous edicts were issued to treat the slaves well, for it was in the obvious interests of the slavers, plantations, businessmen, and countries to deliver as many live, healthy slaves as possible. Brutality was not normal or inevitable, but it occurred. The mortality rate of slave ships in the eighteenth century was estimated at 9 percent.

There were slave ship sinkings. One of the most disgraceful was in 1738, when the Dutch vessel *Leuden* hit the rocks in a storm off the Surinam coast. The crew closed the hatches and escaped, leaving 702 slaves to drown. In 1706, the Danish *Kron-Printzen* was lost in a storm with 820 slaves. The vessels that reached port would disgorge their passengers to humiliating inspections, often performed while the slaves were naked, and ships and slaves would be fumigated.[27]

The similarities between slave ships and hellships is striking. Does this, therefore, excuse the Japanese, who were doing little that was not already practiced for centuries by European powers? Does it excuse the slave traders, owners, or government officials who sanctioned or profited from the trade? Again, this book is not about debating morality. Perhaps what both epochs illustrate is that man's capacity for inhumanity to his fellow man knows no bounds of race, creed, or time.

The most singular contrast between slave ship and hellship was the absence of rebellion on the latter. One slave insurrection broke out about every nine journeys. Many were bloodily put down, with whippings or decapitations the likely punishments. Some were successful. Slaves murdered the crews, fought them, put them off on lifeboats, threw them overboard, deposited them on land, forced surviving crew members to sail the boats to safe havens, or sailed away themselves.[28] If that rebellion ratio held during the war in the Pacific, one might expect that fifteen or more hellships would have experienced prisoner revolts.

There were no revolts on hellships, although the possibility was discussed. On the *Argentina Maru*, which carried the first POWs, officers cased the ship and counted the guards. It was thought they could seize the vessel and sail to San Francisco. The plan, however, was overruled because they could get no positive intelligence on the actual number of armed Japanese aboard. The presence of Navy nurses and an American woman with a baby were also deterrents. Australians on *DeKlerk* talked of taking over the ship and heading for the Borneo coast, where they could escape to join the guerrillas. Had they realized how strong the anti-Japanese feeling there was, and the number of guerrillas in the Sulu Islands, they might have gone through with their plan. There was talk of taking over *Moji Maru* and sailing to India, but the idea was abandoned to the disgust of many. Similar discussion was made on *Rashin Maru* while the guards were seasick during a storm, but the idea was quickly abandoned. On *Canadian Inventor*, officers talked about seizing the ship. The prisoners outnumbered the guards, and there were men aboard who could navigate. However, they were in Japanese waters, the engines were faulty, they had few supplies, and they could barely make it from port to port as it was without being pursued by Japanese warships. Perhaps the closest men came to rebelling was when the survivors of *Rakuyo Maru* and *Kachidoki Maru* were going to be put on a tanker to Japan. Their refusal to sail resulted in their placement on *Kibitsu Maru*, which was not much of an improvement.

Certainly there were many more discussions about the possibility and consequences of rebelling, yet no attempt was ever made. Resistance and sabotage were not as commonplace as popularly believed. In Hollywood movies, television, and other media, prisoners are often depicted as constantly engaged in escape plots or acts of sabotage. In fact, these activities were infrequent in camp and completely absent at sea.[29]

More than fifty years later, a number of former POWs were asked why there had been no revolts. It was not an easy question. Spero Dardaris, who rode *Hokusen Maru* and *Melbourne Maru*, believed that black slaves rebelled because they had nothing to lose, nothing to look forward to but a life of slavery. "We, on the other hand," said Dardaris, "lived in the hope of surviving until the end of the war, and if we were alive, we were free." The armed guards on the hellships were deterrents, he said, and there were always escorts following alongside. "How far would we get if we did succeed?" he asked. "I never once heard a peep from anyone about a revolt."

Robert Dow, who rode *Nissyo Maru*, didn't believe that one could compare slaves with prisoners, because by the time they boarded the ship, they had been captives for longer than two years and were all "a bunch of sick people," suffering from beriberi, malaria, scurvy, dysentery, and other diseases. Once on board they were stuck in the holds, and "armed guards were topside looking down at us" while warships escorted them. "You tell me," Dow asked, "with all the conditions I described, how in the world we were going to take over the ship?" Dow also speculated about the contention that only Americans killed each other on hellships. "Is it possible," he asked, "that the Americans, when writing about their experiences, were more prone to admit how low men can sink?"

Preston Hubbard, also on *Nissyo Maru,* wrote his own book about his POW experiences. "I was rather taken aback by your questions," he said. "I had previously concluded that passenger accommodations aboard the slave ships were comparable to those of the Japanese hellships." However, Hubbard did not believe that conditions aboard the hellships invited prisoner revolts. The ships were too closely guarded, and the men were confined to the holds. The convoys were too deep within Japanese waters, and even if one was captured, they could not have safely reached a friendly port. The primary reason they were unable to rebel was their poor health. By the summer of 1944, said Hubbard, the men "were more like zombies than humans—both mentally and physically unfit."

William Evans, who also wrote of his prisoner experiences, was incensed with the question of why no POWs attempted to take over a ship. "I would appreciate you telling me how we would have overpowered the Japs and taken over the ship?" he asked. "Forget that there were probably a dozen Jap destroyers out there ready to blow us out of the water if this impossible feat was accomplished. Wish you had been aboard to lead us in the charge against rifles, bayonets, and machine guns."

Martin Christie, who was on *Taikoku Maru,* could understand such feelings. "Yes, we are touchy," he said, "particularly if you have talked to, or written members of the 4th Marines. We were surrendered and we resent that fact." He thought that all the American POWs were in too poor a physical condition to have attempted any rebellion, unlike what he heard about the British. "The Brits," Christie believed, "were transported while in excellent physical condition and with full 'kits' as they call them." He concluded that all former prisoners' comments have to be viewed with the understanding that these are "men who for years have suffered from survivor guilt, dreams of POW days, and sudden returns of trauma when confronted with reminders of events they went through."

The responses are legitimate. Yet perhaps the underlying, unspoken reason for the prisoner's acceptance of his lot was a subconscious belief that after four hundred years of renaissance, enlightenment, reason, and science, civilized man would never commit such atrocities on his fellow man. War in itself, however, is an atrocity. It follows no rationale or rules.

WAR CRIMES

Arguments can be endless concerning the right of the victor to try the vanquished for crimes of war. Right or wrong, trials were held. The first, in 1945 and 1946, was the more famous proceedings in Nuremberg, Germany. In the Pacific, the IMTFE was centered in Tokyo and Yokohama, but trials were also held in the Philippines, Marianas, Hong Kong, Singapore, Java, and other Pacific islands. It began in May 1946, and lasted two years and three months, the longest continuous trial in history.

Japanese prisoners were divided into groups: Class A war criminals were accused of "crimes against peace," and were generally those who had planned, initiated, or waged war of aggression; Class B criminals were charged with conventional war crimes, such as murder, ill treatment, plunder, destruction, or deportation for slave labor; and Class C criminals were those accused of "crimes against humanity," such as extermination, enslavement, or persecution. The divisions tended to blur in some cases.

Among the Class A criminals were Gen. Doihara Kenji, the commander of the Kwantung Army, who later ran cruel prison camps in Malaya, Sumatra, Java, and Borneo, while withholding supplies. Gen. Itagaki Seishiro was chief of staff and commander in Korea as well as in Singapore. He was charged with inhumane treatment of Chinese and of prisoners in Singapore. Gen. Kimura Heitaro, commanding the Burma Area Army, was aware of the horrendous treatment of POWs on the Burma Railway and did not alleviate conditions or restrain his troops from committing atrocities. Gen. Muto Akira commanded in Sumatra and later in the Philippines, where his troops murdered, tortured, and massacred civilians. Gen. Tojo Hideki was the Japanese premier from 1941 to 1944. He was in charge of all POWs and internees and issued instructions that all prisoners who did not work, would not eat. Adm. Oka Takasumi was in charge of the Naval Affairs Bureau. He issued orders for transport of POWs and civilian laborers aboard hellships. He believed that survivors of torpedoed hellships should be killed and issued orders to shoot them while they were in the water. All of the above men, except one, were convicted and executed. One—Oka—was given life imprisonment.[30]

Among the Class B criminals, Lieutenant Generals Homma and Yamashita were both tried in Manila and both convicted and executed. There were about forty-two hundred Class C criminals, the ones that would have been most closely associated with day-to-day misery of the prisoners. In a typical hellship trial, Case 154, commander of the guards Lieutenant Toshino and interpreter Wada were accused of mistreating and abusing, causing mental and physical suffering to, and, ultimately, causing the deaths of 1,039 Americans on *Oryoku Maru, Enoura Maru,* and *Brazil Maru.* Corporal Aihara and six other soldiers were accused of shooting, stabbing, and decapitating 15 prisoners. Charges against the ship's captain were dropped. Many former POWs attended the trial, and those who could not, sent depositions. The defense objected to the absentee depositions, stating that the action gave the commission a "canned case" for study, whereas the defense could not follow suit. The objection was overruled. There were ninety-one prosecution exhibits, as opposed to only thirty-five for the defense. In the end, three soldiers were acquitted, three were given prison terms, Wada was given a life sentence, and Toshino and Aihara were sentenced to death by hanging. Afterward, a case reviewer believed that Wada was as culpable, or more so, than Toshino, and should also have been given the death penalty.[31]

Other hellship commanders and guards met with mixed fates. Sgt. Mori ("Blood") and interpreter Kasiyama ("Slime"), who had given the prisoners hell on Haruku, Ambon, and on the *Maros Maru,* were both convicted by the court in Singapore. Mori was hanged; Kasiyama was also sentenced to death, but he served a prison term and was released. Interpreter Niimori, the bane of British and Canadian prisoners on *Lisbon Maru, Shinsei Maru,* and *Toyama Maru,* was convicted of eight war crimes by the British court in Hong Kong, but he only received a fifteen-year prison term. It is said that he jumped up and clapped for joy at his good fortune. Lieutenant Saito, who ordered the executions of five Marines on *Nitta Maru,* committed suicide. Gen. Kou Shiyoku, one-time chief of POW camps in the Philippines, was put to death for command responsibility for the killing of the men escaping from *Shinyo Maru.* Admiral Sakaibara was sentenced to death for the execution of ninety-six construction workers on Wake. Vice Admiral Sakonju and Captain Mayazumi were found guilty of murdering seventy-two crew and passengers off *Behar.* Sakonju was hanged, but Mayazumi received only seven years in jail.[32]

In a Yokohama trial, Case 339, there were forty-four naval officers accused of planning, ordering, conspiring, and murdering more than eight hundred survivors of sunken Allied merchant ships in the Indian Ocean. Orders were given in March 1943 that submarine commanders were not only to sink ships but to "carry out the complete destruction of the crews" after seizing some to extract information. With these orders in mind, fourteen ships were sunk in the Indian Ocean in 1943 and 1944, among them the United States' SS *Jean Nicolet*, SS *Richard Hovey*, SS *John A. Johnson*, and SS *William K. Vanderbilt*; Britain's SS *Daisy Moller*, SS *British Chivalry*, MV *Sutlej*, SS *Ascot*, SS *Nancy Moller*, and SS *Nellore*; Holland's SS *Tjisalak*; and Norway's MV *Scotia*. Commander of the 14th Submarine Flotilla, Rear Adm. Katsuto Haruo, was reprimanded for being too lenient with survivors. After the disposal orders, submarines were mounted with 7-mm light machine guns for the purpose of killing survivors.

After the war, many of the commanders responsible for the killings did not come to trial. Lieutenant Shimizu, who murdered men on the *Nancy Moller*, disappeared. Lt. Cdr. Kudo Kaneo, who disposed of survivors from the *John A. Johnson*, also disappeared. Lieutenant Commander Kusaka, who machine-gunned *Richard Hovey*'s men, was not brought to trial. Lt. Ebato Kazuro, who killed fifty-five men off *Daisy Moller*, received appropriate punishment when his submarine, RO-110, was sunk by the Royal Navy two months later. Lt. Cdr. Ariizumi Tatsunosuke, on I-8, who slaughtered men off *Tjisalak* and *Jean Nicolet*, took his own life. Two Lieutenants aboard I-8, Motonaka Sadao and Hattori Masonori, received seven and five years sentences, respectively.

Despite the evidence against them, twenty-eight of the accused naval officers were acquitted. Sixteen were convicted, but only received sentences that ranged from two to twenty years. A reviewer of the case in the Judge Advocates' Office could find little consistency in comparison with similar cases. He believed the sentences were "grossly inadequate." If they were found guilty, as they were, "the punishment meted out should have fit the crime. It is considered that in no case in past cases have sentences been so lenient."

Pondering this inconsistency, one author speculated that, by this time, boredom or fatigue may have taken over in the trials. Perhaps. Another reason, however, may have been an Allied reluctance to condemn Japanese submarine captains when some of their own captains may have engaged in similar, albeit unsanctioned, behavior. One might compare the punishment received by the Japanese with a similar case at Nuremberg. In March 1944, KLt. Heinz Eck, in his U-852, sank the Greek steamer *Peleus* in the South Atlantic, then had his men machine-gun and lob grenades at the survivors. Eck and two others were sentenced to death, tied to posts, and shot by a British firing squad.[33]

The question is far from settled as to whether or not the Japanese are unique in their apparent capacity for cruelty. Japanese author Tanaka Yuki takes exception with Gavan Daws's book for omitting explanation as to why the Japanese may have appeared so cruel. He believes Daws has fostered the impression that the Japanese are a people with unique characteristics and challenges that interpretation. Japan's past is far from unique. "War crimes," Tanaka says, "were and are the monopoly of no people or nation." Japan's actions were not so different from the Nazis or the Allies or, more recently, from episodes in Vietnam, Iraq, Rwanda, or the former Yugoslavia. Tanaka sees no "inherently peculiar Japaneseness" for the spiral into total war; it was a product of emperor ideology, family-state concepts, and the military takeover of the government. As such, his thesis is similar to a fifty-year-old assessment by naval historian Samuel Eliot Morison, and a recent explanation by Robert Edgerton.

Regardless of whether the Japanese exhibit any unique traits, unlike Germans, they have certainly tried to erase memories of the Pacific war from the national consciousness. During the late 1940s, the Education Ministry admitted Japan's responsibility for the war and tried to see that schoolchildren understood the situation. In the early 1950s, however, the United States itself brought about a sea change when it tried to promote militarism among the Japanese people to gain support for rearmament against new cold war enemies. Japan did an enthusiastic about face, and the Education Ministry began to promote a new interpretation: Japan was a victim of war, it had just cause for fighting, it liberated Asia from the Europeans. Mention of fault and atrocities were removed from textbooks. Ienaga Saburo's school textbook was rejected because it was too critical of Japan's role in World War II, and he fought a crusade for years to rectify the situation. Yet by the 1970s, the idea of Japan as a victim had been firmly entrenched. In the new millennium, the Education Ministry still screens Japanese history textbooks; only one mention of comfort women can be found, and "invasion" or "aggression" are euphemistically described as "advances."

Japan continues to deny and cover up its atrocities. A movie was made from Clay Blair's book *Return from the River Kwai,* detailing prisoners' experiences on the Burma Railway and their subsequent transportation and sinking on the *Kachidoki Maru* and *Rakuyo Maru.* The rights to the movie were originally bought by TriStar in 1989, which then merged with Columbia, which in turn was bought by Sony Corporation. In 1997, Sony CEO Morita Akio, once a Japanese naval officer in World War II, blocked release of the picture in the United States. In a lawsuit, the film's producer alleged that "TriStar didn't want to offend its new Japanese bosses with a film critical of the nation's treatment of WWII POWs."[34] More than fifty years after the war, there are still people on both sides who do not want the full story of the hellships exposed.

The war crimes trials did not reduce future atrocities. Outrageous, inhumane behavior has not slackened, as glancing at the international pages of the daily newspapers over the past decades can attest. Perhaps this will prove too nihilistic an assessment for some tastes, but if survival depended upon the flip of a coin, and governments realized that to kill the foe, sometimes friend too must die, war crimes must be seen as inevitable. Agnes Keith, who suffered through years of civilian internment camps in Borneo, noted, "War is the acceptance of suffering and atrocity, and the sacrifice of decency and good thinking. War itself is the crime against humanity. When we accept war we accept war crime; we then have no grounds to complain."[35]

THE HELLSHIP EXPERIENCE

Some former POWs forgot about the war, some tried to forget, and others remember it with a vengeance. Lester Tenney, who rode *Toko Maru,* could not understand how some former POWs could say that they forgot about the war. "I know without a doubt," he said, "that my experiences during those trying four years shaped my thinking, my philosophies, and attitudes about life for the next fifty years."

For the overwhelming majority, being a prisoner was an indelible experience, and for all of those unfortunate enough to have ridden hellships, the experience was the worst of the worst. Preston Hubbard has been plagued by nightmares of executions, beatings, and dead bodies for five decades. But the worst recurring nightmare was of the human feces that seemed to coat everything in the "unspeakable holds of the *Nissyo Maru.*" Hubbard realized that there is no healthy escape for him. The dreams will always be there. He has an utter revulsion of war, yet is horrified that the last great war has not removed all thoughts of future war from the realm of possibility.

Plagued by his own "caged dragons," Bob Haney, who was aboard *Nagato Maru,* spent forty years trying to avoid anyone and anything that would remind him of his experience. But he could not forget. Living in the cesspool of the ship's hold made an indelible impression. "For much of the rest of my life," said Haney, "this nightmare Pacific passage would color my impression of the Japanese culture."[36]

Prison camps were bad, but hellships were worse. Henry Stanley said of his journey on *Taga Maru,* "That ship was the worst part of the whole deal; that ship made the Death March look like a picnic. They died like flies!" Manny Lawton, who rode *Oryoku Maru* and *Brazil Maru,* had a similar appraisal. His ferry rides, train rides, and truck rides were all substandard, and the sixty-five-mile foot journey called the Death March was not misnamed. Yet, Lawton said, "by far the worst of all was the . . . journey from Manila to Japan on the Hell Ships." Andrew Carson affirmed that the worst night of his life was spent on the *Nissyo Maru.* John McEwan thought that "the infamous Black Hole of Calcutta could not have been worse than the filthy, infested, claustrophobic death-cell on the *England Maru.*" Of *Hokusen Maru,* Bill Donovan said, "The trip on that ship—thirty-nine hellish days—was indescribable, the worst part of the whole war for me." Forrest Knox elaborated about his experience on that same ship:

> It broke me as a soldier. I was a good soldier until then but that ship ruined me. . . . How I survived it I can't really tell. Some survived it because they were kids and never realized just how rotten the situation was. Others survived day to day—bullheaded stubbornness would be a good explanation. But when you got into bad shape, like in the hold of that ship, the ones that got out were the ones that hated. Love never kept anyone alive . . . but if you hated, whether a Jap or those medics or an officer, it seems strange but those that did—I mean hated real hard—they lived. Those that started begging for their mothers, then you'd better start digging a hole for them.
>
> Once you felt sorry for yourself, you were an absolute gone bastard.[37]

For many, the hating would not easily go away. Virgil Vining, who rode *Nissyo Maru,* holds no grudge against the Japanese population as a whole, but against the Japanese sailor and soldier of World War II, he said, "I can retain nothing but hate." Bob Farrands and Cliff Farlow were on *Celebes Maru* and *Rakuyo Maru*. Farrands said of the Japanese, "I will neither forgive nor forget. I will hate them until I die." Farlow declared, "I don't believe I'd ever become prisoner of the Japs again. I think I would rather stand up and shoot or be shot. Even today I don't want to have anything to do with them." Captured pilot Bob Martindale tersely wrote, "Americans have short memories and forgive too easily."[38]

All of the POWs came home scarred to some extent, physically or mentally. Some healed faster than others, but all had a readjustment period. Some found it hard to return to home and family; wives also had a difficult time trying to help their husbands cope. Communication was often difficult and many former POWs found that the only ones they could talk to were other veterans. The bonding is strong between prisoners who shared such horrible experiences—at times stronger than ties between brothers. They are knit together by their war experience, and by their feeling of postwar rejection by their respective governments. Their health is worse than their nations' populations at large, and they die at younger ages. Promises of health care and monetary compensation made by past regimes are not kept. It hurts them to see Germany admit its responsibility and make reparations while Japan does not. It doubly hurts them to see the United States pay twenty thousand dollars to every Japanese American civilian who was placed in a relocation center during the war while they receive no compensation from Japan, which remains unrepentant and continues to deny its history of brutality in the Pacific.

After all is said and done, we can only hope that the surviving former POWs of the Japanese will be able to live out their remaining years somewhat content with the knowledge that they fought for a just cause, regardless of how trite and outdated such sentiment may appear in this age. They took everything the enemy could throw at them. They survived the war and they survived hell. We hope we will never have to face again what they went through, but should the need arise, we hope we will be blessed with another such generation of men.

APPENDIX: HELLSHIP VOYAGES AND POW DEATHS

1942

Ship	Date	POWs	Deaths	Days	Voyage
Argentina Maru	1-10-42	800		5	Guam to Japan
Nitta Maru	1-12-42	1,187	5	11	Wake to Japan
Op Ten Noort	3-4-42	900		1	Bandjarmasin to Makassar
Tatsuta Maru	3-12-42	200		4	Japan to Wake
Maru Ichi (1)	4-2-42	32		14	Makassar to Japan
Celebes Maru	5-15-42	1,000		9	Singapore to Burma (A Force)
Toyohashi Maru	5-15-42	2,000		5	Singapore to Burma (A Force)
England Maru	5-16-42	500		9	Sumatra to Burma
Kyokusei Maru	5-16-42	1,200		5	Sumatra to Burma
Maru Ni (2)	6-4-42	500		5	Java to Singapore
Montevideo Maru	6-22-42	1,053	1,053	8	Rabaul to Hainan

Ship	Date	POWs	Deaths	Days	Voyage
Naruto Maru	7-6-42	79		15	Rabaul to Japan
Ume Maru	7-7-42	1,494		10	Singapore to Sandakan (B Force)
Samurusan Maru	7-26-42	500		10	Timor to Java
Sanko Maru	7-29-42	346		3	Manila to Palawan
Heiyo Maru	7-42	200		5	Wake to Japan
Interisland Steamer	7-42	200		8	Manila to Davao
England Maru	8-12-42	400		17	Singapore to Formosa
Fukkai Maru	8-12-42	1,100		41	Singapore to Takao and Pusan
Nagara Maru	8-12-42	180		2	Manila to Formosa
Maru San (3)	8-15-42	100		12	Mindanao to Formosa and Pusan
Tatu Maru	8-42	300		1	Mergui to Tavoy
Maru Shi (4)	9-3-42	616		8	Hong Kong to Japan
Nishi Maru	9-4-42	1,974		14	Timor to Java to Singapore
Toko Maru	9-5-42	500		32	Manila to Japan
Lima Maru	9-20-42	300	8	13	Manila to Formosa
Tachibana Maru	9-20-42	200		10	Wake to Japan
Dainichi Maru	9-23-42	1,000		6	Timor to Surabaya
Lisbon Maru	9-27-42	1,816	842	8	Hong Kong to Shanghai
Tamahoko Maru	10-3-42	268		3	Mindanao to Manila
Shinsei Maru	10-5-42	840	5	3	Shanghai to Japan

Ship	Date	POWs	Deaths	Days	Voyage
Kenkon Maru	10-8-42	1,500	1	3	Java to Singapore (Williams Force)
Tottori Maru	10-8-42	1,961	30	32	Manila to Pusan
Asama Maru	10-10-42	1,000		13	Makassar to Japan
Ex-British ship	10-10-42	1,846	10	9	Singpore to Kuching to Jesselton
Dainichi Maru	10-11-42	1,000		3	Java to Singapore (Branch Party Five)
Maebashi Maru	10-14-42	1,700		8	Singapore to Burma
Singapore Maru	10-17-42	3,000		8	Java to Singapore
Maru No. 760	10-18-42	1,000		5	Bugo, Mindanao to Davao
England Maru	ca. 10-20-42	1,000	3	17	Singapore to Formosa
No. 1 Yoshida Maru	10-22-42	2,700	10	4	Java to Singapore
Yamagata Maru	10-23-42	1,000		1	Rangoon to Moulmein
Shinyu Maru	10-24-42	500	100	4	Singapore to Burma
Taiko Maru	10-25-42	530		11	Ambon to Hainan
Erie Maru	10-28-42	1,000	2	10	Manila to Davao
Dainichi Maru	10-30-42	1,200	80	26	Singapore to Moji
Singapore Maru	10-30-42	1,100	60	25	Singapore to Moji
Maru Go (5)	10-42	1,000		12	Timor to Singapore
Asama Maru	11-1-42	20		5	Wake to Japan
Nagara Maru	11-7-42	600	1	2	Singapore to Rabaul to Ballale (Gunner 600 Party)

Ship	Date	POWs	Deaths	Days	Voyage
Nagato Maru	11-7-42	1,600	20	17	Manila to Moji
Kamakura Maru	11-28-42	2,213	10	9	Singapore to Nagasaki (C Force)
Panama Maru	12-20-42	130		21	China to Truk
Maru Roku (6)	12-28-42	74		3	Java to Singapore

1943

Ship	Date	POWs	Deaths	Days	Voyage
Usu Maru	1-4-43	1,978		3	Java to Singapore
Aki Maru	1-10-43	74		26	Singapore to Formosa
Moji Maru	1-11-43	800	25	5	Penang to Moulmein
Nichimei Maru	1-11-43	1,000	40	4	Singapore to Moulmein
Small steamer	1-12-43	62		12	Berhala to Kuching (Civilians)
Tatsuta Maru	1-19-43	663		3	Hong Kong to Japan
Roko Maru	2-9-43	500		3	Java to Singapore
Dainichi Maru	2-20-43	86		2	Hankow to Nanking
Kamakura Maru	2-26-43	10		3	Makassar to Singapore to Japan
Koryu Maru	3-4-43	235		3	Shanghai to Nanking
Akikaze	3-17-43	60	60	2	Wewak to Kavieng (Civilians)
Treasure	3-20-43	8		15	Sandakan to Kuching
DeKlerk	3-28-43	1,000		4	Singapore to Kuching (E Force)

Ship	Date	POWs	Deaths	Days	Voyage
DeKlerk	4-3-43	760		5	Kuching to Sandakan (Java One Party)
Taka Maru	4-9-43	500		6	Kuching to Sandakan (E Force)
Amagi Maru	4-22-43	1,071		12	Java to Ambon
Cho Saki Maru	4-22-43	1,000		12	Java to Ambon
Kunitama Maru	4-22-43	1,000		8	Java to Ceram
Kyokko Maru	4-26-43	1,500	2	25	Singapore to Japan (G Force)
Thames Maru	5-5-43	2,022	200	29	Singapore to Palau
Wales Maru	5-16-43	950		22	Singapore to Japan (J Force)
Seikyo Maru	5-18-43	3		4	Shanghai to Canton
Treasure	6-8-43	22		7	Sandakan to Kuching
Sibijac	6-27-43	8		6	Kuching to Singapore
Clyde Maru	7-23-43	500		15	Manila to Moji
Sandakan Steamer	8-16-43	30		10	Sandakan to Kuching
Taga Maru	9-20-43	850	70	15	Manila to Japan
Asama Maru	9-21-43	71		18	Singapore to Japan
Makassar Maru	9-26-43	3,500		3	Java to Singapore
Rio de Janiero Maru	10-2-43	200		2	Makassar to Java
Tiensen	10-16-43	104		18	Sandakan to Kuching
SS Subuk	10-25-43	72		12	Sandakan to Kuching
France Maru	11-5-43	300		5	Batavia to Palembang

Ship	Date	POWs	Deaths	Days	Voyage
Maru Shichi (7)	11-5-43	500		29	Singapore to Japan
No. 7 Hoshi Maru	11-13-43	9		22	Rabaul to Japan
Suez Maru	11-25-43	546	546	4	Ambon to Java
Chuyo	11-30-43	21	20	4	Truk to Japan
Unyo	11-30-43	20		6	Truk to Japan
Soong Cheong	12-15-43	504		5	Hong Kong to Formosa
Kunishima Maru	12-23-43	300		5	Ambon to Makassar
Toyama Maru	12-26-43	504	1	10	Formosa to Japan

1944

Ship	Date	POWs	Deaths	Days	Voyage
Ikoma Maru	1-21-44	611	418	1	Palau to Hollandia
Toka Maru	2-12-44	6		2	Cape Jacquinot to Rabaul
Tango Maru	2-24-44	3,500	3,000	2	Java to Ambon
Tone	2-26-44	111	72	6	Indian Ocean to Java
Kenwa Maru	3-6-44	200		16	Manila to Japan
Taikoku Maru	3-24-44	308		17	Manila to Japan
No. 6 Kotobuki Maru	4-20-44	400		3	China to Japan
Chuka Maru	5-14-44	1,200	5	3	Java to Singapore to Sumatra
Hioki Maru	6-3-44	315		18	Singapore to Moji (Japan Party One)
Hozan Maru	6-3-44	451		18	Singapore to Moji (Japan Party One)
Kokusei Maru	6-3-44	456		18	Singapore to Moji (Japan Party One)

Ship	Date	POWs	Deaths	Days	Voyage
Miyo Maru	6-3-44	208		15	Singapore to Formosa (Japan Party One)
Teia Maru	6-5-44	500		14	Singapore to Moji
Yashu Maru	6-12-44	1,250	56	5	Davao to Cebu
Tamahoko Maru	6-18-44	772	560	6	Formosa to Japan
Singoto Maru No. 824	6-22-44	1,194	1	3	Cebu to Manila
Harugiku Maru	6-25-44	730	178	1	Belawan to Pakanbaroe
Canadian Inventor	7-2-44	1,100	6	62	Manila to Japan
Asaka Maru	7-4-44	738		12	Singapore to Manila (Japan Party Two)
Hakushika Maru	7-4-44	609		12	Singapore to Manila (Japan Party Two)
Hofuku Maru	7-4-44	1,287		15	Singapore to Manila (Japan Party Two)
Rashin Maru	7-4-44	1,065		12	Singapore to Manila (Japan Party Two)
Sekiho Maru	7-4-44	1,024		12	Singapore to Manila (Japan Party Two)
Nissyo Maru	7-17-44	1,600	12	17	Manila to Japan
Hakushika Maru	7-23-44	609		21	Manila to Moji
Sekiho Maru	7-23-44	1,024		21	Manila to Moji
Koshu Maru	7-29-44	1,513	1,239	4	Batavia to Makassar
Asaka Maru	8-9-44	738	31	8	Manila to Takao
Rashin Maru	8-9-44	1,065	15	30	Manila to Moji
Hakusan Maru	8-22-44	707		6	Takao to Japan
Noto Maru	8-27-44	1,135	1	8	Manila to Japan

Ship	Date	POWs	Deaths	Days	Voyage
Nanshin Maru	9-5-44	3		3	Palau to Davao to Manila
Uruppu Maru	9-5-44	5		3	Palau to Davao to Manila
Kachidoki Maru	9-6-44	900	400	6	Singapore to Japan (Japan Party Three)
Kenzan Maru	9-6-44	300	25	23	Makassar to Surabaya
Rakuyo Maru	9-6-44	1,318	1,159	6	Singapore to Japan (Japan Party Three)
Sugi Maru	9-6-44	200	55	23	Makassar to Surabaya
Shinyo Maru	9-7-44	750	667	1	Davao to Manila
Kibitsu Maru	9-10-44	677	8	18	Hainan to Japan
Junyo Maru	9-17-44	6,520	5,620	2	Java to Sumatra
Maros Maru	9-17-44	650	325	67	Ambon to Java
Hofuku Maru	9-21-44	1,289	1,047	1	Manila to Japan
Kaishun Maru	9-21-44	150	4	2	Mindanao to Manila
Maru Hachi (8)	9-44	150		2	Palawan to Manila
Hokusen Maru	10-3-44	1,100	39	39	Manila to Formosa
Trading Vessel	10-8-44	450		3	Ambon to Celebes
Arisan Maru	10-21-44	1,800	1,792	4	Manila to Japan
Fukuji Maru	11-9-44	354		1	Moji to Pusan
Coastal Craft	11-11-44	100	27	3	Celebes to Java
Oryoku Maru	12-14-44	1,620	300	2	Manila to Japan
Awa Maru	12-26-44	525		20	Singapore to Moji
Brazil Maru	12-27-44	250	5	4	Luzon to Formosa

Ship	Date	POWs	Deaths	Days	Voyage
Enoura Maru	12-27-44	1,070	316	4	Luzon to Formosa

1945

Ship	Date	POWs	Deaths	Days	Voyage
OSK Ferry	1-8-45	1,000		3	Java to Singapore
Brazil Maru	1-14-45	925	450	15	Formosa to Japan
Melbourne Maru	1-14-45	500	1	9	Formosa to Japan
Enoshima Maru	1-25-45	564		5	Keelung to Moji
Haruyasa Maru	1-31-45	2,500		9	Singapore to Saigon (Japan Party Four)
Taiko Maru	2-27-45	700		6	Keelung to Moji
Coastal Craft	4-13-45	50		6	Muna to Makassar
No. 17 Nanshin Maru	7-18-45	416	1	12	Makassar to Surabaya
TOTALS	1942–45	126,064	21,039	1,639	

This list represents 156 voyages of 134 ships. For some ships mentioned in the book, complete information was not available. Those ships are not listed.

NOTES

1942: RELOCATING THE POWS

1. Costello, *Pacific War*, 217, 220, 232; Whitman, *Bataan*, 603; Wright-Nooth, *Prisoner of the Turnip Heads*, 85; Kinvig, *Scapegoat*, 224; Daws, *Prisoners of the Japanese*, 94; Toland, *Rising Sun*, 345.
2. Daws, *Prisoners of the Japanese*, 96.
3. Giles, *Captive of the Rising Sun*, 46–47, 60–61; Iannarelli, *Eighty Thieves*, 26; Jordan, *World's Merchant Fleets*, 262, 540; Jentschura, Jung, and Mickel, *Warships of the Imperial Japanese Navy*, 59.
4. Giles, *Captive of the Rising Sun*, 55, 62; LaForte, Marcello, and Himmel, *With Only the Will to Live*, 118.
5. Giles, *Captive of the Rising Sun*, 70–71, 78. The *Argentina Maru* was commissioned as the escort carrier *Kaiyo* in November 1943. It was bombed and ran aground in July 1945.
6. As is the Japanese custom, surnames will appear first, followed by the personal name.
7. Schultz, *Wake Island*, 70; Urwin, *Facing Fearful Odds*, 328, 332, 526, 534–35.
8. Daws, *Prisoners of the Japanese*, 45–47; LaForte, Marcello, and Himmel, *With Only the Will to Live*, 117–18; Urwin, *Facing Fearful Odds*, 544; Jordan, *World's Merchant Fleets*, 258.
9. Daws, *Prisoners of the Japanese*, 48; Urwin, *Facing Fearful Odds*, 544; Kerr, *Surrender and Survival*, 42; Giles, *Captive of the Rising Sun*, 81.
10. Kerr, *Surrender and Survival*, 42–43; Daws, *Prisoners of the Japanese*, 49; Schultz, *Wake Island*, 158–59; Huie, *Can Do!* 71.
11. Kinvig, *Scapegoat*, 201; Shores and Cull, *Bloody Shambles*, 59, 86–87.
12. Shores and Cull, *Bloody Shambles*, 84; Lord Russell, *Knights of Bushido*, 104–5.
13. Winslow, *Fleet the Gods Forgot*, 186, 197, 210, 212, 214, 217, 221, 226, 230–32; Shores and Cull, *Bloody Shambles*, 231.
14. Shores and Cull, *Bloody Shambles*, 239, 307, 311; Roscoe, *United States Submarine Operations*, 82–83.

15. Hara, Saito, and Pineau, *Japanese Destroyer Captain*, 74–75, 87–88, 111; Jordan, *World's Merchant Fleets*, 277. Hara claimed he could only take forty or fifty men on his destroyer, yet during the Battle of the Eastern Solomons, on 24 August 1942, he rescued three hundred Japanese sailors from the carrier *Ryujo*. It was said that the *Op ten Noort* was on a mission to rescue survivors of the Java Sea battle when captured. However, Hara makes it clear that she was taken before the battle.

16. Blain, *Huryo*, 1–3; Morison, *Rising Sun in the Pacific*, 372; Nevitt, "Long Lancers."

17. Michel, *Mr. Michel's War*, 82–90; Winslow, *Fleet the Gods Forgot*, 227–32; Morison, *Rising Sun in the Pacific*, 373–74; Nevitt, "Long Lancers."

18. Winslow, *Fleet the Gods Forgot*, 245–52; Roscoe, *United States Submarine Operations*, 96–99; Hara, Saito, and Pineau, *Japanese Destroyer Captain*, 89–92; Nevitt, "Long Lancers"; Sam Simpson to author, 20 January 1999.

19. Blain, *Huryo*, 3–5; Michel, *Mr. Michel's War*, 91–94, 100; Hara, Saito, and Pineau, *Japanese Destroyer Captain*, 92; Record Group (RG) 38, Orange Translations, Box 992, National Archives and Records Administration (NARA). Michel remembers seeing the *Op ten Noort* at Makassar on 5 March. Hara remembers it in Bandjarmasin on 6 March. It was renamed *No. 2 Hikawa Maru* in April 1943 and was an operational loss in October 1944.

20. Michel, *Mr. Michel's War*, 103–4; Sam Simpson to author, 10 March 1999; RG 38, Box 991, NARA. The exact name and sailing date for this ship is unknown. For convenience, I have named it *Maru Ichi, ichi* meaning "one" in Japanese. Other transports with names unknown will be named similarly: *Maru Ni* (two), *Maru San* (three), and so on.

21. Michel, *Mr. Michel's War*, 183; Winslow, *Fleet the Gods Forgot*, 252.

22. Kinvig, *River Kwai Railway*, 27–30; Thompson, *Thousand Cups of Rice*, 1; Salim, *Prisoners at Kota Cane*, 1, 19.

23. Kinvig, *River Kwai Railway*, 18–25; Daws, *Prisoners of the Japanese*, 183–84; Harries and Harries, *Soldiers of the Sun*, 310.

24. Hall, *Blue Haze*, 15–19; Ken Williams to author, 25 February 1997.

25. Kinvig, *River Kwai Railway*, 39; Komamiya, *Senji Yuso*, 8–9; Jordan, *World's Merchant Fleets*, 248; Hall, *Blue Haze*, 19, 20, 36, 56, 59; Apthorpe, *British Sumatra Battalion*, 71–74. The *Celebes Maru* was bombed by planes in the central Philippines on 15 November 1944.

26. Komamiya, *Senji Yuso*, 8–9; Alden, *U.S. Submarine Attacks*, 11. The *Kyokusei Maru* was sunk on 2 March 1943, in the Battle of the Bismarck Sea.

27. Krancher, *Defining Years*, 25–28.

28. Kinvig, *River Kwai Railway*, 52–53; Tanaka, *Hidden Horrors*, 15–16, 220; Keith, *Three Came Home*, 16, 35, 42; Silver, *Sandakan*, 36; Young, *Return to a Dark Age*, 48–51; Firkins, *From Hell to Eternity*, 9–10. Former POW Don Wall says that the name of this ship was *Ube Maru*, while author Lynette Silver states that it was *Yubi Maru*. The *Ube Maru* was torpedoed by *Seahorse* on 3 November 1943.

29. Wade, *Prisoner of the Japanese*, 53–56; Kinvig, *Scapegoat*, 231–32; Cody, *Ghosts in Khaki*, 299; Lord Russell, *Knights of Bushido*, 60–62; Clarke, Burgess, and Braddon, *Prisoners*

of War, 139; Lamont-Brown, *Kempeitai*, 83–85. The *Fukkai Maru* was torpedoed by *Pogy* on 13 December 1943.

30. Wall, *Heroes at Sea*, 134–37; Tanaka, *Hidden Horrors*, 145; Morison, *Rising Sun in the Pacific*, 259–60; Lord, *Lonely Vigil*, 5–6; Bath, *Tracking the Axis Enemy*, 143; *Sturgeon*, 4th Patrol Report.

31. Wall, *Heroes at Sea*, 135; Tanaka, *Hidden Horrors*, 145; Nelson, "Return to Rabaul," 144; Wigmore, *Japanese Thrust*, 612, 674; Nevitt, "Long Lancers." The *Naruto Maru* was torpedoed by *Whale* on 8 August 1943.

32. Whitman, *Bataan*, 16, 39, 126, 424; Dull, *Battle History of the Imperial Japanese Navy*, 32–34; Breuer, *Devil Boats*, 38; Considine, *General Wainwright's Story*, 83, 86–87, 130–32.

33. Waterford, *Prisoners of the Japanese*, 251–61; Knox, *Death March*, 118–19, 154–55.

34. Morton, *United States Army in World War II*, 499, 577.

35. Stewart, *Give Us This Day*, 67–70; LaForte, Marcello, and Himmel, *With Only the Will to Live*, 124; Wrynn, "Massacre at Palawan," 56–57; Henderson, "Another Tender Sailor's Tale," 4; Donald H. Thomas to author, 24 November 1998; J. D. Merritt to Dennis Wrynn, Fairfax, Virginia, 19 March 1992. *Sanko Maru* was bombed off New Hanover on 16 February 1944.

36. Nordin, *We Were Next to Nothing*, 70; Kerr, *Surrender and Survival*, 107–8; Considine, *General Wainwright's Story*, 157, 169–75, 181–82.

37. Tenney, *My Hitch in Hell*, 113–15; Jentschura, Jung, and Mickel, *Warships of the Imperial Japanese Navy*, 280. Tenney remembered the ship as *Toro Maru*, but the only ship of that name was sunk in December 1941. A possibility is *Toko Maru*, an ex-Chinese, ex-Dutch ship of 4,180 tons, requisitioned during the war. It was built in 1908, closely matching Tenney's age estimation. Being rusted, perhaps the letters in "Toko" appeared to read "Toro."

38. Tenney, *My Hitch in Hell*, 116–22; Matson, *It Tolled for New Mexico*, 364–65.

39. King, "Fall of Corregidor," 5–7. The *Lima Maru* was torpedoed by *Snook* on 8 February 1944.

40. Jordan, *World's Merchant Fleets*, 115, 250, 500; Nelson, *P.O.W. Prisoners of War*, 151–52; Hank Nelson to author, 11 February 1999; Dawson, *To Sandakan*, 42–45; Wall, *Kill the Prisoners!* i, 3; International Military Tribunal Far East (hereafter cited as IMTFE), POW statements. The *Nishi Maru* was bombed near Manila on 13 November 1944.

41. Wright-Nooth, *Prisoner of the Turnip Heads*, 64, 85; Lord Russell, *Knights of Bushido*, 96–98.

42. Lindsay, *At the Going Down of the Sun*, 178; Wright-Nooth, *Prisoner of the Turnip Heads*, 84, 194, 224; Lord Russell, *Knights of Bushido*, 121–22; Kvalheim, "Sinking of the Lisbon Maru," 16; *Grouper*, 2d Patrol Report. Capt. Edwin R. Swinburne, McGregor's superior, was not pleased with his aggressiveness, thinking that he was too tentative in attacking. McGregor blamed poor torpedo performance. Because McGregor did not see what he called a "Lyons Maru class" ship sink, he may not have been given credit for it, until an intercepted Japanese radio message verified that the *Lisbon Maru* (a *Lyons*-class ship) did indeed sink where McGregor had claimed.

43. Lord Russell, *Knights of Bushido*, 122–26; Kvalheim, "Sinking of Lisbon Maru," 16–17. The *Shinsei Maru* was torpedoed by *Tarpon* on 28 August 1943.

44. Jackfert and Miller, *History of the Defenders*, 75; Nordin, *We Were Next to Nothing*, 70; Jordan, *World's Merchant Fleets*, 268; Dreher, "Diary." Jackfert and Miller incorrectly call this ship the *Ama Maru*.

45. Kerr, *Surrender and Survival*, 112; Petak, *Never Plan Tomorrow*, 127–34; Harris, *Factories of Death*, 123–24; Dreher, "Diary"; Cave, *Beyond Courage*, 288–89; Grokett, "Twelve Hundred Days," 15; Alden, *U.S. Submarine Attacks*, 19. The torpedoes may have come from the *Spearfish*, which was operating in the area off northwest Luzon. She fired three torpedoes at a target in an underwater daylight attack and claimed two hits for damage but may have been deceived by end of run explosions.

46. Kerr, *Surrender and Survival*, 112–13; Petak, *Never Plan Tomorrow*, 135–38, 141–43, 147; Dreher, "Diary"; Harris, *Factories of Death*, 124; Cave, *Beyond Courage*, 289. The *Tottori Maru* was torpedoed in the Gulf of Thailand by the *Hammerhead* on 15 May 1945.

47. Urwin, *Facing Fearful Odds*, 544; Jentschura, Jung, and Mickel, *Warships of the Imperial Japanese Navy*, 263; Michel, *Mr. Michel's War*, 136–43; Blain, *Huryo*, 12–17; RG 38, Box 991, 992, NARA.

48. Urwin, *Facing Fearful Odds*, 544; RG 38, Box 992, NARA; Holewinski, "Hell Ships," 6. Holewinski, one of the last twenty servicemen transferred, remembered the name of the ship as the *Asuma Maru* and thought the voyage occurred in May 1942.

49. Dawson, *To Sandakan*, 46–47, 50–52; Wall, *Kill the Prisoners!* 3–7.

50. Hall, *Blue Haze*, 24–26, 52–53, 105; Williams to author, 25 February 1997; IMTFE.

51. Hall, *Blue Haze*, 65–66, 72–73; LaForte and Marcello, *Building the Death Railway*, 79–85; Charles, *Last Man Out*, 45–47.

52. LaForte and Marcello, *Building the Death Railway*, 79, 80, 92; Hall, *Blue Haze*, 282; Fujita, *Foo*, x, xi, 110; Thompson, *Thousand Cups of Rice*, 3, 56–58; Weissinger, *Kitoski, Bakaro!* 81–82. The *Kenkon Maru* was torpedoed by *Gato* near Bougainville on 21 January 1943.

53. LaForte and Marcello, *Building the Death Railway*, 88–89, 186; Daws, *Prisoners of the Japanese*, 180, 190; Charles, *Last Man Out*, 49, 51; Roydon C. Cornford to author, January 1997; Arthur Bancroft to author, 14 December 1998. The *Maebashi Maru* was torpedoed by *Pogy* on 30 September 1943.

54. Hall, *Blue Haze*, 72–73, 120; Charles, *Last Man Out*, 69–71; LaForte and Marcello, *Building the Death Railway*, 186; Daws, *Prisoners of the Japanese*, 180–81; Kinvig, *River Kwai Railway*, 56–57; Krancher, *Defining Years*, 28; Roydon C. Cornford to author, 11 August 1997; Bancroft to author, 14 December 1998. Coincidentally, the *Shinyu Maru* was torpedoed and damaged again, this time by the *Redfin* south of Mindanao, on 15 April 1944. Sailing in the same convoy, the *Yamagata Maru* was torpedoed and sunk by the *Redfin* one day later.

55. Fletcher-Cooke, *Emperor's Guest*, xiii, 2–3, 56–62; Waterford, *Prisoners of the Japanese*, 167. Cooke called the ship the *Yoshida Maru*, a cargo vessel of about 3,000 tons. However, the *Yoshida Maru* was converted to a 2,980-ton gunboat in May 1942, and as such, it would not have been configured with cranes and four cargo holds and would be unable

to carry supplies and twenty-seven hundred men. More likely, this was the larger cargo ship *No. 1 Yoshida Maru*. It was torpedoed by the *Jack* on 26 April 1944.

56. McIntosh, *Hell on Earth*, 66–69; Fletcher-Cooke, *Emperor's Guest*, 63–73, 78; Daws, *Prisoners of the Japanese*, 285; King, "Fall of Corregidor," 8; Lord Russell, *Knights of Bushido*, 127–28.

57. Lord Russell, *Knights of Bushido*, 128. The *Dainichi Maru* was torpedoed by *Gurnard* on 8 October 1943.

58. Nordin, *We Were Next to Nothing*, 70–74.

59. Lawton, *Some Survived*, 46–53; Wills, *Sea Was My Last Chance*, 32–35; Kerr, *Surrender and Survival*, 117–19; Bert Schwarz, telephone interview by author, 15 February 1999. The *Erie Maru* was torpedoed by *Sturgeon* on 11 January 1944.

60. Harrison, *Ambon Island of Mist*, 88, 106, 173, 186–89, 247, 260; Weiss, *Under the Rising Sun*, 165–66.

61. Wall, *Kill the Prisoners!* 111, 112, 115; Komamiya, *Senji Yuso*, 14, 17; Nelson to author, 11 February 1999. Nelson said that Alf Baker, the only survivor of the group who remained at Rabaul to have written his memoirs, claimed that the ship that brought them to Rabaul was an "ex-Liverpool coaler" that carried a considerable number of Japanese troops. Two other survivors stated that the ship was called either the "Eige Maru" or "Masta Maru," neither of which appear in Japanese records. The *Nagara Maru* was bombed near Guadalcanal on 14 November 1942.

62. McEwan, *Out of the Depths of Hell*, 2, 62–63, 64–65, 67. The *England Maru* was torpedoed by *Grayback* in the Admiralties on 17 May 1943.

63. Haney, *Caged Dragons*, 101–6; Miller, *Bataan Uncensored*, 258–63; Boisclaire, *In the Shadow of the Rising Sun*, 93–105. Some POWs believed another ship, the *Umeda Maru*, sailed from Manila with the *Nagato Maru*, also with fourteen hundred prisoners. See Gordon, *Horyo*, 133. Gordon didn't know this for sure but heard of it later. Further independent confirmation is lacking. The *Nagato Maru* was bombed off Wewak on 2 September 1943.

64. LaForte, Marcello, and Himmel, *With Only the Will to Live*, 119; Fujita, *Foo*, 122–25; Wigmore, *Japanese Thrust*, 613; Clarke, Burgess, and Braddon, *Prisoners of War*, 139; Burfitt, *Against All Odds*, 184; McIntosh, *Hell on Earth*, 69; Jentschura, Jung, and Mickel, *Warships of the Imperial Japanese Navy*, 60. The "contraband goods" that Visage saw aboard *Kamakura Maru* in Singapore may have been the relief supplies the ship was carrying after the repatriate–Red Cross exchange at Laurenco Marques in October.

65. LaForte, Marcello, and Himmel, *With Only the Will to Live*, 11; RG 38, Box 992, NARA; Komamiya, *Senji Yuso*, 21.

66. Spector, *Eagle Against the Sun*, 218; Parillo, *Japanese Merchant Marine*, 7, 15, 17.

67. Parillo, *Japanese Merchant Marine*, 239, 240, 242, 243.

1943: AN UNEASY STASIS

1. Beaumont, "Victims of War," 1–6.

2. Kerr, *Surrender and Survival*, 90–91; Wright-Nooth, *Prisoner of the Turnip Heads*, 99;

Lamont-Brown, *Kempeitai*, 116–17; Vance, *Objects of Concern*, 195–96; Nelson, "Return to Rabaul," 139; Herbert Papock diary.

3. Kerr, *Surrender and Survival*, 158–60, 162; Vance, *Objects of Concern*, 196–203; Spector, *Eagle Against the Sun*, 398; Wygle, *Surviving a Japanese P.O.W. Camp*, 91–94; Weissinger, *Kitoski, Bakaro!* 86–87.

4. Lord Russell, *Knights of Bushido*, 163–64; Waterford, *Prisoners of the Japanese*, 153; Dunlop, *War Diaries of Weary Dunlop*, 154–61; Williams, *Wartime Disasters at Sea*, 208.

5. Hall, *Blue Haze*, 282–83; Weissinger, *Kitoski, Bakaro!* 90–94; Thompson, *Thousand Cups of Rice*, 61–65; LaForte, Marcello, and Himmel, *With Only the Will to Live*, 118–19; LaForte and Marcello, *Building the Death Railway*, 95–97; Komamiya, *Senji Yuso*, 24; Bancroft to author, 14 December 1998; Holmes, *Four Thousand Bowls of Rice*, 23–24. In the latter book, Holmes confuses Harry Bishop's narrative, incorrectly placing him, and the bombing, on *Maebashi Maru*.

6. McIntosh, *Hell on Earth*, 2, 27–28; Dancocks, *In Enemy Hands*, 248–49; McCormack and Nelson, *Burma-Thailand Railway*, 163–64; Vance, *Objects of Concern*, 183, 185; Lindsay, *At the Going Down of the Sun*, 178. The *Tatsuta Maru* was torpedoed by *Tarpon* off Honshu on 8 February 1943.

7. Silver, *Sandakan*, 91; Keith, *Three Came Home*, 35, 42, 66, 79, 81–88.

8. RG 38, Box 992, NARA; IMTFE; Chang, *Rape of Nanking*, 72–73. The *Roko Maru* was torpedoed by *Tang* on 11 August 1944. The *Koryu Maru* was bombed on 22 April 1944. The *Kamakura Maru* was torpedoed by *Gudgeon* on 28 April 1943.

9. Tanaka, *Hidden Horrors*, 171–75, 180, 182–86, 190–93; Komamiya, *Senji Yuso*, 185. The *Akikaze* was torpedoed near Manila by *Pintado* on 3 November 1944.

10. Wall, *Kill the Prisoners!* 60–61, 69–71; Dawson, *To Sandakan*, 60–61; Keith, *Three Came Home*, 113–15; Young, "Long Ago in Borneo," 8–9; Wigmore, *Japanese Thrust*, 596; Wall, *Abandoned?*, 24–25; Burfitt, *Against All Odds*, 158–59.

11. Cowling, *My Life with the Samurai*, 77–86, 89; Peacock, *Emperor's Guest*, 70, 73–81; Krancher, *Defining Years*, 48–49; Waterford, *Prisoners of the Japanese*, 160, 333. Waterford lists his source as "Captain Korteweg, DE 1000 van Amahai, Amsterdam, 1946" but spells the maru as "Kuritama" and "Kurimata." The ship, in fact, may have been the *Kunitama Maru*, which was sunk by *Capelin* on 23 November 1943, northwest of Ambon. The *Amagi Maru* was torpedoed near the Andaman Islands by *Tantalus* on 2 May 1944.

12. Kinvig, *River Kwai Railway*, 117, 119, 120–23; Burfitt, *Against All Odds*, 192; Wigmore, *Japanese Thrust*, 613. The *Kyokko Maru* was torpedoed by *Crevalle* on 15 November 1944.

13. Mitchell, *Forty-Two Months in Durance Vile*, 85–97; Burfitt, *Against All Odds*, 182, 189; Komamiya, *Senji Yuso*, 50–51; Alden, *U.S. Submarine Attacks*, 45. The *Wales Maru* was torpedoed by *Lapon* on 23 May 1944.

14. Wigmore, *Japanese Thrust*, chap. 25, n.p.; Lord Russell, *Knights of Bushido*, 171–72; Waterford, *Prisoners of the Japanese*, 166, 335; RG 38, Box 992, NARA; Komamiya, *Senji Yuso*, 67. The *Thames Maru* was torpedoed by *Pompon* on 25 July 1943.

15. Ken Williams to author, 19 March 1997; Harold D. Martin, statement on audiotape, February 1997.

16. Kinvig, *River Kwai Railway*, 100, 103, 124-25, 128, 130-33, 136-38.

17. Cook and Cook, *Japan at War*, 102-3, 421-22.

18. Costello, *Pacific War*, 427-29; Gordon, *Through the Valley of the Kwai*, 67-69, 188, 217; Lomax, *Railway Man*, 268; Kinvig, *River Kwai Railway*, 128.

19. Kerr, *Surrender and Survival*, 182; Knox, *Death March*, 364; RG 38, Box 992, NARA. *Clyde Maru* was torpedoed in Formosa Strait by *Picuda* on 29 January 1945.

20. Kerr, *Surrender and Survival*, 184-85; Waterford, *Prisoners of the Japanese*, 165; Matson, *It Tolled for New Mexico*, passim; LaForte, Marcello, and Himmel, *With Only the Will to Live*, 93-94; Thomas E. Gage Jr. to unknown correspondent, August 1988; Paul Fleming to unknown correspondent, August 1988; Smith L. Green to author, 24 November 2000. Kerr indicates the name of this ship was the *Corral Maru*. I can locate no such ship name in Japanese records. Similar sailing dates, numbers involved, and camp destinations indicate the *Corral Maru* is *Taga Maru*. The *Taga Maru* was torpedoed by *Sargo* on 9 November 1943.

21. Silver, *Sandakan*, 56, 62, 94-96; Young, "Long Ago in Borneo," 10; Young, *Return to a Dark Age*, 103, 114.

22. Wallace, *Escape from Hell*, 188-90; Wall, *Kill the Prisoners!* 78, 84, 102; Dawson, *To Sandakan*, 65-67; Silver, *Sandakan*, 118.

23. Wall, *Kill the Prisoners!* 142-43, 157, 185; Young, "Long Ago in Borneo," 12; Young, *Return to a Dark Age*, 132-37; Silver, *Sandakan*, 119.

24. Wall, *Kill the Prisoners!* 78, 84, 102; Dawson, *To Sandakan*, 65-67; Silver, *Sandakan*, 127, 135.

25. Young, "Long Ago in Borneo," 11, 37; Dawson, *To Sandakan*, 68-70, 74-75; Wall, *Kill the Prisoners!* 108-9, 135-36, 278; Silver, *Sandakan*, 130, 135, 141, 144.

26. IMTFE; Waterford, *Prisoners of the Japanese*, 164; Harrison, *Ambon Island of Mist*, 124; Krancher, *Defining Years*, 29-32; Jentschura, Jung, and Mickel, *Warships of the Imperial Japanese Navy*, 239. The *Rio de Janeiro Maru* was bombed at Truk on 17 February 1944. The *Makassar Maru* was sunk by *Hoe* and *Aspro* on 7 October 1944. The *France Maru* was sunk by naval aircraft off Singapore on 12 January 1945.

27. Martindale, *13th Mission*, 37-38, 41, 64, 67-69, 85; Komamiya, *Senji Yuso*, 112. Since the *Hokkai Maru*, *Makassar Maru*, and *Lyons Maru* were newer and larger ships, and the *Taisho Maru* turned back to Rabaul after sailing, we will place the nine POWs on *No. 7 Hoshi Maru*.

28. Blair, *Silent Victory*, 367-69; Roscoe, *United States Submarine Operations*, 219-21; Kiefer, "Two Faces of Penang," 44-46; IMTFE. The *Asama Maru* was torpedoed off Luzon by *Atule* on 1 November 1944.

29. Braddon, *Naked Island*, 107; Nelson, *P.O.W. Prisoners of War*, 19-20; Roscoe, *United States Submarine Operations*, 156-57; Costello, *Pacific War*, 357-58; Kerr, *Surrender and Survival*, 111.

30. Wall, *Kill the Prisoners!* 111-16; Nelson, "Return to Rabaul," 148-49.

31. Edgerton, *Warriors of the Rising Sun*, 264; Urwin, *Facing Fearful Odds*, 544; Schultz, *Wake Island*, 155–57.

32. Edgerton, *Warriors of the Rising Sun*, 18, 61, 81, 116, 121, 129, 175, 212; Harries and Harries, *Soldiers of the Sun*, 92–93.

33. Lord Russell, *Knights of Bushido*, 54; Edgerton, *Warriors of the Rising Sun*, 235–37; Daws, *Prisoners of the Japanese*, 96–97; Spector, *Eagle Against the Sun*, 39–40.

34. Costello, *Pacific War*, 232–33, 428; Daws, *Prisoners of the Japanese*, 97–98; Lord Russell, *Knights of Bushido*, 54.

35. Edgerton, *Warriors of the Rising Sun*, 322–24; Daws, *Prisoners of the Japanese*, 99.

36. Peacock, *Emperor's Guest*, 114; Cowling, *My Life with the Samurai*, 114, 124; Wall, *Kill the Prisoners!* 120–26; RG 38, Box 991, NARA; *Bonefish*, 3d Patrol Report. Minesweeper 12 was torpedoed in the Flores Sea off Sumbawa Island, by the *Besugo*, on 6 April 1945.

37. Parillo, *Merchant Marine*, 242–43.

38. Layton, *And I Was There*, 81, 471; Stripp, *Codebreaker*, 65, 67–79.

39. Layton, *And I Was There*, 471–73; Stripp, *Codebreaker*, 70–71; Drea, *MacArthur's Ultra*, 74–76; Bath, *Tracking the Axis Enemy*, 174, 176, 186, 192; Holmes, *Double-Edged Secrets*, 117; Prados, *Combined Fleet Decoded*, 405–7.

40. Mendenhall, *Submarine Diary*, 287–89; Roscoe, *United States Submarine Operations*, 288; LaVO, *Back from the Deep*, 36–39, 124–34. Captain Cromwell was posthumously awarded the Congressional Medal of Honor.

41. LaVO, *Back from the Deep*, 134–36, 138–40; Jentschura, Jung, and Mickel, *Warships of the Imperial Japanese Navy*, 58–59; RG 38, Box 991, NARA; Williams, *Wartime Disasters at Sea*, 194–95.

42. LaVO, *Back from the Deep*, 141; Blair, *Silent Victory*, 482–86, 497; Nevitt, "Long Lancers"; Tully, "Kido Butai"; Calvert, *Silent Running*, 98–99.

43. LaVO, *Back from the Deep*, 122–23, 141–42, 145–55; Roscoe, *United States Submarine Operations*, 296–98; Blair, *Silent Victory*, 497–99; Walter P. Murphy to author, 11 February 1999; Tully, "Kido Butai."

44. Waterford, *Prisoners of the Japanese*, 166; Jordan, *World's Merchant Fleets*, 262; McIntosh, *Hell on Earth*, 60–62.

45. In Daws's book, *Prisoners of the Japanese*, 286, the author incorrectly states that 1943 was worse than 1942 for prisoners on hellships.

1944: FLEEING FROM THE ALLIES

1. Bouslog, *Maru Killer*, 71–73; Komamiya, *Senji Yuso*, 151, 166; IMTFE.

2. Komamiya, *Senji Yuso*, 145, 189; Waterford, *Prisoners of the Japanese*, 165; Jordan, *World's Merchant Fleets*, 64, 477; Sasgen, *Red Scorpion*, 140–43; *Rasher*, 3d Patrol Report. Information about prisoners of war on the *Tango Maru* comes from Peter van der Kuil, who was a child in a civilian internment camp in Batavia. His sources included the Dutch publication *Eresalunt Boven Massagraf—Junyo Maru de Vergeten Scheepsramp*, by E. Melis with W. F. van Wamel and T. Jansen.

3. Edwards, *Blood and Bushido*, 137–49. *Tone* was sunk by carrier aircraft at Kure, Honshu, on 24 July 1945.

4. Smith, *Prisoner of the Emperor*, 75–80, 90; Komamiya, *Senji Yuso*, 199; RG 38, Box 991, NARA; Bumgarner, *Parade of the Dead*, 135, 141–46. In the latter book, Bumgarner calls the ship the *Enoura Maru*. Komamiya and intercepted messages indicate the *Kenwa Maru* loaded two hundred medical personnel in Manila.

5. Martin Christie to author, 20 September 1998; Woodrow W. Bennie to author, 25 September 1998; George B. Nelson to author, 9 October 1998; Komamiya, *Senji Yuso*, 206. *Taikoku Maru* was torpedoed by *Sandlance* on 17 May 1944. Colonel Bogey's March had ribald lyrics, enthusiastically sung by the British soldiers. Its tune, however, was only whistled as the theme song in the movie *Bridge on the River Kwai*.

6. RG 38, Box 991, NARA.

7. Bonga, *Eight Prison Camps*, 177–80; Nelson, *P.O.W. Prisoners of War*, 154–56; Browning, *U.S. Merchant Vessel War Casualties*, 188–89, 208–9, 255; Bunker, *Heroes in Dungarees*, 135; Duffy, "Dreadful Saga," 2, 4; Waterford, *Prisoners of the Japanese*, 272–73; RG 38, Box 991, NARA.

8. Kinvig, *River Kwai Railway*, 164, 166, 168–69; Hall, *Blue Haze*, 286, 290–91; Williams to author, 19 March 1997; Power, *Kurrah!* 91; Blair and Blair, *Return from the River Kwai*, 40.

9. Wall, *Heroes at Sea*, 4; Waterford, *Prisoners of the Japanese*, 154; Duffy, "Dreadful Saga," 4; RG 38, Box 991, NARA; IMTFE; John Alden to author, 19 April 1999. The names of some of these ships have caused confusion. Waterford lists the men who embarked on the *Miyo Maru* but did not know the ship's name. Wall calls the ship "Bijou Maru," but there was no such ship. Perhaps it was a mispronunciation of *Miyo Maru*, or even another rendition of what several unknown ships were called—"Benjo [toilet] Maru." One intercepted message identified the ship as "Biyoo Maru," and a subsequent decryption corrected it to "Miyoo Maru." Likewise, the *Hiyoki Maru* is often rendered as "Byoki (sick) Maru." *Kokusei Maru* was torpedoed by *Hammerhead* off Borneo on 1 October 1944. The *Hozan Maru* was sunk by *Redfin* off Formosa on 23 November 1944.

10. Wall, *Heroes at Sea*, 4–5; Nelson, *P.O.W. Prisoners of War*, 149; RG 38, Box 991, NARA; IMTFE; Alden, *U.S. Submarine Attacks*, 105; Alden to author, 19 April 1999.

11. O'Kane, *Clear the Bridge!* 217, 219–26; *Tang*, 3d Patrol Report; RG 38, Box 991, NARA.

12. Wall, *Heroes at Sea*, 6–12; Thompson, *Thousand Cups of Rice*, 173–76; Duffy, "Dreadful Saga," 3; Alden, *U.S. Submarine Attacks*, 108–9; RG 38, Box 991, NARA. In a decoded Japanese message of 5 July, Allied intelligence learned that the *Tamahoko Maru* was sunk, but the uncanny ability of submarines to always be waiting was attributed to signals sent by prisoners on deck. The Japanese couldn't believe that their codes were compromised.

13. McIntosh, *Hell on Earth*, 94–97; Cody, *Ghosts in Khaki*, 318; Jordan, *World's Merchant Fleets*, 46, 456; IMTFE. The *Teia Maru* was torpedoed by *Rasher* on 18 August 1944.

14. Wall, *Heroes at Sea*, 15–16; Waterford, *Prisoners of the Japanese*, 158; McLaggen, *Will to Survive*, 154; *Truculent*, 4th Patrol Report; RG 38, Box 991, NARA; IMTFE.

15. Lawton, *Some Survived*, 79–80, 86, 96, 101; Kerr, *Surrender and Survival*, 140, 144.

16. Nordin, *We Were Next to Nothing*, 143–44; Kerr, *Surrender and Survival*, 195–96; Wills, *Sea Was My Last Chance*, 2–12.

17. Nordin, *We Were Next to Nothing*, 150; Kerr, *Surrender and Survival*, 196. Nordin called the ship "Singoto." Actually, *shigoto* meant "work" in Japanese.

18. Nordin, *We Were Next to Nothing*, 145–48; Lawton, *Some Survived*, 104; Cave, *Beyond Courage*, 281; LaForte, Marcello, and Himmel, *With Only the Will to Live*, 99–100.

19. Roscoe, *United States Submarine Operations*, 508–19; Dissette and Adamson, *Guerrilla Submarines*, 16, 18, 35.

20. Wall, *Abandoned?* 30–31, 34, 36, 38, 40–44; Wall, *Kill the Prisoners!* 142–43, 157, 185; Wallace, *Escape from Hell*, 184–85; Silver, *Sandakan*, 152–54.

21. Wall, *Abandoned?* 48, 54; Wall, *Kill the Prisoners!* 156; Lockwood and Adamson, *Hell and Deep Water*, 29–38; Silver, *Sandakan*, 282, 301, 302, 307.

22. Kerr, *Surrender and Survival*, 196; Nordin, *We Were Next to Nothing*, 148–53; Gautier, *I Came Back from Bataan*, 160–63; Cave, *Beyond Courage*, 291–93; Hoyt, *Bowfin*, 148–49; Komamiya, *Senji Yuso*, 278.

23. Vining, *Guest of an Emperor*, 2, 13, 336; Hubbard, *Apocalypse Undone*, 150; Fitzpatrick, *Hike into the Sun*, 191.

24. Versaw, *Mikado No Kayaku*, 2; Vining, *Guest of an Emperor*, 338–39.

25. Hubbard, *Apocalypse Undone*, 151; Carson, *My Time in Hell*, 148–49; Dow, "Nissyo Maru," 37.

26. Versaw, *Mikado No Kayaku*, 5–6; Carson, *My Time in Hell*, 152–53.

27. Vining, *Guest of an Emperor*, 341; Hubbard, *Apocalypse Undone*, 153; Dow, "Nissyo Maru," 37–38.

28. Komamiya, *Senji Yuso*, 261; Carson, *My Time in Hell*, 159; Hubbard, *Apocalypse Undone*, 155–160.

29. Komamiya, *Senji Yuso*, 262; McCants, *War Patrols*, 207–8, 215–23; Ruhe, *War in the Boats*, 256–57; Alden, *U.S. Submarine Attacks*, 118; Carson, *My Time in Hell*, 169; Hubbard, *Apocalypse Undone*, 162; Dow, "Nissyo Maru," 38; Cave, *Beyond Courage*, 294.

30. Versaw, *Mikado No Kayaku*, 15; Carson, *My Time in Hell*, 163; Vining, *Guest of an Emperor*, 351–52.

31. Martin, *Brothers from Bataan*, 183–96; Cave, *Beyond Courage*, 194; Komamiya, *Senji Yuso*, 281–82; James T. Murphy to author, 25 September 1998. Estimates of the number of men that died on the *Noto Maru* vary greatly, from none or one, up to seventy. It was bombed in Ormoc Bay, Leyte, on 2 November 1944.

32. Komamiya, *Senji Yuso*, 265–66; Alden, *U.S. Submarine Attacks*, 120.

33. Power, *Kurrah!* 92–93; Komamiya, *Senji Yuso*, 254; Jordan, *World's Merchant Fleets*, 264, 541; RG 38, Box 991, NARA; Jackfert and Miller, *History of the Defenders*, 74; IMTFE. Radio decrypts indicate the *Sekiho Maru* carried POWs, as do Jackfert and Miller, but the translation of Komamiya calls the ship the *San Diego Maru*, a 7,269-ton converted oiler. The *Hakushika Maru* is sometimes listed as *Hakuroku Maru*. The *Hofuku Maru* is sometimes called *Toyofuku Maru*.

34. Nelson, *P.O.W. Prisoners of War*, 62, 139–42; Cody, *Ghosts in Khaki*, 306; Power, *Kurrah!* 96–97, 101–2.

35. Komamiya, *Senji Yuso*, 256; Power, *Kurrah!* 98–99; Nelson, *P.O.W. Prisoners of War*, 142; IMTFE. The *Hakushika Maru* was torpedoed by *Bluegill* on 18 October 1944.

36. Power, *Kurrah!* 97–98; Nelson, *P.O.W. Prisoners of War*, 142–43; Cody, *Ghosts in Khaki*, 307; Clarke, Burgess, and Braddon, *Prisoners of War*, 140; IMTFE; RG 38, Box 991, NARA. The 5,135-ton oiler, *Shinei Maru*, was sunk by torpedoes from *Guitarro*. The name of the freighter is unknown.

37. Nelson, *P.O.W. Prisoners of War*, 143–45; Power, *Kurrah!* 99, 102–3; Clarke, Burgess, and Braddon, *Prisoners of War*, 140; Dingman, *Ghost of War*, 31–33; RG 38, Box 991, NARA; IMTFE. In October–November 1944, the *Hakusan Maru* was given safe conduct passage to transport relief supplies to Allied prisoners in Korea. The *Rashin Maru* was torpedoed by *Pargo* in the Sea of Japan on 8 August 1945.

38. Blair and Blair, *Return from the River Kwai*, 19; Hall, *Blue Haze*, 73; M. R. Farrands to author, 20 February 1997.

39. Blair and Blair, *Return from the River Kwai*, 32, 47, 57; Roydon C. Cornford to author, May 1998.

40. RG 457, Japanese Navy Message Translations (hereafter cited as SRN), Entry 9014, Box 44, NARA; LaForte and Marcello, *Building the Death Railway*, 232; Cliff L. Farlow to author, 17 March 1997.

41. RG 457, SRN, Entry 9014, Box 44, NARA; Grover, "Turncoat Transport," 19–24; Grover and Grover, *Captives of Shanghai*, 46, 119; Komamiya, *Senji Yuso*, 288–89.

42. RG 457, SRN, Entry 9014, NARA; Blair and Blair, *Return from the River Kwai*, 61, 68–69, 71; M. R. Farrands to author, 4 August 1999; Cornford to author, May 1998.

43. RG 457, SRN, Entry 9014, Box 44, NARA; Komamiya, *Senji Yuso*, 289.

44. Blair and Blair, *Return from the River Kwai*, 73–75, 100–103; Martin, statement on audiotape.

45. Blair and Blair, *Return from the River Kwai*, 111–13; Farrands to author, 20 February 1997.

46. Blair and Blair, *Return from the River Kwai*, 117, 126–28, 133–34; Cliff L. Farlow to author, May 1998; Farrands to author, 20 February 1997; Cornford to author, May 1998.

47. RG 457, SRN, Entry 9014, Box 44, NARA; RG 38, Office of the Chief of Naval Operations, Operational Records Series (hereafter cited as ONS), Box 195, NARA; Williams to author, 19 March 1997; Blair and Blair, *Return from the River Kwai*, 152–54.

48. RG 457, SRN, Entry 9014, Box 44, NARA; Blair and Blair, *Return from the River Kwai*, 160–63, 166; Komamiya, *Senji Yuso*, 246–49. Japanese sources say that the *Kachidoki Maru* took about fifty minutes to sink. Blair and Blair claim she took two hits, stood on end, and sank in fifteen minutes, taking seven hundred people down with her.

49. RG 38, ONS, Box 195, NARA; RG 457, SRN, Box 45, NARA; Martin, statement on audiotape; Ken Williams to author, February 1997; Farrands to author, 20 February 1997; Roydon C. Cornford to author, August 1999; Blair and Blair, *Return from the River Kwai*, 180–87, 190–93, 202–7; Holmes, *Four Thousand Bowls of Rice*, 77.

50. Lee, *Marching Orders*, 234-35.

51. Padfield, *War Beneath the Sea*, 149, 381; *Pampanito*, 3d Patrol Report; Peillard, *Laconia Affair*, 22, 126, 140-41, 158.

52. Blair and Blair, *Return from the River Kwai*, 210-11; Richard J. Sherlock, interview by Clay Blair Jr., 1977; Gordon Hopper to author, 23 January 1996.

53. Blair and Blair, *Return from the River Kwai*, 211-215; Paul E. Summers, interview by Clay Blair Jr., 1977; William F. Yagemann, interview by Clay Blair Jr., 1977; Charles A. McGuire, statement on audiotape, March 1996; Cliff L. Farlow, statement on audiotape, March 1997; Martin, statement on audiotape; M. R. Farrands to author, 14 March 1997; Cornford to author, January 1997; Williams to author, 19 March 1997; Hopper, "Recollections," 4.

54. Blair and Blair, *Return from the River Kwai*, 220-21; Blair, *Silent Victory*, 683-85; Fluckey, *Thunder Below*, 121-22, 136-37.

55. Blair, *Silent Victory*, 685; Fluckey, *Thunder Below*, 138-47; Bancroft to author, 14 December 1998; John Bennett to author, 10 May 1998.

56. Blair and Blair, *Return from the River Kwai*, 215-18, 235-36, 257; Farrands to author, 20 February 1997; Maurice L. Demers, interview by Clay Blair Jr., 1977.

57. RG 457, Records of the National Security Agency/Central Security Service (hereafter cited as SRNS), Entry 1485, Box 15, NARA.

58. Jentschura, Jung, and Mickel, *Warships of the Imperial Japanese Navy*, 232; Komamiya, *Senji Yuso*, 290; Blair and Blair, *Return from the River Kwai*, 194-96; Holmes, *Four Thousand Bowls of Rice*, 77. Several sources incorrectly call this ship the *Kibibi Maru*.

59. RG 457, SRN, Entry 9014, Box 45, NARA; Komamiya, *Senji Yuso*, 290-91; USS *Plaice*, 2d Patrol Report; Blair and Blair, *Return from the River Kwai*, 231-34, 251-52. *Asaka Maru* was bombed in Formosa Strait on 12 October 1944.

60. RG 38, Box 991, NARA; Jordan, *World's Merchant Fleets*, 250.

61. Lawton, *Some Survived*, 140; Dissette and Adamson, *Guerrilla Submarines*, 157; Knox, *Death March*, 293-98; Schwarz telephone interview; Komamiya, *Senji Yuso*, 292.

62. *Paddle*, 5th Patrol Report; Godfrey Orbeck, "The Shinyo Maru Story," *Polaris* 43, no. 1 (February 1999): 14; Knox, *Death March*, 298-305; Cave, *Beyond Courage*, 302; Schwarz telephone interview; LaForte, Marcello, and Himmel, *With Only the Will to Live*, 41-45; Kerr, *Surrender and Survival*, 200.

63. *Paddle*, 5th Patrol Report; Komamiya, *Senji Yuso*, 292; Knox, *Death March*, 307-11; Blair, *Silent Victory*, 712-13; Lawton, *Some Survived*, 146-47; Dissette and Adamson, *Guerrilla Submarines*, 158-60.

64. Krancher, *Defining Years*, 51-52; Peacock, *Emperor's Guest*, 140-50; RG 38, Box 991, NARA.

65. Lord Russell, *Knights of Bushido*, 129-34; Cowling, *My Life with the Samurai*, 160; Peacock, *Emperor's Guest*, 150-51; Krancher, *Defining Years*, 52; Waterford, *Prisoners of the Japanese*, 161; van der Post, *Prisoner and the Bomb*, 27-28. Lieutenant Blackwood estimated from 17 to 27 bodies were thrown overboard per day. Other death estimates for the entire trip range from 309 to 371.

66. van der Kuil, "Sinking of the Junyo Maru"; Krancher, *Defining Years,* 39–40; Mary Ann Lackey (Miller) to author, 7 November 1998; Jordan, *World's Merchant Fleets,* 200, 495; Alden, *United States and Allied Submarine Successes,* 149. Alden states that the *Junyo Maru* was the ex-British ship *Deslock.* Jordan states that the *Deslock* was indeed captured by the Japanese, but was renamed *Uzan Maru* and sunk by the *Trout* on 2 May 1942.

67. van der Kuil, "Sinking of the Junyo Maru"; Krancher, *Defining Years,* 40–42; Lord Russell, *Knights of Bushido,* 134–35; Waterford, *Prisoners of the Japanese,* 158–59; HMS *Tradewind,* 3d Patrol Report; Lackey to author, 7 November 1998; RG 38, Box 991, NARA. Van Waterford, who wrote the above cited book, is the pen name of Willem Wanrooy, who was on the *Junyo Maru.* Lieutenant Commander Maydon never learned until 1970, the year before his death, that there were POWs aboard the ship he had sunk. The only ship disaster during the entire war with more casualties occurred when the German liner *Wilhelm Gustloff* was torpedoed in the Baltic Sea by a Russian submarine in January 1945. About six thousand passengers were lost, but they were not POWs.

68. Donald H. Thomas to author, 1 January 1999; Henderson, "Another Tender Sailor's Tale," 4; Holmes, *Last Patrol,* 114–15, 117; Roscoe, *United States Submarine Operations,* 348, 356; Jacobson, "Survivor's Story," 2, 4, 17, 49, 60, 63, 78–81.

69. Ashton, *Bataan Diary,* 258–59; Komamiya, *Senji Yuso,* 304; Kerr, *Surrender and Survival,* 201; Waterford, *Prisoners of the Japanese,* 157; Caraccilo, *Surviving Bataan and Beyond,* 182; Hammel, *Air War Pacific,* 432, 450; IMTFE; RG 38, Box 991, NARA; RG 457, SRN, Entry 9014, Box 45, NARA. Noritaka Kitazawa of the Japanese Defense Ministry indicated that the 495-ton *Kaishun Maru,* carrying 150 POWs, was also attacked and sunk by carrier planes on 21 September, near Cebu. Four of the POWs were killed.

70. Donovan and Donovan, *P.O.W. in the Pacific,* 89–90, 98; Coone, *Sequential Soldier,* 158, 162; Goodman, *M.D.P.O.W.,* 114–15; Komamiya, *Senji Yuso,* 314; IMTFE; Josephine Donovan to author, 16 January 1999; Alvin Poweleit to Donna Weigel, 9 October 1992; Noritaka Kitazawa to author, 15 February 1999. Josephine Donovan, daughter of William Donovan, wrote to the National Institute for Defense Studies in Japan to track down the name of the ship. There was no "Haro Maru." I followed up on her lead but was informed by Captain Kitazawa that he was unable to determine the name of the ship that carried POWs in MATA-28. Some prisoners remembered the painted out names on the ships as "Tahan Maru" and "Hwansuka Maru." Subsequent ship losses and tracking of individual routes remove all but three from consideration. "Tahan" might have been *Bunzan Maru,* but this was a subchaser-sized vessel. "Hwansuka" may have been *Hishigata Maru,* or *Hokusen Maru.* The *Hokusen Maru* had been in Manila Bay since 18 September. It is not listed as part of MATA-28 in Komamiya's book, however, its itinerary, per the POWs, matches that of MATA-28 perfectly. Also, Matson's book, *It Tolled for New Mexico,* lists three men who sailed on the *Hokusen Maru* or "Haro Maru," one of whom died on 12 October. Radio intercepts also indicate the *Hokusen Maru* carried the prisoners.

71. Knox, *Death March*, 339-40; Donovan and Donovan, *P.O.W. in the Pacific*, 90-92; Evans, *Kora!* 107, 112; LaForte, Marcello, and Himmel, *With Only the Will to Live*, 97-98, 100, 101; Spero Dardaris to author, 7 October 1998.

72. Donovan and Donovan, *P.O.W. in the Pacific*, 93-94; Komamiya, *Senji Yuso*, 314-15; Knox, *Death March*, 341; LaForte, Marcello, and Himmel, *With Only the Will to Live*, 98; Goodman, *M.D.P.O.W.*, 117. The *Shoei Maru* continued on to Japan, for on 18 October it was sailing in another convoy from Sasebo.

73. Komamiya, *Senji Yuso*, 314-15; Knox, *Death March*, 342-44; LaForte, Marcello, and Himmel, *With Only the Will to Live*, 101; Goodman, *M.D.P.O.W.*, 126; Spero Dardaris to author, 21 October 1998; RG 38, Box 991, NARA. More confirmation that "Haro Maru" was *Hokusen Maru* comes from a radio intercept. A 6 November message from Tokyo stated, "After the temporary quartering in Taiwan of the prisoners who were on board the *Hokusen Maru* (JHDA 2,256T) instructions should be given to transport them using an Army commandeered ship returning to Japan."

74. Komamiya, *Senji Yuso*, 322-23; LaForte, Marcello, and Himmel, *With Only the Will to Live*, 103; Lawton, *Some Survived*, 115, 120-21; Blair, *Silent Victory*, 744-45; Calvin Graef, statement on audiotape, 1983; statements of Donald Meyer, Robert Overbeck, Anton Cichy, 5 December 1944, photocopies in possession of the author; *Snook*, 7th Patrol Report; *Seadragon*, 11th Patrol Report. The *Snook* is sometimes credited with sinking *Arisan Maru*, but POW reports and submarine patrol logs point to *Shark*. Blair speculated that the *Shark* may have been sunk while trying to rescue the POWs, however, the close proximity of the destroyers and their immediate counter-attack preclude this scenario. 24 October 1944, was a black day for the submarine force, as the *Shark*, *Tang*, and *Darter* were all lost.

75. LaForte, Marcello, and Himmel, *With Only the Will to Live*, 104; Lawton, *Some Survived*, 121-27; Cave, *Beyond Courage*, 305-6; Ashton, *Bataan Diary*, 295-96; Komamiya, *Senji Yuso*, 323; statements of Avery E. Wilbur, Meyer, Overbeck, Cichy, 5 December 1944, photocopies in possession of the author.

76. LaForte, Marcello, and Himmel, *With Only the Will to Live*, 104; Lawton, *Some Survived*, 128-30; Knox, *Death March*, 344; Kerr, *Surrender and Survival*, 208; Komamiya, *Senji Yuso*, 328. The convoy that rescued Brodsky and Oliver was probably HOMA-01, which traveled from Hong Kong to Takao, and consisted of the *Hamburg Maru*, *Yasukuni Maru*, *No. 18 Nissho Maru*, *Eiwa Maru*, *Shinetsu Maru*, *Kanshu Maru*, and escorts minesweeper 20, subchaser 33, subchaser 30, and auxiliary subchaser 41.

77. Kerr, *Surrender and Survival*, 131-35; Waterford, *Prisoners of the Japanese*, 155; Coone, *Sequential Soldier*, 162; Spero Dardaris, telephone interview by author, 1 October 1998. More people were lost on the *Arisan Maru* than on the cruiser *Juneau*, with the five Sullivan brothers, the cruiser *Indianapolis*, or the *Titanic*.

78. RG 38, Box 991, NARA. The *Oryoku Maru*, *Brazil Maru*, and *Enoura Maru* are the three hellships most often recalled and written about by American survivors, and their stories are adequately told in many other publications, including Daws, *Prisoners of the Japanese*; Kerr, *Surrender and Survival*; Lawton, *Some Survived*; Knox,

Death March; Cave, *Beyond Courage;* Stamp, *Journey Through Hell;* Stewart, *Give Us This Day;* Machi, *Under the Rising Sun;* Ashton, *And Somebody Gives a Damn;* Lord Russell, *Knights of Bushido;* Hibbs, *Tell MacArthur to Wait;* Berry, *Prisoner of the Rising Sun;* Toland, *Rising Sun;* Bumgarner, *Parade of the Dead.*

79. Ashton, *And Somebody Gives a Damn,* 223; Hibbs, *Tell MacArthur to Wait,* 202, 203; McCants, *War Patrols,* 323; RG 38, Box 991, NARA. The *Momo* was sunk by *Hawkbill* on 15 December.

80. Lawton, *Some Survived,* 156–60, 174; Kerr, *Surrender and Survival,* 222–26; Hammel, *Air War Pacific,* 515, 520; Stamp, *Journey Through Hell,* 83; Brown, "Oryoku Maru Story," n.p.; Peart, "Peart's Journal," 3–8; Bodine, "No Place for Kindness," 9–23; Alden, *U.S. Submarine Attacks,* 167.

1945: LAST OF THE HELLSHIPS

1. Parillo, *Merchant Marine,* 242, 243; Lawton, *Some Survived,* 192, 196, 206; Stewart, *Give Us This Day,* 158, 168; Bodine, "No Place for Kindness," 32; Brown, "Oryoku Maru," n.p.; Peart, "Peart's Journal," 9–18; Knox, *Death March,* 346–47; Dardaris to author, 7 October 1998; RG 38, Box 991, NARA. *Brazil Maru* struck a mine off Shikoku on 12 May 1945.

2. Henderson, "Another Tender Sailor's Tale," 6; RG 38, Box 991, NARA. There were at least five *Taiko Marus.* It is not known if this was the same *Taiko Maru* that carried Aussies from Ambon to Hainan in 1942.

3. Lott, *Most Dangerous Sea,* 150, 155, 157, 160; RG 38, Box 991, NARA; LaForte and Marcello, *Building the Death Railway,* 270–72; Charles, *Last Man Out,* 167; Wall, *Heroes at Sea,* 115; Komamiya, *Senji Yuso,* 355.

4. Blair, *Silent Victory,* 811–13; Roscoe, *United States Submarine Operations,* 459–60; Dingman, *Ghost of War,* 7, 39, 41–43, 50–51, 73, 91, 95, 157, 236; RG 38, Box 991, NARA.

5. Peacock, *Emperor's Guest,* 152–53, 158–59, 163, 165; Krancher, *Defining Years,* 52–53; Nelson, *P.O.W. Prisoners of War,* 139; Komamiya, *Senji Yuso,* 375; RG 38, Box 991, NARA; IMTFE.

6. Cowling, *My Life with the Samurai,* 141–44, 148–52, 156–59, 162–64; RG 38, Box 991, NARA: IMTFE.

7. Wrynn, "Massacre at Palawan," 58–60; Harvey Carlisle to author, 13 September 2000. In RG 38, Box 991, NARA, there is evidence that at least four of *Robalo*'s crew may not have been on Palawan for the massacre. Radio intercepts indicate that four submariners, "Rafuin, Posuton, Maten, Taika" (Laughlin, Poston, Martin, Tucker), were placed aboard the *Takao Maru* on 19 August and the light cruiser *Kinu* on 22 August 1944. The *Kinu* had just come from Palau with captured airmen Mooney and Gilbert. *Kinu* took them to Manila on 25 August, and from there they disappear from the record. They may have been killed on board or taken to Ofuna, where many other pilots and submariners were kept, then killed later.

8. Sakaida, *Siege of Rabaul,* 19, 21; Gregory Boyington, *Baa Baa Black Sheep,* 232–33; Tanaka, *Hidden Horrors,* 155–57.

9. Goodwin, *Shobun*, 44, 46–47, 68–69, 81; Cook and Cook, *Japan at War*, 110–12.

10. Goodwin, *Shobun*, 35; Ienaga, *Pacific War*, 192; Tanaka, *Hidden Horrors*, 119–20, 124, 126.

11. Wall, *Kill the Prisoners!* 155, 160–61, 186, 207, 294–95; Young, "Long Ago in Borneo," 12–19, 40.

12. Lott, *Most Dangerous Sea*, 193; Cave, *Beyond Courage*, 391; Daws, *Prisoners of the Japanese*, 334, 340, 345.

13. Nelson, "Return to Rabaul," 142; Tanaka, *Hidden Horrors*, 120; Silver, *Sandakan*, 267.

14. RG 38, Boxes 991, 992, NARA.

15. Smyth, *Will to Live*, 39, 44, 47, 52, 67, 114–15, 121; Wigmore, *Japanese Thrust*, 540.

16. Urwin, *Facing Fearful Odds*, 551; Grover and Grover, *Captives of Shanghai*, 88, 123; Considine, *General Wainwright's Story*, 225, 239; Waterford, *Prisoners of the Japanese*, 157; Michel, *Mr. Michel's War*, 230–34; Blain, *Huryo*, 33; Feifer, *Tennozan*, 90.

17. IMTFE.

18. Hicks, *Comfort Women*, 11, 19, 51, 59, 83, 115, 121, 134, 138, 143, 154, 164.

CONCLUSION

1. Parillo, *Japanese Merchant Marine*, 242, 244.

2. Dunnigan and Nofi, *Dirty Little Secrets*, 49.

3. Daws, *Prisoners of the Japanese*, 360. According to the Center for Internee Rights, the Nazis captured 93,941 American combatants and 1,121 died, a rate of 1 percent. The Japanese captured 36,260 Americans and 13,851 died, a rate of 38 percent.

4. Gordon, *Through the Valley of the Kwai*, 52; Daws, *Prisoners of the Japanese*, 360; McCormack and Nelson, *Burma-Thailand Railway*, 56, 163; Kerr, *Surrender and Survival*, 292; LaForte, Marcello, and Himmel, *With Only the Will to Live*, xxix; Ashton, *Bataan Diary*, x.

5. Kinvig, *River Kwai Railway*, 198; Daws, *Prisoners of the Japanese*, 297; Waterford, *Prisoners of the Japanese*, 167–68.

6. Parillo, *Japanese Merchant Marine*, 151; Dunnigan and Nofi, *Victory at Sea*, 63; Dunnigan and Nofi, *Dirty Little Secrets*, 264.

7. Kerr, *Surrender and Survival*, 162–64; RG 38, Box 991, NARA.

8. Shores and Cull, *Bloody Shambles*, 234; Cook and Cook, *Japan at War*, 88–89; Edgerton, *Warriors of the Rising Sun*, 266.

9. Petak, *Never Plan Tomorrow*, 135; Waterford, *Prisoners of the Japanese*, 153; LaForte and Marcello, *Building the Death Railway*, 92; Feifer, *Tennozan*, 80–82.

10. Browne, *Tojo*, 228.

11. Burfitt, *Against All Odds*, 182; Wigmore, *Japanese Thrust*, 612; Daws, *Prisoners of the Japanese*, 284, 286.

12. Knox, *Death March*, 337.

13. Hubbard, *Apocalypse Undone*, 146.

14. Daws, *Prisoners of the Japanese*, 23, 26, 297.

15. Ibid., 23–24, 138, 222–23.

16. Winslow, *Ghost that Died,* xvii; Bancroft to author, 14 December 1998; Thompson, *Thousand Cups of Rice,* 1, 173–76; Matson, *It Tolled for New Mexico,* 11, 18–19; Tenney, *My Hitch in Hell,* 4, 211–13; Duffy, "Dreadful Saga," 2–4; Urwin, *Facing Fearful Odds,* 542; Tanaka, *Hidden Horrors,* 11; Holmes, *Four Thousand Bowls of Rice,* 158; Charles, *Last Man Out,* 167.

17. Braddon, *Naked Island,* 141.

18. Waterford, *Prisoners of the Japanese,* 356.

19. Winton, *Ultra in the Pacific,* 192–93; Drea, *MacArthur's Ultra,* xiv; Prados, *Combined Fleet Decoded,* 524; Holmes, *Double-Edged Secrets,* 140; Griffith, *MacArthur's Airman,* 79; Stripp, *Codebreaker,* 67, 118; Lewin, *American Magic,* 255.

20. Dingman, *Ghost of War,* 73, 236; Don Wall to author, 13 March 1997; Lewin, *American Magic,* 238; Wall, *Kill the Prisoners!* 207; Kinvig, *River Kwai Railway,* 194.

21. Breuer, *MacArthur's Undercover War,* 54, 114, 121, 132–33, 136–37, 200; Sakakida, *Spy in their Midst,* 156–58; Drea, *MacArthur's Ultra,* 129–30; Komamiya, *Senji Yuso,* 213.

22. RG 457, SRNS, Entry 1485, Box 15, NARA; RG 38, ONS, Box 195, NARA; Lewin, *American Magic,* 220.

23. Stripp, *Codebreaker,* x.

24. Capt. Harry L. Pence, USN, Personal Papers, University of California–San Diego Library, Box 2, Folder 3; Lockwood is cited in Winton, *Ultra in the Pacific,* 193.

25. Tanaka, *Horrors of War,* 75–76; Dower, *War Without Mercy,* 11.

26. Thomas, *Slave Trade,* 9, 12, 125, 203, 275, 311, 387, 411–14, 541.

27. Ibid., 416–19, 424, 428, 432.

28. Ibid., 424–27.

29. Iannarelli, *Eighty Thieves,* 28–29; Nelson, *P.O.W. Prisoners of War,* 112; Powers, *Kurrah!* 99; Cave, *Beyond Courage,* 291–92; LaForte, Marcello, and Himmel, *With Only the Will to Live,* 23.

30. Ginn, *Sugamo Prison,* 6–7, 18, 20, 22, 24, 25, 31, 33, 34.

31. Ibid., 77, 85–87; Piccigallo, *Japanese on Trial,* 86.

32. Cowling, *My Life with the Samurai,* 173–74; Wright-Nooth, *Prisoner of the Turnip Heads,* 227; Kerr, *Surrender and Survival,* 295; Edwards, *Blood and Bushido,* 231.

33. Ginn, *Sugamo Prison,* 108–11, 118–19, 139; Edwards, *Blood and Bushido,* 230–31; Padfield, *War Beneath the Sea,* 380–82.

34. Tanaka, *Hidden Horrors,* 4–9; Ienaga, *Pacific War,* 180, 254–56; Hicks, *Comfort Women,* 273; Sun Tzu Newswire, "Japan's Sony Squelches Movie on 'Hell Ships.'"

35. Keith, *Three Came Home,* 237.

36. Tenney, *My Hitch in Hell,* 194; Hubbard, *Apocalypse Undone,* 252–54; Haney, *Caged Dragons,* 104, 221.

37. LaForte, Marcello, and Himmel, *With Only the Will to Live,* 93; Lawton, *Some Survived,* 221; McEwan, *Out of the Depths of Hell,* 69; Donovan and Donovan, *P.O.W. in the Pacific,* 89; Knox, *Death March,* 345.

38. Vining, *Guest of an Emperor,* 422; Farrands to author, 14 March 1997; Farlow to author, May 1998; Martindale, *13th Mission,* 237.

BIBLIOGRAPHY

BOOKS

Alden, John D. *United States and Allied Submarine Successes in the Pacific and Far East During World War II Chronological Listing.* Pleasantville, N.Y.: By the Author, 1999.

——. *U.S. Submarine Attacks During World War II.* Annapolis: Naval Institute Press, 1989.

American Psychiatric Association, eds. *Diagnostic and Statistical Manual of Mental Disorders: DSM III-R.* Washington, D.C.: American Psychiatric Association, 1987.

Apthorpe, A. A. *The British Sumatra Battalion.* Lewes, Sussex: Book Guild, 1988.

Ashton, Paul. *And Somebody Gives a Damn!* Santa Barbara, Calif.: Ashton Publications, 1990.

——. *Bataan Diary.* Santa Barbara, Calif.: Ashton Publications, 1984.

Bath, Alan Harris. *Tracking the Axis Enemy: The Triumph of Anglo-American Naval Intelligence.* Lawrence: University Press of Kansas, 1998.

Beach, Cdr. Edward L. *Submarine!* New York: Holt, Rinehart and Winston, 1952.

Bergerud, Eric. *Touched with Fire: The Land War in the South Pacific.* New York: Viking Penguin, 1996.

Berry, William A., with James Edwin Alexander. *Prisoner of the Rising Sun.* Norman: University of Oklahoma Press, 1993.

Blain, Geoffrey. *Huryo: The Emperor's Captives.* New York: Vantage Press, 1995.

Blair, Clay, Jr. *Silent Victory: The U.S. Submarine War Against Japan.* Book club ed. New York: J. B. Lippincott, 1975.

Blair, Joan, and Clay Blair Jr. *Return from the River Kwai.* New York: Simon & Schuster, 1979.

Boisclaire, Yvonne. *In the Shadow of the Rising Sun.* Bella Vista, Calif.: Clearwood Publishers, 1997.

Bonga, Dieuwke W. *Eight Prison Camps: A Dutch Family in Japanese Java.* Athens: Ohio University Press, 1996.

Bouslog, Dave. *Maru Killer: The War Patrols of the USS Seahorse.* Sarasota, Fla.: Seahorse Books, 1996.

Boyington, Gregory. *Baa Baa Black Sheep.* New York: Bantam Books, 1977.

Braddon, Russell. *The Naked Island.* Garden City, N.Y.: Doubleday, 1953.

Breuer, William B. *Devil Boats.* Novato, Calif.: Presidio Press, 1987.

——. *MacArthur's Undercover War: Spies, Saboteurs, Guerrillas, and Secret Missions.* New York: John Wiley & Sons, 1995.

Browne, Courtney. *Tojo: The Last Banzai.* New York: Da Capo Press, 1998.

Browning, Robert M., Jr. *U.S. Merchant Vessel War Casualties of World War Two.* Annapolis: Naval Institute Press, 1996.

Bumgarner, John R., M.D. *Parade of the Dead: A U.S. Army Physician's Memoir of Imprisonment by the Japanese, 1942-1945.* Jefferson, N.C.: McFarland, 1995.

Bunker, John. *Heroes in Dungarees: The Story of the American Merchant Marine in World War II.* Annapolis: Naval Institute Press, 1995.

Burfitt, James. *Against All Odds: The History of the 2/18 Battalion, AIF.* Sydney: 2/18 Battalion Association, 1991.

Calvert, James F. *Silent Running: My Years on a World War II Attack Submarine.* New York: John Wiley & Sons, 1995.

Caraccilo, Dominic J., ed. *Surviving Bataan and Beyond: Colonel Irvin Alexander's Odyssey as a Japanese Prisoner of War.* Mechanicsburg, Pa.: Stackpole Books, 1999.

Carson, Andrew D. *My Time in Hell: Memoir of an American Soldier Imprisoned by the Japanese in World War II.* Jefferson, N.C.: McFarland, 1997.

Cave, Dorothy. *Beyond Courage: One Regiment Against Japan, 1941-1945.* Las Cruces, N.M.: Yucca Tree Press, 1996.

Chang, Iris. *The Rape of Nanking: The Forgotten Holocaust of World War II.* New York: Basic Books, 1997.

Charles, H. Robert. *Last Man Out.* Austin, Tex.: Eakin Press, 1988.

Clarke, Hugh V. *A Life for Every Sleeper: A Pictorial Record of the Burma-Thailand Railway.* Sydney: Allen & Unwin, 1986.

Clarke, Hugh, Colin Burgess, and Russell Braddon. *Prisoners of War.* Sydney: Time Life (Australia), 1988.

Cody, Les. *Ghosts in Khaki: The History of the 2/4th Machine Gun Battalion 8th Australian Division A.I.F.* Carlisle, Western Australia: Hesperian Press, 1997.

Considine, Robert, ed. *General Wainwright's Story: The Account of Four Years of Humiliating Defeat, Surrender, and Captivity by General Jonathan M. Wainwright Who Paid the Price of His Country's Unpreparedness.* Garden City, N.Y.: Doubleday, 1946.

Cook, Haruko T., and Theodore F. Cook. *Japan at War: An Oral History.* New York: New Press, 1992.

Coone, Herbert W. *The Sequential Soldier.* Baltimore: Gateway Press, 1992.

Costello, John. *The Pacific War.* New York: Rawson, Wade Publishers, 1981.

Cowling, Anthony. *My Life with the Samurai.* Kenthurst, New South Wales: Kangaroo Press, 1996.

Dancocks, Daniel G. *In Enemy Hands: Canadian Prisoners of War, 1939-45.* Edmonton, Alberta: Hurtig Publishers, 1983.

Daws, Gavan. *Prisoners of the Japanese: POWs of World War II in the Pacific.* New York: William Morrow, 1994.

Dawson, Christopher. *To Sandakan: The Diaries of Charlie Johnstone Prisoner of War, 1942-45.* St. Leonards, New South Wales: Allen & Unwin, 1995.

Dingman, Roger. *Ghost of War: The Sinking of the Awa Maru and Japanese-American Relations, 1941-1995.* Annapolis: Naval Institute Press, 1997.

Dissette, Edward, and Hans Christian Adamson. *Guerrilla Submarines.* New York: Ballantine Books, 1972.

Donovan, William N., M.D., and Josephine Donovan, ed. *P.O.W. in the Pacific: Memoirs of an American Doctor in World War II.* Wilmington, Del.: Scholarly Resources, 1998.

Dower, John. *War Without Mercy: Race and Power in the Pacific War.* New York: Pantheon Books, 1986.

Drea, Edward J. *MacArthur's Ultra: Codebreaking and the War Against Japan, 1942-1945.* Lawrence: University of Kansas Press, 1992.

Dull, Paul S. *A Battle History of the Imperial Japanese Navy (1941-1945).* Annapolis: Naval Institute Press, 1978.

Dunlop, E. E. *The War Diaries of Weary Dunlop: Java and the Burma-Thailand Railway, 1942-1945.* Ringwood, Victoria: Penguin Books Australia, 1990.

Dunnigan, James F., and Albert A. Nofi. *Dirty Little Secrets of World War II.* New York: William Morrow, 1994.

———. *Victory at Sea: World War II in the Pacific.* New York: William Morrow, 1995.

Edgerton, Robert B. *Warriors of the Rising Sun: A History of the Japanese Military.* New York: W. W. Norton, 1997.

Edwards, Bernard. *Blood and Bushido: Japanese Atrocities at Sea, 1941-1945.* New York: Brick Tower Press, 1997.

Evans, William R. *Kora!* Rogue River, Oreg.: Atwood, 1986.

Feifer, George. *Tennozan: The Battle of Okinawa and the Atomic Bomb.* New York: Ticknor & Fields, 1992.

Firkins, Peter. *From Hell to Eternity.* Perth, W. Austral.: Westward Ho, 1979.

Fitzpatrick, Bernard T. *The Hike into the Sun: Memoir of an American Soldier Captured on Bataan in 1942 and Imprisoned by the Japanese Until 1945.* Jefferson, N.C.: McFarland, 1993.

Fletcher-Cooke, John. *The Emperor's Guest, 1942-1945.* London: Leo Cooper, 1994.

Fluckey, Eugene B. *Thunder Below! The USS Barb Revolutionizes Submarine Warfare in World War II.* Urbana: University of Illinois Press, 1992.

Fujita, Frank. *Foo: A Japanese-American Prisoner of the Rising Sun. The Secret Prison Diary of Frank "Foo" Fujita.* Denton: University of North Texas Press, 1993.

Gautier, Sgt. James Donovan, Jr. *I Came Back from Bataan.* Greenville, S.C.: Blue Ridge, 1997.

Giles, Donald T., Jr., ed. *Captive of the Rising Sun: The POW Memoirs of Rear Admiral Donald T. Giles, USN.* Annapolis: Naval Institute Press, 1994.

Ginn, John L. *Sugamo Prison, Tokyo: An Account of the Trial and Sentencing of Japanese War Criminals in 1948, by a U.S. Participant*. Jefferson, N.C.: McFarland, 1992.

Goodman, Julien M. *M.D.P.O.W.* New York: Exposition Press, 1972.

Goodwin, Michael J. *Shobun: A Forgotten War Crime in the Pacific*. Mechanicsburg, Pa.: Stackpole Books, 1995.

Gordon, Ernest. *Through the Valley of the Kwai*. New York: Harper & Brothers, 1962.

Gordon, Richard M. *Horyo: Memoirs of an American POW*. St. Paul, Minn.: Paragon House, 1999.

Griffith, Thomas E., Jr. *MacArthur's Airman: General George C. Kenney and the War in the Southwest Pacific*. Lawrence: University Press of Kansas, 1998.

Grover, David H., and Gretchen G. Grover. *Captives of Shanghai: The Story of the President Harrison*. Napa, Calif.: Western Maritime Press, 1989.

Hall, Leslie. *The Blue Haze: POWs on the Burma Railway*. Kenthurst, New South Wales: Kangaroo Press, 1996.

Hammel, Eric. *Air War Pacific Chronology: America's Air War Against Japan in East Asia and the Pacific, 1941-1945*. Pacifica, Calif.: Pacifica Press, 1998.

Haney, Robert E. *Caged Dragons: An American POW in WWII Japan*. Ann Arbor, Mich.: Sabre Press, 1991.

Hara, Capt. Tameichi, Fred Saito, and Roger Pineau. *Japanese Destroyer Captain*. New York: Ballantine Books, 1961.

Harries, Meirion, and Susie Harries. *Soldiers of the Sun: The Rise and Fall of the Imperial Japanese Army*. New York: Random House, 1991.

Harris, Sheldon H. *Factories of Death: Japanese Biological Warfare, 1932-1945, and the American Cover-up*. London: Routledge, 1994.

Harrison, Courtney T. *Ambon Island of Mist: 2/21st Battalion AIF (Gull Force) Prisoners of War, 1941-45*. North Geelong, Australia: T. W. and C. T. Harrison, 1988.

Hibbs, Ralph Emerson, M.D. *Tell MacArthur to Wait*. New York: Carlton Press, 1988.

Hicks, George. *The Comfort Women: Japan's Brutal Regime of Enforced Prostitution in the Second World War*. New York: W. W. Norton, 1997.

Holmes, Harry. *The Last Patrol*. Shrewsbury, England: Airlife, 1994.

Holmes, Linda Goetz. *Four Thousand Bowls of Rice: A Prisoner of War Comes Home*. St. Leonards, New South Wales: Allen & Unwin, 1993.

Holmes, W. J. *Double-Edged Secrets: U.S. Naval Intelligence Operations in the Pacific During World War II*. New York: Berkley Books, 1981.

Hoyt, Edwin P. *Bowfin: The True Story of a Fabled Fleet Submarine in World War II*. Short Hills, N.J.: Burford Books, 1983.

Hubbard, Preston John. *Apocalypse Undone: My Survival of Japanese Imprisonment During World War II*. Nashville, Tenn.: Vanderbilt University Press, 1990.

Huie, William Bradford. *Can Do! The Story of the Seabees*. Annapolis: Naval Institute Press, 1997.

Iannarelli, Anthony N., Sr. *The Eighty Thieves: American P.O.W.s in World War II Japan*. San Diego: Patriot Press, 1991.

Ienaga, Saburo. *The Pacific War, 1939-1945: A Critical Perspective on Japan's Role in World War II.* New York: Pantheon Books, 1978.

Jackfert, Edward, and Andrew Miller, eds. *History of the Defenders of the Philippines, Guam and Wake Islands.* Paducah, Ky.: Turner, 1991.

Jentschura, Hansgeorg, Dieter Jung, and Peter Mickel. *Warships of the Imperial Japanese Navy, 1869-1945.* Annapolis: Naval Institute Press, 1986.

Jordan, Roger. *The World's Merchant Fleets 1939: The Particulars and Wartime Fates of 6,000 Ships.* Annapolis: Naval Institute Press, 1999.

Keith, Agnes Newton. *Three Came Home.* New York: McFadden Books, 1965.

Kerr, E. Bartlett. *Surrender and Survival: The Experience of American POWs in the Pacific, 1941-1945.* New York: William Morrow, 1985.

Kinvig, Clifford. *River Kwai Railway: The Story of the Burma-Siam Railroad.* London: Brassey's, 1998.

———. *Scapegoat: General Percival of Singapore.* London: Brassey's, 1996.

Knox, Donald. *Death March: The Survivors of Bataan.* New York: Harcourt Brace, 1981.

Komamiya, Shinshichiro. *Senji Yuso Sendan Shi* (Wartime Transportation Convoys History. Part 1). Translated by William G. Somerville. Tokyo: Shuppan Kyodosha, 1987.

Krancher, Jan A., ed. *The Defining Years of the Dutch East Indies, 1942-1949: Survivors Accounts of Japanese Invasion and Enslavement of Europeans and the Revolution that Created Free Indonesia.* Jefferson, N.C.: McFarland, 1996.

LaForte, Robert S., and Ronald E. Marcello, eds. *Building the Death Railway: The Ordeal of American POWs in Burma, 1942-1945.* Wilmington, Del.: Scholarly Resources, 1993.

LaForte, Robert S., Ronald E. Marcello, and Richard L. Himmel, eds. *With Only the Will to Live: Accounts of Americans in Japanese Prison Camps, 1941-1945.* Wilmington, Del.: Scholarly Resources, 1994.

Lamont-Brown, Raymond. *Kempeitai: Japan's Dreaded Military Police.* Gloucestershire, England: Sutton, 1998.

LaVO, Carl. *Back from the Deep: The Strange Story of the Sister Subs Squalus and Sculpin.* Annapolis: Naval Institute Press, 1994.

Lawton, Manny. *Some Survived.* Chapel Hill, N.C.: Algonquin Books of Chapel Hill, 1984.

Layton, Rear Adm. Edwin T. *"And I Was There": Pearl Harbor and Midway—Breaking the Secrets.* New York: William Morrow, 1985.

Lee, Bruce. *Marching Orders: The Untold Story of World War II.* New York: Crown Publishers, 1995.

Lewin, Ronald. *The American Magic: Codes, Ciphers and the Defeat of Japan.* New York: Farrar Straus Giroux, 1982.

Lindsay, Oliver. *At the Going Down of the Sun: Hong Kong and South/East Asia, 1941-45.* London: Hamilton, 1981.

Lockwood, Charles A. *Down to the Sea in Subs.* New York: W. W. Norton, 1967.

Lockwood, Charles A., and Hans Christian Adamson. *Through Hell and Deep Water.* New York: Greenberg Publisher, 1956.

Lomax, Eric. *The Railway Man: A True Story of War, Remembrance, and Forgiveness.* New York: Ballantine Books, 1995.

Lord, Walter. *Lonely Vigil: Coastwatchers of the Solomons.* New York: Viking Press, 1977.

Lord Russell of Liverpool. *The Knights of Bushido: A Short History of Japanese War Crimes.* London: Cassell & Company, 1958.

Lott, Arnold. *Most Dangerous Sea.* New York: Ballantine Books, 1959.

Machi, Mario. *Under the Rising Sun: Memoirs of a Japanese Prisoner of War.* Miranda, Calif.: Wolfenden, 1994.

Martin, Adrian R. *Brothers from Bataan: POWs, 1942-1945.* Manhattan, Kans.: Sunflower University Press, 1992.

Martindale, Robert R. *The 13th Mission: The Saga of a POW at Camp Omori, Tokyo.* Austin, Tex.: Eakin Press, 1998.

Matson, Eva Jane. *It Tolled for New Mexico: New Mexicans Captured by the Japanese, 1941-1945.* Las Cruces, N.M.: Yucca Tree Press, 1994.

McCants, William R. *War Patrols of the USS Flasher: The True Story of One of America's Greatest Submarines, Officially Credited with Sinking the Most Japanese Shipping in World War II.* Chapel Hill, N.C.: Professional Press, 1994.

McCormack, Gavan, and Hank Nelson, eds. *The Burma-Thailand Railway: Memory and History.* St. Leonards, New South Wales: Allen & Unwin, 1993.

McEwan, John. *Out of the Depths of Hell: A Soldier's Story of Life and Death in Japanese Hands.* South Yorkshire, England: Leo Cooper, 1999.

McIntosh, Dave. *Hell on Earth: Aging Faster, Dying Sooner—Canadian Prisoners of the Japanese During World War II.* Whitby, Ontario: McGraw-Hill Ryerson, 1997.

McLaggen, Douglas. *The Will to Survive: A Private's View as a POW.* Kenthurst, New South Wales: Kangaroo Press, 1995.

Mendenhall, Rear Adm. Corwin. *Submarine Diary: The Silent Stalking of Japan.* Annapolis: Naval Institute Press, 1991.

Michel, John J. A. *Mr. Michel's War from Manila to Mukden: An American Navy Officer's War with the Japanese, 1941-1945.* Novato, Calif.: Presidio Press, 1998.

Miller, Col. E. B. *Bataan Uncensored.* Long Prairie, Minn.: Hart Publications, 1949. Reprint, Little Falls, Minn.: Military Historical Society of Minnesota, 1991.

Mitchell, R. Keith. *Forty-Two Months in Durance Vile: Prisoner of the Japanese.* London: Robert Hale, 1997.

Morison, Samuel Eliot. *History of United States Naval Operations in World War II.* Vol. 3, *The Rising Sun in the Pacific.* Boston: Little, Brown, 1948.

Morton, Louis. *United States Army in World War II: The Fall of the Philippines.* Washington, D.C.: Center of Military History United States Army, 1989.

Nelson, Hank. *P.O.W. Prisoners of War: Australians Under Nippon.* Sydney: ABC Enterprises, 1985.

Nordin, Carl S. *We Were Next to Nothing: An American POW's Account of Japanese Prison Camps and Deliverance in World War II.* Jefferson, N.C.: McFarland, 1997.

Norman, Elizabeth M. *We Band of Angels: The Untold Story of American Nurses Trapped on Bataan by the Japanese.* New York: Random House, 1999.

O'Kane, Richard H. *Clear the Bridge! The War Patrols of the U.S.S. Tang.* Novato, Calif.: Presidio Press, 1989.

———. *Wahoo: The Patrols of America's Most Famous World War II Submarine.* Novato, Calif.: Presidio Press, 1987.

Padfield, Peter. *War Beneath the Sea: Submarine Conflict During World War II.* New York: John Wiley & Sons, 1995.

Parillo, Mark P. *The Japanese Merchant Marine in World War II.* Annapolis: Naval Institute Press, 1993.

Peacock, Donald. *The Emperor's Guest: The Diary of a British Prisoner-of-War of the Japanese in Indonesia.* Cambridge, England: Oleander Press, 1989.

Peillard, Leonce. *The Laconia Affair.* New York: Bantam Books, 1983.

Petak, Joseph A. *Never Plan Tomorrow: The Saga of the Bataan Death March and Battle of Corregidor Survivors, 1942-1945.* Fullerton, Calif.: Aquataur, 1991.

Piccagallo, Philip R. *The Japanese on Trial: Allied War Crimes Operations in the East, 1945-1951.* Austin: University of Texas Press, 1979.

Power, F. W. G. *Kurrah! An Australian POW in Changi, Thailand and Japan, 1942-1945.* McCrae, Australia: R. J. & S. P. Austin, 1991.

Prados, John. *Combined Fleet Decoded: The Secret History of American Intelligence and the Japanese Navy in World War II.* New York: Random House, 1995.

Roscoe, Theodore. *United States Submarine Operations in World War II.* Annapolis: United States Naval Institute, 1949.

Ruhe, Capt. William J. *War in the Boats: My World War II Submarine Battles.* Washington, D.C.: Brassey's, 1994.

Sakaida, Henry. *The Siege of Rabaul.* St. Paul, Minn.: Phalanx, 1996.

Sakakida, Richard, with Wayne S. Kiyosaki. *A Spy in their Midst: The World War II Struggle of a Japanese-American Hero.* Lanham, Md.: Madison Books, 1995.

Salim, Leon. *Prisoners at Kota Cane.* Ithaca, N.Y.: Cornell University Press, 1986.

Sasgen, Peter T. *Red Scorpion: The War Patrols of the USS Rasher.* Annapolis: Naval Institute Press, 1995.

Schultz, Duane. *Wake Island: The Heroic, Gallant Fight.* New York: St. Martin's, 1978.

Sellwood, A. V. *The Damned Don't Drown: The Sinking of the Wilhelm Gustloff.* Annapolis: Naval Institute Press, 1996.

Shores, Christopher, and Brian Cull, with Yasuho Izawa. *Bloody Shambles.* Vol. 2, *The Defence of Sumatra to the Fall of Burma.* London: Grub Street, 1993.

Silver, Lynette Ramsay. *Sandakan: A Conspiracy of Silence.* Burra Creek, New South Wales: Sally Milner, 1998.

Smith, Stanley W. *Prisoner of the Emperor: An American POW in World War II.* Niwot: University of Colorado Press, 1991.

Smyth, Sir John. *The Will to Live: The Story of Dame Margot Turner D.B.E., R.R.C.* London: Cassell & Company, 1970.

Spector, Ronald H. *Eagle Against the Sun: The American War with Japan.* New York: Vintage Books, 1985.

Stamp, Loren E. *Journey Through Hell: Memoir of a World War II American Navy Medic Captured in the Philippines and Imprisoned by the Japanese.* Jefferson, N.C.: McFarland, 1993.

Stewart, Sidney. *Give Us This Day: A True Story of the Survivors of the Bataan Death March.* New York: Popular Library, 1957.

Stripp, Alan. *Codebreaker in the Far East: How Britain Cracked Japan's Top Secret Military Codes.* New York: Oxford University Press, 1995.

Tanaka, Yuki. *Hidden Horrors: Japanese War Crimes in World War II.* Boulder, Colo.: Westview Press, 1996.

Tenney, Lester I. *My Hitch in Hell: The Bataan Death March.* Washington, D.C.: Brassey's, 1995.

Thomas, Hugh. *The Slave Trade: The Story of the Atlantic Slave Trade, 1440–1870.* New York: Simon & Schuster, 1997.

Thompson, Kyle. *A Thousand Cups of Rice: Surviving the Death Railway.* Austin, Tex.: Eakin Press, 1994.

Toland, John. *The Rising Sun: The Decline and Fall of the Japanese Empire, 1936–1945.* New York: Random House, 1970.

Urwin, Gregory J. W. *Facing Fearful Odds: The Siege of Wake Island.* Lincoln: University of Nebraska Press, 1997.

Vance, Jonathan F. *Objects of Concern: Canadian Prisoners of War Through the Twentieth Century.* Vancouver: University of British Columbia Press, 1994.

van der Post, Laurens. *The Prisoner and the Bomb.* New York: William Morrow, 1971.

Versaw, Donald L. *Mikado no Kayaku.* N.p.: Published by the Author, 1997.

Vining, Virgil V. *Guest of an Emperor.* New York: Carlton Press, 1968.

Wade, Tom Henling. *Prisoner of the Japanese: From Changi to Tokyo.* Kenthurst, New South Wales: Kangaroo Press, 1994.

Wall, Don. *Abandoned? Australians at Sandakan, 1945.* Mona Vale, New South Wales: Don Wall, 1990.

——. *Heroes at Sea.* Adelaide, South Australia: Griffin Press, 1991.

——. *Kill the Prisoners!* Mona Vale, New South Wales: Don Wall, 1996.

Wallace, Walter. *Escape From Hell: The Sandakan Story.* London: Robert Hale, 1958.

Waterford, Van. *Prisoners of the Japanese in World War II: Statistical History, Personal Narratives, and Memorials Concerning POWs in Camps and on Hellships, Civilian Internees, Asian Slave Laborers and Others Captured in the Pacific Theater.* Jefferson, N.C.: McFarland, 1994.

Weiss, Edward W. *Under the Rising Sun: War, Captivity and Survival, 1941–1945.* Erie, Pa.: Edward Weiss, 1992.

Weissinger, William J., Jr. *Kitoski, Bakaro! Attention, Fool!* Austin, Tex.: Eakin Press, 1998.

Whitman, John W. *Bataan: Our Last Ditch, the Bataan Campaign, 1942.* New York: Hippocrene Books, 1990.

Wigmore, Lionel. *The Japanese Thrust: Australia in the War of 1939-1945.* Canberra: Australian War Memorial, 1957.

Williams, David. *Wartime Disasters at Sea: Every Passenger Ship Loss in World Wars I and II.* Somerset, England: Patrick Stephens, 1997.

Wills, Donald H. *The Sea Was My Last Chance: Memoir of an American Captured on Bataan in 1942 Who Escaped in 1944 and Led the Liberation of Western Mindanao.* Jefferson, N.C.: McFarland, 1992.

Winslow, Capt. W. G. *The Fleet the Gods Forgot: The U.S. Asiatic Fleet in World War II.* Annapolis: Naval Institute Press, 1982.

——. *The Ghost that Died in Sunda Strait.* Annapolis: Naval Institute Press, 1984.

Winton, John. *Ultra in the Pacific: How Breaking Japanese Codes and Cyphers Affected Naval Operations Against Japan, 1941-1945.* London: Leo Cooper, 1993.

Wright-Nooth, George, with Mark Adkin. *Prisoner of the Turnip Heads: Horror, Hunger and Humour in Hong Kong, 1941-1945.* London: Leo Cooper, 1994.

Wygle, Peter R. *Surviving a Japanese P.O.W. Camp: Father and Son Endure Internment in Manila During World War II.* Ventura: Pathfinder Publishing of California, 1991.

Young, Bill. *Return to a Dark Age.* Allawah, New South Wales: Privately Published, 1991.

JOURNALS AND PERIODICALS

Beaumont, Joan. "Victims of War: The Allies and the Transport of Prisoners-of-War by Sea, 1939-45." *Journal of the Australian War Memorial* 2 (April 1983): 1-7.

Dow, Robert J. "Nissyo Maru: Hellship." *Ex-POW Bulletin* 49, no. 5 (May 1992): 37-38.

Grover, David H. "The Turncoat Transport: President Harrison." *Sea Classics* 21, no. 3 (March 1988): 18-26, 61.

Holewinski, Ralph. "Hell Ships." *Quan* 54, no. 4 (January 2000): 6.

Jacobson, Alvin E. "Survivor's Story: Submarine U.S.S. *Flier.*" *Submarine Journal* (Spring 1998): 1-118.

Kiefer, Edwin A. "The Two Faces of Penang—Part III." *Submarine Journal* (Summer 1998): 1-96.

Kvalheim, Val. "Lisbon Maru Survivors Meet." *Polaris* 42, no. 6 (December 1998): 23.

——. "The Sinking of the Lisbon Maru." *Polaris* 39, no. 1 (February 1995): 16-17.

Nelson, Hank. "'A Bowl of Rice for Seven Camels': The Dynamics of Prisoner-of-War Camps." *Journal of the Australian War Memorial* 14 (October 1989): 33-42.

——. "The Return to Rabaul, 1945." *Journal of Pacific History* 30, no. 2 (1995): 131-41.

——. "Travelling in Memories: Australian Prisoners of the Japanese, Forty Years after the Fall of Singapore." *Journal of the Australian War Memorial* 3 (October 1983): 13-24.

Orbeck, Godfrey. "The Shinyo Maru Story." *Polaris* 43, no. 1 (February 1999).

Peters, Betty. "The Life Experience of Partners of Ex-POWs of the Japanese." *Journal of the Australian War Memorial* 28 (April 1996): 1-11.

Wrynn, V. Dennis. "Massacre at Palawan." *World War II* (November 1997): 56-62.

SUBMARINE PATROL REPORTS

U.S. Reports

Submarine Force Library, Groton, Connecticut
Bashaw (SS 241), Third; *Bonefish* (SS 223), Third; *Cabrilla* (SS 288), Sixth; *Drum* (SS 228), Eleventh; *Grouper* (SS 214), Second; *Growler* (SS 215), Tenth; *Icefish* (SS 367), First; *Paddle* (SS 263), Fifth; *Pampanito* (SS 383), Third; USS *Plaice* (SS 390), Second; *Rasher* (SS 269), Third; *Raton* (SS 270), Third; *Sawfish* (SS 276), Eighth; *Seadragon* (SS 194), Eleventh; *Sealion II* (SS 315), Second; *Snook* (SS 279), Seventh; *Sturgeon* (SS 187), Fourth; *Tang* (SS 306), Third; *Whale* (SS 239), Ninth.

British Reports

Royal Navy Submarine Museum, Gosport, England
HMS *Tradewind,* Third; HMS *Truculent,* Fourth.

CORRESPONDENCE, INTERVIEWS, AND STATEMENTS

Correspondence With Author

Alden, John D. 8 July 1997; 18 February 1998; 19 April 1999.
Bancroft, Arthur (POW). 14 December 1998.
Bennett, John. 10 May 1998.
Bennie, Woodrow W. (POW). 25 September 1998.
Bruckart, William L. 2 February 1997.
Carlisle, Harvey. 13 September 2000.
Christie, Martin (POW). 20 September 1998.
Cocking, Jack (POW). April 1998.
Cornford, Roydon C. (POW). January, 11 August 1997; May 1998; August 1999.
Dardaris, Spero (POW). 7 October, 21 October 1998.
Donovan, Josephine. 16 January, 15 February 1999.
Dow, Robert J. (POW). 16 August, 27 August 1998; 15 March 1999.
Duffy, George W. (POW). 24 September, 7 October 1998.
Evans, William R. 5 March 1999.
Farlow, Cliff L. (POW). 17 March 1997; May 1998.
Farrands, M. R. (POW). 20 February, 14 March 1997; 4 August 1999.
Green, Smith L. (POW). 24 November 2000.
Grokett, Russell, Jr. January 1998.
Hocking, John R. (POW). 22 May 1997.
Hopper, Gordon. 23 January, 20 May, 20 June 1996.
Hubbard, Preston J. (POW). 19 September 1998; 9 March 1999.
Kitazawa, Noritaka. 15 February 1999.
Lackey, Mary Ann. 7 November 1998.
Martin, Harold D. (POW). 10 February 1997.

McGregor, Rob Roy. January 1997.

McGuire, Charles A., Jr. 23 December 1995.

Murphy, James T. (POW). 25 September 1998.

Murphy, Walter P. 11 February 1999.

Nelson, George B. (POW). 9 October 1998.

Nelson, Hank. 11 February 1999.

Papock, Herbert (POW). 25 January, 4 February 1999.

Schwarz, Bert (POW). 1999.

Sherlock, Richard J. 10 February, 18 February, 17 May 1996.

Simpson, Sam (POW). 20 January, 10 March 1999.

Thomas, Donald H. (POW). 24 November 1998; 1 January 1999.

van der Kuil, Peter. 14 March 1998.

Wall, Don (POW). 13 March, 17 July 1997; 25 February, 18 March 1999.

Weigel, Edwin, and Donna Weigel. 19 April, 22 September, 4 October, 18 October 1998.

Wheeler, Ray (POW). August 1999.

Williams, Ken. (POW). 25 February, 19 March 1997; May 1998.

Interviews Conducted By Clay Blair Jr.

All in the Clay Blair Jr. Papers, University of Wyoming American Heritage Center, Laramie.

Demers, Maurice L. 1977.

Hauptman, Anthony C. 1977.

McGuire, Charles A., Jr. 1977.

Sherlock, Richard J. 1977.

Summers, Paul E. 1977.

Yagemann, William F. 1977.

Telephone Interviews Conducted By Author

Dardaris, Spero (POW). 1 October 1998.

Hopper, Gordon. 3 November 1996.

Schwarz, Bert (POW). 15 February 1999.

Statements On Audiotape (Self-Conducted)

Farlow, Cliff L. (POW). March 1997.

Graef, Calvin (POW). 1983.

Martin, Harold D. (POW). February 1997.

McGuire, Charles A., Jr. March 1996; May 1997.

PERSONAL PAPERS

Bodine, Roy L., Jr. "No Place for Kindness: The Prisoner of War Diary of Roy L. Bodine." Manuscript. Ft. Sam Houston Museum, Ft. Sam Houston, Tex., 1983.

Brown, Charles M. "The Oryoku Maru Story." Manuscript. Magalia, Calif., 1983.

Dreher, Alfred B. "Diary, 7 October 1942–11 November 1942." Photocopy in possession of the author.

Hopper, Gordon. "*Pampanito* Recollections—the Boat, the Crew, the Experiences, 1993." Photocopy of typed manuscript.

Kooi, Muriel, with Donald H. Thomas. "The Wrigley Peace Pact of August 17, 1945." Undated, privately printed booklet.

Papock, Herbert. "Diary, 8 December 1941–18 September 1944." Photocopy in possession of the author.

Peart, Cecil J., USN. "Peart's Journal." Photocopy. Personal Papers Unit, Marine Corps Historical Center, Washington, D.C.

Pence, Capt. Harry L., USN. Personal Papers. Mandeville Special Collections Department, University of California–San Diego Library, La Jolla, California.

Young, Bill. "Long Ago in Borneo." Allawah, New South Wales, n.d. Unpublished booklet, photocopy in possession of the author.

INTERNET SOURCES

"A Brief History of NYK." Http://www.nyk.com/corpinfo/history.

Duffy, Capt. George. "The Dreadful Saga of the MV American Leader and Her Crew." Http://www.usmm.org/duffyamerlead.

Grokett, Russell A., Sr. "Twelve Hundred Days." Http://www.jacksonville.net/˘7Ergrokett/pow/1200days.

Henderson, Henry Clay. "Another Tender Sailor's Tale: Diary of Henry Clay Henderson." Http://www.home.cybertron.com/˘7Ecomcents/tendertale.

"Japan's Sony Squelches movie on 'Hellships.'" Http://www.ccnet.com/˘7Esuntzu75/pirn9734.

King, Otis H. "Fall of Corregidor." Http:www.virtualtexan.com/veterans/memories/otisking.htm.

Nevitt, Allyn D. "Long Lancers." http://www.combinedfleet.com/lancers.htm.

Tully, Anthony P. "Kido Butai! Stories and Battle Histories of the IJN's Carrier Fleet." Http://www.combinedfleet.com/cvlist.htm.

van der Kuil, Peter. "The Sinking of the Junyo Maru." Http://www.omen.com.au/˘7Evanderkp/junyopg3.

NATIONAL ARCHIVES AND RECORDS ADMINISTRATION SOURCES

Japanese Navy Message Translations (SRN).

Record Group 38. Office of the Chief of Naval Operations. Operational Records Series (ONS).

Record Group 457. Records of the National Security Agency/Central Security Service (SRNS).

INDEX OF HELLSHIPS

SUBJECT INDEX

Green, Charles B., 18
Green, Smith L., 118
Grenadier, 126–27, 147
Gripsholm, 89, 91, 173, 278
Grockett, Russell A., 51
Gronow, Mervyn, 83
Grouper, 44–45
Growler, 205, 206, 207, 210–11
Guavina, 270–71
Gudgeon, 144, 324n. 8
Guerrero, Josefina, 294
Gunnel, 144
Gurnard, 294, 323n. 57
Guyton, Benson, 180

Haddo, 177
Hague Convention, 131–32
Haguro, 10, 13
Hakko Maru, 218
Halbrook, Alton C., 246
Hamanaka Shuichi, 10
Hamilton, G. C., 46–47
Hancock, 260
Haney, Robert E., 78, 80–82, 306
Hannum, Earl R., 6
Hara Tameichi, 9–10, 12, 14, 320n. 15, 320n. 19
Harder, 178
Harima Maru, 218
Harrington, Neal, 179–80
Harris, Reginald J., 207
Hartenstein, Werner, 212
Harukaze, 250, 253, 255
Hatsukaze, 12
Hatsushimo, 191
Hattori Masonori, 303
Hauptman, Tony, 212–14
Hawkbill, 258, 333n. 79
Hayabusa Maru, 193

Hayate, 3
Heath, L. M., 36
Heinen, Julius B., 62
Hekking, Henri, 64, 291
hellships, Japanese accommodations on, 52, 62–63, 80, 92, 121, 159, 284–86
Henderson, Henry Clay, 33–34, 241, 266
Hewlett, Thomas H., 182
Hikawa Maru, 232
Hiramatsu Aitaro, 197
Hishigata Maru, 247–48, 331n. 70
Hiyodori, 77, 188, 196
Hocking, John R., 206
Hoe, 248, 325n. 26
Hogan, Thomas, 134, 136
Hokkai Maru, 125, 325n. 27
Hokurei Maru, 247
Holland, H. M., 25
Holmes, Wilfred J., 218–19, 293
Homma Masaharu, 30, 31, 302
Hong Kong, massacre at, 42
Hopper, Gordon, 213, 215, 218
Hornet, 243, 260–61
Hoshijima Susumu, 105, 119, 120
Hoshino, Sgt., 124
Houston, 8, 60, 61, 62–63, 95, 290, 291
Hubbard, Preston J., 184–88, 288, 300, 305
Hughes, Charles, 257, 266
Hugh L. Scott, 284
Huie, William Bradford, 7
Hull, Cordell, 283
Hurt, David A., 12–13, 14, 15
Hutchison, Russell, 175

Icefish, 250
Ienega Saburo, 304

ABOUT THE AUTHOR

Greg Michno was born in Detroit, Michigan, in 1948.

He attended Michigan State University and received a master's degree in history at the University of Northern Colorado. His interest in naval history began as a child, when his father, a submariner who served on the USS *Pampanito*, told him tales of torpedoings and sea rescues such as those in *Death on the Hellships*.

Michno has written a score of articles that have appeared in various journals and magazines, including *Montana, Journal of the West, Research Review,* and *Wild West.* He has won several awards for his articles and books. The Indian wars in the American West were the subjects of his first two volumes: *The Mystery of E Troop* and *Lakota Noon.* His third, *USS Pampanito: Killer Angel,* was the story of a fleet submarine in the Pacific war.

Greg and his wife, Susan, live in Westland, Michigan. Along with his work for the State of Michigan's Family Independence Agency, he continues to research both the American West and World War II in the Pacific. His current projects include Indian conflicts during the Civil War and U.S. submarine wolfpacks.